Charlotte, NC

Charlotte, NC

The Global Evolution of a New South City

Edited by William Graves
and Heather A. Smith

The University of Georgia Press
Athens and London

© 2010 by the University of Georgia Press
Athens, Georgia 30602
www.ugapress.org
All rights reserved

Designed by April Leidig-Higgins
Set in Garamond PremierPro by Copperline Book Services
Printed and bound by Thomson-Shore and Swift Print Press

The paper in this book meets the guidelines for
permanence and durability of the Committee on
Production Guidelines for Book Longevity of the
Council on Library Resources.

Printed in the United States of America
14 13 12 11 10 C 5 4 3 2 1

Library of Congress Cataloging-in-Publication Data
Charlotte, NC : the global evolution of a new South city /
edited by William Graves and Heather A. Smith.
   p. cm.
Includes bibliographical references and index.
ISBN-13: 978-0-8203-3561-2 (hardcover : alk. paper)
ISBN-10: 0-8203-3561-4 (hardcover : alk. paper)
   1. Charlotte (N.C.) — Economic conditions.
2. Charlotte (N.C.) — Social conditions.
3. Social change — North Carolina — Charlotte.
4. Urbanization — North Carolina — Charlotte.
5. Globalization — Social aspects — North Carolina — Charlotte.
6. City and town life — North Carolina — Charlotte.
7. Social change — North Carolina — Charlotte.
8. Cities and towns — Southern States — Growth — Case studies.
9. Social change — Southern States — Case studies.
10. Globalization — Social aspects — Southern States — Growth —
Case studies.   I. Graves, William, Ph. D.   II. Smith, Heather A.
III. Title: Charlotte, N.C.   IV. Title: Charlotte, North Carolina.
HC108.C33C54   2010
330.9756'76 — dc22   2009051210

British Library Cataloging-in-Publication Data available

Contents

vii   Acknowledgments

viii–x   Maps

1   HEATHER A. SMITH AND WILLIAM GRAVES
Introduction. From Mill Town to Financial Capital:
Charlotte's Global Evolution

10   DAVID GOLDFIELD
A Place to Come To

24   MATTHEW D. LASSITER
Searching for Respect:
From "New South" to "World Class"
at the Crossroads of the Carolinas

50   RONALD L. MITCHELSON AND DEREK H. ALDERMAN
Red Dust and Dynamometers:
Charlotte as Memory and Knowledge Community
in NASCAR

87   WILLIAM GRAVES AND JONATHAN KOZAR
Blending Southern Culture and International Finance:
The Construction of a Global Money Center

102   RONALD V. KALAFSKY
Beyond Local Markets:
The Export Performance and Challenges
of Charlotte Manufacturers

119   TYREL G. MOORE AND GERALD L. INGALLS
A Place for Old Mills in a New Economy:
Textile Mill Reuse in Charlotte

141 HEATHER A. SMITH AND EMILY THOMAS LIVINGSTONE
Banking on the Neighborhood:
Corporate Citizenship and Revitalization
in Uptown Charlotte

160 GERALD L. INGALLS AND ISAAC HEARD JR.
Developing a Typology of African American
Neighborhoods in the American South:
The Case of Charlotte

189 STEPHEN SAMUEL SMITH
Development and the Politics of School
Desegregation and Resegregation

220 DAVID WALTERS
Centers and Edges:
The Confusion of Urban and Suburban Paradigms
in Charlotte-Mecklenburg's Development Patterns

247 TOM HANCHETT
Salad-bowl Suburbs:
A History of Charlotte's East Side and
South Boulevard Immigrant Corridors

263 JOSÉ L. S. GÁMEZ
Mi Reina:
Latino Landscapes in the
Queen City (Charlotte, N.C.)

284 OWEN J. FURUSETH
Epilogue:
Charlotte at the Globalizing Crossroads

291 Contributors

297 Index

Acknowledgments

Charlotte, NC: The Global Evolution of a New South City has truly been a collaborative enterprise, and the editors wish to express their deepest thanks to the book's author team for their contributions and dedication to this project. We are especially appreciative of their willingness to adjust early drafts and chapter structures so that we could ensure a cohesive and compelling volume. We are also deeply grateful to our editor at the University of Georgia Press. Derek Krissoff's unwavering patience and counsel were invaluable throughout the manuscript development process.

Patrick Jones of the Cartography and Graphics Lab in the Department of Geography and Earth Sciences at UNC Charlotte provided his expertise to the development and standardization of the volume's tables and figures. We would like to thank Carlan Graves, for her copyediting of the entire book prior to its initial submission to the press, and Linda Wessels for her thoughtful and careful editing during the pre-production phase. To Dennis Rash we convey our appreciation for his enduring enthusiasm about our work. We would also like to acknowledge our students at UNC Charlotte for their patience and understanding as looming deadlines translated into rescheduled meetings and distracted professors.

In many ways our family stories parallel the central theme of this book — the hybridization of identity and the richness of experience that comes through a complex blending of the southern and the global. While Bill and his family are native southerners with longstanding North Carolina roots, Heather's family (but one) are immigrants coming from the already global cities of Toronto, London, and Vancouver. The different lenses through which we view, and the different ways in which our families experience, Charlotte's globalizing transition provided the genesis for this project. It is to our tremendously supportive spouses and to our globally-aware, Charlotte-raised daughters that we dedicate this book.

Heather Smith and Bill Graves

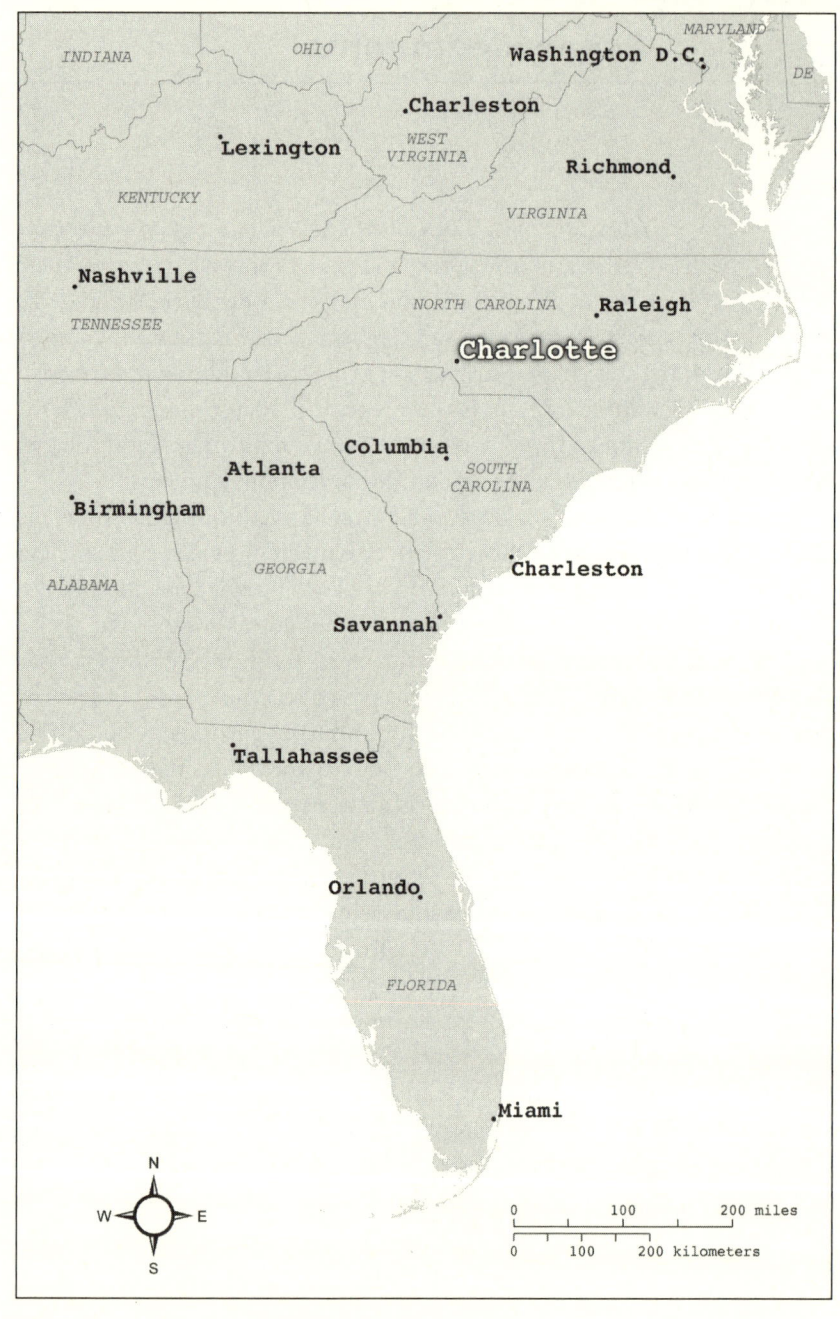

Charlotte is in an unlikely location for a globalizing city.
(Source: UNC Charlotte Cartography Lab.)

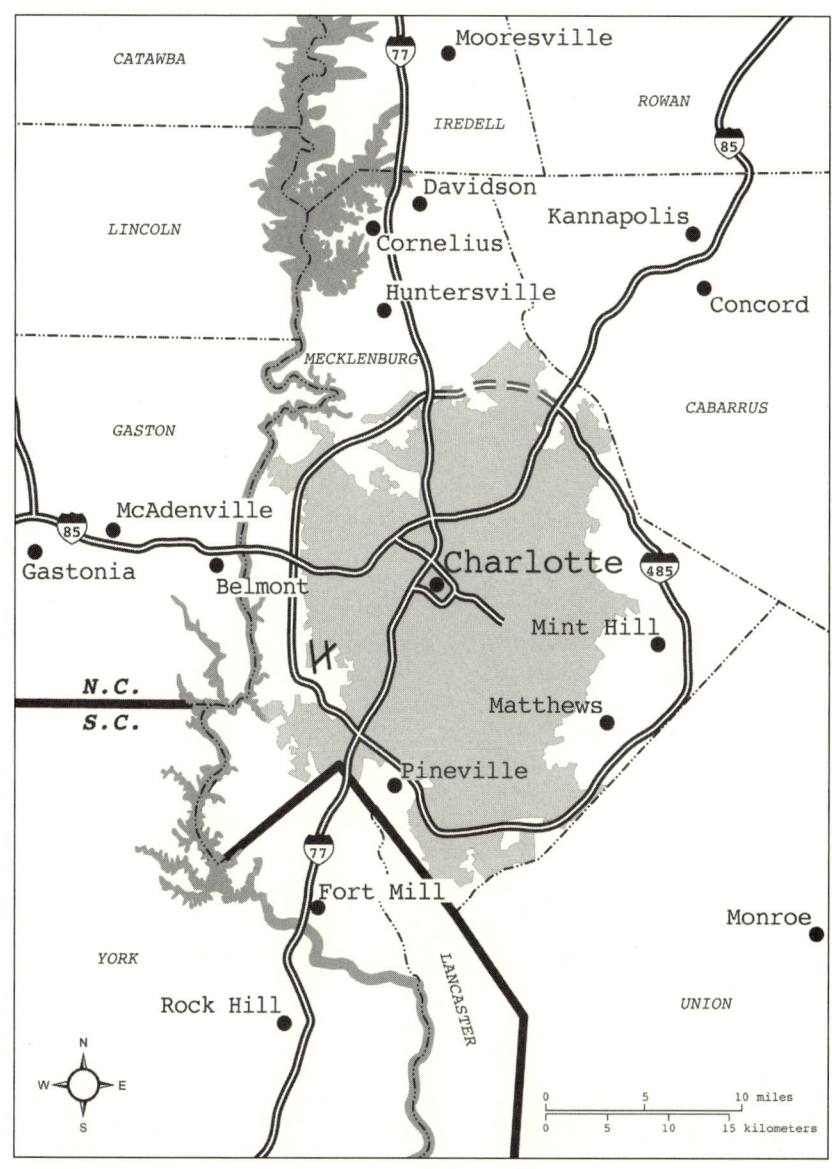

Metropolitan Charlotte. (Source: UNC Charlotte Cartography Lab.)

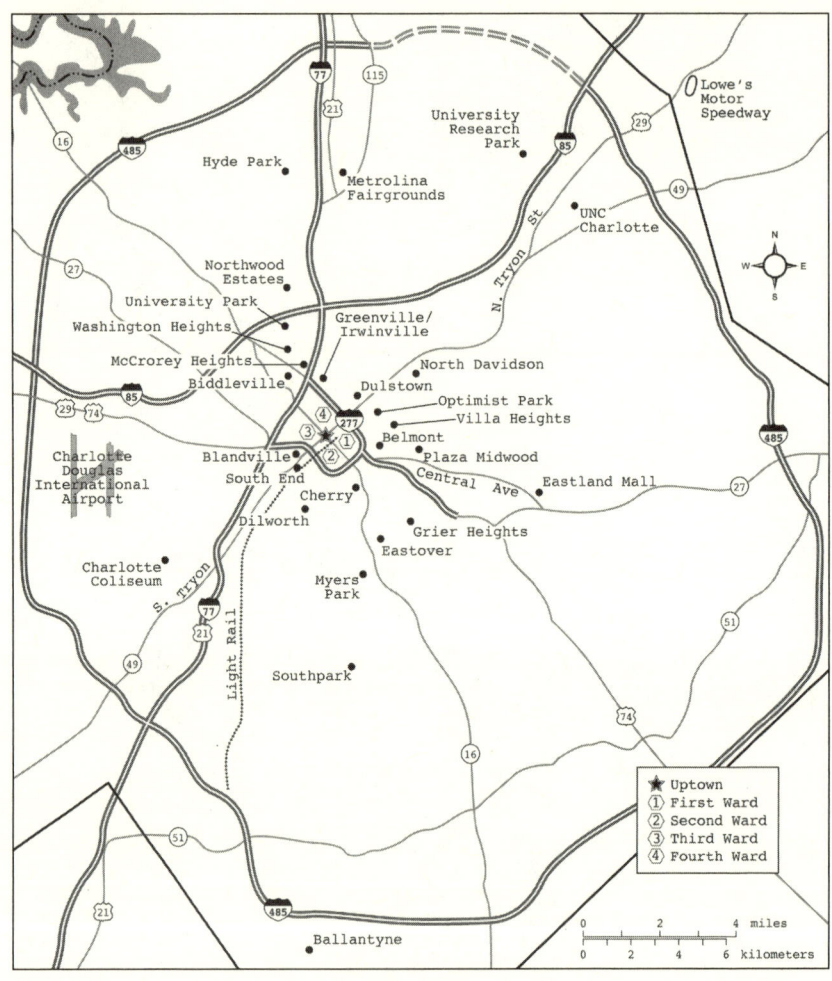

Noted Charlotte neighborhoods and landmarks. (Source: UNC Charlotte Cartography Lab.)

Heather A. Smith and William Graves

Introduction.
From Mill Town to Financial Capital
Charlotte's Global Evolution

Charlotte, North Carolina, is not a "global city."[1] It is, however, a globalizing one.

In less than four decades, Charlotte has transformed itself from a regional backwater into a globally ascendant but still distinctively southern city. Once a regional manufacturing and textile center, Charlotte is now one of the nation's premier banking and finance cores with tendrils reaching firmly into global markets.[2] This once black-and-white, distinctively bicultural city has also emerged as one of the country's leading Hispanic hypergrowth metros and is now considered a rising immigrant gateway.[3]

While a restructuring economy and changing demographics are the bedrock on which Charlotte's emerging global status rests, the hallmarks of a globalizing city are many and varied. Expanding connectivity with global economic markets; a rapidly growing foreign-born and increasingly transnational population; broadening social and cultural diversity; a widening gap between the city's disenfranchised poor and its globally networked elite; fixed capital investment in the form of corporate headquarters, production facilities, condominium skyscrapers, and multinational hotel towers; major public transit and infrastructure development; the centralization and construction of cultural and sporting venues; and gentrification in the historic core and streetcar suburbs are features shared by Charlotte and other globalizing cities.[4]

Charlotte's evolution into what scholars view as an incipient world city is remarkable given its regional disadvantages.[5] The city's unexceptional location (far from ports, navigable rivers, or mountain gateways), the cultural baggage of its impoverished southern heritage, its economic history as a low-wage industrial center, and its politically peripheral position in state politics make it an unlikely site for a globally ascendant center. And yet, Charlotte is today included among cities "like Atlanta, Georgia; Rochester, New York; [and] Columbus, Ohio . . . where an imaginative and aggressive leadership has sought to carve out distinctive niches in the global marketplace."[6] It is a credit to the city's leaders that they were able to envision a globally connected future despite the place-based disadvantages and obstacles. Indeed, it could be argued that Charlotte's peripheral economic and geographic history was an advantage that shielded the city from much of the social and economic unrest that engulfed the region post-Reconstruction. This, in turn, provided an opportunity for the city's leadership to blaze an alternative path. Forged through ceaseless self-promotion and, in some cases, a willingness to bend the rules of southern economic development, this path led Charlotte beyond the literal and figurative boundaries of both the traditional and the New South. The city stands today at the vanguard of a globalizing South that is less "a world apart" than it is "a part of the world."[7]

As the chapter authors of this volume detail, the effects of globalization on Charlotte are widespread and undeniable. The city's expanding and contracting fortunes are tied to the vagaries of the global economy. Its spatial reorganization is achieved through processes of redevelopment and revitalization. The city's neighborhood landscapes are undergoing cultural hybridization, and faces and accents are changing within its labor force and leading entrepreneurial efforts. Charlotte's position as a nascent immigrant gateway is affected by global geographies of poverty, while its role as a destination for American-born labor is a function of deindustrialization in the North and ballooning costs of living in the West. Challenges face school and health care systems reshaped by the expectations and needs of newcomers. And there is the extraregional reach and growing global appeal of NASCAR.

Despite these realities, the city's evolution and global rank are frequently dismissed by native Charlotteans and overlooked by globalization scholars. Locals scoff, citing Charlotte as a global city as an "overblown claim" or grousing that few people outside the South have heard of the city or can "point it out on a map."[8] In the scholarly realm, Charlotte's position is treated with only a little less skepticism. Some argue that the city does not "bear convincing objective markers of global status."[9] Others cite Charlotte as a "wannabe world city" focusing only on its conscious attempts to attract "big city functions like banking" away from higher-tier global cities like New York and San Francisco.[10]

Still others take a different tack and point to Charlotte's command-and-control function (as measured by the nature and number of its corporate headquarters and multinational firms) as evidence of its global position as a subregional specialized service center subordinate to its regional and national counterparts, Atlanta and New York.[11] Recent writing even places Charlotte within the global city hierarchy categorizing it as a fifth-tier global city.[12]

While its recognition as a city of note within the global city literature is certainly significant, the intent of this volume is neither to position Charlotte within the global city hierarchy nor to provide an inventory of the ways in which Charlotte meets or fails to meet global-city criteria. Its aim is to explore how the external forces of globalization combine with the city's internal dynamics and history to reshape the local structures, landscapes, and identities of a once quintessentially southern place. It examines the process of globalization as it meets the tradition of the South and restructures a single city — Charlotte, North Carolina.

Most previous work on globalization examines the character and connectivity of established (already global) cities, systems, and institutions. Charlotte has only recently begun its transformation and, as such, presents an exceptional opportunity to explore the local effects of global change as they unfold. The tendency to view places as products of either global or provincial forces has led scholars to ignore the process of places *becoming* global. Charlotte's status as *globalizing* allows the authors of this volume to look beyond the traditional all-or-nothing dichotomies of global research. This emphasis on process develops a more robust picture of the evolution of a global place and broadens the traditional geographic settings and approach of global research. By focusing on the process of a regional city's transformation into a globalizing city, we look beyond the standard global pantheon of New York, London, and Tokyo and beyond even the second- and third-tier cities such as San Francisco, Toronto, and Buenos Aires. Our view looks farther down the hierarchy to a city in the earliest tentative stages of a potential global becoming.

We also diverge from traditional studies by focusing on the interplay between local and global to ask not only how Charlotte is being affected by the external forces of globalization but also how these external forces are being affected by their encounter with the regional identity, traditions, and dynamics of the South. In many cases the driving question for our authors is how the global fits into the southern and not the other way around. This collection suggests that the adoption of global traits without losing the valued aspects of the traditional South has produced a hybridized globalization not seen elsewhere. Here, perhaps, the South maintains a strong enough hold to reshape the global into something different.

It is our hope that these chapters will illuminate the multiple ways in which the local and global intertwine in Charlotte to undergird its ascendency as a globalizing city and shape the structures, spaces, and relationships of daily lives in a way that makes those who call this city their home — both newly arrived and long established — distinctively, globally southern.

Charlotte, NC: The Global Evolution of a New South City begins with an essay by David Goldfield that provides an overview of Charlotte's evolution from "a big small town with a nice canopy of trees" into a globalizing yet still southern center. Goldfield connects the region's history of poverty to the rise of industry, banking, and an urbane culture. He attributes the emergence of this protoglobal urbanity, in part, to the city founders' freedom from the tradition of the old South and their constant willingness to embrace change. This adaptability was a boon to development but has diluted the city's collective identity, and in turn, made it more accessible to newcomers. As Goldfield remarks, "it may be too early, or it may be entirely irrelevant, to assess whether or not Charlotte is a 'world class city,' but it is certainly now a city of the world."

The theme of Charlotte emerging from its small town status is continued by Matthew Lassiter. Lassiter focuses on the city's struggle to overcome its southern roots via its self-promotion to outside interests. The city's efforts to appear to be more than a southern city and the tensions that this creates with the traditional culture in the region illustrate some of the early difficulties in moving toward global status. This struggle for identity not only forms a foundation for Charlotte's initial economic development but also underlies much of the city's contemporary political process.

The theme of globalizing the southern is picked up by Ronald Mitchelson and Derek Alderman in their discussion of NASCAR as a major local industry. The popular racing circuit was born from the poverty that enveloped the region in the early twentieth century. The industry that emerged from the region's small towns became one of the area's most recognized cultural products and one of its most sophisticated manufacturing and marketing machines. While stock-car racing has become one of the most watched sports in the nation, some of the region's decision makers increasingly resent the sport's embrace of certain elements of traditional southern culture, which they believe place a drag on global growth. This case study eloquently illustrates that, despite the tensions it may cause, there is value in adapting selected aspects of the region's traditional culture to suit the desires of global consumers.

Charlotte's other iconic industry is banking. William Graves and Jonathan Kozar explore the development of two of the nation's largest banks in a region that was once one of the country's poorest. Banking, like NASCAR, also leveraged elements of traditional southern culture into a globally competitive economic cluster. As with NASCAR, the continued significance of traditional culture has become a barrier to the expansion of the most global of the city's industries. Banking is also the element of Charlotte's economic structure that is most vulnerable to external shocks. The global credit crisis that began in 2008 threatens the continued survival of Charlotte's largest private employers.

Ronald Kalafsky addresses the reach of Charlotte's manufacturers and the degree to which the city meets their needs as participants in a global production system. The Charlotte region has long been known for its plentiful supply of low-skill, low-wage workers. According to Kalafsky, the value of this workforce has diminished as the barriers to global trade have eroded, and the region's supply of human capital places manufacturers at a productive disadvantage in global markets. In this context the manufacturing industry's struggles to adapt to the demands of a global economic system form a stark contrast to the city's successes in creating a knowledge industry that has found firm footing on the global stage.

Tyrel Moore and Gerald Ingalls connect the tangible landscape of the region's industrial past to the architectural demands of its postindustrial present. The reuse of the textile mills that make up the discarded industrial-era landscape may be the most visible element of Charlotte's changing economic and cultural orientation. Moore and Ingalls also illustrate how this adaptive reuse expresses the uneven nature of economic globalization as mills in less desirable locations are simply abandoned and dismantled. While the theme of adapting historic landscapes to contemporary uses forms the core of the chapter, an equally important element is Charlotte's pervasive public-private partnership strategy in the redevelopment process.

Partnership and corporate leadership are also at the heart of Heather Smith and Emily Livingstone's chapter about gentrification as a strategy that not only revitalized a declining but historically significant central city neighborhood but also helped the city convey an image that would attract the human capital necessary to buoy corporate goals of extraregional growth and expansion. In Charlotte's Fourth Ward, the gentrification process combined corporate philanthropy with the banks expansionary strategy and resulted in neighborhood revitalization that launched the wholesale redevelopment of the center city (see the map at the front of this volume for the locations of Charlotte neighborhoods).

Gerald Ingalls and Isaac Heard Jr. address the intersection between the region's legacy of segregation and its globalizing future by constructing a typology of the evolution of African American neighborhoods. While some of the historic African American neighborhoods have been consumed and transformed by the forces of economic globalization, others have been bypassed. The variety of transformations discussed in the chapter demonstrates that the economic globalization forces that have buffeted the region are unevenly distributed and their impact is contingent on more than just geography.

Charlotte's transformation from a traditional southern city is perhaps most visible in the context of the local school system. Stephen Samuel Smith traces changes in school board politics as the city's business-led political structure is transformed by the arrival of newcomers from other regions of the country. Particularly noteworthy is the connection between the arrival of large numbers of nonsouthern voters and the political rejection of the busing strategies that had integrated the Charlotte-Mecklenburg school system since the early 1970s. Smith also discusses the changes to urban form triggered by the newcomers and how that suburban sprawl was reflected in the political makeup of the education establishment.

The role of urban form in the city's evolution is the focus of David Walters' chapter on the local politics of planning. Walters' discussion outlines a traditional culture of suburban development that conflicts with the high-density urbanism required for global knowledge industries. In this sense development and planning in Charlotte-Mecklenburg is a mirror image to the school system: traditional strategies detracted from Charlotte adapting to the global economy, while newcomers played a pivotal role in the development of the dense, transit-oriented development desired by global knowledge industries and their workforces.

The book's last chapters address the demographic and cultural change Charlotte has experienced as a function of the globalizing forces of migration. A destination city for both domestic and foreign-born migrants, Charlotte has a growing multicultural community at the heart of what many see as the clearest tension between traditional southern culture and a new, more globalized, southern identity. Whether northerners coming from cities in which globalizing forces have led to deindustrialization, job losses, and declining quality of life or Mexican immigrants fleeing their country's poverty and limited opportunity, newcomers have brought with them differing cultures and perspectives that at once reinforce and challenge traditional southern norms.

Tom Hanchett provides stories of how the residential, institutional, and commercial landscapes of Charlotte's east and south sides, once sorted along the lines of race and class, have evolved into intermingled microcosms of the world's many cultures, faiths, and languages. Given the local and national emphasis on Charlotte's unexpected large-scale Hispanic population growth, Hanchett's chapter about the "salad-bowl suburbs" reminds us to look beyond the immediately apparent to see the true diversity, historic significance, and entrepreneurial spirit of these transitioning areas.

José Gámez's chapter takes us to the scale of lived experience and into the neighborhoods of east and south Charlotte where the city's most recent international arrivals are transforming the physical landscapes of their daily lives and claiming the Queen City as their own. Through Gámez's work we come to understand that even though international borders may have been crossed on the journeys to Charlotte, new and unexpected borders emerge after arrival. Sometimes these borders are encountered or created as Latinos reshape neighborhood spaces by blending cultural elements from their old and new homelands. By comparing such practices — and the resistance they frequently encounter — in Charlotte and East Los Angeles, Gamez shows how Latinos in both global and globalizing cities are central to an evolving understanding of transnational culture's role in the restructuring of public, private, and hybridized urban space.

An epilogue by Owen Furuseth reminds us of the stark differences between W. J. Cash's 1940 image of Charlotte as a southern city and the globalizing view collectively painted by the authors of this volume. Furuseth emphasizes the reality that as cities globalize they also tend to liberalize. Profiling religion and immigration in the city, he shows how conservative perspectives have given way to more progressive ones. Once firmly rooted in a church-going Protestant tradition, Charlotte's religious landscape today reflects a broader range of faiths and spiritual practices. Such changes have made migration to Charlotte a complex and contested issue in which political and business leadership do not always see eye to eye and where reactive policy approaches and personal opinions are still in flux. As Furuseth lays out, Charlotte is at the globalizing crossroads with a promising future that is far from "middling," far from "unimportant," and far from fully written.

In aggregate, the chapters of *Charlotte, NC* vividly illustrate not only the complexity and multiscalar nature of globalization but also that it is an evolutionary and variable process. While some of Charlotte's experience is typical (e.g., increased plurality, a postindustrial knowledge-driven economy), in other cases the integration of the traditional with the global (e.g., banking, NASCAR) has produced a potentially unique — distinctively southern — set of responses. Within the city, as globalization unfolds, some aspects of urban life remain relatively untouched (sprawl continues, poverty remains concentrated within particular African American communities), while others are dramatically changed (more than 120 languages are now spoken among students in the Charlotte-Mecklenburg school system).[13] And, while the impact of globalization has only recently been felt in realms such as religion, in the neighborhood of Fourth Ward, global forces have been shaping and reshaping socioeconomic and demographic change since the early 1970s. The globalization of any place is not an all-or-nothing process. Nor is it a predictable one. As world economic events of late 2008 and 2009 reveal, there is always the possibility that globalizing trajectories may be halted or reversed. Only time will tell if this will be the case for Charlotte. Whether accelerated or slowed, however, as the city continues along its globalization path, we fully anticipate that the melding of internal and external forces will continue to yield a place and people shaped and defined by both a southern past and global future.

Notes

1. See John Friedmann, "The World City Hypothesis," *Development and Change* 17 (1986): 69–83, and Saskia Sassen, *The Global City* (Princeton, N.J.: Princeton University Press, 1991) for benchmark definitions of global cities.

2. This remains the case even in the context of the 2008–09 economic downturn.

3. See Roberto Suro and Audrey Singer, *Latino Growth in Metropolitan America: Changing Patterns, New Locations* (Washington, D.C.: Brookings Institution and Pew Hispanic Center, 2002); Audrey Singer, Susan W. Hardwick, and Caroline B. Brettell, eds., *Twenty-First-Century Gateways: Immigrant Incorporation in Suburban America* (Washington, D.C.: Brookings Institution Press, 2008); and Audrey Singer, *The Rise of New Immigrant Gateways,* Living Cities Census Series (Washington, D.C.: Brookings Institution, 2004).

4. Peter J. Taylor and Robert E. Lang, *U.S. Cities in the 'World City Network'* (Washington, D.C.: Brookings Institution, 2005), 1–17; Paul L. Knox, "Globalization and Urban Economic Change," *Annals of the American Academy of Political and Social Science* 551 (1997): 17–27; and John R. Short and Yeong-Hyun Kim, *Globalization and the City* (London: Addison Wesley Longman, 1999).

5. See Taylor and Lang, *U.S. Cities in the 'World City Network,'* 1–17; Knox, "Globalization," 17–27; Paul L. Knox, "World Cities," in *Globalization: The Reader,* ed. John Beynon and David Dunkerley (New York: Routledge, 2000), 66–68; and Leonard I. Ruchelman, "Cities in the Next Century," in *The Urban Society Reader,*

Annual Editions, 11th ed. (Guildford, Conn.: McGraw-Hill/Dushkin, 2003), 198–202.

6. Knox, "World Cities," 66.

7. James C. Cobb and William Stueck, *Globalization and the American South*, (Athens, Ga.: University of Georgia Press, 2005), xi.

8. Emily Thomas Livingstone, "Contemporary Gentrification Processes in a Globalizing City: Super-gentrification, New-build Gentrification and Charlotte, North Carolina" (master's thesis, University of North Carolina at Charlotte, 2008), 164.

9. D. E. Paul, "World Cities as Hegemonic Projects: The Politics of Global Imagineering in Montreal," *Political Geography* 23 (2004): 572.

10. John R. Short and Yeong-Hyun Kim, *Globalization and the City* (London: Addison Wesley Longman,1999), 99.

11. Donald Lyons and Scott Salmon, "World Cities, Multi-national Corporations, and Urban Hierarchy: The Case of the United States," in *World Cities in a World System*, ed. Paul Knox and Peter J. Taylor (Cambridge: Cambridge University Press, 1995).

12. See Taylor and Lang, *U.S. Cities in the 'World City Network,'* 5; Knox, "Globalization," 23; and Knox, "World Cities," 66.

13. *Charlotte: Innovation and Excellence in Education,* (Charlotte: Charlotte Chamber, 2008), 3.

David Goldfield

A Place to Come To

In November 1986 the Southern Historical Association (SHA) held its annual convention in Charlotte. Comprised primarily of academics who either teach southern history or teach at southern institutions, the SHA brought about thirteen hundred participants to the Queen City. Most of the delegates stayed at the Adams Mark Hotel, a property that left guests a seven-block uphill walk to the heart of Uptown. Rumors of safety issues and the unseasonably frigid weather rendered the walk even more problematic. The hotel staff was pleasant though clearly overwhelmed and generally clueless about the most frequently asked questions during the four days of meetings: "Where should we eat?" and "What's there to do here?"

In fairness to the staff, those questions would have challenged the expertise of most Charlotteans. The few restaurants in the area were hardly sites of culinary wizardry. For the meeting's participants, who in previous years had enjoyed the fine food of New Orleans, Houston, Memphis, Louisville, Nashville, Atlanta, Washington, D.C., and yes, Birmingham, the idea of eating six meals of Carolina barbecue, whatever its well-earned merits, did not whet many appetites.

The annoyance at the distance of Uptown (which is downtown in the rest of the world, but here in Charlotte the designation implies a city on a hill and all the messianic connotations that accompany such a designation) dissipated after the few intrepid souls who wandered out in the cold night air to experience the city center reported back that there was no there there. Not much nightlife except for a few panhandlers whom the delegates were glad to see as evidence that a stealth nuclear explosion had not occurred during their trek up the hill. The verdict was clear from the membership: "Let's not meet here again."

Couldn't blame them, really. I thought about that meeting, which I attended and apologized for time and again, eight years later when Charlotte hosted the NCAA Final Four, an extravaganza that rivals the Olympic Games for pomp and revelry, except that it is an annual event. Uptown still exuded the aura of a demilitarized zone, but civic leaders hit upon the idea of creating a vibrant city center where none existed. It was totally *ersatz*, of course, but it kept the fans in their cups for nearly a week. It was not difficult to conclude that Charlotte had succeeded only in turning the state motto on its head: "To Seem Rather Than to Be."

What Charlotte seemed to be, or at least what visitors saw of it, was a big small town with a nice canopy of trees that covered neighborhoods somewhere beyond the concrete hill of banks and office buildings. Charlotte was urban, but not urbane. Even an attempt at urbanity came off either slightly ridiculous or slightly sinister. In the 1960s, city planners in Minneapolis constructed aerial walkways to connect downtown buildings at their second stories. Considering the long and brutal Minneapolis winters, creating an enclosed street system connecting workers with garages, shops, restaurants, and their offices seemed like a capital idea; and it was. Charlotte's winters are quite mild and relatively short. Critics panned Charlotte's version as an imitation gone bad. Or worse: some suggested darkly that the walkways were functional after all — a way to help white office workers and executives avoid mingling with African Americans waiting for buses on the street level. The tale may be apocryphal, though civic leaders hailed the erection of a city bus terminal several blocks off the Square (the heart of Uptown) where African Americans could now congregate off the street and out of sight.

It is easy to poke fun at such foibles of an urban wannabe, let alone a "world-class" city. The fact is, however, that Charlotte's history has been more "hit" than "miss," and even when you could hear the echoes of your footsteps on the Uptown pavement at night, things were percolating that would change the city and region in a major way. As the southern historians happily bid good riddance to Charlotte, Hugh McColl, the head of NCNB, concluded the Southeastern Banking Compact that enabled banks in the region to open branches wherever they wanted. So successful was this entrepreneurial endeavor that by the time NCNB became NationsBank in the early 1990s, it was gobbling up failed savings and loan institutions at bargain prices and transforming Charlotte into a major banking center.

McColl was part of a long line of brash, innovative entrepreneurs who all had one thing in common: they were not from Charlotte. Most were not even from North Carolina. In the slavery era, Charlotte sat in the middle of a modest agricultural region with a relatively modest black population and an equally modest white population churning out a modest living from the clay soil. Then the railroad came. By the mid-1850s, Charlotte boasted three railroads, including the North Carolina Railroad that stretched all the way east to Goldsboro. Charlotte's main connections, however, ran north and south with what became the Southern Railway system. It was easier to get to Philadelphia than to Wilmington, and it was certainly a snap sending goods along the river or railroad into South Carolina and eventually to the wider world from Charleston. Thus, Charlotte always had a cosmopolitan outlook, beyond the state, and even beyond the region.

What this meant in practical terms was that Charlotte was not a city of tradition, either in ideas or families. Richmond, Charleston, and Savannah were hidebound; like dowager sisters they clung to a faded past and eschewed new ideas. After the Civil War, the future of the South belonged to places such as Charlotte, Atlanta, Birmingham, and Nashville. The old port cities were dead in the water. The energy of Dixie lay in the interior towns with good railroad connections and go-getters aplenty.

Daniel A. Tompkins, from Edgefield, South Carolina, was one of those go-getters. An engineer by training, educated up north, he came to Charlotte in the 1870s, purchased a newspaper called the *Charlotte Observer* and set about promoting the town much as folks in other interior cities of the South were doing. Standing at the railroad depot one day, he noticed that porters were loading cotton bales on cars bound for the Northeast. Why, he wondered, could not the South take its greatest raw material — cotton — and turn it into yarn and cloth instead of shipping it off for someone else to reap the profits from the finished product?

Tompkins launched his "cotton-mill campaign" in the early 1880s. By 1905, more than half of the looms in the South were located within a hundred-mile radius of Gastonia, North Carolina, and the Carolina Piedmont was challenging New England for textile manufacturing supremacy. Young workers coming down from the impoverished farms in the mountains and foothills traveled up and down the Southern Railway to one mill-town job or another, and when the automobile became popular and affordable in the 1920s, they drove back and forth from farm to town eking out a hard living, but at least not starving.

Child labor and union busting accompanied the industrial boom as boosters touted a docile Anglo-Saxon labor force that was not so much quiet as cowed. The mill owners controlled the local police, politicians, ministers, and schools and rented houses to their workers in tight-knit company towns. These towns and most of the mills were located outside Charlotte's borders. Charlotte civic leaders liked it that way. They did not mind the city's image as the "linthead capital of the world," as long as there were few lintheads about.

Local capital financed the mills for the most part. That is how Charlotte got into the banking business. The progenitors of Bank of America and Wachovia originated as groups of well-heeled farmers and merchants raising money, obtaining a bank charter, and lending out funds to promising entrepreneurs in places like Belmont, Gastonia, McAdenville, and Kannapolis. It beat begging up north where interest rates and loan terms were always more onerous. Charlotte boosted its banking credentials even further when the federal government made a surprise announcement in 1927 that it would locate a branch of the Federal Reserve Bank in Charlotte. Everyone assumed that Columbia, South Carolina, would receive the nod for the branch.

It would not be the last time that Charlotte surprised the pundits. The hallmark of the Charlotte style was evident in the Reserve Bank bid: hard work behind the scenes. Charlotte leaders have relished underestimation. While Atlanta kept its eye on Birmingham in the late 1930s, its mayor, William B. Hartsfield, built his folly south of town — an airport that was ten years ahead of its time — which meant that when World War II ended, Atlanta was already well ahead of rivals for air postal service, freight, and eventually passenger traffic. Mayor Ben Douglas in Charlotte meanwhile quietly built an air terminal to serve the city the same year, 1941, that Hartsfield Airport opened in Atlanta. Later, both Atlanta and Charlotte became major airline hubs, and, as any civic leader will tell you, being a hub is golden. The great convenience to go nonstop most any place in the United States where you would want to go (and a few places in Europe as well) is a significant recruiting tool, not only for companies, but for families eager to see their relatives, children, and friends on holidays and vacations.

Charlotte came out of the Second World War poised to go someplace important. True, textiles still dominated the surrounding area, an industry that did not create much consumer buying power among its work force. True, Charlotte, as a southern city, pretty much wrote off at least one-quarter of its population with inferior schools, slipshod urban services, and a benign indifference that passed for good race relations. African Americans built culturally rich if monetarily modest neighborhoods and institutions, as they did elsewhere in the South. There was a thriving middle class of teachers and preachers, but segregation was never equal.

The city also lacked a first-class institution of higher education. It was the hallmark of northern cities such as Philadelphia, New York, Boston, and

Chicago to boast some of the finest universities in the nation. In the South, however, the best state institutions were wrapped in the magnolia of small towns like Chapel Hill, Athens, Tuscaloosa, Knoxville, Charlottesville, and Lexington. The great Methodist schools, such as Duke in Durham, Emory in Atlanta, and Vanderbilt in Nashville, grew in an urban context, but they hardly connected with their environment. Again, an outsider, an entrepreneur, and a woman no less — Bonnie Cone — came with a vision for a great institution of higher education in Charlotte. The state legislature chartered Charlotte College (and its black counterpart, Carver College) as a two-year branch of the Chapel Hill campus in 1946.

The state created the college on a shoestring as the GI Bill filled the pockets of returning veterans eager to obtain a college degree. The lawmakers perceived Charlotte College as a temporary solution to enable the vets to work and go to school at the same time without having to traipse to Chapel Hill, Greensboro, or Raleigh. Bonnie Cone had other, grander ideas. In the tradition of Daniel A. Tompkins, Ms. Bonnie, as everyone called her, dreamed large, in her case of a university in the growing metropolitan area. She persuaded the legislature that the demand in the Charlotte region was significant enough for the state to expand Charlotte College into a four-year institution.

It was a hard sell. North Carolina lawmakers have not always cherished the assets that Charlotte brings to the state and often the bankers and developers need to remind the eminents in Raleigh. This is not surprising, as many Charlotte residents have historically come from outside the state, particularly from South Carolina. Charlotte looked north and south for commerce and people, not east and west. Columbia, South Carolina, is a more easily accessible capital than Raleigh, and for all Raleigh has done for the city, Charlotte's capital might just as well be in South Carolina. From road building to education, getting Raleigh's attention has always been difficult. Yet, Ms. Bonnie persisted, and UNC-Charlotte debuted as a four-year institution in 1949.

The tenuous and contentious connection with Raleigh should not imply that Charlotte is an island in the midst of an indifferent state. Hugh McColl recognized before many others that Charlotte had the good fortune of being in the right geographic place at the right time. A major demographic shift occurred in the United States between the 1960s and the turn of the twenty-first century, a trend that persists to this day. Millions of Americans (ten million since 1990) have moved into the Southeast from other parts of the country, mainly from the Rust Belt regions of the Midwest and the Northeast.

The migration added a new dimension to the city's traditional mix of newcomers, many of whom came from adjacent counties and states, rather than from the North. The newcomers also fueled growth in Atlanta, Raleigh-Durham-Chapel Hill, and Nashville. They brought with them good education, high skill levels, and a demand for quality urban and cultural services. They enjoyed the fine barbecue here and appreciated the occasional "meat-and-three" lunches, but they wanted more creative fare, better bagels, pizza that reminded them of home, and places to shop for organic produce. Much as the folks who migrated down the Great Valley Road from Pennsylvania in the eighteenth century gave shape to Charlotte and the Piedmont, so now another wave of Yankees would make a significant mark on the community and region.

The prevailing myth is that this migration stream appeared mainly because the city solved its racial crises, desegregating its public accommodations in the 1960s and then its public school system in the 1970s. Racial segregation by law demanded its own code of silent assent on the part of whites and made life very difficult for those who dissented. Contrary to the theme of southern hospitality, the South was not a very welcoming place in the segregation era unless you kept your mouth shut and went about your business.

Projecting a positive image has always been a major concern among Charlotte's civic leaders. They wanted the world, or at least the rest of the country, to know that the more insidious aspects of Jim Crow were unwelcome in the city. In fact, Charlotte's leaders were much more concerned about labor unions than about fractious black people. Still, the early 1960s were volatile years throughout the South and Charlotte did not want to emulate Little Rock, New Orleans, and certainly not Birmingham. Two years prior to the 1964 Civil Rights Act, which mandated the desegregation of public accommodations, white civic leaders got together with their black counterparts and went out to lunch, thus desegregating Uptown restaurants, and soon other public facilities followed. Lunching rather than lynching characterized Charlotte's approach to race relations.

Desegregating public education came more slowly and with greater difficulty. Although the U.S. Supreme Court had declared segregated education unconstitutional in the landmark *Brown v. Board of Education of Topeka* decision (1954), Charlotte-Mecklenburg's schools were essentially still segregated when the Court handed down its opinion in *Swann v. Charlotte-Mecklenburg School Board* in 1971. The story of what followed is well known and has attained a hagiographic eminence in the community, much of it deserved.

What is problematic, however, is the connection between the peaceful and temporarily successful desegregation of the public schools and Charlotte's rapid rise to regional and then national preeminence. The major migrations into the region did not occur until the late 1980s and after, long after the desegregation of the schools. Ironically, the migration probably abetted the move toward resegregation. Northerners were unaccustomed to integrated schools for the most part. Many northern whites came from suburbs where schools were predominantly white. They associated quality education with white education. Considering the low performance of inner-city northern school systems, that association was not far-fetched. Simultaneously, African Americans around the country, and not just in Charlotte, began to question the value of desegregation, especially since most of its burdens — busing and the closing of black schools — fell on black children and teachers.

There was also a concern in the black community that behind the desegregation effort was an assumption that a black child had to sit next to a white child in order to learn. Some in African American communities engaged in "segregation nostalgia." For all of the difficulties of the Jim Crow era, they asserted, there was a sense of community, of looking after one another, of close-knit extended families, of rock-solid churches, and of schools that, for all their shortcomings, imparted more than book knowledge to their charges. Separate was never equal, however, and the context of the era devalued black education. That context is mostly gone, and there is no saying that single-race schools cannot succeed. It is a rare thing, though, whether in Charlotte-Mecklenburg, Topeka, or Atlanta, that an all-black school is a high-performing school. That this may reflect socioeconomic status more than race is probably true, but segregated schools still shortchange a significant portion of the Southeast's urban population.

Again, Hugh McColl was right. His support of the decision not to appeal the rescission of the busing order for the city-county school system made sense from a business point of view. There are good public schools in Charlotte; there are even better private schools, and the better neighborhoods where most of the newcomers reside have a good choice. Atlanta is booming, Washington, D.C., is undergoing a remarkable renaissance, and Richmond is thriving; few educators, however, would give high or even mid-range marks to the public school systems in those cities. The reality is that the fortunes of cities and their public school systems are not complementary.

Charlotte continues to be "a place to come to," with most of its population hailing from someplace else, primarily because of the job demands of the knowledge economy that has supplanted though not entirely replaced the old industrial economy. The workers accrued their skills and education elsewhere, and there are enough educational alternatives in the region for their children to receive a fine education.

Charlotte is still "a good place to make money," as the early twentieth-century motto declared. And few northern white transplants bother themselves with racial issues, refighting the Civil War, or debating the finer points of evangelical theology. They are just here to raise a family, make some money, and enjoy the fine climate and what this city has to offer.

That does not make for much of a sense of community, a shortcoming that became increasingly obvious by the late 1980s when subdivisions erupted like hives on the county's periphery. The city became more fragmented, as was reflected in the school bond defeat and in the contention on the school board. Political leaders were ineffective in drawing the disparate and increasingly far-flung areas of the city and county together. Traffic congestion increased, as did crime. It seemed that Charlotte was becoming like Atlanta after all. In a city whose day-to-day operations are run by the city manager, with a weak mayor, it fell to the business community to develop a comprehensive vision, a role to which it was accustomed.

Five events between 1992 and 1998 relaunched the Charlotte star and secured its unprecedented rise as one of the nation's major banking centers and innovators in city planning. These five episodes may reflect the city's good fortune, but they are also indicative of the significant role entrepreneurs have played in guiding Charlotte's development. The first event involved the opening of a missing piece in any city's urban repertoire; the second, a milestone sport announcement that had nothing to do with NASCAR; the third, the establishment of a new institution; the fourth, the defeat of an old philosophy; and the fifth, an audacious business deal that built on the city's renewed energy.

The first event was the opening of the Blumenthal Center for the Performing Arts in 1992. As with many landmark episodes in the 1990s, the Center reflected the changing demographics of the Charlotte region. Charlotte had a decent symphony orchestra and occasionally hosted some good theater and classical music performers, but it lacked a major venue for these attractions. Though it is easy to poke fun at Charlotte's "world-class-city" preening, civic leaders understood that recruiting creative and talented people to the city required a certain level of urbanity. This urbanity did not require burying the city's southern heritage — Charleston and Savannah had been urbane for three centuries. It has long been a misconception that cities, true cities, are somehow unsouthern, a myth that ranks up there with the notion that our ancestors subsisted on shrimp and grits. The Blumenthal family provided the key financial gift. The family's patriarch, I. D. Blumenthal — another outsider — came to Charlotte from his native Savannah in the 1930s.

A year later, another cultural event generated great community elation: the award of a National Football League (NFL) franchise. The NFL endorsement meant that the Charlotte region possessed enough wealth and marketing clout to support a professional football franchise. It became another key recruiting tool and business entertainment opportunity that would wear well in the coming years.

What city is complete without a first-class history museum? The Museum of the New South, imagined by a small group of civic leaders and academics in 1991, functioned as a museum without walls at numerous venues until it formally opened its doors to the public in 1996. The idea of the museum was to tell the story of Charlotte and the Carolina Piedmont to the public, but especially to those who came from outside the region. Charlotte has a hazy image beyond its borders. Sure, there's NASCAR, barbecue, and banking, but what that adds up to in terms of a definable image is not clear. The museum presented the region's history and how it came to its present moment, especially with its core exhibit, "From Cotton Fields to Skyscrapers."

Schoolchildren marched through the museum and, often, their parents followed. The hope was that visitors would place their own stories within the context of the stories told by the museum, and through that process come to identify with their home, new or old. Temporary exhibits on race, on immigration, on foodways, and on religion, among others, provided an in-depth perspective on themes presented in the core exhibit. I recall when we first discussed the museum with then-mayor Richard Vinroot. He scratched his head and stated that he liked the concept, but what could a Charlotte history museum show? Richmond, for example, had a history, he noted, but Charlotte? Well, with all due respect to His Honor, Charlotte and the Carolina Piedmont have a very rich history.

Funding is the bane of museums everywhere, but through some deft fund-raising both at the state level and through private donations, the museum remained afloat until Leon and Sandra Levine offered a substantial gift that enabled the museum to thrive and fulfill its mission even better. Leon Levine, the founder and chairman of Family Dollar stores, is one of the South's great philanthropists. Not only the Levine Museum of the New South, but the Levine Children's Hospital and the Levine Campus of Central Piedmont Community College as well as the Levine Jewish Community Center reflect the family's commitment to the city and region. Levine, like so many before him, was not a native. He hailed from down east in Rockingham, North Carolina.

It also happens that the Blumenthals and Levines are active in Charlotte's Jewish community, as well. As in most southern cities, the dividing line has typically been black and white, not religious, as long as one professes a religion. Mutt Evans, the Jewish six-term mayor of Durham, North Carolina, always put his synagogue affiliation on his yard signs.

Such public displays of religion are jarring to settlers from the North who are accustomed to viewing religion as a private, personal matter. Moving into a neighborhood in a southern city, a newcomer's first encounter with neighbors is likely to elicit the question, "What church do you go to?" It is less of a quiz than a way to place the newcomer and invite him or her to the neighbor's church. It would be highly unusual for a neighbor, say, on Long Island to approach a newcomer at first sight with that question.

There is no mistake about the important role of religion in Charlotte, but the unwritten rule is that it must not intrude on the city's major task of making money. It was only 1979 that Charlotte voted to have liquor by the drink. The fact that professional football games often start at 1 pm on Sunday meant that banning Sunday alcohol sales or delaying them until game time were not options for thirsty fans. So, the county rolled back the time by an hour.

Alcohol is no longer the flash point it once was in the region: too many newcomers and too many parties. Homosexuality, on the other hand, remains a very touchy issue. As in most of the South, evangelical Christians predominate in Charlotte's religious community. Jim and Tammy Faye Bakker prospered here, until the *Charlotte Observer* exposed their excesses. Billy Graham called Charlotte his home and if you arrive in the city at the airport, it is likely you will be whisked Uptown, at least part of the way, on the Billy Graham Parkway. Unlike most of the South, however, the Presbyterians are particularly prominent, which is perhaps one reason why, early on, the city never really allowed religion to get in the way of the main chance.

In 1997, a controversy erupted over the staging of Tony Kushner's play

Angels in America. There is a particularly annoying tendency among some people these days to equate a presentation with an advocacy. The charge was that the play advanced and encouraged homosexuality. For those people who derive their morals, values, and day-to-day operating instructions from television and movies, I suppose such confusion is understandable. For the rest of us, however, we realize that we are not witnessing reality but an artistic representation of it and, in good theater, which this is, it will engage us and give us something to think about. Fine, the opponents of the play said, but no public money should be allocated to support such a performance. The ringleader of this opposition, Hoyle Martin, a black evangelical Democrat, and the four white Republicans on the County Commission cut $2.5 million funding to the Arts and Science Council, which funded the Charlotte Repertory Theater. At that point, as noted elsewhere in this volume, the business leaders, particularly Joe Martin of NationsBank, swung into action and the play was staged.

The issue was not whether one should or should not accept homosexuality — that is a private decision — but whether the community should censure certain artistic expressions because some members of that community oppose them on religious grounds. Should religious belief, in other words, translate to public policy? The business leaders recognized that, with the growing religious diversity in the region and with Charlotte's heightened economic profile, the mixture of religion and politics could generate the equivalent of the Scopes trial and all the accompanying ridicule. The *New York Times* picked up the story and many were pegging Charlotte as a pesthole of intolerant Bible thumpers. This was not an issue over sexual orientation, but of freedom of speech and expression. Though letters to the editor of the *Charlotte Observer* continue to this day to rail against the alleged "homosexual agenda" of this book or that play or that policy, religion has remained outside public policy ever since. This is not to say that the religious beliefs of city and county political leaders are irrelevant, just that they are private and no longer the explicit basis of public policy.

The most stunning event of the decade of the 1990s was the merger of NationsBank with Bank of America in 1998 and the removal of the international headquarters from San Francisco to Charlotte. The banking consolidation proved contagious as First Union and Wachovia merged three years later. The recent upheavals in the banking industry, including the merger of Wells Fargo with Wachovia at the end of 2008 and the change in leadership at Bank of America in late 2009, shook the city's confidence. The banks are recovering, however, and the talented men and women drawn to the city in the past two decades ensure a synergy of creativity and prosperity.

Perhaps the most exciting transformation of Charlotte during and after this time period, 1992–98, was not an event, but rather a continuous stream of immigrants into the Southeast. The migration constitutes not so much a new trend in southern history as a renewal of a stream dating from the colonial era that was cut off during the decades of economic stagnation following the Civil War. Scotch-Irish and German families settled the Carolina Piedmont in the 1730s and 1740s, many of them descending from Pennsylvania along the Great Wagon Road. German Jewish peddlers and Irish workers moved south along the rail network in the 1850s and settled in several southern cities and towns. By the 1890s, however, when immigrants from southern and eastern Europe crowded into northern cities, the urban South, including Charlotte, was overwhelmingly native-born. Entrepreneurs touted this Anglo-Saxon stock to outside investors and industrialists, appealing less to their patriotism than to the fact that these homegrown laborers did not bring radical European ideas with them to the job site, and wages and overhead in the South were bound to be lower. Just as industrial jobs moved offshore beginning in the 1980s, eviscerating the textile industry in the Carolina Piedmont, so they moved from New England to the South in the early twentieth century, and for the same reasons.

Industrial labor in the Carolina Piedmont today, however, is just as likely to be foreign-born as homegrown. In some of the smaller communities, industrial workforces, especially in meat-processing plants, are overwhelmingly Hispanic. The Hispanic, primarily Mexican, migration to the Carolinas has become a major demographic theme of the early twenty-first century. Initially migrating to pick crops beginning in Florida and working their way northward, the booming economies of the urban Southeast drew Hispanics to the cities, to work in construction and landscaping in particular.

In true southern urban fashion, there is no Hispanic ghetto in Charlotte, but there are pockets of residential and commercial concentration. A similar residential pattern exists in Atlanta. The Hispanic influence on Charlotte is evident in restaurants, on supermarket shelves, in schools with the immense popularity of Spanish language classes, and in the ethnic culture of the community. There is also a strong and increasing presence of Asian immigrants and political refugees from Africa and Eastern Europe.

They all pursue the age-old American dream for immigrants. The dream remains the same, even if the latitude has changed somewhat. That Hispanics have not made common cause with African Americans on a variety of issues including education is not surprising. As immigrants, Hispanics, Asians, Africans, and Eastern Europeans want to emulate their immigrant predecessors, not the unique and often unfortunate history of black Americans. This reflects a national phenomenon. As historian David Roediger has noted, the process of becoming American for immigrants is the process of becoming "white," something that Africans and newcomers from the Caribbean can attain, but not African Americans for the simple reason that they did not come to this country for a better life. They are what one might call involuntary immigrants. In a nation of immigrants, African Americans remain the outlier, written out of the American story. That is a dilemma far beyond Charlotte, but it is an issue that white and black Americans must confront eventually.

Few would argue that Charlotte's rapid growth, especially since the mid-1990s, has been without negative consequences. However, growth has made possible a vibrant Uptown quite different from the barren desert the southern historians encountered in 1986 or the phony oasis basketball fans strolled through in 1994. There are more than twelve thousand residents Uptown, and that figure is growing. The increased density has helped to make the light rail system inaugurated in 2007 a great success, with various parts of the city and region now clamoring to get on board the planned extensions of the main line. There are discussions now of Charlotte becoming a green capital, not as in "money," but as in "environment." Growth and prosperity provide the business leadership the opportunity to be creative, bold, and decisive.

It has usually been the case in Charlotte's history that there were few people around to say "No." Old families concerned about their patrimony and old traditions that encrusted and paralyzed decision making were simply not part of the way Charlotte did business. The leadership and the newcomers had something in common: they came from someplace else, they often brought new ideas with them, and they always brought a desire to succeed. If America is an immigrant nation, then Charlotte is its prototypical city in the sense that its great leaders and its ordinary citizens came from someplace else. It may be too early, or it may be entirely irrelevant, to assess whether or not Charlotte is a "world-class city," but it is certainly now a city of the world.

Chapel Hill sociologist John Shelton Reed is fond of saying that Atlanta is what 350,000 Confederate soldiers died trying to prevent. The great Georgia writer Flannery O'Connor remarked that there were neighborhoods in Atlanta where not a southerner lived — and that was back in the 1950s. There are frequent lamentations that Charlotte has lost its southern charm, assuming it once possessed that attribute. In fact, Charlotte's overheated boosterism, its occasional lapses into theological thuggery, and its disdain for government restrictions on development are some of the least attractive remnants of southern civilization, and thankfully, they are fading as it becomes apparent that managed growth is good business, religion thrives best in homes and churches, not in public policy, and diversity is an asset not a threat to a city on the make. As if to add an exclamation point to this sentiment, the Southern Historical Association has agreed, after nearly a quarter century absence, to meet again in Charlotte in 2010. The members will find a very different city.

Matthew D. Lassiter

Searching for Respect
From "New South" to "World Class" at the Crossroads of the Carolinas

"One way to tell that you're from Buffalo," the *New York Times* informed readers in 2000, "is that half of your friends moved to Charlotte, N.C., and the other half went to Raleigh."[1] This gloomy joke that made the rounds in Erie County, New York, captures the iconography of Rust Belt decline and Sun Belt ascendance that has shaped the national imagination about regional trends since the 1970s. A similar script, though boastful rather than mournful, has characterized the century-long booster project to market the fast-growing cities of the New South as the antithesis of the fading industrial centers of the Northeast and Midwest, with warmer weather, better living standards, progressive race relations, and a prosperous business climate.[2] In Charlotte, a midsized southern metropolis with civic aspirations to catch up with Atlanta and keep ahead of Raleigh, the Chamber of Commerce has always taken the lead in promoting the Queen City on the national stage. The corporate priorities of economic growth and metropolitan expansion have therefore dominated the presentation of Charlotte as a full-throttled embodiment of American capitalism, from the early 1900s "Watch Charlotte Grow" campaign to the frank 1970s slogan declaring the city "A Good Place to Make Money."[3] Charlotte business leaders and politicians pursued this public relations strategy in order to overcome a regional inferiority complex based on persistent national stereotypes about southern racial and economic backwardness by converting these liabilities into the virtuous synthesis of New South interracial harmony and Sun Belt metropolitan development.[4]

Charlotte's boosters, along with many ordinary residents, have spent the past century on a perennial search for respect, both in terms of an obsessive regard for the city's national reputation and in the sense of a collective crisis of civic identity. "Charlotte should have been Charlotte without the N.C.

a long time ago," asserted former mayor Harvey Gantt in 1993, expressing a common lament of city leaders frustrated over being confused for Charleston (South Carolina) or Charlottesville (Virginia). "The nightmare is always there," the *Washington Post* explained, "the worst possible combination of the Old South and the fantasies of arrogant Yankees." Instead of a New South city, a national metropolis with American values — "the terrible vision of trailer trash, bare-bulb tent revivals, ... overalls, straw hats, Bull Connor's attack dogs, rickets, missing teeth, old ladies smoking pipes, six-fingered hillbillies chasing their sisters through the woods."[5] By the 1980s and 1990s, Charlotte appeared to have transcended these gothic and mythic images of southern exceptionalism by veering all the way to the other extreme, leading to a pervasive anxiety that the New South/Sun Belt project had succeeded too well in creating a bland bankers' paradise with no unique character, no true soul, no sense of place at all. Charlotte is "the city without a past," in the conventional wisdom cited by a local columnist; "Potemkin Village with a drawl," in a sarcastic *New York Times* assessment; "a nice place to live," according to a self-deprecating local joke, "but you wouldn't want to visit there."[6] "Charlotte is overwhelmingly ... average," charged the *Raleigh News and Observer* in 1987. "It is a fine, rich, upstanding city. It just isn't much of a fine, rich, upstanding Southern city. It has all of the quaint Southern appeal of Des Moines." And then the ultimate insult from the cross-state rival, pinpointing the greatest fear of all: "Charlotte's raging inferiority complex, as witnessed by its overwhelming need to boost its image, comes about because nobody else pays much attention to it."[7]

Charlotte's latest incarnation as an "international city" adapts the New South/Sun Belt framework to the contemporary hype surrounding globalization, an updated quest for identity and respect based on an unstable fusion of past and future evident in the Chamber of Commerce's branding Charlotte as a "world-class city with small town charm." Corporate boosters celebrate the transformation of the "Crossroads of the Carolinas" into the distribution and transportation hub of America's fifth-largest urbanized region by 2008 (7.1 million people within a hundred-mile radius), a "pro-business environment" with the presence of more than three-fifths of the nation's Fortune 500 firms, and a global "magnet that attracts foreign-owned companies and valuable employees." In the tradition of the civil rights era, when business leaders in the New South emphasized the direct links between racial progress and economic prosperity, the Charlotte Chamber promises international migrants that they will find a "multicultural metropolitan area that embraces diverse ideas, opinions, business operations and residents." As a global metropolis with a small-town feel, "Charlotte means many things to many people — Southern hospitality, the second-largest banking center in the country, a city of trees, home of major-league sports teams, a 'can-do' city filled with big dreams and friendly neighbors."[8] This enthusiastic willingness to abandon history altogether — to become whatever anyone with sufficient dollars or dreams wants it to be — is the secret of Charlotte's successes and the simultaneous source of its failures, a combination that is not unique to the Queen City's path of development but rather intrinsic to the New South/Sun Belt model and the updated world-class city manifestation. Each of these categories of corporate marketing has sought to reconcile Charlotte's elusive civic identity with its concrete economic mission through a functional embrace of the city's crossroads relationship to the Southeast, the rest of the nation, and, increasingly, the world.[9]

New South City

Back in 1791, George Washington dismissed Charlotte as a "trifling place" while passing through on his way to somewhere else. This oft-cited tale resonates among Charlotte's builders and promoters less because subsequent history proved the nation's first president to be wrong and more because the comment reinforces their own remarkable achievements in dreaming into existence a city with no compelling reason to exist where it does.[10] Without the natural advantage of a river or port, according to a 1926 publication by the Charlotte Chamber of Commerce, the now "thriving metropolis" of sixty thousand residents overcame Washington's verdict through the "phenomenal progress" brought by the textile mills, railroads, and highways that turned the city into a regional manufacturing base and distribution center. In addition, Charlotte boasted nearly perfect weather for anyone "looking for a climate that does not exhibit the extremes of the Northeast, yet possesses sufficient variation to break the monotony of sameness of that of California or Florida." Instead of sweltering humidity, this temperate atmosphere was "dry enough to make the heat of the summer days endurable, yet contains enough moisture to make it healthy; that has no destructive winds, yet sufficient circulation to purify the air and prevent stagnancy." At the height of the Jim Crow era, the primary concern of Charlotte's business leadership revolved around the perceived problem of modernizing a region with a substantial black population. "Is it possible," the Chamber wondered, "for Mecklenburg whites to reach their highest and best development alongside of an illiterate, unsanitary, immoral negro race?"[11]

Beginning in 1905, the businessmen who formed the Greater Charlotte Club adopted the straightforward slogan "Watch Charlotte Grow." A decade later, the renamed Chamber of Commerce was already looking beyond the textile economy of the Carolina Piedmont and marketing Charlotte's status as a regional powerhouse: the "Queen City of the South" and the "Open Gateway to the New South." During the first half of the twentieth century, the Chamber's industrial recruitment pamphlets explicitly contrasted Charlotte's fair weather and compliant workforce with the disagreeable conditions of the Northeast and Midwest. Charlotte's climate was "characterized by long but not unpleasantly warm summers and by mild winters," while the white laboring class was 99.3 percent "native born of old American stock." Thanks to this nonimmigrant population of "the pure Anglo-Saxon and Scotch," the Chamber of Commerce explained in 1928, "Charlotte is probably freer from industrial trouble than any other city in the South. We have none." In the metropolitan region, businesses seeking to expand or relocate would find workers "of a better type than in the older industrialized sections of the North and East, intelligent, loyal, easily trained, 100 per cent American and inclined to be contented with decent treatment and fair wages." During World War II, the Chamber launched a new marketing campaign highlighting the "Industrial Center of the Carolinas," including the conspicuous and mathematically creative message that more people lived within a hundred-mile radius of Charlotte (1.972 million) than of Atlanta (1.904 million). In a city that only managed to break the one hundred thousand population threshold in the 1940 census after desperate business leaders funded two recounts, the Chamber of Commerce even made the ambitious claim that 4.5 million people lived within Charlotte's trading zone of shopping and product distribution.[12]

During the boom years of the early Cold War, the Chamber of Commerce jettisoned the overt language of white supremacy and emphasized instead Charlotte's "progressive" philosophy and the full embrace of national ideals in "an American city which is proud of its American people." Charlotte offered the best of all worlds for a nation on the move, "a cosmopolitan society which enjoys a healthy balance between time-honored traditionalism and modern progressivism." Postwar business leaders reoriented their sales pitch away from low-paying jobs in industries such as textiles in favor of higher-salaried opportunities in the service sector, pointing to the arrival of retail stores such as Sears, Roebuck as evidence that "Charlotte has become one of the great trading centers of the Southeast." The Illinois-based company responded in kind: "Charlotte's future is determined by the progressive thinking and actions of its commercial and industrial enterprises." A 1948 diagram produced by the Chamber of Commerce portrayed Charlotte (the nation's ninety-first largest city) at the center of a distribution network covering the entire eastern half of the United States, with lines stretching as far north as New York and Chicago and southward (well past Atlanta) to New Orleans and Miami. At midcentury, in literature sent to thousands of business contacts in the Northeast and Midwest, the Chamber boasted that Charlotte was "sizing up her larger rivals," Richmond and Atlanta, in the battle for regional primacy. "The South is moving forward. Charlotte is leading the way."[13]

In the postwar period, national magazines began featuring the upstart Queen City as a major new player on the economic landscape. An upbeat *Business Week* profile in 1949 observed that while textiles remained the most important industry in Charlotte, the area's healthy and diversified economy increasingly revolved around merchandising, finance, and the distribution of northern-made products throughout the Southeast. (The earlier natural disadvantage of no river or port had turned into the modern advantage of a crossroads for rail freight shipping and interstate trucking). Two years later, *Business Week* returned to the Carolinas for a lengthy story titled "Charlotte: Unsouthern, Untypical." Because Charlotte's economic growth focused on distribution networks rather than manufacturing jobs, "white-collar workers make up the bulk of the city's newer residents, dilut[ing] southern provincialism with cosmopolitan flavor." With language that could have come straight from a Chamber of Commerce press release, *Business Week* praised the collective "attitude" in Charlotte, the "aggressiveness and progressiveness" that had made the city one of the most dynamic in the nation. Race relations received no mention at all, with the absence of conflict marking another sign of New South progress. There were some drawbacks to being a white-collar business town run by Protestant family men: no "decent auditorium," not a single "really good" restaurant, "no night life at all." This critique of Charlotte's cultural deficiencies would remain a familiar refrain for decades, as would other problems listed as the consequences of rapid growth: terrible traffic and overcrowded schools. Ignoring the downside, the Chamber of Commerce celebrated the attention from *Business Week* and other national publications, which had "put Charlotte in the nation's eye in a way that will bring firms and families to the fastest growing business center in the South." And four years later, with great fanfare, the city opened the Charlotte Coliseum and the adjacent Ovens Auditorium.[14]

The very effective "Spearhead of the New South" motto accompanied the rise of the civil rights movement, which required boosters to send a strong message that Charlotte's progressive reputation meant the intertwined commitment to racial moderation and economic growth. The Chamber of Commerce deployed the slogan from the mid-1950s through the late 1960s, usually with a logo featuring a queen's crown riding on a flying arrow, sometimes with the "Spearhead of the New South" phrase superimposed on an aerial photograph of skyscrapers in the downtown business district (see figure 1).[15] In the era of racial desegregation that followed the 1954 *Brown v. Board of Education* decision, Chamber literature avoided any explicit mention of civil rights, indeed avoided almost any recognition at all that African Americans constituted one-third of the population of Charlotte and surrounding Mecklenburg County. Behind the scenes, however, the Chamber played a critical role in establishing a biracial forum, the Community Relations Committee, which negotiated civil rights issues with the public relations objective of preventing black demonstrations and white violence alike. In the political arena, Mayor Stanford Brookshire (a former Chamber president) engineered the business establishment's accommodation to the civil rights movement, including the desegregation of public facilities in advance of the 1964 Civil Rights Act, through an agenda that he labeled "peaceful progress in race relations." In his speeches, Brookshire insisted that Charlotte "has a heart and a social conscience that embraces the interests of all of our citizens regardless of race, color, religion, economic or social status."[16]

Charlotte received glowing national publicity for the peaceful implementation of racial desegregation, including a 1964 report by a civil rights organization praising the progressive New South city for "mov[ing] its racial concerns into the mainstream of American thought and activity." The liberal editorial page of the *Charlotte Observer* labeled this philosophy the "Charlotte Way" — "the highest and best example in matters of racial transition ... resolved because of the good sense and basic good will of community leaders, white and black." Mayor Brookshire repeatedly linked economic growth to racial harmony and equal treatment under the law, contrasting the disastrous path taken by Birmingham and other defiant southern cities with the enlightened philosophy of Charlotte, "heart of the Piedmont, crossroads of the Carolinas and the spearhead of the New South." In private, corporate leaders in Charlotte bluntly acknowledged that their permanent drive to recruit new industry to the Carolinas required their moderate stance on race relations, a necessary means to a more important end.[17]

What most excited the business establishment in the early 1960s, beyond the annual celebration of "new industry ... new jobs ... new money," was the

Figure 1. Charlotte: "Spearhead of the New South." (Source: Charlotte Chamber.)

arrival of big jets at Douglas Airport. "Charlotte is on the jet map . . . that tells which cities will be the distribution points of the future," the Chamber of Commerce announced in 1961, with daily Eastern Air Lines flights to New York, Pittsburgh, Miami, and New Orleans.[18] Charlotte had become the "Action City," according to the promotional campaign that began in 1963, "*the* best place to build, grow, and live!" The Action City combined the

Searching for Respect 31

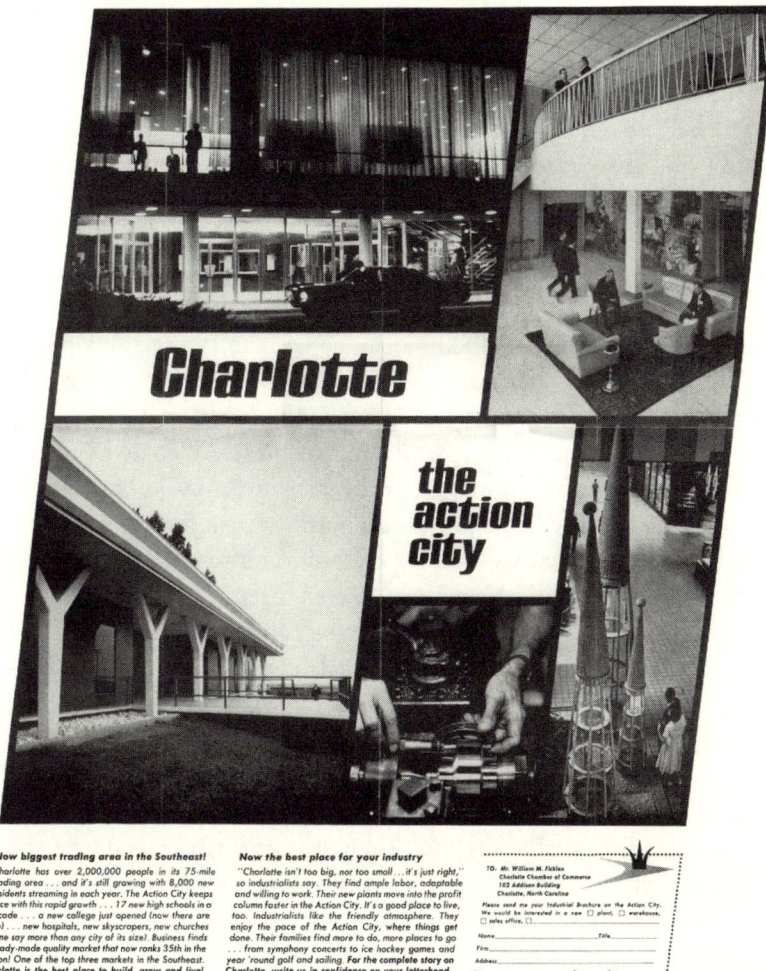

Figure 2. "Charlotte: The Action City," 1963. (Source: Charlotte Chamber.)

"tradition of Southern hospitality" with the "spirit of the New South," from downtown skyscrapers to suburban shopping malls, from cultural events at the Coliseum to seventy daily flights at the airport (see figure 2). "Like other Southern cities, Charlotte has embraced the dream of becoming another Atlanta," the *Observer* explained. "Anything that indicates that the dream is coming true is trumpeted northward to the men and money who can make it wholly true."[19]

In 1963, instead of simply basking in the new national prominence, the Chamber of Commerce pledged that "Charlotte will prove to the world that she deserves attention." The world beyond the United States first became a significant presence on the booster radar a decade earlier, not long after business recruiters had boasted of the absence of foreign immigrants in the Carolina Piedmont, and a quarter-century before their successors began touting the "international city." The Chamber of Commerce established its first Foreign Trade Committee in 1955 in order to "create an awareness among our citizens of the ever increasing importance of export-import trade on our daily lives." The city held its inaugural Foreign Trade Week in 1958; a Brazilian diplomat delivered the keynote speech. An annual week-long World Trade Festival soon followed, along with an International Fun Festival for children, to underscore the nearly $1 billion annual import-export business conducted in the state of North Carolina. In 1964, the Chamber of Commerce convinced the federal government to designate Douglas Airport a port of entry for imported products. But for five more years, until Charlotte secured federal approval as a port of origin for exports, corporations based in the metropolitan region had to move overseas-bound shipments through Norfolk, New York, or even Atlanta. Finally, in 1969, the Chamber could launch the next marketing campaign featuring Charlotte as a full-service international port, the nucleus of a "great metropolitan area [to] be recognized throughout the nation and the world as a major trading and population center."[20]

Political and business leaders in Charlotte had insisted for decades that the city was located at the center of the "biggest trading area in the Southeast," a claim dismissed in Atlanta, disputed by census data, and treated with skepticism even by the loyal boosters at the *Charlotte Observer*. Atlanta, the nationally recognized headquarters of the New South, was the "yardstick for other Southern cities to measure themselves with," the *Observer* acknowledged. "Whenever a company establishes anything in Charlotte — a sales office, a manufacturing facility, a warehouse — it becomes not merely a victory for Charlotte but a victory for Charlotte over Atlanta."[21] Among the many maneuvers by the Charlotte Chamber of Commerce in the long intraregional struggle for primacy in the New South, the most ill-fated was almost certainly the unveiling of Metrolina in 1968. The Chamber introduced Metrolina (an amalgam of "Metropolitan" and "Carolina") in an effort to rebrand a twelve-county region surrounding Charlotte as "the million plus market of the Carolinas." Metrolina embodied the new "regional city" — "the city too large in its economic, cultural and social importance to be contained within the limits of any municipality." Rival newspapers in North Carolina pointed out the transparent attempt to expand Charlotte's metropolitan region by unilateral action because the population within the official census-designated SMSA (Standard Metropolitan Statistical Area) had fallen behind the metropolitan total of Greensboro/Winston-Salem. The *Raleigh News and Observer*, speaking for a city that had never appreciated its involuntary inclusion in Charlotte's 150-mile (as the crow flies) trading radius, mocked Metrolina as nothing more than "a high tech made up word that Charlotte boosters have adopted." The Chamber persevered into the 1980s in its discursive quest to transform metropolitan Charlotte into Metrolina, but the name never caught on with the public, resistant outer-ring suburbs, or the national business press.[22]

Charlotte's corporate establishment spent much of the 1970s on the political defensive, a consequence of its failure to provide constructive leadership during the city's protracted crisis over court-ordered busing combined with a powerful grassroots backlash against the gospel of growth and the presumption that Charlotte should keep aspiring to become the next Atlanta. The successful resolution of school desegregation earned Charlotte national acclaim as "the city that made busing work" and prevented massive white flight from crippling the business climate and sabotaging the urban tax base. At the same time, the busing controversy accelerated a neighborhood-based revolt against the domination of local government by the Chamber of Commerce and the broader growth-is-good mantra that had led to unconstrained suburban sprawl throughout Mecklenburg County. In the early 1970s, the *Charlotte Observer* sided with neighborhood activists and accused the Chamber of Commerce of imperiling the region's future through a vision modeled on "the downtown of Atlanta combined with the suburbanized world of Los Angeles."[23] In the face of heavy public criticism, the Chamber released an unprecedented declaration that "uncontrolled growth is like cancer and will eventually cause the community to die. For that reason, growth for the sake of growth alone is not the aim of the Chamber. Our continued goal is selective growth . . . which will make Charlotte a better place in which to work and live." After decades of planning policies that openly favored downtown financial interests and the affluent suburbs of southeast Charlotte, corporate leaders pledged "more equitable growth" through the "broadest base possible of community effort" in the planning process. Then in 1975, Chamber president Don Bryant delivered the most remarkable statement of all: "Nobody that I know wants Charlotte to become another Atlanta. But there's nothing wrong with trying to become the finest middle-sized city in the country."[24]

This modest and attainable goal, to make livability and equitable development higher priorities than as much growth as possible everywhere in the metropolitan region, emerged from the most inclusive public debate in Charlotte's history. For a relatively brief period, roughly from the late 1960s through the early 1980s, substantial voices at the grassroots combined with at least some influential members of the business establishment to contemplate the possibility that Charlotte should change course and emulate Portland, Oregon, rather than Atlanta. Back in 1957, an admiring portrait of Charlotte's dynamic economy in *Manufacturers Record* reported that corporate leaders unanimously wanted and expected to become "as big as Atlanta."[25] By 1980, a profile of the city in *South Business* quoted the president of a major financial institution summarizing the conventional wisdom: "If you took a vote on whether Charlotte wanted to be another Atlanta or not, there'd be a resounding vote for no, we don't want to be." According to the business community, "head-over-heels growth simply isn't Charlotte's style anymore," the article explained. Instead, "Charlotte aims to be the 'Best Mid-Sized City' in the South." But the tensions that were already undermining this halfhearted commitment to equity and restraint could be seen everywhere, from the latest sprawling suburbs that exacerbated residential segregation, traffic, and air pollution to the continued use of eminent domain to "clear out the worst of the slums" and remove poor black residents from the financial and entertainment district rechristened "Uptown" (more "upbeat sounding" than downtown).[26] "Charlotte-Mecklenburg is a focus for businesses and families choosing to move into the Sunbelt," the Chamber of Commerce proclaimed in 1980. Now "this vibrant Sunbelt city" had a new identity as a banking capital of national influence and international reach.[27]

Sun Belt Banking Center

Hugh McColl, chief executive of North Carolina National Bank (NCNB), "lives by a creed," *Fortune* magazine reported: "Once you stop growing, you start dying." Charlotte's rising status as a major center of banking and finance profited from the free-wheeling capitalism of the Reagan era and the continued power shift to the metropolitan Sun Belt. During the economic boom of the 1980s, thanks to the relaxation of federal regulation of interstate banking, NCNB under McColl's leadership expanded through acquisitions in Florida and Texas. Then in 1991, NCNB took over Atlanta's most venerable financial institution, Citizens & Southern National Bank (which had recently merged with Richmond-based Sovran), to form a new Charlotte-based powerhouse renamed NationsBank. The combined presence of NationsBank and First Union, which also aggressively pursued mergers and acquisitions, turned Charlotte into the nation's third-largest banking headquarters, surpassing Los Angeles and trailing only San Francisco and New York City. With NationsBank's new sixty-story Uptown skyscraper, and with New South capitalists no longer hat-in-hand dependent on the whims and prejudices of northern investors, Charlotte's traditional booster vision of besting Richmond and matching Atlanta now seemed insufficiently ambitious. Instead of the short-lived goal of restrained growth and finding contentment as a midsized southern city, the Chamber of Commerce adopted a new slogan in 1991: "The Sky's the Limit." The NationsBank merger represented "a triumphant event for a city with a historic longing for recognition of almost any kind," concluded the *New York Times*. Charlotte finally had a legitimate claim to "rival Atlanta as the financial capital of the New South," the *Washington Post* agreed. NationsBank "brings what many of Charlotte's 400,000 residents seem desperately to want: recognition as a world-class city."[28]

The "world-class city" mantra began gathering steam under the leadership of Harvey Gantt, an architect who became Charlotte's first African American mayor in 1983. For Gantt, a fervent advocate of what is now called Smart Growth, the mission to secure Charlotte's prosperous future meant curbing suburban sprawl and redirecting resources to the urban core. The mayor lobbied IBM (unsuccessfully) to relocate from its suburban office park to Uptown in order to "demonstrate that our center city is truly world class," called for a European-style central business district aimed at pedestrians and in-town residents as well as commuting bankers, and told neighborhood groups that environmentally sensitive infill development and a focus on improving quality of life "will make Charlotte a 'world class' city."[29] While the liberal mayor envisioned controlled growth inside the city limits as the overriding priority, his unreliable allies at the Chamber of Commerce never really abandoned their belief in the inherent value of any new growth anywhere in the sprawling Metrolina region. Despite protests to the contrary, Charlotte's business leadership was still trying to catch up to Atlanta, whose own boosters had launched a marketing campaign to promote "The World's Next Great International City" more than a decade earlier. In 1985, the Chamber of Commerce released a new manifesto, "Visions for a Greater

Charlotte," with the goal of regaining the dominant role in political affairs and public discourse that the corporate establishment had seen diminished during the previous decade and a half. The Chamber called for the transformation of Uptown into a regional destination for arts and entertainment, the realization of Charlotte's potential as one of the nation's leading convention centers, and the attraction of international firms (almost always located in suburban office parks) from Europe, Asia, and Latin America.[30]

A survey of corporate executives in the mid-1980s revealed widespread sentiment that the Charlotte/Metrolina region must "attract more foreign investment" and "seek to become an international trade center."[31] The Chamber of Commerce carefully marked the outside world's growing presence in Charlotte: 55 foreign-owned companies in Mecklenburg County by 1976; trade delegations from Germany, Switzerland, Japan, and Nigeria in 1977; 146 international firms by 1985. Civic leaders also welcomed federal designation of the Charlotte Foreign Trade Zone, which would "expand an already thriving international flavor to the area economy."[32] And in 1983 business executives joined with UNC-Charlotte to form the Carolinas Council on World Affairs (soon renamed the World Affairs Council of Charlotte), an alliance dedicated to expanding "Carolinians' awareness of the world and the world's awareness of Charlotte and the Carolinas."[33] To help make this happen, the Chamber of Commerce and elected officials began lobbying the federal government to permit international flights to London and Frankfurt, which meant outmaneuvering competitors such as Raleigh and Pittsburgh. "We are an attraction for foreign investment and travel, and we are aggressive in our outreach to foreign markets and international concerns," Mayor Gantt informed the Department of Transportation during the successful campaign for a London flight from Charlotte's US Air hub. "The airport is a very important economic generator for Charlotte," his successor Sue Myrick declared in 1989, shortly before the renamed Charlotte Douglas International Airport added a direct flight to Frankfurt via Lufthansa. (Fifteen thousand Germans lived in metropolitan Charlotte, and more than sixty West German firms operated in Mecklenburg County).[34] "Charlotte: A City on the Move," the Chamber of Commerce responded in its next public relations campaign. "Home for two of the nation's leading banks; home of a brand-new NBA franchise; home of an International Airport; home to an orchestra which has made a name for itself in Europe; headquarters for over 200 foreign-based firms."[35]

Charlotte's acquisition of professional sports teams seemed to cement its status as a major American metropolis, and even a rising world-class city, especially in the views of local partisans. In the mid-1980s, a group of corporate investors initiated Charlotte's quest for a National Basketball Association franchise and supportive city officials began constructing the new Charlotte Coliseum before learning the verdict. "Having a pro basketball team raises your profile in the convention and trade-show business," according to the pragmatic analysis of the head of the coliseum authority. The collective civic spirit mattered as well, as Harvey Gantt informed NBA commissioner David Stern: "We are willing and feel able to make Charlotte one of the best NBA cities in the country!" The Queen City secured equal bragging rights with Sun Belt rivals Dallas and Atlanta in 1987, when the NBA awarded Charlotte the Hornets franchise and fifty thousand people turned out for the celebration. First Union provided the financing for the NBA team, which meant that NASCAR alone would no longer define Charlotte's national image as a sports town. "Charlotte is the New South at its finest," remarked Hornets president Spencer Stolpen, who had recently relocated from New Jersey. "It's a blend of the old southern charm and a new sophistication brought in by business people coming in from out of town."[36] Six years later, the National Football League chartered the Carolina Panthers franchise, so named to highlight Charlotte's central location in a multistate regional market. Civic pride exploded in a public celebration at the NationsBank Corporate Center amid widespread appreciation that Hugh McColl had made it all possible. "Forevermore," the *Charlotte Observer* rejoiced, "this single decision will likely change the way people across the country feel about what lies between Washington and Atlanta." "This is a can-do city, a city that believes in itself," Mayor Richard Vinroot proclaimed. "We don't have any self-doubt."[37]

The constant bluster and intrinsic braggadocio of New South boosterism suggest a deep-seated inferiority complex that in turn functions as a defensive response to the resilient national stereotypes of southern exceptionalism and regional backwardness. During the 1950s and 1960s, the perceived gulf between New South progress and Old South bigotry seemed so wide that civil rights groups struggled to draw attention to the thoroughly national patterns of residential segregation and racial inequality emerging in leading southern cities such as Atlanta and Charlotte. During the 1980s and 1990s, with the civil rights era fading into myth and the new zero-sum equation of Rust Belt crisis and Sun Belt prosperity, every New South triumph celebrated in Charlotte precipitated a new outpouring of condescension and clichés. "Charlotte Hits the Big Time," mocked the *Los Angeles Times* after the city's NBA coup. How did a real-life Mayberry that was "too small, too rural, too backward," in a state where everyone still watched "Andy, Opie,

Barney, and Goober" on television, fool the NBA's market researchers? "The town of 400,000 is trying to be a big city," the *Chicago Tribune* explained after the Panthers announcement. "Sports fans may wonder what all the fuss is about. The city's skyline, which did not even exist 25 years ago, is only four blocks long. The streets are practically devoid of people and cars during a weekday lunch hour." Charlotte residents welcomed the creation of NationsBank, according to the *Washington Post*, because they were "tired of being thought of by the rest of the nation as a bunch of country bumpkins, rednecks, and 'NASCAR numskulls.'" Even Hugh McColl, the South Carolina native who became the most successful man in Charlotte, could not always disguise the resentment that fueled his banking empire. "I always felt that the New York banks looked down on us and snubbed us," he told the *Post* during the Panthers celebration. "I always wanted to be big enough to be able to take them on ... There are Northerners who still haven't accepted the fact that there are people from below the Mason-Dixon line who have fine minds."[38]

Despite the boom times of the 1980s and 1990s, Charlotte's boosters and business leaders found it difficult to overcome pervasive national presumptions that their New South city must be a stereotypical Bible Belt backwater. "I know what the Bible Belt feels like," First Union CEO Ed Crutchfield insisted to the *New York Times* in 1987. "Charlotte never had the feel of the Bible Belt." That summer, the Hornets acquisition competed for national media coverage with the ongoing sex scandal involving Jim and Tammy Faye Bakker, the *PTL Club* televangelists who operated the giant Heritage USA theme park in the Charlotte suburbs. (Charlotte partisans pointed out that the Bakkers were based across the South Carolina state line, although Heritage USA was certainly located inside the boundaries of Metrolina). "Charlotte has come a long way," the *Times* profile conceded, "from hot rods, night riders, and revival tents."[39] But in the mid-1990s, when conservative ministers demanded censorship of a local run of Tony Kushner's *Angels in America*, the *New York Times* was back to emphasizing the "cultural tensions created when a Bible Belt town tries to move quickly into the first rank of American cities." The director of the Charlotte Repertory Theater requested that opponents of gay rights (and visiting reporters) recognize that "this is a progressive city ... I don't want us portrayed as a hick town or a redneck town." The conflict escalated after the Mecklenburg Board of County Commissioners drew national headlines by voting to deny public funding to local arts groups that encouraged "perverted forms of sexuality." Activists affiliated with the Religious Right charged that the corporate establishment wanted to turn Charlotte into "some kind of wanna-be world-class city," no matter what the cost to tradition and moral values. In rapid response, Hugh McColl of NationsBank and Ed Crutchfield of First Union launched an initiative to reinstate public funding for the arts, support "pro-tolerant" local politicians, and restore what McColl called the city's once "common purpose — make money, build nice things, make it happen."[40]

In a *Washington Post* editorial published during the arts controversy, a media executive who recently had relocated to Charlotte framed the city's future in stark terms: the potential to become "the next great Southern city," or the danger of remaining "a small town with delusions of grandeur: Mayberry with skyscrapers." National media coverage in the 1990s stressed that Charlotte's goal of "becoming the region's next Atlanta" (as the *Wall Street Journal* phrased it) faced even larger obstacles, most notably the widespread sense that the Queen City offered nice suburban living and plenty of opportunities to make money, but not much at all in terms of downtown entertainment for younger professionals or out-of-town visitors (especially in the "ghost town" of Uptown after the bankers left in the evening). In 1994, when the *New York Times* took the unusual step of featuring Charlotte in its travel section, the profile began by promising readers that the local culture had more to offer than the two most widely known exurban destinations: the NASCAR speedway and the Bakkers' now defunct evangelical theme park. Uptown Charlotte had performing arts centers, museums, and occasional crafts shows, although the NationsBank Corporate Center remained the most popular tourist attraction. A year later, when the city hosted the NCAA Final Four basketball tournament, out-of-town journalists mocked the fabricated "movie set" of temporary nightlife installed in vacant storefronts, a "Street of Champions" boarded up again as soon as the games were over.[41] In a local poll on Charlotte's "major-league" status, residents demonstrated a previously unacknowledged sense of humor about their city's desperate quest for national respect. Asked to encapsulate Charlotte's character, the top selections included "a big old country-fried Southern town with an attitude," "a little town with penis envy that wants to be world class," and "a city of rich Christian hypocrites who steal from the poor to pay for their parties and golf."[42]

The constant debate over Charlotte's identity crisis, and the difficulty in uncovering the actual metropolis beyond the incessantly constructed version, reflects not only the city's relentless pursuit of external validation but also the direct consequence of its primary mission of serving as a crossroads for the rest of the nation and the world. Charlotte had a "nebulous image," business leaders acknowledged in the mid-1980s, without "anything especially unique about itself to set it apart in a positive way from many of its 'competitor' cities."[43] "We exist for no other reason," a real estate broker admitted following the NationsBank merger, "than to deliver goods and services to other people." "Charlotte is more like a Northern city than a Southern city," remarked an advertising executive required to relocate from Wall Street. "Most of the people you meet here in business are from the North or the Midwest." "We're not a final destination for people," a marketing official at the Charlotte Convention Bureau conceded to the *Washington Post* in 1993, but that meant corporate visitors "don't get distracted the way they would by Disney World if they were having a convention in Orlando."[44] Even granted the public relations impulse to turn weaknesses into virtues, surely Charlotte had more to offer than an efficient hotel and convention complex with nothing too exciting to divert out-of-towners from getting down to business. The *Raleigh News and Observer* hammered this critique home on every possible occasion, such as when Charlotte bested the state capital in the battle to secure direct flights to and from London. "What awaits those European visitors when they get off the plane in Charlotte?" the Raleigh newspaper wondered. "Charlotte's problem is there isn't any reason for it to be there. There are no natural or man-made wonders to behold in Charlotte unless you have a particular fascination for condos, asphalt and smoked glass... A foreign tourist would wither from visual deprivation in Charlotte."[45]

International Horizons

For Charlotte's political and business leadership, the quest for both national approval and international standing meant a new mission to sell the metropolitan region as "America's New Business Horizon." In the 1980s, Chamber of Commerce literature mainly addressed transplants from the Northeast and Midwest who presumably had been "bombarded with numerous rumors about the people and lifestyles of the South. Many expect to see residents chewing on corncob pipes and wearing coveralls. Rest assured this is not the case. Like any thriving metropolis, Charlotte is a city whose skyline is marked with gleaming skyscrapers... and whose population is outfitted in three-piece suits as well as blue jeans... Some of the friendliest people in the world live down South."[46] By the 1990s, the Chamber of Commerce had established a new marketing group, the Carolinas Partnership, to "create a cohesive region that is prepared to compete successfully in the global economy" and "target those industries both domestic and international that would support and advance the quality of life in the Charlotte region." The Carolinas Partnership sponsored an advertising campaign (in New York, Chicago, Los Angeles, and Toronto) to convince skeptical national and international executives that Charlotte *really was* the third-largest banking center in the United States, while also tapping into their presumed frustrations with cold winters and/or congested freeways.[47] The coalition also distributed trilingual promotional materials selling the "Charlotte Region: America's New Business Horizon" in Great Britain, Germany, and Japan. The booklets included images of the Blue Ridge Mountains, the nation's twenty-first busiest airport, sporting events and cultural venues, skyscrapers in the Uptown financial district, international firms based in suburban office parks, and a multinational and multiracial population in peaceful pursuit of business and pleasure.[48]

The city government supplemented the Carolinas Partnership with an "international city" initiative launched in 1992 under Mayor Richard Vinroot. He established the Mayor's International Cabinet to focus on three main goals: "for Charlotte to be recognized as the best city of its size" in the global marketplace, to collaborate with local banks to become "a new money center for the conduct of world commerce," and to ensure "a welcoming and accepting community for an increasingly diverse mix of cultural, religious, and ethnic groups." As much spin as substance, the International Cabinet pledged to "ensure that Charlotte is recognized (and recognizes herself) as an international city." Mayor Vinroot claimed that Charlotte was "the only city [in the United States] with an international vision and action plan," although the initiative primarily publicized trends already underway on the metropolitan landscape. The International Cabinet called for more overseas flights, multilingual signs at the airport, additional Uptown hotels, better mass transit options, more study-abroad programs at local universities, citizenship training for new immigrants, and English as a second language classes in the secondary schools (to serve the rapidly growing Latino population).[49] Marketing remained the overriding focus of the international city campaign, which welcomed conventioneers and tourists to the "growing metropolitan city with a touch of Southern Charm! We boast world-class sporting events, attractions, arts and entertainment, shopping, dining and a wide variety of accommodations." For foreign tourists who did not plan to spend their whole vacation either Uptown or in the "world-class" suburban shopping malls, Charlotte would serve as the "international gateway to the Carolinas," with direct flights to ten destinations in Europe and the Caribbean. By the end of the decade, 379 foreign-owned firms from 35 different nations also operated in Charlotte-Mecklenburg, one of the fastest-growing regions in the United States.[50]

Without question, the most significant event in Charlotte since the civil rights era took place in the spring of 1998 when NationsBank announced its merger with San Francisco–based BankAmerica Corp. The new financial giant adopted the Bank of America name but kept its headquarters in Charlotte, which immediately became the nation's second-largest banking center ($774 billion in assets) trailing only New York City ($1.6 trillion). Anxious leaders in Charlotte expressed relief that Bank of America would remain based in the South; in fact, Hugh McColl had broken off merger talks three years earlier over the refusal of his West Coast counterparts to compromise on the issue. Hailed as a hometown hero, McColl took the occasion to boast: "You see our [NationsBank's] hand in almost everything. I've had more fun building a city than I have, perhaps, in building the bank." In a typically backhanded compliment, the *Wall Street Journal* observed: "This deal means Charlotte may finally get some respect. For years the city has played second fiddle to Atlanta in the South and been confused for similar-sounding cities, such as Charlottesville, Va., and Charleston, S.C." Evidencing little awareness of Charlotte's century-long quest for New South recognition, national media coverage repeatedly (and erroneously) marveled at the recent and rapid transformation of the "sleepy Southern Bible Belt town" and brought up the Jim and Tammy Faye Bakker scandal again for good measure. Charlotte residents also expressed shock and anger over the vituperative portrayals of their city in the San Francisco newspapers: a redneck Mayberry of "grits and stock car races," a "nouveau riche" boomtown run by barely mannered good old boys. Lamented one columnist in the *San Francisco Examiner*: "Why is BofA moving its headquarters from glorious San Francisco to soulless Charlotte?"[51]

True to form, Bank of America proceeded to take over the FleetBoston bank a few years later, in addition to expanding its global operations throughout Europe and Asia and staking its claim as the third-largest bank in the world. Across the street, First Union merged into Wachovia in 2001 while maintaining the Charlotte headquarters and consolidating its place as a national and international player in its own right. Closer to home, Bank of America and First Union/Wachovia continued to invest hundreds of millions of dollars in the horizontal expansion of Uptown, especially mixed-use office, retail, and residential complexes that required "slum clearance" of the poor and mostly minority population of existing in-town neighborhoods. After the dispiriting defection of the Hornets to New Orleans, the two banks also teamed up to bring professional basketball back to Charlotte by financing a new arena for the NBA Bobcats expansion team. Charlotte's leading financial institutions embraced the civic responsibility of downtown redevelopment in large part to neutralize the constant criticism that the New South banking center remained a cultural wasteland that shut down with the evening traffic rush to the suburbs. "Our objective is to have a European model center city in Charlotte," a Bank of America executive told the *Financial Times* of London. "We want that vitality." To accomplish this ambitious goal, corporate leaders launched a semicoercive civic fundraising campaign that the *New York Times* labeled "one of the country's most effective systems" for building up cultural institutions in an urban center. "This has become part of our business culture," Hugh McColl said. "If you want to be a player, part of the larger power structure, then you've got to play."[52]

During the past fifteen years, the transformation of Charlotte's central business and entertainment district has been fairly dramatic, and the revision of the city's cultural reputation as a barren wilderness has involved at least as much makeover of substance as image. By the late 1990s, as NationsBank executed its West Coast power play, visiting journalists were praising Charlotte's cultural amenities in language that no longer seemed diametrically opposed to the promises made by the Chamber of Commerce. The *Washington Post*, while noting politely that "a single weekend may be the ideal amount of time to devote to Charlotte's charms," praised the new restaurants, the lively microbreweries, and Uptown's three major museums (Discovery Place, the Mint Museum, and the Museum of the New South). "Despite its rapid growth, Charlotte is still a city with soul," according to the revisionist wisdom of Toronto's *National Post*, "a city that appreciates its art and culture." Charlotte had much more to offer than just a big airport for connecting flights, the *Boston Globe* agreed in 2005. "New museums, new sporting facilities, new ways to explore the city, even a new culinary flair . . . A city in search of its 'cool' self and, in places, finding it."[53] Not everyone was convinced, of course, especially not the cross-state rivals at the *Raleigh News and Observer*, which continued to publish broadsides against the Queen City for being "addicted not only to growth but — even worse — to approval . . . Charlotte, surely you can see how absurd you are. You're not a world-class city, and you invite ridicule when you say it. You are a fairly large city in the South. That's all, and that should be enough."[54] But Charlotte had become comfortable or cool enough, at last, to satirize itself through a musical revue portraying area residents as "sports-loving, Fourth of July–rioting, suburban-sprawling, snow-fearing rednecks" who all had migrated from somewhere else.[55]

Few places in the United States are as obsessed with issues of civic identity, and as driven in their searches for both internal and external respect, as the boomtowns of the Sun Belt South. And both for better and for worse, few places in the nation are as cavalier toward history and tradition, and as willing to destroy or deny the past, in the rush to create a new future on whatever terms seem most desirable to outsiders and newcomers. During the past decade, Charlotte-Mecklenburg effectively has abandoned the most significant accomplishment in the city's history, the comprehensive commitment to a racially and economically integrated public school system, as a direct consequence of the higher priorities of metropolitan growth and suburban sprawl, no matter what the cost.[56] At the same time, the global version of New South boosterism has ushered in the aura of the international city, and the official 2004–05 visitors guide promises that "multicultural Charlotte embraces and celebrates an ever-changing mosaic of cultures, faiths, and races." The civil rights era is altogether absent in the new marketing literature. Instead, the guide chronicles a metropolis "built upon the crossroads of two Native American trading paths. It would seem destiny played a role in Charlotte's evolution into the second largest banking capital of the country ... with the excitement of a cosmopolitan city and the ease of Southern charm."[57] And then comes the Chamber of Commerce sales pitch: "Moxie. Chutzpah. Whatever you call that spirit of daring, of making your dreams come true, Charlotte's got it. There are some cities where you feel as if its glory days are past. In Charlotte, you get the sense the best is yet to come ... What we dream, we do."[58] The more things change, the more they stay the same in this New South city of dreams, this self-proclaimed gateway to a world-class future, this sprawling metropolitan region where the sky's always been the only limit to be acknowledged.

Notes

1. *New York Times*, April 9, 2000.
2. James C. Cobb, *The Selling of the South: The Southern Crusade for Industrial Development, 1936–1980* (Baton Rouge: Louisiana State University Press, 1982); James C. Cobb, *Industrialization and Southern Society, 1877–1984* (Lexington: University Press of Kentucky, 1984); Paul M. Gaston, *The New South Creed: A Study in Southern Mythmaking* (New York: Knopf, 1970); Bruce J. Schulman,

From Cotton Belt to Sunbelt: Federal Policy, Economic Development, and the Transformation of the South, 1938–1980 (New York: Oxford University Press, 1991).

3. Peter Applebome, *Dixie Rising: How the South Is Shaping American Values, Politics, and Culture* (New York: Harcourt Brace, 1996), 148–81; Jack Claiborne, *Crown of the Queen City: The Charlotte Chamber from 1877 to 1999* (Charlotte: KPC Custom Publishing, 1999).

4. Matthew D. Lassiter, *The Silent Majority: Suburban Politics in the Sunbelt South* (Princeton: Princeton University Press, 2006).

5. *Washington Post*, November 5, 1993.

6. *Charlotte Observer*, September 30, 1992; *New York Times*, April 2, 1994; *Norfolk Virginian-Pilot*, December 3, 1995.

7. *Raleigh News and Observer*, reprinted in *Charlotte Observer*, February 1, 1987.

8. Charlotte Chamber of Commerce, "Economic Development," <http://www.charlottechamber.com/index> (accessed February 28, 2008). Also see Bea Quirk, *Charlotte, City at the Crossroads: A Contemporary Portrait* (Chatsworth, Ca.: Windsor Publications, 1989).

9. Lassiter, *Silent Majority*, 109–31, 206–21, 324–29.

10. For an early reference to the George Washington comment, see Edgar T. Thompson, *Agricultural Mecklenburg and Industrial Charlotte: Social and Economic* (Charlotte: Charlotte Chamber of Commerce, 1926), 307. Numerous Chamber of Commerce publications, along with newspaper and magazine profiles, repeated the anecdote over the years. See, for example, Doug Mayes, *Charlotte: Nothing Could Be Finer* (Memphis: Towery Publishing, 1996).

11. Thompson, *Agricultural Mecklenburg and Industrial Charlotte*, 31, 307, 310, 316. Also see Claiborne, *Crown of the Queen City*, 1–25.

12. Charlotte Chamber of Commerce, "Know Charlotte" (1928), "Facts about Charlotte: The Queen City of the South" (1937), "Charlotte: The Industrial Center of the Carolinas" (1940), Publications and Brochures Folder, Robinson-Spangler Carolina Room, Public Library of Charlotte and Mecklenburg County (hereinafter cited as CMPL); Claiborne, *Crown of the Queen City*, 27–67.

13. Charlotte Chamber of Commerce, "This Is Charlotte: Key City of the Southeast" (1948), Special Section, *Charlotte News*, May 10, 1948, C. Chamber of Commerce 1940s and 1950s Folder, CMPL; Charlotte Chamber of Commerce, "Charlotte" (January 1950), Publications and Brochures Folder, CMPL.

14. "'Queen City' Keeps Her Crown," *Business Week* (May 21, 1949), 92–98; "Charlotte: Unsouthern, Untypical," *Business Week* (August 11, 1951), 70–84; "Charlotte, P.C.," *Manufacturers Record* (February 1957), 31–49; Charlotte Chamber of Commerce, Annual Report, 1951, Publications and Brochures Folder, CMPL.

15. Charlotte Chamber of Commerce, "1956 Membership Roster and Finger Tip

Facts about Charlotte," C. Chamber of Commerce 1940s and 1950s Folder, CMPL; Charlotte Chamber of Commerce, 1958 Annual Report, 1964 Annual Report, C. Chamber of Commerce 1980– Folder, CMPL.

16. Speeches by Mayor Stanford Brookshire collected in Folder 1, Box 6, Stanford R. Brookshire Papers, UNC Charlotte Manuscript Collection 41, University of North Carolina at Charlotte Library; Lassiter, *Silent Majority*, 123–31; Davison M. Douglas, *Reading, Writing, and Race: The Desegregation of the Charlotte Schools* (Chapel Hill: University of North Carolina Press, 1995).

17. Pat Watters, *Charlotte* (Atlanta: Southern Regional Council, 1964); *Charlotte Observer*, January 30, 1970; Brookshire speeches.

18. Charlotte Chamber of Commerce, 1961 Annual Report, 1964 Annual Report, C. Chamber of Commerce 1980– Folder, CMPL.

19. Charlotte Chamber of Commerce, "Charlotte: The Action City" (October 1963), Publications and Brochures Folder, CMPL; *Charlotte Observer*, March 24, 1963.

20. Charlotte Chamber of Commerce, 1955 Annual Report, 1958 Annual Report, 1963 Annual Report, 1965 Annual Report, 1969 Annual Report, C. Chamber of Commerce 1980– Folder, CMPL; Charlotte Chamber of Commerce, "The Third Century: 'For the People'" (1969), C. Chamber of Commerce 1960s Folder, CMPL; *Charlotte News*, September 21, 1968.

21. Charlotte Chamber of Commerce, "Charlotte: The Action City" (October 1963), Publications and Brochures Folder, CMPL; *Charlotte Observer*, March 24, 1963.

22. Charlotte Chamber of Commerce, Press Release, December 4, 1968, Folder 20, Box 1, Brookshire Papers; Charlotte Chamber of Commerce, "The Third Century: 'For the People'" (1969), *Greensboro Daily News*, December 5, 1968, C. Chamber of Commerce 1960s Folder, CMPL; *Raleigh News and Observer*, February 1, 1987.

23. Lassiter, *Silent Majority*, 131–221; *Charlotte Observer*, November 4, 1973.

24. "On the Way Up: Four Cities Show How It Can Be Done," *U.S. News and World Report* (April 5, 1976), 62–64; Chamber of Commerce Research Committee, "A Concept for Charlotte's Future," November 3, 1972, Charlotte Chamber of Commerce, 1978 Annual Report, Bryant quoted in *Charlotte Observer*, undated (1977), C. Chamber of Commerce 1970s Folder, CMPL; Charlotte Chamber of Commerce, "Greater Charlotte Metroguide" (1974–75), Chamber of Commerce 1980– Folder, CMPL.

25. "Charlotte, P.C.," *Manufacturers Record* (February 1957), 49.

26. Otis White, "Charlotte Aims To Be the 'Best Mid-Sized City' in the South," *South Business* (June 1980), reprint in Folder 4, Box 3, Harvey B. Gantt Papers, University of North Carolina at Charlotte Library. According to the *Charlotte Observer*, many local residents referred to the central business district as "uptown" until the 1950s, when merchants began pushing for the "downtown" designation in order to emphasize that Charlotte had become a major city with a vibrant busi-

ness center (rather than a small town with an upscale residential enclave). In the 1980s, the Downtown Merchants Association changed its name to the Uptown Merchants Association and publicized the new label, which evokes the slogans of the neotraditional planning movement and seeks to escape the racial stigmatization of "downtown" with crime and urban decay. See *Charlotte Observer*, February 14, 1987.

27. Charlotte Chamber of Commerce, "Greater Charlotte Metroguide" (1980), 4–11, Chamber of Commerce 1980– Folder, CMPL.

28. Gary Hector, "Merger Mania for More Banks?" *Fortune* (July 29, 1991), 18; Josh Eppinger, "Charlotte Sheds its Small-Town Image," *Adweek* (June 25, 1990), 22; *Washington Post*, August 14, 1991; *New York Times*, August 24, 1991; *Charlotte Observer*, December 3, 1991; *Wall Street Journal*, July 8, 1993; *St. Petersburg Times*, September 7, 1997.

29. Harvey Gantt to Roger W. Owens, February 27, 1985, Folder 29, Charlotte Community Concert Association, Resolution, May 17, 1987, Folder 21, Box 1, Harvey Gantt, Speech to the Charlotte Condominium Council, January 25, 1984, Folder 14, Box 5, Gantt Papers; *Charlotte Observer*, November 29, 1984.

30. Charlotte Chamber of Commerce, "Visions for a Greater Charlotte" (1985), reprinted in *Charlotte Observer*, October 13, 1985; Charles Rutheiser, *Imagineering Atlanta: The Politics of Place in the City of Dreams* (New York: Verso, 1996), 65–73.

31. Charlotte Economic Development Study Commission, "Summary of Community Leader Interviews," April 10, 1985, Folder 29, Box 1, Gantt Papers.

32. Charlotte Chamber of Commerce, "Greater Charlotte Metroguide" (1977–78), "Greater Charlotte Metroguide" (1981), Chamber of Commerce 1980– Folder, CMPL; Charlotte Chamber of Commerce, 1978 Annual Report, C. Chamber of Commerce 1970s Folder, CMPL; Charlotte Chamber of Commerce, "The Charlotte Economy" (March 1985), Publications and Brochures Folder CMPL.

33. Carolinas Council on World Affairs, "Mission Statement," 1983, "Statement," n.d., Folder 15, Box 1, Sue Myrick Papers, University of North Carolina at Charlotte Library.

34. Harvey Gantt to Secretary of Transportation Elizabeth Dole, August 18, 1986, Folder 2, Box 1, Gantt Papers; Sue Myrick, State of the City Address, 1989, Folder 9, Box 5, Myrick Papers; *Charlotte Observer*, March 23, 1988.

35. Charlotte Chamber of Commerce, "Charlotte: In Detail" (n.d., ca. 1988), Publications and Brochures Folder, CMPL.

36. Maria E. Recio, "Build an Arena Now, Get a Team Later — Maybe," *Business Week* (April 20, 1987), 90; Harvey Gantt to NBA Commissioner David Stern, June 30, 1986, Folder 1, Box 3, Gantt Papers; *Washington Post*, August 14, 1991; *Wall Street Journal*, April 30, 1997.

37. *Washington Post*, August 6, 1991, October 31, 1993; *New York Times*, October 28, 31, 1993; *USA Today*, November 1, 1993; Jeff Jensen, "How Charlotte Snared

Panthers," *Advertising Age,* November 15, 1993, 31. *Charlotte Observer* quoted in *New York Times,* October 31, 1993.

38. *Los Angeles Times,* June 7, 1987; *Chicago Tribune,* November 25, 1993; *Washington Post,* August 14, 1991, October 31, November 5, 1993.

39. *New York Times,* June 24, 1987.

40. *New York Times,* March 22, 1996; *Wall Street Journal,* April 23, 1997, November 4, 1998; *Philadelphia Inquirer,* June 23, 1997.

41. *Washington Post,* February 15, 1998; *Wall Street Journal,* March 1, 1995; *New York Times,* February 27, 1994.

42. *Washington Times,* April 2, 1994.

43. Charlotte Economic Development Study Commission, "Summary of Community Leader Interviews," April 10, 1985, Folder 29, Box 1, Gantt Papers.

44. *Washington Post,* August 14, 1991, November 5, 1993; *New York Times,* June 24, 1987.

45. *Raleigh News and Observer,* reprinted in *Charlotte Observer,* February 1, 1987.

46. Charlotte Chamber of Commerce, "Charlotte Newcomer" (1982), Publications and Brochures Folder, CMPL.

47. Carolinas Partnership, "Statement of Purpose," n.d. (early 1990s), Folder 20, Box 1, Richard Vinroot Papers, University of North Carolina at Charlotte Library; Suzanne Wittebort, "Life in the Big Leagues," *Business North Carolina* (April 1, 1992); "Ad Campaign Hits Execs' Hot Buttons," *Business Journal* (March 22, 1993).

48. Carolinas Partnership, "Our Future Grows Brighter Every Day," n.d. (1990s), "Prospect Charlotte," n.d. (1990s), Publications and Brochures Folder, CMPL.

49. Mayor's Office, "International Vision: Working Draft," 1992, Mayor's International Cabinet, "International Strategic Plan," December 7, 1992, Folder 17, "City of Charlotte Mayor's International Cabinet," n.d., Folder 22, Box 6, Press Release, July 14, 1994, Folder 2, Box 7, Vinroot Papers.

50. Charlotte Convention and Visitors Bureau, "Charlotte: Official Visitors Guide" (Spring/Summer 2000), Publications and Brochures Folder, CMPL; Charlotte Chamber of Commerce, *Charlotte's Largest Employers Directory and Career Guide* (Charlotte: Charlotte Chamber of Commerce, 2000), 11–13.

51. *St. Louis Post-Dispatch,* May 31, 1998 (McColl quotation); *Wall Street Journal,* April 14, 1998; *Washington Times,* April 14, 1998; *Philadelphia Inquirer,* June 7, 1998; *St. Petersburg Times,* April 26, 1998 (includes quotations from San Francisco newspapers).

52. *Boston Globe,* October 28, 2003, September 7, 2004; *Financial Times of London,* September 11, 1997, September 11, 2000, September 24, 2003; *Wall Street Journal,* October 7, 1998; *New York Times,* April 2, 1994, November 12, 2001.

53. *Washington Post,* October 18, 1998; *National Post* (Canada), September 25, 2000; *Boston Globe,* July 24, 2005.

54. *Raleigh News and Observer*, August 5, 2001.

55. *Charlotte Observer*, January 27, 2007.

56. Lassiter, *Silent Majority*, 206–21, 324–29; Stephen Samuel Smith, *Boom for Whom? Education, Desegregation, and Development in Charlotte* (Albany: State University of New York Press, 2004).

57. Charlotte Convention and Visitors Bureau, "The New Accent of the South: Charlotte Official Visitors Guide" (2004–2005), Publications and Brochures Folder, CMPL.

58. Charlotte Convention and Visitors Bureau, "Charlotte: Official Visitors Guide" (Spring/Summer 2000), C. Chamber of Commerce 1980– Folder, CMPL.

Ronald L. Mitchelson
and Derek H. Alderman

Red Dust and Dynamometers
Charlotte as Memory and Knowledge
Community in NASCAR

On June 19, 1949, the Charlotte Speedway hosted NASCAR's first official race of "strictly stock" cars, serving as the inaugural event for a division that ultimately grew into the prominent Sprint Cup Series operating today. Although modest by current standards, the Charlotte Speedway was larger than many other tracks in the South at the time. It was a three-quarter-mile, slightly banked dirt track. The race attracted a crowd of over twenty thousand spectators who watched thirty-three drivers compete for a then-generous $5,000 purse. Drivers included Lee Petty, the father of the famous Richard "the King" Petty and a superstar in his own right, Hall of Fame driver Red Byron, and Sara Christian, the first woman driver in NASCAR history. The race, successful on many levels, began the process of mythologizing the sport and its participants. Glenn Dunnaway of Gastonia, North Carolina, was initially declared the winner but disqualified when his car, which he used for bootlegging moonshine, was found to have been illegally modified.[1] Lee Petty raced a Buick Roadmaster borrowed from a friend. He eventually wrecked the car (after rolling it four times), forcing him and his family, including eleven-year-old son Richard, to hitch a ride home.[2]

Racing in Charlotte dates back to the early 1900s, but that 1949 race was the beginning of an active and lucrative relationship with NASCAR, the major sanctioning body for stock-car racing. The official birthplace of NASCAR is Daytona Beach, Florida, where Bill France and a few others established the racing association at the Streamline Hotel in 1947 and named France its first president. However, Charlotte and its surrounding towns (such as Mooresville and Concord) are, without question, the industrial and cultural home of the sport. Unlike other professional sports in Charlotte, like football and basketball, which have at times received lukewarm public support, interest in stock-car racing has remained consistently high in the region. In the words of one racing enthusiast, "Auto racing is to Charlotte as hockey is to Canada."[3] Yet, in the sixty years since that seminal race in Charlotte, much has changed in stock-car racing. An average Sprint Cup event now attracts almost two hundred thousand attendees, winning purses are well over $1 million, and small dirt tracks that once covered drivers and spectators with red dust have been replaced by large, paved superspeedways.[4] For example, the Lowe's Motor Speedway, where major races are now held in the Charlotte area, is a one-and-a-half-mile track that, when filled with spectators, becomes the fourth-largest city in North Carolina behind Charlotte, Raleigh, and Greensboro.[5]

NASCAR has expanded beyond its traditional southern base to become one of the fastest-growing professional sports in the country. Like Charlotte, NASCAR is undergoing intense development and spatial restructuring, as is evident from the widening distribution of tracks and drivers participating in the sport. NASCAR officials continue to aggressively identify and cultivate new markets, including international ones.[6] Races are now held in several cities outside the South, including the fabled open-wheel racing capital of Indianapolis. Until the 1970s, most of leading NASCAR drivers were from the Carolinas, Virginia, and Georgia.[7] Now driving talent comes from across the nation and world. One of the most talked about drivers as of late is Juan Pablo Montoya of Colombia. That's Colombia, South America — not South Carolina. The days of drivers racing and wrecking the family Buick at the track are gone; they now drive highly engineered cars that undergo extensive testing using digital simulations, wind tunnels, and dynamometers, which measure horsepower and torque.

In the face of NASCAR's increasing national (and even global) influence, the centrality of Charlotte within the sport has not waned but increased. Charlotte serves as an important gathering place within the expanding geography of stock-car racing — a point of convergence or contact zone for industry promoters, racing teams, technology development, drivers, and fans. The region serves as an important economic cluster or "knowledge community" around which stock-car racing teams, mechanics and engineers, and related firms interact with each other as they develop car innovations and maintain a competitive advantage in the industry. At the same time, however, this cluster is not just technologic in nature. Charlotte is also the destination for an important racing heritage tourism industry, serving as a "memory community" for visiting and local fans to connect with NASCAR's southern roots and mythologies, particularly the reputational power and allure of its drivers. In return, NASCAR-related activities currently contribute about $6 billion to the North Carolina economy with approximately 75 percent of that total concentrated within the Charlotte region.[8] This economic impact promises to become even larger with the planned 2010 opening of the NASCAR Hall of Fame in Charlotte's already well-developed downtown financial district.

To understand how and why Charlotte remains so central to a growing sport that, according to some critics, is losing its unique regional identity,[9] one must recognize the dynamic and hybrid nature of the American South. According to noted historian James Cobb, the region is an inseparable synthesis of tradition and transition, and the southern landscape can embody continuity, change, or both.[10] Regions — and by extension their cities — are not fixed and tightly bounded entities, but sets of changing relations and structures "constituted by a dialectic of social, economic, and political interactions between individuals, groups, and institutions."[11] Similarly, NASCAR is "transcultural" in nature and can be seen as dynamic interactions and relations that seek to extend the popularity of stock-car racing into new markets while keeping the sport tied to the South in selective ways.[12] Hence, it is Charlotte's position within an array of flows (including NASCAR's) along with the city's other external networking that yield cultural exchanges and interrelationships that characterize and (re)construct the city. Charlotte's centrality in NASCAR demonstrates that regional economies and identities are not necessarily at odds with the forces of nationalization and globalization.[13] Rather, Charlotte is a site for the ongoing negotiation of change and continuity in NASCAR. It is a place where regional, national, and global forces meet, give and take, and even clash. Indeed, while stock-car racing contributes greatly to Charlotte's economy and public image, conflict and tension have also arisen as social actors and groups in the city debate the impact of NASCAR on their lives and livelihood.

This chapter explores the important place of Charlotte within NASCAR and vice-versa, how the clustering of the racing industry around Charlotte developed, the contemporary dimensions of the city's role as a knowledge and memory community, and the stresses that underlie the negotiation of the regional and the national/global via Charlotte's relationship with stock-car racing.

Early NASCAR: Why in Charlotte and not Atlanta?

In observing the present clustering of NASCAR activities within the Charlotte region, it is easy to assume that it has always been this way. In reality, Charlotte's emergence as NASCAR's preeminent city is a result of a long history of growth processes that are, in some ways, national and global in nature but highly contingent on local agents and culture. Among those who study regional agglomeration and competitiveness, there is recognition that economic clusters of specialization evolve initially for "accidental" reasons, although once established, such clusters are sustained by external industrial forces that attract even greater economic opportunities.[14] In particular, it is insightful to examine how such a cluster actually gets its "accidental" start. Today's NASCAR industrial center did not have to be Charlotte. It could just as easily have been Atlanta if not for certain historical contingencies and technological developments as well as the decisions, actions, and rivalries of key individuals and social groups.

At least two dimensions of historic significance figure in the emergence of NASCAR in the South: southern moonshine and New South urban boosterism.[15] Despite "Big Bill" France's best efforts to obscure it, early NASCAR history was dominated by moonshiners. The geography of moonshining in the 1920s reveals an important ingredient for the growth of stock-car racing as a distinctive southern enterprise in the late 1920s and 1930s and ultimately the start of NASCAR in 1948. The rural Appalachian hills of Georgia (6,155 moonshine still seizures in 1923–24 by law enforcement officials), Tennessee (4,232 seizures), Virginia (3,919 seizures), and North Carolina (3,287 seizures) provided the production of corn whiskey, and the residents of southern cities like Nashville, Knoxville, Chattanooga, Birmingham, Atlanta, Greenville, Charlotte, Greensboro, Winston-Salem, and Richmond provided the consumption.[16]

The repeal of prohibition did nothing to alter this system of supply and demand. The trip from rural Appalachia to the urban South with an illegal load of corn whiskey required the ability to outrun local, state, and federal officers. That need for velocity and car handling yielded great mechanics providing exceptionally strong cars to very talented drivers. No two moonshine routes surpassed the volume and notoriety of Dawson County (Dawsonville) to Atlanta in Georgia and Wilkes County (North Wilkesboro) to Charlotte in North Carolina. These two routes to selective and limited Appalachian prosperity provided the best mechanics, the best cars, and the best drivers. For a while, these same cars and drivers that ran the whiskey would show up on weekends to run on red-clay tracks like Lakewood in Atlanta and Southern States Fairgrounds in Charlotte. Southerners, deprived of professional sports (baseball and football) in general, flocked to these racing events by the thousands.

In the case of Atlanta, almost all of the successful cars were built by a mechanic named Red Vogt and owned by a wealthy Georgian (a moonshiner originally from Dawsonville) named Raymond Parks.[17] They took Ford cars right off the Atlanta assembly line from the 1920s to the late 1930s, modified them greatly, and ran them much faster than anything else on the road. Dawsonville was arguably the hub of American moonshining in the 1930s and it was essential to cover the sixty winding miles to Atlanta as fast as possible. Georgia drivers like Robert and Ray Seay, Roy Hall, and Red Byron ran whiskey during the week and raced on the weekends.

In the case of Charlotte and North Carolina, the cars were built and owned by a wider variety of individuals. The make of cars also was more diverse and included Fords, Oldsmobiles, Pontiacs, Chevrolets, and Hudsons. Wilkes County was the hub of North Carolina moonshine production. In 1935, police and federal IRS agents raided Ingle Hollow in Wilkes County to make the largest moonshine bust in U.S. history. As a result, Robert Johnson Sr. was jailed while his four-year-old son, "Junior" Johnson, watched as agents found 7,100 gallons of the white lightning. Junior would be running moonshine by age fourteen and would become one of NASCAR's early superstars. Curtis Turner, whom some claim to be NASCAR's best driver ever, was making the Charlotte bootlegging run by age ten. Other drivers of this time from North Carolina or with strong North Carolina connections included Buck Baker (a bus driver in Charlotte and father of Buddy Baker), Buddy Shuman (a moonshiner from Charlotte), and Glenn "Fireball" Roberts, who drove the number 11 "White Lightning" car and died in a race crash in Charlotte in 1964.

Prior to NASCAR's first races in 1948, most of the officially sanctioned auto racing in the United States was open wheeled, costly, exclusive, elitist, largely northern, and used professional drivers. The Indy 500 was the model. In contrast, "stock" car racing was largely ignored by the northern establishment. Its popularity in the South grew in the late 1920s and throughout the 1930s. Most of the cars were Fords significantly modified for bootlegging and most of the drivers were "amateurs." Of the early red-clay tracks, Lakewood (in Atlanta) was considered the "Indy of the South." Twenty thousand spectators showed up at Lakewood in November 1938. Among the drivers were Atlanta's bootleggers, Charlotte's bootleggers, and Bill France; France lost to the Atlanta bootleggers. His dislike for that particular group was confirmed and would be reinforced frequently during the first decades after he established NASCAR in 1947. According to Thompson, it frustrated France that a small group of moonshiners could dominate his sport. By 1941, France was quickly transitioning from driver to promoter. His consistent losses to moonshiners only hastened that transition.[18]

Stock-car racing continued sporadically during the World War II era as many of its drivers and mechanics served during the war; the sport's growth could not be fully reestablished until after 1945. Within days of Japan's surrender, the federal ban on motor racing was lifted and a Labor Day stock-car race was planned for Lakewood Speedway in Atlanta. However, Atlanta's religious leaders (especially Methodist and Baptist clergy) pressured the mayor's office to limit race entries by requesting that bootleggers and racketeers be excluded. Mayor William Hartsfield provided the names of five drivers to be banned from the Labor Day race. Three were drivers of Raymond Parks's team and included the best of the Atlanta drivers, Roy Hall. The Atlanta fans were particularly upset with this exclusion because Hall was their clear favorite. The attack on Hall and other bootleggers was continued in editorials in the Atlanta newspaper. This was the start of Atlanta's complicated relationship with stock-car racing. Atlanta Police Chief Marion Hornsby vowed to support Hartsfield's ban on bootleggers at Lakewood races. In 1947, bootlegger Bob Flock entered a race at Lakewood under an alias, an Atlanta police officer recognized him, and the officer chased Flock down the straightaway and off the track.[19]

Many stock-car drivers looked for venues outside of Atlanta, most notably those located in North Carolina, whose official reception of stock-car racers, regardless of criminal history, was far more enthusiastic than Atlanta's. For instance, when Bill France started organizing a race in Charlotte in 1945, he found willing partners at the Southern States Fairgrounds and he also received sage advice from the *Charlotte Observer's* sports editor, Wilton Garrison. France credits Garrison with asserting the importance of creating structure and uniformity and a point system for determining a champion if stock-car racing was ever to become legitimate. While moonshining provided the necessary cars and driving talent, the organizing of races was aided by a booster environment in which civic promoters and elites saw racing as a way "to bring attention to their cities and to their business potential."[20] This early distinction between Atlanta's and Charlotte's reception of stock-car culture provided an initial condition that fostered Charlotte's strong relationship with NASCAR.[21]

In the decade from 1939 to 1949, eleven stock-car championship titles were at stake. Ten of those were won by bootlegger drivers or owners and almost all drove cars from Atlanta created by Red Vogt. In fact, the greatest rivalries of 1948 and 1949 involved Atlantan rivalries and the first NASCAR season of 1948 did feature Atlanta's top mechanics and drivers. But Atlanta's dominance had peaked. The late 1940s witnessed the eroding of Red Vogt's mechanical preeminence and increasing challenges to Raymond Parks's position as the sport's first and most successful team owner.[22] Because of these Atlantans' decline, the Atlanta region's centrality within the sport also diminished. NASCAR's importance and centrality were headed eastward with a multitude of new investors, new teams, and new tracks in North Carolina. Drivers like Buddy Shuman of Charlotte pushed France for a purse that would be 40 percent of ticket sales (instead of France's favored and cheaper flat rate). France would not negotiate. In protest, a few drivers like Shuman and Curtis Turner pulled out of NASCAR and joined the rival NSCRA circuit in 1949. Charlotte's O. Bruton Smith took over the NSCRA at that time and announced plans for "strictly stock" races. In reaction to Smith's creativity, France immediately started his own plans for a strictly stock event to be held in Charlotte. Smith (based in Charlotte) and France (based in Daytona) would remain intense rivals for decades.[23]

NASCAR's first strictly stock race is a major turning point in motorsports history. That event was run at Charlotte Speedway, which had been built during the summer of 1948 by well-known Charlotte bootleggers Pat and Harvey Charles. Their conviction on bootleg charges in 1949 prevented them from witnessing this historic race on June 19, 1949. With a strictly stock format, the cars had to be recent models (less than three years old) and this immediately brought a wider array of competitive cars (not just Fords). The intent was to provide a class of car that "Mr. and Mrs. America drove to the Piggly Wiggly grocery store." This connectedness of fans with drivers and with vehicles provided the sport with key parts of its marketing strategy.[24]

NASCAR's strict form of "stock" regulation immediately devalued Atlanta's racing community, which had previously dominated with modified Fords. In fact, during the 1950 racing season no Ford won a strictly stock race and it would be 1955 before Ford won again. Of the thirty-three drivers that qualified for that first strictly stock race in Charlotte in 1949, about half were southern bootleggers. Other notable drivers were Lee Petty (a North Carolina bakery truck driver), Buck Baker (a Charlotte bus driver), and Herb Thomas (a North Carolina tobacco farmer).

Charlotte radio personality Grady Cole issued the order for the "gentlemen" to start their engines at this first stock race. Glenn Dunnaway seemingly won the 200-lap (150-mile) race with a lead of more than three laps driving a whiskey car owned by bootlegger Hubert Westmoreland. But Al Crisler (NASCAR's first technical inspector) found steel wedges welded to Dunnaway's springs, which improved his handling. Dunnaway was disqualified. NASCAR won the subsequent lawsuit filed by Westmoreland. This solidified NASCAR's regulatory power and intensified the long-standing antagonism between NASCAR (France) and the bootleggers. Additionally, France had been triumphant in promoting a very successful race in rival Bruton Smith's hometown of Charlotte. NASCAR was positioned to dominate stock-car racing.[25]

France immediately scheduled seven more strictly stock events for 1949 and renamed the strictly stock series as NASCAR's Grand National Division. Grand National races quickly surpassed modified races as the fan and driver favorites. The Grand National Series was later named the Winston Cup, then the Nextel Cup, and now the Sprint Cup Series, reflecting the growing importance of corporate sponsorship. From the perspective of competition between Charlotte and Atlanta, it should be noted that Atlanta was largely excluded as a venue from the first few years of Grand National racing. In fact, NASCAR would not run a Grand National event in Atlanta until 1951. The birth and formalization of strictly stock altered the technologic landscape, significantly devaluing Atlanta's Ford specialization and reducing the importance of Atlanta as a venue for racing. Race car regulation and track selection, both under Bill France's (NASCAR's) purview, had elevated the importance of the Charlotte region relative to Atlanta.[26] Thus, the origin of the current NASCAR cluster in Charlotte was no "accident."

Growing Dominance of Charlotte in NASCAR

The Charlotte region's prominence in NASCAR grew throughout the 1950s and the 1960s. The reasons for this concentration included the high densities of driver talent, auto mechanic talent, and venues in the region during the 1950s and 1960s. Herb Thomas (Olivia, North Carolina) was Grand National champion in 1951 and 1953; Lee Petty (Randleman, North Carolina) was champion in 1954, 1958, and 1959; Buck Baker (Charlotte) was champion in 1956 and 1957; Rex White (Taylorsville, North Carolina) was champion

Figure 3. The original Charlotte Speedway was made completely of wood with forty-degree banking. It hosted its first open-wheel event in 1924 and closed in 1927. (Source: Robinson-Spangler Carolina Room at the Public Library of Charlotte and Mecklenburg County.)

in 1960; Ned Jarrett (Newton, North Carolina) was champion in 1961 and 1965; Richard Petty (Randleman, North Carolina) won his first of seven championships in 1964. Other regional notables during this early period included Buddy Shuman (Charlotte), winner of fifty Grand National races Junior Johnson (Wilkes County), and Ralph Earnhardt (Kannapolis, father of Dale Earnhardt, and grandfather of Dale Jr.). Early champions from outside of North Carolina were not very far removed from Charlotte's influence.[27]

The first notable venue in Charlotte, the original Charlotte Speedway, was completed in 1924 and was regarded as the premiere racing facility in the entire South. It was a one-and-a-quarter-mile, steeply banked oval constructed entirely (including the racing surface) of pine and cypress wood (see figure 3). There were several of these wooden tracks in the North. Demonstrating the importance of urban boosterism and investment, Osmond Barringer, a local Charlotte car dealer, led a group that built this track for open-wheel racing. Although only operating for three years, it hosted seven national-level open-wheel events during that time. It was a very different type of facility and different type of racing than the stock-car events that would take place on red-clay tracks starting in the late 1920s.

Most of those early stock events and facilities were associated with county and state fairs; fairground tracks dotted the southern landscape. One such facility, Charlotte's Southern States Fair Ground, was a half-mile dirt track

Figure 4. The second Charlotte Speedway was built in 1948 and hosted NASCAR's very first "strictly" stock-car race in 1949. (From *Dirt Tracks to Glory* by Sylvia Wilkinson. © 1983 by Sylvia Wilkinson. Reprinted by permission of Algonquin Books of Chapel Hill. All rights reserved.)

built in 1926 at the intersection of Sugar Creek Road and North Tryon Street. The track hosted regularly scheduled events after 1937 and hosted NASCAR events between 1949 and 1960. Another historically important dirt track venue was Charlotte Speedway, which was built in 1948 west of Charlotte on Wilkinson Boulevard (see figure 4). As mentioned earlier, this track was the site of the first strictly stock race and a key NASCAR venue throughout the 1950s.[28]

Dirt track racing remained popular in the South and in the Charlotte region in particular even after paved tracks ushered in the superspeedway era. Other dirt tracks in the region included Concord Speedway, which hosted racing between 1955 and 1979 and several Grand National events in the late 1950s and early 1960s. The half-mile track at the Metrolina Fairgrounds in northeast Charlotte started out as a dirt track in 1965, was paved in 1974, ran intermittently throughout the 1980s, and closed in 1998. Dale Earnhardt won his first race on asphalt at Metrolina. Queen City Speedway, another short clay track, was built in the late 1960s near the airport. Neighbors complained bitterly about track noise and the facility closed in 1968.[29]

Figure 5. The Charlotte Motor Speedway was the project of driver Curtis Turner (pictured) and Charlotte race promoter O. Bruton Smith. Completed in 1960, it is now known as Lowe's Motor Speedway. (Source: *Charlotte Observer*.)

Although stock-car racing was born on red-clay tracks, this sport came of age on the South's paved superspeedways. Darlington Raceway in South Carolina, which opened on Labor Day in 1950, is considered the oldest superspeedway. North Carolina's first modern speedway with pavement, lights, and banked turns was Southland Speedway (later known as Raleigh Speedway and Dixieland Speedway) completed north of Raleigh in 1952. The Charlotte (later Lowe's) Motor Speedway resulted from the combined efforts of Charlotte promoter Bruton Smith and legendary driver Curtis Turner (see figure 5). They originally started independent projects, but united in 1959 and initiated construction north of Charlotte near Concord. The first event at Charlotte Motor Speedway was the World (later Coca-Cola) 600, which was run on June 19, 1960, with the first purse of $100,000 in NASCAR history.[30]

Charlotte's emergence as the center for technological advancement in stock-car racing was concurrent with Atlanta's demise throughout the 1950s and 1960s. Atlanta's technological leadership, particularly that provided by Parks and Vogt, did not cope well with the strictly stock category. They had specialized themselves out of competition with their myopic focus on old modified Fords. New automobile mechanical talent in the Charlotte region included Lee Petty (voted NASCAR's mechanic of the year in 1950), Buck

Figure 6. This 1960 photo of the famous Holman-Moody shop near the Charlotte airport illustrates the scale and sophistication of that facility. Most shops were backyard affairs. Its fleet of Ford Fairlanes became the standard for NASCAR stock racing in the 1960s. This facility became a model and a draw for future team facilities. (Source: *Charlotte Observer*.)

Baker's crew of Joe Rumph and Jimmy Ross, Ralph Earnhardt (in addition to being a driver he was a master mechanic and the first to install crash bars for driver protection), and Curtis Turner's crew at Schwam Motor Company in Charlotte, among others.[31]

Charlotte's technologic preeminence was achieved (ironically) with Ford's return to stock-car success from the mid 1950s through the early 1970s. That success resulted from the Charlotte partnership of John Holman and Ralph Moody. The Holman-Moody shop was created in 1957 (the two teamed up after Ford and other car manufacturers withdrew sponsorship of stock-car racing) and it was significantly different from anything that NASCAR had ever seen. The shop was much larger in scale (at least a dozen full-time mechanics) and far more sophisticated than the humble backyard garages that typified this sport in the 1950s and 1960s (see figure 6). In terms of scale, technologic sophistication, and branding ("the best-known name in racing"), the Holman-Moody shop was a glimpse into NASCAR's future. The shop had its own NASCAR race teams with drivers like Joe Weatherly, Curtis Turner, Marvin Amick, Fireball Roberts, Fred Lorenzen, Mario Andretti, and David Pearson. The shop also built engines and performance parts for other teams in NASCAR as well as for other motorsports.[32]

As a clear indicator of dominance, Holman-Moody Fords won forty-eight of fifty-five NASCAR Grand National Races in 1965, a record that has never been matched. From the shop's location next to the Charlotte airport, their innovations included fuel cells, full-floater rear axle, on-board fire systems, quick change disk brakes, square tube frames, and tube shocks. In fact, the 1966 Holman-Moody Ford Fairlane was the basis for all NASCAR racecars until very recently. The Holman-Moody shop, with its combination of large scale and technical innovativeness, became a major attraction for other shops to locate in the Charlotte region. It also became the model for NASCAR shop development, with scale and technical innovation at the heart of shop success. As the knowledge intensity of this motorsports industry increased, the extent of clustering in the Charlotte region increased proportionately. By 1987, twenty-nine of the forty-two teams that made the lineup for that year's Coca-Cola 600 had their shops within one hundred miles of Charlotte. In turn, the need for this specialized knowledge derived, at least in part, from the highly regulated environment that NASCAR maintains. The desire for highly competitive racing is at the heart of that regulatory environment. The level of regulation is much higher than in most other forms of racing.[33]

Charlotte as Knowledge Community

Charlotte's current cluster of NASCAR-related activities is impressive: the Charlotte Regional Partnership lists 425 motorsports companies in the Charlotte region.[34] According to an economic impact study commissioned by the North Carolina Motorsports Association (NCMA was formed in 2002), North Carolina motorsports generated approximately $5.1 billion in 2003 (updated and estimated at $7 billion in 2006) and was responsible for just under 25,000 jobs.[35] These include direct activities and all multiplier effects. On average, these jobs are much higher paying than most North Carolina jobs; mean compensation is just over $70,000. Most of this economic impact, approximately three-fourths, is felt within the Charlotte region. At the very heart of this Charlotte cluster are the race shops and their teams. Nearly all (90 percent) of NASCAR's Sprint Cup teams are based in the greater Charlotte region. With all of the dominant teams — Hendrick, Gibbs, Roush, Earnhardt, Penske, Childress, Waltrip, Yates, Petty, and Evernham — located within an easy commute of Charlotte, their center of gravity is powerful, and they attract a large assortment of other upstream and downstream activities.

It is this cluster of nearly twenty Sprint shops that is responsible for Charlotte's technologic superiority (see figure 7). Collectively, they constitute a knowledge community not unlike the Formula One motorsports center located in the South of England, the British Motor Sports Valley.³⁶ *Knowledge communities* are spatial systems of innovation that generally operate most effectively at a relatively local regional level, that is, within a fifty-mile radius. Such communities interact formally and informally. Frequent face-to-face interactions are transactional (with money exchanged) and nontransactional. This highly localized "buzz" is complemented by "global pipelines," the ties to select external technological facilities and racing venues.³⁷ Knowledge flows through the community as the result of technologic component sales, labor mobility between competitors, shared suppliers, observation at practice sessions, and informal communications (see figure 8). Knowledge institutions play an important role in supporting this regional system of innovation with applied research, consultancy, and education of skilled labor. Universities, community colleges, and technical institutes all play an important role in support of the community. According to Kimmo Viljamaa, the motorsport industry is highly specialized, competitive, and sophisticated and incremental innovation and engineering skills have great importance. The industry is regarded as post-Fordist in the sense that it involves technologic innovation on the one hand and a widely popular spectacle on the other.³⁸

As mentioned above, at the heart of innovation is the collection of firm race teams. To be competitive, each team requires approximately $20 million annually. Each team has an explicit relationship (commercial and technical) with an auto manufacturer. These now include Chevrolet, Dodge, Ford, and Toyota (since 2007). Sponsors vary widely in nature and are attracted by NASCAR fans' high level of brand recognition and loyalty. A recent study conducted by James Madison University (Center for Sports Sponsorship) found that 36 percent of one thousand NASCAR fans could name the sponsor of every car in the top thirty. Primary sponsorship can cost as much as $15 to $20 million (in 2008). Primary sponsors include such corporate and brand notables as Office Depot, Lowe's, FedEx, Target, UPS, Best Buy, Budweiser, Miller Lite, DuPont, Valvoline, Mountain Dew, Tide, Bass Pro Shops, AT&T Mobile, Shell, Kellogg's, Texaco, NAPA, Alltel, Mobil, DeWalt, Little Debbie, and M&Ms. Each race team has primary and secondary sponsors.

Team facilities are impressive; larger facilities can include multiple buildings totaling over five hundred thousand square feet. While the number of firm-team employees varies substantially, the largest shops (limited to four Sprint cars) have over 500 employees. For example, Hendrick Motorsports

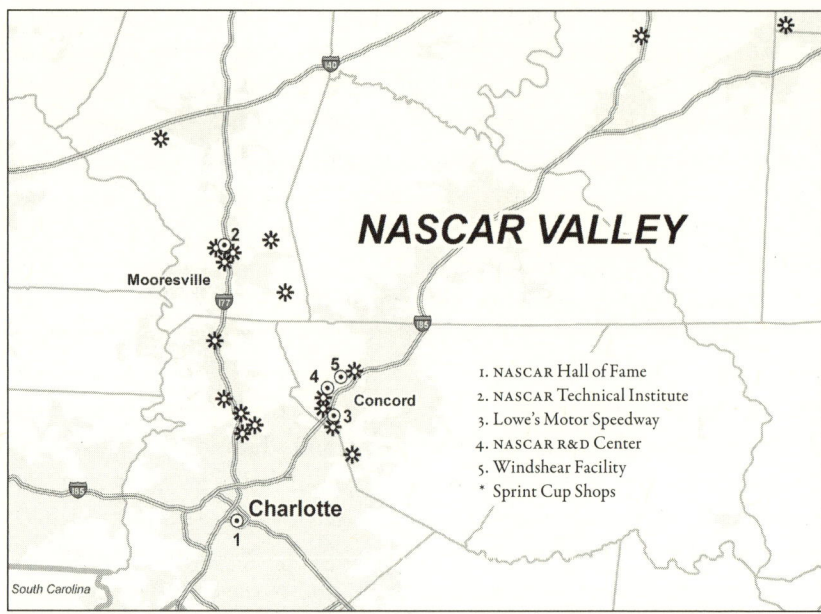

Figure 7. Eighteen out of twenty Sprint Cup shops lie at the very heart of Charlotte's NASCAR knowledge and memory communities and form the basis of the region's technological dominance. (Source: Ronald Mitchelson)

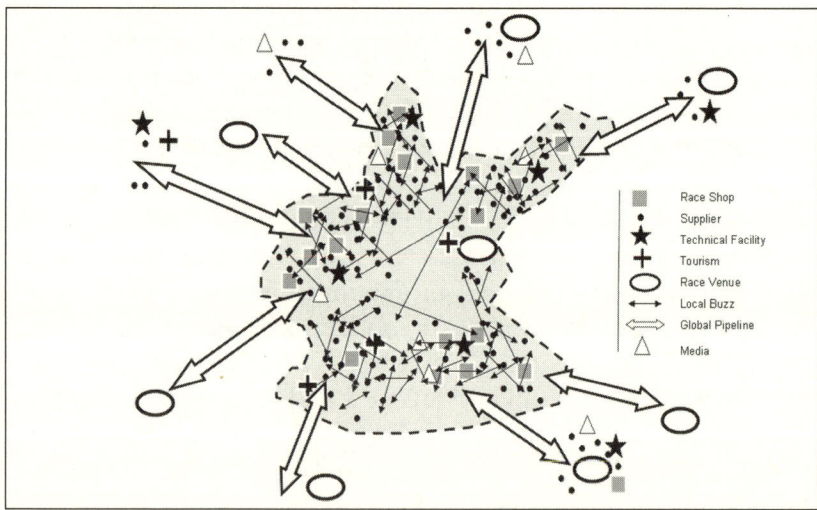

Figure 8. The firms attract a variety of activities that yield local buzz (frequent and often informal interactions) and global pipelines (less frequent but more formal external-internal interactions). (Adapted from Harald Bathelt, Anders Malmberg, and Peter Maskell, "Clusters and Knowledge: Local Buzz, Global Pipelines, and the Process of Knowledge Creation," *Progress in Human Geography*, 28, no. 1 (2004), 31–56, fig. 1.)

Figure 9. Hendrick Motorsports is located near Lowe's Motor Speedway in Concord. Visitors can observe cars being worked on in Hendrick's garage. (Source: Derek H. Alderman.)

employs over 550 individuals, including 60 engineers (see figure 9). A fundamental benefit of larger multicar shops is NASCAR's allocation of practice time on a per-car basis (laps per car). Multiple cars provide the racing firm with more data for improved performance across the entire shop. Single car shops are at a distinct disadvantage.

Each of these teams has functional specializations that include management, marketing, retailing, tourism, engines, fabrication, assembly, safety, communications, engineering, and research and development. Teams spend about 20 percent of their budgets on research and development. In contrast to the present, engineers were rare in these shops as recently as the 1980s. The enhanced draw of the Charlotte region and its upscale facilities is illustrated by the 2008 move of Petty Enterprises from its historic, small, and fragmented facilities located in Level Cross, North Carolina, to Mooresville, which is just north of Charlotte and home to many NASCAR teams. According to ESPN, the Pettys desired a larger and less fragmented facility, closer proximity to suppliers, and an improved location to attract key skilled labor.[39]

While the production side of NASCAR is increasingly clustered within the Charlotte region, the consumption of its race-day spectacle is widely and increasingly dispersed to an estimated 75 million fans.[40] Charlotte benefits in disproportionate fashion as revenues flow back into the cluster from an expanding market. In addition to North Carolina, NASCAR now runs events in Florida, California, New Mexico, Arizona, Kansas, Texas, Tennessee, Virginia, Georgia, Delaware, South Carolina, Michigan, Pennsylvania, Illinois, Indiana, New York, and New Hampshire. Thirty-eight events (not all point producing) are run at twenty-two different venues. Every major track in the United States wishes to host a Sprint Cup event. In the case of Kentucky's recently constructed track, the owners sued NASCAR to gain an event based on antitrust legislation; the suit was dismissed in 2007. Subsequently, the track was purchased by SMI (Bruton Smith) in 2008.[41]

Television coverage has expanded the consumption of NASCAR's weekend spectacles greatly since the first live and complete coverage of the Daytona 500 in 1979. ESPN was crucial to the early live programming of NASCAR events during the 1980s and 1990s. NASCAR television revenues grew from $67 million in 2001 to $163 million in 2006. By 2007, NASCAR could sign an eight-year contract with ABC and ESPN worth nearly $4.5 billion. Much of that revenue filters to NASCAR teams and venues. In 2008, the fiftieth Daytona 500 was watched by 33.5 million American viewers. There was modest concern for reduced viewership of Nextel Cup events between 2006 and 2007 with 10.7 million viewers on average in 2006 and 9.7 million in 2007 (a 9 percent reduction). Despite this decline, Fox sold all of its advertising slots for the 2008 Daytona 500 at $550,000 per thirty-second spot. NASCAR's declining TV ratings follow a more general trend for reduced viewing of sporting events. Since the strongest NASCAR fan loyalties lie with individual drivers, most analysts associate the decline in viewing to the retirement (or semiretirement) of popular drivers like Rusty Wallace, Mark Martin, and Bill Elliott along with the lack of recent success by Dale Earnhardt Jr., NASCAR's most popular driver.[42]

The Charlotte region remains home to one of the premiere race venues in all of NASCAR, Lowe's Motor Speedway (see figure 10). Lowe's hosts three major events, including the Coca-Cola 600, each year. The Speedway was the first to accept a corporate identity (Lowe's in 1999) with $35 million in revenues spread over ten years. The Speedway is located on 1,300 acres in Concord and has permanent seating of 162,000 along with 113 luxury suites and two residential condo buildings. In addition to that venue, Speedway Motorsports, Inc., (SMI) is headquartered in Concord. Bruton Smith, long-

Figure 10. Lowe's Motor Speedway, one of NASCAR's premiere venues, is located in Concord. It hosts three Sprint Cup events annually including the Coca-Cola 600. The speedway is owned by SMI, also headquartered in Concord. (Courtesy Derek H. Alderman.)

time rival of Bill France, is the chairman and CEO of this large, publicly traded corporation.

SMI's growth throughout these expansion years has been substantial. In addition to Lowe's Motor Speedway, SMI owns Atlanta Motor Speedway, Bristol Motor Speedway, Infineon (California) Raceway, Las Vegas Motor Speedway, Texas Motor Speedway, and newly acquired New Hampshire Motor Speedway (purchased for $340 million in cash in November 2007) and Kentucky Speedway in 2008. SMI total permanent seats (all venues) is just under one million. The value of owned properties easily exceeds $1 billion. While revenues have tripled from roughly $190 million in 1997 to $570 million in 2006, the share of revenues attributable to TV has increased from 8.2 percent to 28.7 percent.[43]

Specialized facilities that support firm teams serve as an essential part of NASCAR's knowledge community in the Charlotte region. Two are located near each other in Mooresville: the NASCAR Technical Institute (NTI) and Performance Instruction and Training (PIT). NTI opened in 2002 in a new

Figure 11. NASCAR Technical Institute in Mooresville is among an impressive array of facilities in close proximity to the cluster of NASCAR shops that support the knowledge community in NASCAR Valley. (Source: Derek H. Alderman.)

146,000-square-foot facility equipped with forty classrooms and labs for welding, fabrication, shock absorbers, engines, transmissions, and chassis all equipped with dynamometers (see figure 11). The school operates with 150 instructors and staff. The fifty-seven-week curriculum includes eighteen weeks of NASCAR-specific training. The new PIT facility is located on a five-and-one-half-acre campus with 32,000 square feet of facility space including a quarter-mile approach track with six pit stalls, a complete fitness conditioning center with physical therapy and medical services, and meeting facilities. PIT primarily serves the motorsports industry but also offers services and programs to the general public.

In addition to specialized training, support facilities within the region offer advanced aerodynamic infrastructure. AeroDyn Wind Tunnel in Mooresville was designed primarily for Sprint, Nationwide, and Truck Series vehicles. It employs twenty-two 100-hp fans to achieve full scale analyses at wind speeds of 130 mph. A new 40,000-square-foot wind tunnel facility ("Windshear") was opened in September 2008 near Concord by Haas racing at a cost of $40 million (see figure 12). It uses a twenty-two-foot, 5100-hp

Figure 12. The Haas Windshear Tunnel in Concord is one of the most advanced testing facilities in all motorsports. (Source: Derek H. Alderman.)

fan to achieve 180 mph wind, and it permits tethered race cars to run on a stainless steel conveyor belt at 180 mph. Sensors measure downforce on each of the wheels independently. The rental rate is $1650 per hour. NASCAR has constructed its own 61,000-square-foot Research and Development Center near Concord (see figure 13). The Car of Tomorrow (COT), NASCAR's basic vehicle configuration used by all Sprint Cup teams in all events since 2008, was developed at the Center with a focus on driver safety and car durability. The Center also houses NASCAR regional corporate offices, rules officials, accident investigators, and directors of the Sprint, Nationwide, and Truck Series.[44]

The corporate structure of stock-car racing benefits from being part of an intense pro-business environment in and around Charlotte. NASCAR is historically antiunion and, even today, it is the only major professional sporting organization without significant labor representation.[45] It is not insignificant that the industrial core of stock-car racing remains centered in a right-to-work state with some of the lowest rates of unionization in the nation.

Charlotte as Memory Community

Charlotte provides NASCAR not only a center of technologic and industrial development but also a place for constructing a common heritage that fans can consume and contribute to as they visit the birthplace of stock-car racing. The flow of tourists destined for the large cluster of race shops, retail centers, museums, commemorative landmarks, speedways, and a new Hall of Fame that is scheduled to open in 2010 is an important part of NASCAR's economic and cultural development within the Charlotte region.

The concept of *memory community* refers to more than these places for remembering and memorializing the history of stock-car racing. Perhaps more importantly, the notion of memory community recognizes the important role that Charlotte plays in providing a setting for communicating and exchanging historical narratives about racing and creating a shared sense of the past and what is important historically. As Mark Howell has asserted, NASCAR is a sport "rooted in cultural mythology" that draws on and utilizes "symbols, rituals, and images" to increase its popularity.[46] Building these places of racing memory is of general benefit to Charlotte. As geographer

Figure 13. NASCAR's Research and Development Center, birthplace of the Car of Tomorrow, is located in the Concord area. (Source: Derek H. Alderman.)

Lily Kong has shown, cities often accumulate cultural capital and icons, including memorials and monuments, in their attempt to enhance their status and identity.[47]

While NASCAR's history is not exceptionally long (sixty years), that heritage is significant and eventful and already has undergone some revision. For instance, despite the wider recognition that NASCAR's early history was dominated by moonshine and bootleggers, NASCAR itself has obscured or sanitized that portion of its history.[48] Like most histories, this one too is contested as fans and historians alike debate the true origins of the sport. A reputational politics surrounds the way NASCAR rewrites its history through tourism sites in Charlotte. Such politics dictate that the reputations or images of past and present drivers be constructed and cultivated in selective ways, drawing attention to certain biographical aspects and cultural values over others.[49] Much of NASCAR history is scripted in ways that affirm the mutual, simple, working-class roots of the sport, its participants, and its fans.

The Earnhardt men are good examples of the developed driver identity resembling the cars that they drive: "strictly stock." The Dale Trail in the Kannapolis area, a driving tour dedicated to the deceased icon, illustrates the manner in which the region takes economic advantage of the constructed memory of Dale Earnhardt as "one of us." Fans travel down Dale Earnhardt Boulevard and can visit the original Earnhardt Road where the family's hog slaughterhouse once stood, or visit the site of Eddleman's Garage where Ralph Earnhardt built cars for moonshiners like Junior Johnson, or eat the same type of tomato sandwich that was Dale's favorite at Paunchy's Diner, or visit Dale's nine-foot, nine-hundred-pound bronze statue, clad in jeans and cowboy boots, at the Dale Earnhardt Plaza (see figure 14). Earnhardt's reputation, like his statue, is larger than life. Fans exhibit an enthusiasm for staying connected with this heroic figure and Kannapolis appears ready to accommodate. Promotional accounts of the Dale Trail claim that tourists "may run into local residents who are more than willing to share their memories of [Dale] with you."[50]

Although not dead, Dale Earnhardt Jr. is being mythologized in similar ways. At his Nationwide Series shop in Mooresville, fans are able to purchase Jr. Nation souvenirs, view exhibits that recount Dale Jr.'s life, and inscribe their sentiments about him on a whiteboard wall (see figure 15). The inscriptions reveal the depth to which fans connect with the Earnhardts while also reminding us that the writing of their reputational glory is directed not only by the NASCAR industry but also by the tourists who make the pilgrimage to Charlotte's racing memory community and participate in the process.

Figure 14. Statue of iconic NASCAR racer Dale Earnhardt in Kannapolis. (Source: Derek H. Alderman.)

Figure 15. Dale Earnhardt Jr. provides the type of driver identity that NASCAR thrives on. Dale Jr. is NASCAR's most popular driver. His image is actively cultivated at his Jr. Nation facility in Mooresville. (Source: Derek H. Alderman.)

Figure 16. Economic development downstream from Charlotte's cluster of shops includes many tourist opportunities ranging from NASCAR art, merchandise, and museums to the Hall of Fame scheduled to open in downtown Charlotte in 2010. In this fashion, knowledge and memory communities are physically integrated. (Source: Derek H. Alderman.)

The planned NASCAR Hall of Fame indicates the value that NASCAR places on maintaining and enhancing the reputational allure of its drivers and providing fans with a central place to consume and contribute to this image-making activity. Instead of a Hall of Fame, the racing association could have proposed that a general museum to stock-car racing be built, but this would not have fulfilled the ideology of individualism and the folk-heroic values that NASCAR has long cultivated among fans. Charlotte's selection as the location for a new $150 million Hall of Fame resulted from a stiff competition between Charlotte, Richmond, Kansas City, Atlanta, and Daytona Beach. The density of teams in the region was a major draw. NASCAR also preferred Charlotte's financing plan which is reliant on a hotel-tax increase that was approved prior to the agreement as well as private financing led by Charlotte-based Wachovia and Bank of America. The 100,000-square-foot facility will provide interactive exhibits, a Hall of Honor, restaurants, and retail outlets (see figure 16). NASCAR will develop a method for nomination and election to the Hall and there will be an annual induction ceremony.

The Hall is to be state-of-the-art and very technologically advanced. It is being designed by the same firm that designed the Rock and Roll Hall of Fame in Cleveland and the Holocaust Museum in Washington, D.C. The Hall is intended to be Charlotte's downtown anchor in drawing tourists from national and international origins.[51]

Numerous other tourist attractions are associated with the NASCAR industrial cluster in Charlotte. For example, each of the major firm race teams provides a gift shop and shop tours that celebrate the team's history and NASCAR's larger legacy. Attendance can be quite significant with up to two hundred thousand visitors per year. Several tour companies provide day-long regional excursions that make stops at several shops. In addition, many stand-alone facilities contribute to the construction and maintenance of NASCAR's memory community within the Charlotte region. The highest densities of museums are found amidst the highest density of firm-team facilities in Mooresville and Concord. Both areas are well organized with printed brochures, tour maps, and Web sites.

The media are well represented in the Charlotte region and can have profound effects on the current perceptions of stock-car racing and how it is (and will be) remembered. Three large media corporations located in the Charlotte region focus on NASCAR or motorsports in general: NASCAR Images, Speed Channel, and Performance Racing Network. NASCAR Images, co-owned by NASCAR Digital Entertainment and Fox Cable Network, produces TV programming of current NASCAR activities and events as well as documentary films. It is the exclusive licensor of all NASCAR racing footage. It engages in production of material for other networks, corporate videos, home videos, digitization services, and event planning. One of its best-known productions is the 2006 documentary "Dale" (narrated by Paul Newman) released by its CMT Movies division. Speed Channel moved from Stamford, Connecticut, in order to be closer to the Charlotte knowledge and memory communities. Speed Channel is an affiliate of Fox Cable Network. Half of its programming is focused on NASCAR, much of which originates with NASCAR Images. Performance Racing Network, a radio production facility located in Concord, is an affiliate of Speedway Motorsports, Inc. It produces five different shows, including qualifying, Nationwide, and Sprint races, and postrace shows for events at SMI venues. The network includes 723 radio stations in the United States and the Armed Services Network.[52] A substantial number of marketing and public relations firms in the Charlotte region focus on NASCAR clients. The majority of these are situated in Mooresville or Concord, close to teams. These are typically small firms with ten to fifteen employees. According to the N.C. Motorsports Association, there are about seventy such firms with total employment of nearly nine hundred.⁵³

The Charlotte area serves as a powerful and profitable site for tourists to connect with stock-car-racing heritage, but the importance of memory is not limited to visitors. Racing pervades the everyday landscape of locals, including the names of streets. In a part of Kannapolis known as "Car Town," one can find neighborhood roads named Cadillac, Dodge, Plymouth, Ford, Packard, Chevrolet, Sedan, Coupe, Edsel, and even V-8. During the campaign to land the NASCAR Hall of Fame, Charlotteans asserted that their city was the historically logical location. In addition to delivering a large financial investment to the Hall of Fame ($100 million in public money), boosters covered billboards, T-shirts, and bumper stickers with the slogan "Racing was built here. Racing belongs here."⁵⁴ This strong ownership of NASCAR memory is not just important economically; for many people living in the Charlotte area, it is also part of a larger identification with southern heritage. In the words of one enthusiast: "Stockcar racing is embedded in our culture, the sports equivalent of pork barbecue."⁵⁵ Having the NASCAR Hall of Fame located in Charlotte has important implications for maintaining this local and regional identity as the racing industry expands into other markets and, in doing so, abandons some traditional southern tracks.

Tensions in NASCAR Valley

It is not all smooth sailing for NASCAR and Charlotte. As a point of convergence for so many influences, organizations, and people, Charlotte's relationship with stock-car racing does not come without tensions. In general, there is too much money and too much identity at stake. Some of the stressors facing NASCAR in Charlotte are related to community quality of life. The first strictly stock race back in 1949 at Charlotte Speedway raised so much dust that seven nearby homeowners sued, won, and NASCAR painted their houses. When Bruton Smith proposed a drag strip to be located on his property next to Lowe's Motor Speedway in Concord, his construction permit was originally denied due to noise and property value concerns of residents. When Smith then threatened to move Lowe's Motor Speedway and the Coca-Cola 600 to another venue, the city conceded the drag strip and provided $80 million in development incentives. Municipal leaders even renamed Speedway Boulevard, which runs from Interstate 85 to Lowe's Motor Speedway, for the billionaire racing tycoon.⁵⁶ Smith was taken seriously (or even feared) because of his financial clout and his history of manipulating tracks and moving race dates to meet his financial needs. In 1996, Smith and Bob Bahre bought the historic North Wilkesboro Track simply for the purpose of claiming its two NASCAR Winston Cup races and moving them to new tracks in Texas and New Hampshire. North Wilkesboro lost millions of dollars in annual spectator spending and has never recovered financially. Although the Charlotte area has clearly benefitted from the ongoing expansion of stock-car racing, this prosperity has come at a cost. Concord officials realized that they were economically vulnerable to the loss of the Lowe's race, forcing them to abandon the neighbors' property concerns.[57]

Penske Racing South, located on the north side of Mooresville, is attempting to build a $21 million, three-quarter-mile oval test track next to its 400,000-square-foot shop. Noise is the major community concern. Penske has promised to limit the number of cars and to restrict test hours between 8:00 a.m. and 6:00 p.m. Other environmental concerns about NASCAR might hinder future acceptance and development. NASCAR is not "green." Consumers are increasingly rejecting forms of technology (internal combustion engines, pneumatic rubber tires) that are essentially one hundred years old and viewed as responsible for much of the planet's environmental degradation. Also, the decentralization of NASCAR's venues juxtaposed with the increasing centralization of NASCAR's production creates a tension, especially in terms of the environmental distribution costs (getting race cars and teams to venues). If production were to decentralize in response, it would have a significant effect on Charlotte's existing cluster of race teams and shops.[58]

In addition to environmental concerns, NASCAR must contend with the imperative of market expansion. NASCAR has successfully nationalized its market so that it can claim a fan base of approximately 75 million, most of whom are not the original fan base of southern white males. There are two strategies for future expansion. Within the national market, NASCAR has increased female participation (at the tracks and TV viewing) so that females now account for roughly 40 percent of NASCAR's fan base, but NASCAR has been less successful in attracting minority markets. Given fans' allegiance to individual drivers, this lack of success is unsurprising. The lack of African American drivers is historic and persistent. The only African American to successfully compete at the Grand National (Winston, Nextel, Sprint) level is Wendell Scott, who broke the NASCAR color barrier in 1961. According to NASCAR, diversity is a top corporate initiative. The Drive for Diversity Combine, designed to develop minority and female drivers and crew members, has existed since 2004. To date, the Combine has never produced a

Cup Series driver. The most visible black in NASCAR today is Brad Daugherty. Daugherty is a former UNC-Chapel Hill and NBA basketball star. He is a former Busch and Truck Series owner and current NASCAR TV analyst. Daugherty attributes a chance thirty-second conversation at age twelve with Richard Petty at the 1977 Daytona 500 with fueling his desire to be involved in NASCAR. That sort of connectivity between NASCAR's stars and its fans has been a foundation of success. Most of the NASCAR firm teams have not engaged the diversity goal in any significant way. An exception is Joe Gibbs Racing (JGR). JGR drivers Chris Bristol and Marc Davis are black drivers who have won at several stock levels (including historic Hickory Motor Speedway). Davis in particular has attained considerable notoriety and rang the closing bell at the New York Stock Exchange in observance of Black History Month in February 2008.[59] Still, the commonly held notion that Sundays are the most segregated day of the week continues to apply not just to religion, but to NASCAR.

The stress of diversifying NASCAR's traditionally strong southern white following is evident in Charlotte, particularly as the city participates in racialized debates about heritage and commemoration. Some critics connect the unpopularity of stock-car racing among African Americans to the flying of the Confederate Battle Flag at races.[60] Despite the fact that the flag is interpreted by many blacks (and some whites) as a symbol of racism and oppression, Confederate supporters claim that it is a legitimate part of their heritage and refuse to leave the emblem at home when traveling to tracks. Some observers have suggested that the expansion of NASCAR into new markets has led to uneasiness among southern fans, perhaps leading them to express a connection with the Confederacy even more passionately and defensively.[61] NASCAR officials recognize the importance of the issue; CEO Brian France criticized the flying of the Confederate flag in a 2005 "60 Minutes" show.[62] In reaction to what they interpret as NASCAR's "antisouthern" stance, Confederate heritage defense organizations have condemned the racing association, leading to public demonstrations at races. For example, the North Carolina Division of the Sons of Confederate Veterans carried out a NASCAR protest in Charlotte during the Coca-Cola 600 race on May 26, 2007. While Charlotte serves as an important memory community for celebrating and promoting stock-car-racing history, it also serves as a memory arena for debating southern heritage and NASCAR's connection with its (white) southern past.

As NASCAR continues to grow and seeks to rewrite its cultural image, Charlotte deals with its own struggles over southern memory and identity.

In 2004 and 2005, Charlotte faced an intense debate over whether a Confederate flag should continue flying over the city-owned Elmwood Cemetery. The flag was stolen before officials could officially remove it.[63] Cabarrus County tourism officials made the controversial decision of recruiting and agreeing to host the annual meeting of Sons of Confederate Veterans in July 2008.[64] Repeated attempts to rename a Charlotte street for slain civil rights leader Martin Luther King Jr. met with resistance until city leaders agreed in 2006 on Second Street.[65] Martin Luther King Jr. Boulevard is one of three streets bordering the site of the much-anticipated NASCAR Hall of Fame—an ironic location, given the cold reception that stock-car racing receives from African Americans. But perhaps NASCAR can use this association with King to its advantage as it pursues more diverse markets that transcend the sport's still potent "good ole boy," Confederate-flag-waving image.

Some people complain about NASCAR's changing image, connecting it with larger cultural and economic changes supposedly threatening the Charlotte area. For instance, one observer suggested that southerners avoid Lake Norman, a popular, upscale residential area northwest of Charlotte that is the home of many NASCAR drivers. He said: "A beautiful place, great lake, but now heavily overrun by over-development . . . You see as many NY and NJ tags as you do NC tags. Complete loss of southern identity, and complete commercialism of NASCAR."[66] NASCAR can be a source of tension not only for long-time Charlotteans, but also for the growing number of people moving to the city from outside the South. A participant in a newcomer blog remarked: "I have been here [in Charlotte] one year now. At first it was hard to make friends due to the culture shock and the fact that some natives don't have an appreciation for those from different parts of the world. To them, sweet tea, 'bless your heart,' and NASCAR are part of everyday life for all earthlings."[67] Whether people argue that stock-car racing is too much part of the South or not southern enough, it is clear that the sport and its relationship with Charlotte can be a source of stress as people engage in the larger politics of place and personal identity.

In addition to expanding markets within the United States (among women and minorities), NASCAR seeks to expand markets beyond national boundaries. To date, those efforts have not met with great success. NASCAR has run exhibition Cup events in Canada, Mexico, and Japan and Nationwide points events in Mexico and Canada. New drivers to Sprint Cup competition include former open-wheel drivers coming from outside the United States. The reason is simple: the money is much better than in the open-wheel circuits. Perhaps the popular movie and NASCAR spoof *Talladega Nights: The Ballad of Ricky Bobby* captures a glimpse of NASCAR's future. Will Ferrell plays the very stereotypical southern stock-car driver, Ricky Bobby. Ricky is challenged by another stereotype, the sophisticated European Formula One driver, Jean Girard (played by Sacha Baron Cohen). Ricky ultimately prevails with the help of his African American crew chief, Lucius Washington (played by Michael Clarke Duncan). (Dale Earnhardt Jr. even makes a cameo appearance.) The movie grossed $47 million in its first weekend and was the number one movie during the summer of 2006. If nothing else, Hollywood probably assisted in widening the sport's fan base.[68]

The 2007 and 2008 NASCAR seasons saw the involvement of transplanted Formula One drivers Juan Montoya, Dario Franchitti, and Jacques Villeneuve. Toyota entered new teams in Nextel and Sprint Cup competition in 2007 (Michael Waltrip Racing) and 2008 (Joe Gibbs Racing). Humpy Wheeler (former president of Lowe's Motor Speedway) views globalization in drivers and fans as inevitable and likens it to the NBA and NFL. He believes that the NASCAR spectacle can be effectively exported to Latin America, Europe, and the Pacific Rim. When Montoya showed up in Daytona in 2007, media crews from Russia, Sweden, Germany, Mexico, Canada, Italy, and Colombia were there to record his transition from Formula One to stock cars. The Chip Ganassi Racing team reports that their Web site now attracts visitors from 150 countries in contrast to just seven before Juan Montoya joined the team. Their primary sponsor, Texaco/Havoline, unleashed major advertising campaigns in Russia, Turkey, Bulgaria, and Colombia in the months following Montoya's switch. Dario Franchitti (a Scot of Italian descent) has the same sort of international name power and is married to internationally known American actress Ashley Judd. He started driving full time for the Ganassi team in the 2008 season. The 2008 Daytona 500 had more drivers from outside the country than from the historic center of driver origins, North Carolina. Despite these visible developments, there remains considerable skepticism by portions of the fan base, and within the NASCAR industry itself, to these internationalization efforts. Kyle Petty (Richard's son and driver) believes globalization of the market will not take place and that any strong effort to do so would be a mistake resulting in significant erosion of the traditional fan base. He does not believe that stock-car racing can compete with Formula One racing in places like Brazil or Europe. Even Humpy Wheeler bemoans the fact that no one in NASCAR is really working on those potential new and global markets.[69]

NASCAR and Charlotte Down the Road

Randal Hall has suggested that the study of automobile racing in the South can reveal a great deal about the region. According to Hall, southern racing is an important indicator of "the larger processes of economic development, civic boosterism, cultural change, and regional interaction."[70] Embracing this perspective, we have explored the nature and implications of the strong relationship between NASCAR and Charlotte, recognizing that both the sport and the city are in a state of significant growth and change.

In important ways, these development trajectories are complementary. Within the ever-expanding geography of stock-car racing, Charlotte benefits from serving as core to the sport's knowledge and memory communities, from persisting as the industrial and cultural center of NASCAR. This centrality, however, is not simply a stubborn holdover or historical artifact. It is also a product of Charlotte's growing financial and corporate prominence and globally ascendant status. In the words of Mark Dwyer, a NASCAR vice president and lead negotiator on the Hall of Fame site-selection process, "Charlotte sees the Hall of Fame as a catalyst for economic development downtown — and there is a lot of momentum downtown already with office and residential and restaurants in place and on the move." NASCAR sees Charlotte as important to both the sport's future and its past. While the city is a platform for technologic innovation and economic expansion, it also serves as a guardian of stock-car racing's heritage and the reputational value of its drivers.

Certain tensions and stresses occur in the Charlotte area as it sits at the intersection of the forces of change and continuity within motorsports and within the larger changing South. Down the road, NASCAR will increasingly face the challenge of balancing its need to maintain its historic, place, and region-based identity while continuing its evolution into the mainstream national (even global) culture. Like all knowledge-intensive industries, NASCAR faces a challenge to balance the value of local buzz with global pipelines. If either is left unattended, then the cluster suffers. In the case of NASCAR, there are important questions about whether or not the industry's historical (and more local) roots should be so strongly maintained, particularly in light of how this history is framed to new and widening markets that are both geographic and social in nature. How these questions are ultimately answered will have a major impact on the geography of stock-car racing and its largest and most important center of knowledge and memory, Charlotte.

Notes

1. Richard Pillsbury, "Stock Car Racing," in *The Theater of Sport*, ed. Karl Raitz (Baltimore: Johns Hopkins University Press, 1995), 270–295.

2. Richard Pillsbury, "Carolina Thunder: The Changing Scene," in *Snapshots of the Carolinas: Landscapes and Cultures*, ed. G. Gordon Bennett, 53–56 (Washington, D.C.: Association of American Geographers, 1996), 55; Neal Thompson, *Driving with the Devil: Southern Moonshine, Detroit Wheels, and the Birth of* NASCAR (New York: Three Rivers Press, 2006), 291; Mark Bechtel, "Richard Petty: The People's King," *Sports Illustrated* 109, no. 2 (July 14, 2008), 74–77.

3. Quoted in Marc P. Singer and Ryan L. Sumner, *Auto Racing in Charlotte and the Carolina Piedmont* (Charleston, S.C.: Arcadia Publishing, 2003), 7.

4. Derek H. Alderman, Preston W. Mitchell, Jeffrey T. Webb, and Derek Hanak, "Carolina Thunder Revisited: Toward a Transcultural View of Winston Cup Racing," *Professional Geographer* 55, no. 2 (2003), 238–249.

5. Lowe's Motor Speedway, "Track Facts," http://www.lowesmotorspeedway.com/speedway/track%5Ffacts/.

6. A systematic look at changes in the location of NASCAR tracks and the geographic origins of drivers is provided by Douglas A. Hurt, "Dialed In? Geographic Expansion and Regional Identity in NASCAR's Nextel Cup Series," *Southeastern Geographers* 45 (2005), 120–37.

7. Richard Pillsbury, "Carolina Thunder: A Geography of Southern Stock Car Racing," *Journal of Geography* 73 (1974), 39–47.

8. John E. Connaughton and Ronald A. Madsen, "The Economic Impacts and Occupational Analysis of the North Carolina Motorsports Industry for 2005," Report to North Carolina Motorsports Association (Charlotte, N.C.: University of North Carolina-Charlotte Belk College of Business, January 2006).

9. Richard Pillsbury has been an especially harsh critic of modern day stock-car racing, arguing that the sport's ongoing expansion is eroding its connection to the South and southerners. Richard Pillsbury, "A Mythology at the Brink: Stock car racing in the American South," in *Fast Food, Stock Cars and Rock-n-Roll: Place and Space in American Pop Culture*, ed. George O. Carney, 239–48 (Lanham, Md.: Rowman & Littlefield Publishers, 1995).

10. James C. Cobb, *Redefining Southern Culture: Mind and Identity in the Modern South* (Athens, Ga.: University of Georgia Press, 1999), 192.

11. Robert Ostergren, "Concepts of Region: A Geographical Perspective," in *Regionalism in the Age of Globalism*, vol. 1, *Concepts of Regionalism*, eds. Lothar Honnighausen, Marc Frey, James Peacock, and Niklaus Steiner, 1–14 (Madison, Wis.: Center for the Study of Upper Midwestern Cultures, University of Wisconsin, 2005), 9.

12. Alderman, et al., "Carolina Thunder Revisited," 238–49.

13. The relationship between the American South and globalization is of increasing interest to scholars. See James L. Peacock, *Grounded Globalism: How The*

U.S. South Embraces the World (Athens, Ga.: University of Georgia Press, 2007); James L. Peacock, Harry L. Watson, and Carrie R. Matthews, eds., *The American South in a Global World* (Chapel Hill, N.C.: University of North Carolina Press, 2005); James C. Cobb and William Stueck, *Globalization and the American South* (Athens, Ga.: University of Georgia Press, 2005).

14. Paul Krugman, *Strategic Trade Policy and the New International Economics* (Cambridge, Mass.: MIT Press, 1986); Paul Krugman, "Increasing Returns and Economic Geography," *Journal of Political Economy*, 99 (1991), 483–99; Michael Porter, *The Competitive Advantage of Nations* (London: Macmillan, 1990).

15. The moonshine connections with NASCAR's early history are detailed in Thompson, *Driving with the Devil*, while urban boosterism is emphasized in Randal L. Hall, "Before NASCAR: The Corporate and Civic Promotion of Automobile Racing in the American South, 1903–1927," *Journal of Southern History* 68 (2002), 629–68. Our interpretation of this early history relies on a balance of both interpretations.

16. This strong correlation between the geography of moonshining and southern stock-car racing is contained in many accounts, including Joe Menzer, *The Wildest Ride: A History of NASCAR* (New York: Touchstone Press, 2001), 77–98; Jeff MacGregor, *Sunday Money* (New York: HarperCollins Publishers, 2005), 24–26; and, Thompson, *Driving with the Devil*, 50–71.

17. Much of Thompson's narrative focuses on Atlanta's organized bootlegging with Raymond Parks providing the capital and Red Vogt providing the technical expertise. See Thompson, *Driving with the Devil*, 11–24.

18. Bill France's disdain for Atlanta bootleggers has been well chronicled by several authors, including Mark D. Howell, *From Moonshine to Madison Avenue: A Cultural History of the NASCAR Winston Cup Series* (Bowling Green, Ohio: Bowling Green State University Popular Press, 1997), 21–24; and Thompson, *Driving with the Devil*, 72–100.

19. Atlanta's awkward relationship with stock-car racing and bootleggers appears to have started immediately after World War II. The Flock incident is referenced in several locations, including http://www.legendsofnascar.com/Bob_Flock.htm and in Thompson, *Driving with the Devil*, 168–75.

20. Hall, "Before NASCAR," 635.

21. The contrast between Atlanta's relative rejection and Charlotte's relative reception of stock-car racing and its cultural baggage is a point that is lost in the literature but one that we find to be essential to understanding Charlotte's NASCAR emergence. Thompson, *Driving with the Devil*, 177–81.

22. Menzer, *The Wildest Ride*, 77–98; Thompson, *Driving with the Devil*, 295–309.

23. Howell, *From Moonshine to Madison Avenue*, 21–24; and Thompson, *Driving with the Devil*, 300–309.

24. Thompson, *Driving with the Devil*, 283–86.

25. The legal ruling established NASCAR's regulatory authority and had a profound influence on Atlanta's technical prowess. MacGregor, *Sunday Money*, 24–26.

26. The effect of NASCAR's avoidance of Atlanta between 1949 and 1951 should not be overlooked. Menzer, *The Wildest Ride*, 77–98; Thompson, *Driving with the Devil*, 302–3.

27. North Carolina's dominance is revealed in part by the geographic distribution of champion drivers derived from a variety of sources including William Burt, NASCAR*'s Best: Stock Car Racing's Best Drivers, Past and Present* (St. Paul, Minn.: Motorbooks International, 2004); Singer and Sumner, *Auto Racing in Charlotte and the Carolina Piedmont*; Peter Golenback, NASCAR *Confidential: Stories of Men and Women Who Made Stock Car Racing Great* (St. Paul, Minn.: Motorbooks International, 2004); and Dan Hunter and Ben White, NASCAR *Legends* (St. Paul, Minn.: Touchstone Publishing, 2004).

28. Significant venues within the Charlotte region are nicely documented in Singer and Sumner, *Auto Racing*.

29. Dirt tracks were and continue to be popular venues in the South. These are highlighted in Singer and Sumner, *Auto Racing*, 32–48. As of 2008, there were still twenty-three dirt tracks operating in North Carolina alone. http://www.namotorsports.com/Tracks/NC/#DirtOvalTracks

30. Menzer, *The Wildest Ride*; Singer and Sumner, *Auto Racing*, 49–75.

31. Alex Gabbard, NASCAR*'s Wild Years: Stock Car Technology in the 1960s* (North Branch, Minn.: Cartech, 2005); Singer and Sumner, *Auto Racing*.

32. Tom Cotter and Al Pearce, *Holman-Moody: The Legendary Race Team* (St. Paul, Minn.: MBI Publishing, 2002).

33. Gabbard, NASCAR*'s Wild Years;* Tom Higgins, "Race Week '87: Charlotte Racing's Hub," *Charlotte Observer*, May 22, 1987, 1B.

34. The current motorsports industry in the Charlotte region is nicely summarized at http://www.charlotteusa.com/Regional/regional_industry_motorlist.asp.

35. These impact statements are contained in several reports, including John E. Connaughton, et al., "The Economic Impacts of the Motorsports Industry on the North Carolina Economy," (UNC Charlotte: Belk College of Business Administration, 2004); Sanford Holshouser Group, "Motorsports: A North Carolina Growth Industry Under Threat," (Charlotte, N.C.: North Carolina Motorsports Association, 2004); and a 2005 update in Connaughton and Madsen, "Economic Impacts."

36. The geographic nature of motorsports clusters is analyzed in Steven Pinch and Nick Henry, "Paul Krugman's Geographical Economics, Industrial Clustering, and the British Motor Sport Industry," *Regional Studies* 33 (1999): 815–27; Nick Henry and Steven Pinch, "Spatialising Knowledge: Placing the Knowledge Community of Motor Sport Valley," *Geoforum* 31 (2000): 191–208; Beverly Aston, "Advanced Auto-Engineering: A Technology-Led UK Cluster," *Business Strategy Review* 9 (1998): 45–53.

37. The phrases "local buzz" (local communications and transactions) and "global pipelines" (external communications and transactions) are introduced in Harald Bathelt, Anders Malmberg, and Peter Maskell, "Clusters and Knowledge: Local Buzz, Global Pipelines, and the Process of Knowledge Creation," *Progress in Human Geography*, 28, no. 1 (2004), 31–56.

38. Charlotte's NASCAR cluster has been examined as a knowledge community with a focus on educational support facilities in Kimmo Viljamaa, "Technological and Cultural Challenges in Local Innovation Support Activities: Emerging Knowledge Interactions in Charlotte's Motor Sport Cluster," *European Planning Studies* 15 (2007): 1215–32.

39. David Newton, "Changing Times Forced Pettys to Uproot from Beloved Level Cross, N.C.," ESPN.com, http://sports.espn.go.com/espn/print?id=3191681&type=story, January 11, 2008.

40. Market expansion is covered in Hurt, "Dialed In," 120–137; Alderman, et al., "Carolina Thunder Revisited," 238–49; and M. Graham Spann, "NASCAR Racing Fans: Cranking up an Empirical Approach," *Journal of Popular Culture* 36 (2002): 352–60.

41. Terry Blount, "Lawsuit's Dismissal a Late Christmas Gift for NASCAR," ESPN.com, http://spots.espn.go.com/espn/print?id=3187097&type=story, January 8, 2008.

42. John Consoli, "Fox Sells Out Daytona 500," *AdWeek.com*, http://printthis.clickability.com/pt/cpt?action=cpt&title=Fox+Sells+Out+Daytona+500, February 19, 2008; Jenny Burzanko, "Daytona 500 TV Rating Higher than Last Year," *Scenedaily.com,* http://www.scenedaily.com/news/articles/sprintcupseries/Daytona_500_tv_rating_higher_than_last_year.html, February 18, 2008.

43. Speedway Motorsports, Inc., *2006 Annual Report,* http://phx.corporate-ir.net/phoenix.zhtml?c=99758&p=irol-reports. The purchase of New Hampshire Speedway is reported at http://phx.corporate-ir.net/phoenix.zhtml?c=99758&p=irol-newsArticle&t=Regular&id=1071914&.

44. These facilities are inventoried from a variety of sources that include the Charlotte Chamber, "Charlotte: Where Racing Means Business," (Charlotte N.C.: www.charlottechamber.com, 2006); Charlotte Regional Partnership, "Charlotte USA: Motorsports," (Charlotte, N.C.: www.charlotteusa.com, 2007); Alex Hutchinson, "NASCAR's New Treadmill," *Popular Mechanics*, March 2008, 13; Gary Graves, "Haas CNC Ready to Share Its New Wind Tunnel Technology," *USA Today,* January 23, 2008, 12C; Jim McGraw, "NASCAR Technical Institute," *Popular Mechanics*, June 2002, 20–24; the Performance Instruction and Training (PIT) Web site, http://www.50ff5on.com/; and Ellen Siska, "Leader in Safety Research Steers NASCAR Improvements," ESPN.com, http://sports.espn.go.com/espn/print?id=2945792&type=story, July 23, 2007.

45. NASCAR's strong handed dealings with labor are chronicled in Dan Pierce, "The Most Southern Sport on Earth: NASCAR and the Unions," *Southern Cultures* 7 (2001): 8–33.

46. Howell, *From Moonshine to Madison Avenue*, 5.

47. Lily Kong, "Cultural Icons and Urban Development in Asia: Economic Imperative, National Identity, and Global City Status," *Political Geography* 26 (2007): 383–404.

48. Thompson, *Driving with the Devil*, 7–10.

49. The concept of reputational politics is drawn from the work of sociologist Gary Fine. Gary A. Fine, "John Brown's Body: Elites, Heroic Embodiment, and the Legitimation of Political Violence," *Social Problems* 46, no.2 (1999): 225–49. For the special case of NASCAR, see Robert Edelstein, NASCAR *Generations: The Legacy of Family in* NASCAR (New York: HarperCollins, 2000).

50. For an on-line version of the Dale Trail, see http://www.daletrail.com/the trail.html.

51. Viv Bernstein, "NASCAR Chooses Charlotte for Its Hall," *New York Times*, http://www.nytimes.com/2006/03/07/sports/07nascar.html, March 7, 2006; and, NASCAR, "NASCAR Tabs Charlotte as Site for Hall of Fame," http://nascar.com/2006/news/headlines/cup/03/06/hof_charlotte/index.html, March 6, 2006. See the Hall of Fame Web site at http://www.nascarhall.com/.

52. Chris Pursell, "NASCAR Images Revs Up Business," *Television Week*, September 17, 2007, 6–34; Marty Smith, "NASCAR Says 'Dale' Believed to be Top Selling DVD," http://sports.espn.go.com/espn/print?id=3267457&type=story, February 27, 2008; Sanford Holshouser Group, "Motorsports," 49–51.

53. Sanford Holshouser Group, "Motorsports," 51–53.

54. Scott Dodd, "Charlotte: Where Hall 'Needs to Be' in the End," *Charlotte Observer*, March 7, 2006, 1A.

55. "Built Here, Belongs Here," *Charlotte.com*, August 17, 2005, www2.nccommerce.com/eclipsfiles/11866.pdf.

56. Adam Bell, "Bruton Will Get Street Name," *Charlotte Observer*, December 7, 2007, 1B.

57. The North Wilkesboro decline is juxtaposed with Charlotte's NASCAR-related prosperity in Alderman, et al., "Carolina Thunder Revisited," 238–49.

58. Examples of development tensions are taken from Ken Elkins, "Penske's Test Track Getting Caution Flag in Mooresville," *Charlotte Business Journal*, http://charlotte.bizjournals.com/charlotte/stories/2007/09/17/story16.html, September 17, 2007; Alex Reed, "Group Working to Build a 'Green' Race Track," WCNC TV http://www.wcnc.com/news/topstories/wcnc-120507-krg-greentrack.6f2cbb42.html, December 6, 2007; Adam Bell, "Smith Breaks Ground on Concord Drag Strip," *Charlotte Observer* http://www.charlotte.com/business/v-print/story/480493.html, February 6, 2008; and Sanford Holshouser Group, "Motorsports" 25–30.

59. Market expansion is covered in Hurt, "Dialed In," 120–37; Alderman, et al., "Carolina Thunder Revisited," 238–49; Spann, "NASCAR Racing Fans," 352–60. NASCAR's troubles with expanding into minority markets are addressed in Raygan Swan, "Diversity Still a Struggle for NASCAR Despite Programs," NASCAR.com, http://www.nascar.com/2007/news/headlines/cup/12/13/drive.diversity.struggles

.strides/index.html, December 14, 2007; and Raygan Swan, "Gibbs Youngster Davis Campaigning for Cup Ride," NASCAR.com, http://www.nascar.com/2008/news/headlines/cup/01/24/jgibbs.mdavis.cup, January 24, 2008.

60. Ina Hughs, "NASCAR 'color' is Alarmingly All White," *Knoxville News-Sentinel*, March 31, 2002, E1.

61. Ed Hardin, "This Latest Incident Shows Just How Far NASCAR Still Has to Go," *Greensboro (N.C.) News & Record*, August 13, 1999, C1.

62. "The Real NASCAR Family," *60 Minutes*, October 6, 2005. Transcript available at www.cbsnews.com/sections/60minutes/.

63. Michelle Crouch, "Panel Ready to Strike Confederate Battle Flag; Some Say Controversial Emblem Should Remain," *Charlotte Observer*, January 10, 2005, 1A; Michelle Crouch, "Controversial Flag is Missing; City has Studied Whether to Remove Confederate Banner," *Charlotte Observer*, January 19, 2005, 2B.

64. Adam Bell, "Cabarrus County, N.C., Recruits Confederate Convention," *Charlotte Observer*, July 9, 2005, 1A; Adam Bell, "Cabarrus Lands '08 Meeting," *Charlotte Observer*, July 22, 2005, 1B.

65. "Street Signs Changing in Time for MLK Holiday," *Charlotte Observer*, January 11, 2007, 1B.

66. Carolina_native, "Where don't northerners relocate to?" *City-data.com* forum http://www.city-data.com/forum/north-carolina/21801-where-dont-northerners-relocate.html, October 30, 2006.

67. Bailey, "Comment on 'Is it difficult to make friends in Charlotte?'," *Charlotte Newcomer Blog*, http://charlottenewcomers.blogspot.com/2006/10/is-it-difficult-to-make-friends-in.html, October 25, 2006.

68. David Caraviello, "The World Knocks and NASCAR Opens the Door," NASCAR.*com*, http://www.nascar.com/2007/news/opinion/12/19/dcaraviello.world.South/index.html, December 20, 2007; Joe Menzer, "Global NASCAR? Petty and Wheeler Differ in Opinion," NASCAR.*com*, http://www.nascar.com/2007/news/headlines/cup/01/24/kpetty.cganassi.changes/index.html, January 24, 2007; Associated Press, "Talladega Nights Races to Number 1," *CBSNews.com*, http://cbsnews.com/stories/2006/08/06/entertainment/printable1868289.shtml, August 6, 2006; Susan Wloszczyna, "Hollywood Pit Stop," *USA Today*, http://www.usatoday.com/life/movies/news/2006-08-03-nascar-hollywood_x.htm, August 3, 2006.

69. Lars Anderson, "Foreign Affairs: Dario Franchitti and Jacques Villeneuve Lead the Latest Invasion of NASCAR," *Sports Illustrated*, October 15, 2007, 68; Erik Spanberg, "In the Fast Lane, NASCAR Draws Plenty of Converts," *Christian Science Monitor*, November 9, 2007, 12–16; Nate Ryan, "Open-Wheel Drivers Take Stock," *USA Today*, October 16, 2007.

70. Hall, "Before NASCAR," 629.

William Graves and Jonathan Kozar

Blending Southern Culture and International Finance
The Construction of a Global Money Center

Two trillion dollars. The number, without additional scale, has little meaning. Two trillion dollars is roughly equal to the GNP of China and Canada combined. The number also approximates the total accumulation of bank assets in Charlotte, a metro area of 1.6 million. It is no exaggeration to say that a small group of executives in downtown Charlotte controls assets equal to one-fifth of U.S. annual economic output.

While the rise of banking in Charlotte has been well documented,[1] no one has explored the degree to which the industry connects Charlotte to the broader world. This chapter surveys the creation and evolution of Charlotte's most influential industry and the blend of local culture with the demands of the global economy. The historical and cultural foundations of Charlotte's current global integration also garner closer examination. Charlotte's volume of financial assets is noteworthy on its own, but when contextualized in the historic poverty, cultural conservatism, and once-backward image of the region, this accumulation of wealth represents one of the most dramatic economic achievements in our nation's history.

The recent rise of Charlotte's globally significant financial center is, in part, a product of a long history of Charlotte industrialists recognizing the value of developing connections beyond their own region. It can be argued that the city's bankers, surrounded by the extreme poverty of nineteenth- and twentieth-century southern Piedmont, felt the necessity of expansion more than any other business. However, the desire to expand was frustrated first by limits of technology and later by federal regulation. Only since the mid-1980s have Charlotte bankers been free to expand their business beyond the state's borders.

Banking from the Periphery

Southern historian C. Vann Woodward observed that nineteenth-century southern bankers were among the first agitators for modernization in the agricultural economy.[2] The bankers, few of whom came from the planter class, observed that the most lucrative lending opportunities were in manufacturing, and thus became vocal proponents of industrial development. The southern banking market was inaccessible to northern bankers due to the limited transportation and communications technologies of the era. The resulting capital shortage stunted growth and, when large loans were needed, local industrialists were forced to travel to New York to obtain financing.

The necessity of relying on northern banks for large capital infusions was seen as both economically and culturally problematic. Hugh McColl, former CEO of Bank of America, frequently invoked the image of hometown industrialists having to travel "hat in hand" to the money center banks of New York for large loans.[3] McColl posited: "I actually think part of what drove the southerners was that we had been poor so long and were looked down upon."[4] As McColl's quotes suggest, this sense of southern subjugation was a common motivation for expansion.[5] This pride of place dictated that the creation of a southern source of capital was a critical first step in the modernization of the region.

In the mid-twentieth century, when expansion became technologically feasible, North Carolina was one of only nine states that did not impose limits on branching in the post-Depression era.[6] This laissez-faire regulatory environment existed, in part, in recognition that North Carolina banks would struggle to be sufficiently capitalized when operating in a single community.[7] This regulatory regime, coupled with a stable if relatively poor economy, ultimately produced a handful of large banks with experience managing a far-flung network of branches. This benign regulatory environment allowed Winston-Salem-based Wachovia to become the largest bank in the South by the mid-1950s and for Bank of America forerunner NCNB to achieve this status by 1972.[8]

Interstate banking expansion was thwarted by federal regulation. The McFadden Act of 1927, which explicitly prohibited interstate bank branching, was intended to enhance the competitive position of small banks. The legislation had the side effect of compounding southern poverty by limiting the size of banks while simultaneously preventing the entry of extraregional banks into the southern market. The net result was that southern bankers struggled to develop a sufficient supply of capital to finance the region's growth.[9]

North Carolina bankers' frustration with the prohibition on interstate banking triggered a search for regulatory loopholes. In 1982 a weakness in Florida banking legislation was spotted that enabled NCNB's purchase of tiny First National Bank of Lake City, Florida. The legality of this interstate acquisition was uncertain. During the litigation that followed the purchase agreement, NCNB corporate counsel Paul Polking commented: "In Washington, we were told, 'you can't do that,' we said, 'Now, wait just a minute and let us explain it to you.' "[10] Polking's remarks illustrate the willingness of the Charlotte bankers to bend regulations beyond what was tolerated in the genteel industry. While the purchase was ultimately approved, the Florida legislature closed the legal loophole within one week after the purchase.[11] The tiny transaction did not go unnoticed. *Florida Trend*, a statewide business publication, commemorated the event with a cartoon that "characterized NCNB as a rolling armored car flying a rebel flag and with large guns pointed south."[12] The message was clear: Charlotte bankers were an invading army of financiers, an image that the two banks never shook.

The First National Bank of Lake City acquisition was miniscule but put regulators on notice that the era of interstate banking was unavoidable. If southerners wanted to continue to control their own financial institutions the Southern bankers would need to be proactive in establishing protective legislation for the industry.

Interstate banking remained prohibited until 1984 when a cooperative agreement between bankers and legislatures established the Southeastern Regional Banking Compact. The compact permitted interstate bank acquisitions of southern banks by southern banks, but protected their independence by blocking acquisitions by banks from outside the Southeast. The compact's intent was to foster the development of large southern banks that could ultimately compete with money center banks in the coming era of deregulation.[13] This goal was partially a matter of pride, and partially a product of fear that national banks based outside the region would be reluctant to lend in the South. Hugh McColl described the Southeastern Regional Banking Compact as "a protective wall ... It became a Berlin Wall, which was an interesting wall because it kept us in as well as keeping the Yankees out."[14]

The compact succeeded in nurturing a set of southern banks that developed into five of the twenty-five largest in the country by the dawn of deregulation in 1994.[15] Once restrictions on interstate banking were relaxed, both NationsBank (a Bank of America precursor) and First Union (precursor to Wachovia) had leveraged their protected status to span the South and grow to become the third and sixth largest banks in the country, respectively. Their dominance in the growing South made the Charlotte banks some of the most powerful institutions in the newly deregulated market.

National Expansion of Southern Banking

Thanks to the Southeast Regional Banking Compact, Charlotte banks were well positioned to expand nationally. While there was considerable academic debate on the merits of bank expansion,[16] the chief executives of both Charlotte banks wanted to make their institutions the largest and most powerful in the industry. Hugh McColl and Edward Crutchfield (former CEO of the bank presently known as Wachovia) made no secret of their personal desires to operate the largest banks in the country[17] as well as their unwillingness to be topped by their hometown rival.[18] When pressed on the source of their ambition both men cited their personal experience with southern poverty. McColl in particular spoke many times about southern industrialists (his father included) being unable to obtain capital locally and then finding only unfavorable terms at northern banks.[19] This desire for economic independence was heightened as the Charlotte banks began to expand outside the South — mergers that threatened to dilute southern control were met with hostility. When negotiating the "merger of equals" with San Francisco–based BankAmerica (not to be confused with Bank of America) in 1997 McColl said:

> We carried on negotiations with their CFO ... He came to talk to me on a Saturday morning. He said we can get a deal, but they don't want to be a southern company. I said, "Tough ... ! That's what we are." I really did say that. "We are a southern company, so we are not going anywhere with this conversation." They blinked, and the rest is history. The California press attacked us unbelievably ... They thought we were bumptious barbarians...
> We aren't ashamed of being from the South.[20]

Some power sharing was ultimately offered in the final agreement. The merger was completed in 1998 with the stated intention of the merged bank (named Bank of America) being run by McColl from dual headquarters facilities in Charlotte and San Francisco. It was further stipulated that BankAmerica CEO David Coulter would ascend to the CEO position of the merged bank upon McColl's scheduled retirement in 2001. Both these power-sharing agreements were abrogated when, shortly after the merger, Coulter was dismissed for legacy losses in the BankAmerica investment banking arm. The quick demise of power-sharing was not a surprise to longtime observers of McColl; the "merger of equals" was in fact simply an acquisition.[21]

The Southeastern Regional Banking Compact, the First National Bank acquisition, and the contentious BankAmerica merger indicate the oppositional stance that Charlotte bankers took against their own industry. This cultivation of an oppositional identity in Charlotte banking is consistent with the development of southern culture, a culture that, according to James Peacock, is a product of a consistent southern desire to be seen apart from the larger national identity.[22] The oppositional attitudes in banking are expressed in the preference for acquisition rather than partnership and aggressiveness over compromise. McColl eloquently outlined the significance of southern opposition in his management style: "Do I think Northerners are evil? Absolutely not. Do they think less well of us because we're Southern? Yes, I think so. Do I take pleasure in demonstrably being successful against all comers? Absolutely."[23]

When viewed in the context of the oppositional culture, the BankAmerica merger and the creation of the Southeastern Regional Banking Compact can be seen as actions that broadcast a formal opposition to all those who did not share the goal of southern economic independence. The oppositional stance also facilitated aggressive cost-cutting strategies in the acquired banks. The rapid rise of Charlotte banks from regional power to the nation's largest reinforced the utility of this mindset in the expansion process.

This acquisition binge cemented Charlotte's position atop the nation's financial hierarchy (see table 1). Charlotte's oft-cited status as the second-largest U.S. banking center was touted as evidence the city had achieved national prominence and evolved into the southern source of capital that had been long desired by McColl, Crutchfield, and their predecessors.

Moving Beyond Branch Banking

Charlotte's financial center expansion began to slow after Bank of America's 2005 purchase of Fleet Financial. The purchase of the Boston-based bank pushed Bank of America to the brink of the 10 percent cap of deposits that triggered a regulatory moratorium on retail banking acquisitions.[24] This

Table 1. Bank assets by metropolitan area.

3rd Quarter 2008[a]		1st Quarter 2009[b]	
Metro area	Total assets (billions)	Metro area	Total assets (billions)
New York	$3,491.5	New York	$4,118.8
Charlotte	$2,363.5	Charlotte	$2,321.9
San Francisco	$578.5	San Francisco	$1,300.3
Boston	$276.3	Pittsburgh	$288.1
Chicago	$250.5	Minneapolis	$263.6
Minneapolis	$242.6	Atlanta	$181.6
Cleveland	$239.3	Washington	$179.6
Wilmington, Del.	$180.2	Boston	$150.5
Atlanta	$170.0	Birmingham	$146.9
Birmingham	$139.6	Winston-Salem	$145.4

[a]Source: Compiled by author from FDIC Top 100 Banks
[b]Source: SNL Financial

event forced Bank of America to shift its expansion strategy outside of traditional retail banking and to look to investment banking and to global markets for growth.[25] Although growth in these areas drew upon existing expertise, Bank of America faced significant disadvantages of both geography and culture in these new businesses.

The geographic barriers were a result of Charlotte's peripheral location with respect to global financial markets, corporate headquarters, and financial research. Charlotte's remoteness made the face-to-face contact necessary for the large-scale transactions involved in investment banking awkward.[26] This disadvantage was in stark contrast to the city's low costs and unparalleled infrastructure for domestic retail banking.

The oppositional corporate culture compounded the geographic obstacles to international expansion. Ventures into foreign markets were particularly difficult due to dramatic differences in regulation, language, and customs. These barriers are typically overcome via local partnerships and a process of compromise, strategies that were not previously an element of Charlotte banks' expansion strategy.

Since the Fleet purchase, Bank of America acquired firms in the mortgage brokerage industry, credit card processing, wealth management, and brokerage and investment banking. This diversification strategy was effective, but in 2006 Bank of America still generated more than half of its revenue from

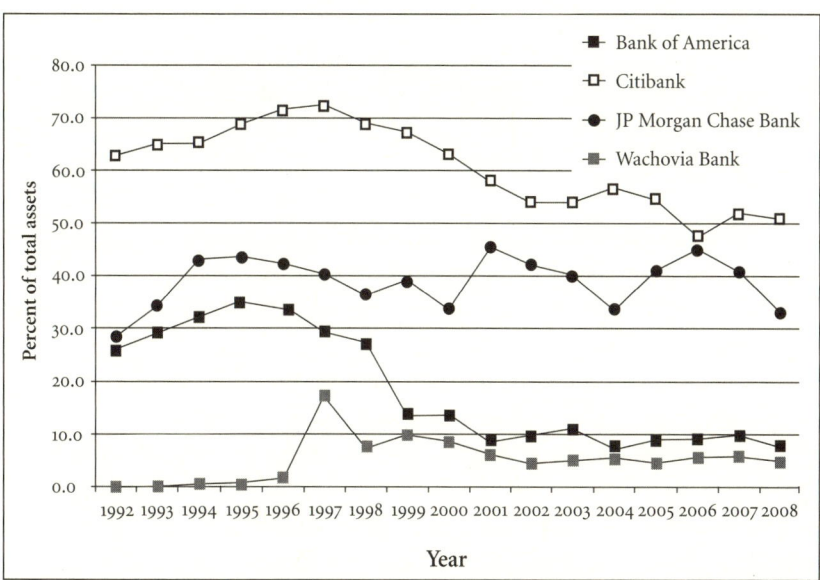

Figure 17. Share of foreign assets for major U.S. banks, 1992–2008. (Source: William Graves and Jonathan Kozar.)

its retail banking franchise; chief competitors Citibank and Chase earned less than 40 percent of revenue from retail bank activities.[27] More significantly, Charlotte banks' international activities pale when compared to New York-based competitors. Both Bank of America and Wachovia obtained less than 10 percent of their assets from foreign sources whereas Chase and Citibank obtained approximately half of their assets from foreign sources in 2006 (see figure 17).

Bank of America and Wachovia's domestic expansion had been driven by their oppositional identity. This mindset of conquest only worked in settings where fine points of law, culture, and public relations were known. Oppositional attitudes made domestic retail bank expansion cost effective, efficient, and nonthreatening to the existing executive corps. The difficulties of oppositional culture in international expansion were recognized by bank executives. Current CEO of Bank of America Ken Lewis addressed this point in a speech in Singapore in 2006:

> Over the years, we learned that serving customers in California or North Carolina is not exactly the same as it is in Florida or Massachusetts. Even as we learned to run a consistent franchise, we also learned to adapt to the needs of local markets and cultures.

We will continue to build our businesses, our capabilities and relationships in this part of the world ... and around the world ... as we work to integrate markets, and drive global economic growth. As your companies and ours pursue these goals in partnership, I look forward to all we'll accomplish together.[28]

Lewis's statement acknowledges the need for a more conciliatory footing to facilitate global growth. As Bank of America extends its global reach it will encounter a new group of competitors, multinational banks experienced with local customers and with a long history of international partnership. With the purchase of a partnership position in the China Construction Bank in 2005, Bank of America implemented a new growth strategy. The partnership was, according to press releases, a means of disseminating Bank of America's consumer banking technology into the Chinese banking system to benefit its local partner,[29] a clear departure from its domestic expansion style. The profitable China Construction Bank partnership offers a model for navigating cultural and regulatory obstacles encountered in global expansion.

While the China Construction Bank partnership suggests that the oppositional corporate culture has been realigned in the international context, Bank of America has continued to struggle to merge its culture with the investment banking industry. Retail and investment banking were kept separate by statute until the mid-1990s. The separation fostered starkly different corporate cultures; retail banking focused on low costs and conservative asset management while investment banking took risks to exploit business cycles. Combining these business models was difficult. Investment bankers chaffed under the hierarchical compensation schemes of retail banks while retail bankers resented the excessive and freewheeling attitudes of their new colleagues. This incompatibility was never more visible than after the NationsBank purchase of San Francisco–based Montgomery Securities in 1997. The blending of incompatible cultures (and compensation schemes) quickly resulted in the exodus of the skilled investment bankers from the newly acquired firm.[30]

The distinct geographies of the retail and investment industries compounded the cultural divide. Investment banking intermediaries, capital sources, and customers were located in New York, London, and a proliferating number of Asian financial centers. Charlotte bank executives were distant from sources of vital high-order information about trading and underwriting activities,[31] and the provincial reputation of the southern financial center made it an unappealing option for investment banking professionals looking to relocate.³² Bank of America's geographic and cultural barriers to success in the industry, combined with a $1.5 billion loss in investment banking in the third quarter of 2007, led to Ken Lewis declaring the end of the firm's involvement in investment banking, a strategy that lasted less than a year.³³

Despite struggles of culture and geography, the Charlotte banking complex reached what may have been the pinnacle of its success in 2007. Bank of America became the nation's largest bank and Wachovia, thanks to the purchase of Golden West Financial of Oakland, California, became only the second U.S. bank with a coast-to-coast presence. Symbolic of this success, both banks began headquarters-related construction projects that substantially expanded Charlotte's skyline.

Charlotte Banks and the Financial Crisis of 2008

The expansionary era of Charlotte's bank cluster began to fade in mid-2007. Summer brought the signs of weakness in previously booming residential real estate markets. The first wave of mortgage defaults triggered large-scale credit market illiquidity. The speed of the credit market collapse resulted in increased volatility in fixed-income and equity markets worldwide. The combination of credit market illiquidity and equity market volatility forced the restructuring of the financial industry and permanently altered the face of Charlotte's iconic industry.

The forces that restructured Charlotte banking originated long before the credit bubble of 2008 was evident. Wachovia, long eager to establish a national presence, purchased California-based Golden West Financial at the height of the credit boom in 2006. Golden West specialized in controversial option ARM mortgage loans, which, since they did not require principal payments, allowed loan balances to increase over time. Since these loans were concentrated within the extravagantly priced California housing market, they were exceptionally vulnerable to default in the event of declining real estate prices. Numerous observers criticized Wachovia for paying a premium for the high-risk portfolio of loans at what was clearly a housing market peak. However, given Wachovia's history of successful empire building, some viewed the cost of Golden West as acceptable due to the foothold it offered in the California market. Others viewed the extravagant price and unfortunate timing of the deal as another example of a Charlotte bank ignoring conventional wisdom to further its growth.³⁴

By the summer of 2008 the crisis had spread beyond credit markets. Rising loan defaults triggered a liquidity crisis and regulatory seizure at both Indymac Bank and Washington Mutual Savings. Investors and depositors saw similar loan defaults looming in Wachovia's Golden West portfolio. On Friday, September 26, Wachovia's dwindling deposit base,[35] combined with the refusal of investors to purchase the short-term securities necessary to finance the day-to-day operations of the bank, forced federal regulators to threaten seizure if the firm was not sold before market opening on Monday. A sale of Wachovia's retail banking operations to Citigroup was announced on Sunday, September 28. Citigroup agreed to pay Wachovia shareholders stock valued at $1 per Wachovia share (the stock had traded above $20 per share less than a month before). Amid widespread shareholder discontent with the forced sale, Wells Fargo of San Francisco extended an offer of $15 billion (or $7 per share) five days later. Wachovia ceased to exist as a North Carolina institution on January 1, 2009, when the acquisition by Wells Fargo was complete. Wells plans to maintain its eastern headquarters in Charlotte but has yet to determine the magnitude of these operations.

Bank of America's approach to the housing boom was considerably more conservative. Bank of America had exited the subprime lending market in 2001,[36] a strategic decision that made it one of the best capitalized banks at the beginning of the credit crisis in 2008. This footing allowed Ken Lewis to make substantial acquisitions at the start of the crisis.[37] The situation in 2008 mirrored NCNB's strategic position in 1988 (the dawn of modern interstate banking) when a collapse in oil prices led to the insolvency of several Texas banks; regulators were willing to waive restrictions on interstate acquisitions to avoid regulatory seizure.[38] Lewis viewed the 2008 credit crisis as an opportunity for Bank of America to play a prominent role in stabilizing the U.S. financial system in addition to an opportunity to increase market share. It was hoped that these actions would cement Bank of America's position at the top of the U.S. financial hierarchy and gain the bank the respect that had previously been withheld by the New York financial community.[39]

As credit markets began their descent in 2007, Bank of America spent $2 billion to purchase 16 percent of struggling Countrywide Financial, the country's largest mortgage lender. The investment was lauded as substantially reducing short-term stresses in credit markets. The initial investment was temporarily well received by markets, but credit markets (and Countrywide stock) resumed their rapid disintegration two months later. In an investment that was said to "build a bulwark against the mortgage-default crisis by protecting one of its biggest casualties from collapse," Bank of America purchased the remaining 84 percent of Countrywide in early 2008 for $4 billion.[40] In less than a year Bank of America had transformed itself from a minor player in mortgage markets into the largest mortgage originator in the nation.

By the summer of 2008 the credit crisis had spread to the investment banking industry. Bank of America's Countrywide purchase encouraged the Federal Reserve to view Bank of America as a private instrument for future bailouts.[41] The September bankruptcy of Lehman Brothers provided an opportunity for Bank of America to reenter investment banking.[42] While the most logical acquisition for Bank of America was the nearly bankrupt Lehman, Lewis desired the more prestigious Merrill Lynch. Lewis was eager to add Merrill's extensive brokerage and wealth management network to the Bank of America portfolio. However, Merrill's exposure to the credit market meltdown was unclear. Despite the considerable uncertainty, the acquisition was negotiated in less than two days, using due diligence conducted by a third party.[43] Lewis was criticized for overpaying, given the Treasury's insistence that Merrill acquire capital and Bank of America's historic difficulties with merging corporate cultures. In this case, Merrill's aggressive commission-based compensation system clashed with Bank of America's self proclaimed "Wal-Mart of Banking" image.[44] The deal, however, brought considerable visibility to a bank that had long struggled for respect outside its home region.

The Merrill acquisition closed on January 1, 2009. Symbolically the purchase represented the reversal of more than a century of southern poverty — Wall Street had been forced to turn to Charlotte bankers as a source of capital.[45] The purchase allowed Bank of America to ascend to the position of largest U.S. bank by assets[46] and control an iconic Wall Street firm. Just before the deal closed, Lewis was interviewed for a national television segment documenting Bank of America's status as the nation's largest bank. Lewis was asked directly if he felt he had defeated Wall Street. He hedged, but conceded that he had achieved the longtime goal of Charlotte bankers — eclipsing Wall Street.[47]

Bank of America's ascendance to the top of the financial world may be shockingly brief. Merrill Lynch's last quarter as an independent firm featured a $15 billion loss — a surprise to Bank of America shareholders who had voted for the merger just three weeks before. Once the magnitude of the Merrill loss became visible to Lewis, he traveled to Washington to inform regulators that Bank of America sought to abort the deal, citing a material adverse change in Merrill's condition. It was reported that the Federal Reserve Chairman and Treasury Secretary "forcefully urged" that the deal be completed. Regulators subsidized the transaction with a loss-sharing agreement on Merrill's liabilities and an additional $20 billion of Troubled Asset Relief Program (TARP) payments.[48]

As news of Merrill's losses and the fuzzy role of federal intervention in the deal were made public, financial markets reacted quickly. Bank of America's market capitalization was cut in half (to $25 billion) in late January 2009. This market value was less than the total paid to acquire Merrill and was less than one-sixth the value of the cash and guarantees from the U.S. Treasury. The collapse in share price led the media to speculate throughout January and February 2009 on the possibility of the nationalization of Bank of America.[49] In less than a month Bank of America went from Wall Street savior to the brink of seizure.

Charlotte Banks in a Global Financial Market

The development of banking in Charlotte illustrates the truism that global systems are inextricably tied to local cultures. The ascent of Charlotte banks into the global economic system was a result of a two-way interaction between traditional culture and the competitive realities of global markets. The cultivation of an oppositional corporate culture built around the regional mythology of poverty and marginalization facilitated national acquisition and cost cutting but did not prepare the banks for growth in the more nuanced global financial system. In the case of Wachovia, aggressive national expansion led to heavy losses and its eventual sale to Wells Fargo. The future of Wachovia/Wells Fargo in Charlotte remains uncertain. Bank of America is, as of this writing, the largest U.S. bank by assets but is simultaneously struggling to avoid nationalization. Assuming Bank of America survives the current credit crisis, the bank will operate in a starkly different competitive environment. As domestic market share becomes more difficult to acquire, international expansion will become a priority. This will place a new emphasis on partnership, a strategy that will require a break from the past. Charlotte bankers will need to modify their oppositional corporate culture to a more diplomatic stance in order to operate in a world without the protectionist conditions that nurtured their early growth.

Despite the banks' recent stumbles, C. Vann Woodward's 1951 observation that southern bankers were the most eager for modernization holds true today. Charlotte bank leadership built a globally significant financial center in what was one of the most impoverished regions of the country.

Perhaps most remarkably, the creation of Charlotte's financial cluster was accomplished by incorporating southern culture into the most global of all industries.

Notes

1. William Graves, "Charlotte's Role as a Financial Center: Looking Beyond Bank Assets," *Southeastern Geographer* 41, no. 2 (2001): 230–45; J. D. Lord, "Interstate Banking and the Relocation of Economic Control Points," *Urban Geography* 8 (1987), 501–19; J. D. Lord. "Geographic Deregulation of the U.S. Banking Industry and Spatial Transfers of Corporate Control," *Urban Geography* 13 (1992), 25–48; James O. Wheeler and Patrick Dillon, "The Wealth of a Nation: Spatial Dimensions of U.S. Metropolitan Commercial Banking, 1970–1980," *Urban Geography* 6 (1985), 297–315.

2. C. Vann Woodward, *Origins of the New South, 1877–1913* (Baton Rouge: Louisiana State University Press, 1951), 152.

3. Craig Whitlock and Irwin Speizer, "Hugh McColl: Tar Heel of the Year 1997," *Raleigh News and Observer*, December 17, 1997.

4. Thomas Hills, "The Recent Rise of Southern Banking: An Examination of the Southeastern Region Banking Compact and Some Resulting Disparities among the Banking Industries of the Leading Southern States" (masters thesis, Georgia State University, 2006), 150.

5. Hills, "The Recent Rise"; Whitlock and Speizer, "Hugh McColl."

6. Lord, "Geographic Deregulation"; Randall Kroszner and Philip Strahan, "What Drives Deregulation? Economics and Politics of the Relaxation of Branching Restrictions," *Quarterly Journal of Economics* 114, no. 4 (1999): 1437–67.

7. Lissa Lampkin Broome, "The First One Hundred Years of Banking in North Carolina," *North Carolina Bank Institute* 9 (April 2005): 129; Hills, "The Recent Rise."

8. Hills, "The Recent Rise."

9. Paul Foster, *Bank Expansion in Virginia 1962–1966 The Holding Company and Direct Merger* (Charlottesville: The University of Virginia Press, 1971), 16.

10. Howard Covington and Marion Ellis, *The Story of NationsBank: Changing the Face of American Banking* (Chapel Hill: University of North Carolina Press, 1993), 175.

11. Hills, "The Recent Rise."

12. Covington and Ellis, *The Story of NationsBank*, 175.

13. Pat Watters, *Commission on the Future of the South: Final Report* (Research Triangle Park: Southern Growth Policies Board, 1980), 30.

14. Hills, "The Recent Rise," 125.

15. Federal Deposit Insurance Corporation, "Top 50 Banks by Total Domestic Deposits," http://www.fdic.gov (accessed January 28, 2009).

16. Sheila Dow, "The Stages of Banking Development and the Spatial Evolution of Financial Systems," in *Money and the Space Economy*, ed. Ron Martin (New York: Wiley, 1999); Jane Pollard, "Globalisation, Regulation and the Changing Organization of Retail Banking in the United States and Britain," in *Money and the Space Economy*, ed. Ron Martin (New York: Wiley, 1999).

17. Hills, "The Recent Rise."

18. Whitlock and Speizer, "Hugh McColl."

19. Ross Yockey, *McColl: The Man with America's Money* (Atlanta: Longstreet, 1999); "Under New Ownership: Bank Of America. CEO of the Nation's Largest Bank Talks about the Treasury Department's Plans for Buying into Financial Firms," *60 Minutes*, October 19, 2008, http://www.cbsnews.com/stories/2008/10/19/60minutes/main4531244.shtml.

20. Hills, "The Recent Rise," 135.

21. Sam Zuckerman, "Breaking the Bank: The Untold Story of how David Coulter Lost BofA," *San Francisco Chronicle*, September 30, 1999.

22. James Peacock, *Grounded Globalism: How the U.S. South Embraces the World* (Athens: University of Georgia Press, 2007), 3–76.

23. Whitlock and Speizer, "Hugh McColl."

24. The Riegle-Neal Interstate Banking and Branching Efficiency Act of 1994 imposed a 10 percent cap on nationwide deposits held by U.S. banks expanding via acquisition. While this cap did not prevent the organic growth of deposits, it was enacted to placate fears of consolidation leading to a monopolistic banking industry. See Cybil Whitedoc, "Riegle-Neal's 10% Nationwide Deposit Cap: Arbitrary and Unnecessary," *North Carolina Banking Institute* 9 (2005): 347–72.

25. Peacock, *Grounded Globalism*.

26. Meric Gertler, "Tacit Knowledge and the Economic Importance of Context, or the Undefinable Tacitness of Being (There)," *Journal of Economic Geography* 3 (2003): 75–99.

27. Larry Light, "Money for the Masses," *Forbes,* October 1, 2007, 77–81.

28. Kenneth Lewis, "Remarks to Bank of America Global Leaders Breakfast" (Singapore, September 18, 2006), http://newsroom.bankofamerica.com/index.php?s=speeches&item=152.

29. Bank of America, "Bank of America and China Construction Bank to Collaborate on Credit Card Business Aims to Capture Dramatic Growth of Chinese Credit Card Market," press release, April 16, 2007, http://newsroom.bankofamerica.com/index.php?s=press_releases&item=7735.

30. Valerie Bauerlein, "CEO Vows to Fix Bank of America," *Wall Street Journal*, October 19, 2007.

31. Matthew Zook, "The Knowledge Brokers: Venture Capitalists, Tacit Knowledge and Regional Development," *International Journal of Urban and Regional Research* 28, no. 3 (2004): 621–41; Pollard, "Globalisation" ; David Porteous, "The Development of Financial Centers: Location, Information, Externalities and Path

Dependence," in *Money and the Space Economy*, ed. Ron Martin (New York: Wiley, 1999).

32. Heather Smith and William Graves, "Gentrification as Corporate Growth Strategy: The Strange Case of Charlotte, North Carolina and the Bank of America," *Journal of Urban Affairs* 27, no. 4 (2005): 403–18.

33. Valerie Bauerlein, "How Moynihan Aims to Right BofA Investment Banking Ship," *Wall Street Journal,* October 31, 2007.

34. A. Ross Sorkin and J.Creswell, "Wachovia to Acquire Bank in West," *New York Times,* May 8, 2006.

35. Wachovia experienced a net outflow of $29 billion in deposits in the third quarter of 2008. Will Boyle, "Wachovia Vet Kelly Makes Return to Regional Banking," *Charlotte Business Journal,* February 20, 2009.

36. Valerie Bauerlein, "Bank of America CEO in Spotlight After Deal," *Wall Street Journal,* August 27, 2007.

37. Eric Dash, "Purchase of Merrill Fulfills Quest for a Bank Top of Form," *New York Times,* September 14, 2008.

38. Carrick Mollenkamp and Dan Fitzpatrick, "BofA to the Rescue Again?" *Wall Street Journal,* September 12, 2008.

39. Damian Paletta, Valerie Bauerlein, and James Hagerty, "Countrywide Rescued by Bank of America," *Wall Street Journal,* January 14, 2008; Mollenkamp and Fitzpatrick. "BofA to the Rescue Again?"

40. Paletta, Bauerlein, and Hagerty, "Countrywide Rescued."

41. Susanne Craig, Jeffrey McCracken, Aaron Lucchetti, and Kate Kelly, "The Weekend That Wall Street Died," *Wall Street Journal,* December 29, 2008.

42. Bank of America's previous efforts to develop investment banking expertise were unsuccessful due to cultural incompatibilities.

43. Craig et al., "The Weekend That Wall Street Died."

44. Randall Smith and Dan Fitzpatrick, "Cultures Clash as Merrill Herd Meets 'Wal-Mart of Banking,'" *Wall Street Journal,* November 14, 2008.

45. Craig et al., "The Weekend That Wall Street Died."

46. "BofA Becomes Nation's Largest Bank with Completion of Merrill Lynch Acquisitions," *Triangle Business Journal,* January 2, 2009.

47. "Under New Ownership."

48. Dan Fitzpatrick, Susanne Craig, and Deborah Solomon, "In Merrill deal, U.S. Played Hardball," *Wall Street Journal,* February 5, 2009.

49. Ari Levy, "Citigroup, Bank of America May Look 'Nationalized,'" Bloomberg.com, January 23, 2009; David Sanger, "Nationalization Gets a New, Serious Look," *New York Times,* January 25, 2009; Damian Paletta, David Enrich, and Dan Fitzpatrick, "U.S. Seeks to Stem Bank Fears," *Wall Street Journal,* February 21, 2009; Peter Coy, "Bank Nationalization: Who Would Bear the Pain?" *Business Week,* February 25, 2009.

Ronald V. Kalafsky

Beyond Local Markets
The Export Performance and Challenges of Charlotte Manufacturers

The manufacturing sector has long been viewed as a catalyst for economic growth in the southern United States. For the past several decades, states, counties, and cities have regarded the manufacturing sector as a vehicle for further regional economic development and therefore directed their recruitment efforts accordingly.[1] The impacts of production-related activities are readily evident in manufacturing-based employment numbers, wages, and in the downstream support of other industries, especially for component suppliers and across numerous facets of the service sector. To witness the sustained importance of manufacturing, one needs only to look at recent automobile assembly plant construction across the South and the continued attention that is paid to recruiting such firms. So despite the move toward service-based economies, manufacturing remains a viable economic sector in the South.

At the same time, it is obvious that there is an ongoing crisis within the manufacturing sector in the southern United States. Overall manufacturing employment has decreased, especially in relatively manufacturing-intensive states such as North Carolina and South Carolina. These tumultuous changes have resulted from heightened global competition (a majority of it cost-based) within many once-key regional industries such as textiles and apparel production.

As pointed out by Glasmeier and Leichenko and by Johnson over a decade ago, the central challenge for countless producers across the South has been to move beyond comparative advantages centered predominantly on lower labor costs and to make the transition toward higher value-added manufacturing.[2] This places most manufacturers in the position of developing new products and implementing new processes — both of which can be difficult at a time when firms are already significantly challenged. In addition to internal production changes, firms often need to reach beyond spatially proximate customers and to engage the international marketplace if they intend to survive. This strategy can have positive impacts at both the firm level and regionally, as producers that succeed in selling outside of their home regions have significantly higher average salaries and are generally more innovative than those selling locally.[3] Exporting is not a necessarily easy process however, as in most cases manufacturers essentially need to reinvent themselves in order to compete within geographically wider markets.[4]

As mentioned throughout this book, Charlotte is a prime example of a rapidly changing U.S. metropolitan area and certainly an example of the evolving economic geography of the South. Its transition into a national financial center has radically transformed the city's landscape, including its industrial environment. It is important to note, however, that manufacturing still plays an important role in Charlotte's economy, despite obvious declines in employment within this sector. In some counties of the metropolitan area, for example, the percentage of the workforce employed in manufacturing exceeds 15–20 percent (figures well above the national average). The challenges of Charlotte-based manufacturers, in many regards, are very similar to their competitors and counterparts across the southern United States. Decreasing local customer bases, for example, are plaguing many producers across the region.[5]

Given falling employment numbers in manufacturing and the Charlotte region's overall economic transition, how can the remaining producers continue to be healthy components of the local economy? This chapter examines one aspect with which firms can possibly remain commercially viable: export activities. Several interlinked questions will be addressed in this chapter. First, with the obvious moves of many manufacturing activities (e.g., textiles) to offshore sites, how could Charlotte manufacturers connect with distant markets and potential customers? Are export activities related to growth metrics or other firm-level characteristics? If firms are exporters, where are their primary destinations? And finally, do firms encounter difficulties when exporting, and are they ready for this next step?

Background

Manufacturing firms throughout the southern United States have been faced with a dilemma. One of the prime advantages of manufacturing in the region once stemmed from lower costs, primarily in terms of labor but also in terms of land.[6] Yet, as industrial history has shown, no location remains a low-cost site forever. For a number of years, researchers have been concerned about this inevitable evolution for southern manufacturers.[7] An upside, however, is that there is evidence of rapidly increasing value-added from manufacturing workers — specifically, in higher-end industries.[8] Most of this upsurge stems from advanced manufacturing sectors, such as machinery and even some textile production. Numerous studies have examined the growing industrial transition of the southern United States and have clearly demonstrated that this region and its manufacturing activities are intimately linked with global economic trends.[9]

Manufacturing firms, like any other companies, evolve over time. And, on a related note, customer demands for their products change as well. Seminal works by Hirsch and Vernon on the product life cycle demonstrated that essentially all manufactured goods follow distinct patterns of demand and production.[10] In its development stages, there is relatively little demand for a product, as it must catch on in the marketplace. If the product does indeed develop a market following, then the product often undergoes an expansion period of rapidly rising sales. During this stage, manufacturers also begin to look at export markets to both supplement and to expand beyond their domestic sales. Eventually, however, demand levels off as the product matures and the production process becomes increasingly standardized.

As the manufactured good becomes a commodity, cost considerations come into play and at this point, location increasingly becomes a factor in the manufacturer's success. Vernon provided an influential examination of international production dynamics in terms of the product life cycle.[11] As a product becomes standardized, production will move overseas in order to be at first closer to international markets. But eventually, production moves in order to achieve lower cost advantages, a point also discussed by MacLachlan.[12] Accordingly, firms themselves can also fall into these patterns of commodity manufacturing and should strive to remain at the innovative end of the spectrum.

How does the product life cycle construct apply to the case of southern manufacturing? If production is to remain in mature industrialized regions (in this case, the Charlotte metropolitan area), the key strategy for manufacturers is to always stay at the front end of the product life cycle, creating newer products with sustained sales and growth trajectories. The obstacle is that many manufacturing firms in the South once relied largely on local and/or regional customers and had decidedly mature product lines. According to tenets of the product life cycle, manufacturers are expected to evolve into generating higher value-added products and move away from commodities if they intend to survive and retain domestic production. It is imperative, therefore, that Charlotte-region manufacturers shift toward developing advanced product lines and implementing new production processes.

As Grabher's research found, if firms remain tied principally to local customers for any length of time, a form of "path dependence" can often set in, slowing innovation and eventually reducing long-range competitiveness.[13] It has long been maintained that firms should explore outside their traditional market ranges, but this is a challenge, in that it requires significantly updated approaches, processes, and products. A key part of the innovative process is for manufacturers to explore export opportunities.

The transitions toward higher-end manufacturing and toward export markets are not easy. Like many manufacturers in the southern United States, and indeed across most industrialized economies, Charlotte-area manufacturers are faced with a number of competitive issues. These firm-level concerns extend beyond product life cycle and innovation issues. Among these are several global-trade-related issues such as diminished local customer demand, import competition, and increased materials costs.[14] Beyond these issues, many firms are finding it difficult to locate skilled workers—the cornerstones of any innovative production activities. These challenges are difficult in relatively stable times, but place additional strains on firms that are already seeing difficulties in adjusting to global market realities.

How does the manufacturing situation in the Charlotte metropolitan statistical area (MSA) compare with national trends? Figure 18 shows that both for Charlotte and the United States as a whole, manufacturing employment has entered a steep decline. The Charlotte MSA, however, has been hit particularly hard, registering a decline of over 38 percent during a ten-year period, set against a decline of just under 25 percent nationally. Interestingly, however, these overall manufacturing patterns contrast with national trends toward high-skilled, advanced production. Research from Deitz and Orr demonstrated that advanced manufacturing employment in the United States actually *increased* by over 36 percent since the 1980s.[15] The South Atlantic Region, in which Charlotte is located, reported an increase of over 60 percent in skilled manufacturing jobs. The data, then, point to quantitative and qualitative changes in the manufacturing landscape, both nationally and certainly within the South. Overall manufacturing employment is declining, but advanced, internationally competitive manufacturing remains.

So despite the recent declines in employment and the closures (or decreases) of many mature industries such as textiles and steel, manufacturing

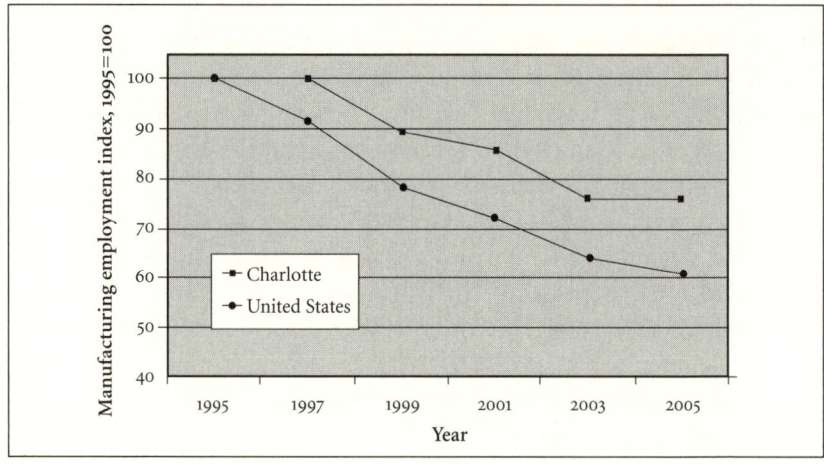

Figure 18. Manufacturing employment trends, 1995–2005. Based on data from the Bureau of Labor Statistics, the Employment Security Commission of North Carolina, the South Carolina Employment Security Commission, and the U.S. Census Bureau. (Source: Ronald Kalafsky.)

remains an important part of the southern economic landscape. No doubt much of this is due to the relatively high wages and multiplier effects on downstream industries that manufacturing provides. Not only do Charlotte manufacturers produce for the consumer, but also a significant number of firms serve as suppliers to other industries. What happens when these industries shrink or cease operations altogether, as was the case of so many textile firms throughout the region? Given that many Charlotte manufacturers never exported or felt the need to do so, is exporting a difficult option? Is it especially difficult for firms that never explored this option before? What is the status of exporting among Charlotte's manufacturing firms?

Export Activities and Relationships

Primary evidence for this study of export activity comes from a 2005 survey of manufacturers in the Charlotte MSA. A survey instrument was sent to the director or owner at a representative sample 850 establishments across the region, with 122 valid responses. Tests compared the set of respondents against known population metrics such as the number of employees in each firm and product lines; no statistically significant differences were found between the two groups. The original goal of the survey was to ascertain the human capital shortage for Charlotte manufacturers, a critical competitive concern. Accordingly, most questions centered on skills needs, the local labor market, and recruitment/training matters. The survey instrument also included several questions on export activities and other firm performance measures. Additional support comes from open-ended answers on the surveys and from a series of post-survey, follow-up conversations with over thirty manufacturers. It should be mentioned that during the firm-level conversations, the discussions often moved to trade-related topics; many open-ended survey comments turned to these concerns as well.

At the outset, what are the geographical sales ranges of the surveyed manufacturers and, specifically, what are the export intensities (percentage of sales coming from exports) of these firms? Figure 19 offers the geographical sales breakdowns for Charlotte-area manufacturers responding to the survey. The results indicate that proximity matters: over three-fifths of the average firms' sales are destined to points within the Charlotte MSA or the southern United States. The evidence intimates that the decline or relocation of many local manufacturers has most likely hurt a number of these firms. It should be noted that on the survey, problems with decreased local customer demand was the second-ranked competitive concern for the respondents.

The high intraregional sales percentages are contrasted against a mean export intensity of just over 10 percent. These numbers would suggest that international markets are not fully accessed by a large number of firms. On the other hand, this also indicates that exports could be a course to potential sales growth. The survey data did indeed show that fully 30 percent of the respondents reported export growth of greater than 5 percent during 2005,

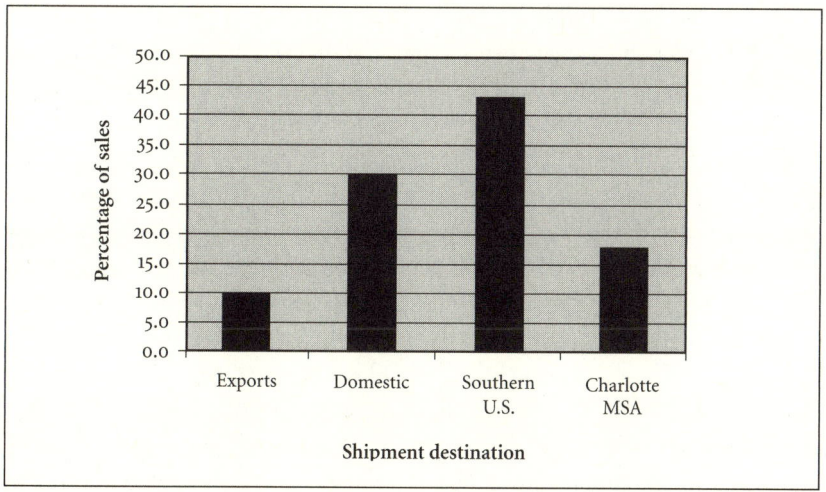

Figure 19. Percentage of sales by geographic region. (Source: Ronald Kalafsky.)

Table 2. Relationships between firm-level growth metrics (gamma statistics).

Growth measure	Exports	Sales	Market share	Employment
Exports	1.000			
Sales	*0.208	1.000		
Market share	**0.366	**0.616	1.000	
Employment	0.111	**0.800	**0.569	1.000

*Significant at $p \leq 0.05$.
**Significant at $p \leq 0.01$.

while only 11 percent indicated a decline in export sales. Exporting, then, should at least be considered by Charlotte manufacturers. If nothing else, exporting provides an opportunity to move beyond local markets, which, in most cases, are in decline.

While the literature points to the benefits of exporting, is it a worthwhile goal for Charlotte manufacturers? Is export expansion related to other company-level growth metrics? The relationships between four firm-level growth measures included on the survey instrument are illustrated in table 2. Export growth exhibits a significant, positive statistical relationship with growth in both sales and market share. These relationships would stand to reason, as exports have long been viewed as a means to expand sales outside of traditional areas and customers. Furthermore, these correlations suggest that manufacturers could possibly use exports to help impel additional sales, especially in a region where overall manufacturing activity is suffering.

In many ways, it is not unexpected that three of these measures of growth — market share, sales, and exports — would be statistically correlated. If firms intend to see any sustained increase in market share, then exporting would appear to be a means to do so. In fact, all of the growth metrics correlate significantly, with the exception of employment and exports. The lack of significant correlation between the export and employment growth measures is not surprising, given that since the economic downturn of the early 2000s, many manufacturers have been somewhat reluctant to hire new workers. In general, Charlotte manufacturers have also held back on staffing increases due to high benefit costs and difficulties locating skilled labor.[16] Informal follow-up discussions also indicated that a number of exporting firms are either quite small or are running "lean" manufacturing operations in order to remain competitive.

Table 3. Correlations between export intensities[1] and selected variables (Spearman's tests).

Variable	Export intensity[1]
Charlotte MSA sales	*-0.343
Southern sales	*-0.260
R&D intensity[2]	*0.284
New product intensity[3]	0.176
Firm size	*0.302

1. Percentage of sales from exports.
2. Percentage of sales spent on research and development.
3. Percentage of sales from products developed within the last five years.
*Significant at $p \leq 0.01$.

Growth in sales exhibits a significant relationship with growth in market share and employment (at $p \leq 0.01$). Note the high degree of statistical correlation between sales growth and employment growth. If Charlotte-based manufacturers begin to explore international customer possibilities and if sales growth is then spurred by export growth, an increase in employment could possibly follow. The fact that export growth correlates with sales growth offers support for firms that are evolving and moving to wider markets.

Whether export intensity is related to other measures of performance and innovation should also be examined. Previous work has suggested that relatively research-intensive firms that produce for wider markets, especially export markets, have demonstrated higher growth rates than their more localized counterparts.[17] Grabher also found that innovative firms have moved beyond local markets.[18] Table 3 investigates the extent to which this is true of Charlotte manufacturers. Of immediate interest are the correlation tests between export intensity and the other geographic sales components. Note the negative, significant correlation between export intensity and both Charlotte-area and broader southern sales intensities. Additionally, there is a positive and significant relationship with wider U.S. sales outside of the South.

These results suggest firms that are active in export markets do not concentrate (and/or do not rely) on spatially proximate sales (i.e., local customers). Or conversely, firms that have been largely reliant on local or regional customers are not successfully globalizing their products. This could be for one of two reasons: manufacturers that originally relied on nearby customers have not explored export markets or the products that these firms marketed are not attractive to export customers. At any rate, the results of the survey indicate that a large number of firms are not ready for the leap to serving global markets, in that they have older product lines and/or have relied for too long on a relatively small customer base. Conversely, this evidence also indicates that the relatively export-intensive firms would be somewhat insulated from recent declines in the local and wider southern manufacturing bases.

Do expenditures on research and development (R&D) lead to innovation, better products, and optimistically, increased sales within geographically expanded markets? The survey data indicate that there are significant positive correlations between this R&D measure and export intensity. One would expect forward-looking firms to be more successful on international markets. There is a statistically significant correlation between R&D and the percentage of recent sales derived from new products. This relationship is no surprise given the technology-related demands for new product lines that are of interest to current and potential customers. If firms intend to compete with new and technologically advanced products, this evidence points to the importance of R&D expenditures. Moreover, there are initial indications that a research-intensive focus helps producers to expand to wider regional markets. A point worth noting, however, is that the median R&D intensity for the sample of Charlotte manufacturers was just 1 percent of sales. Another point worth mentioning regards the workforce requirements of the R&D-intensive, advanced manufacturing environment: competitive manufacturing will demand a highly skilled workforce, which will be discussed later in the chapter.

There is a negative and significant relationship between R&D intensity and Charlotte-region sales, which stands in contrast to the relationship with export-led sales. This is not particularly surprising given that newer and more innovative products tend to sell over wider markets. But there is no statistically significant relationship between firm size and new product intensity (percentage of sales from products developed within the previous five years), which provides evidence that small- to medium-sized producers are engaging in innovative activities.

The new product share and R&D measures — and their relationships with other variables — are important to mention here in order to provide at least some measure of the innovation level of Charlotte firms. It is difficult to enter new and faraway markets without innovative product lines. However, it should also be noted that there is no statistical relationship between R&D expenditures and any of the growth metrics discussed in table 2. So at least

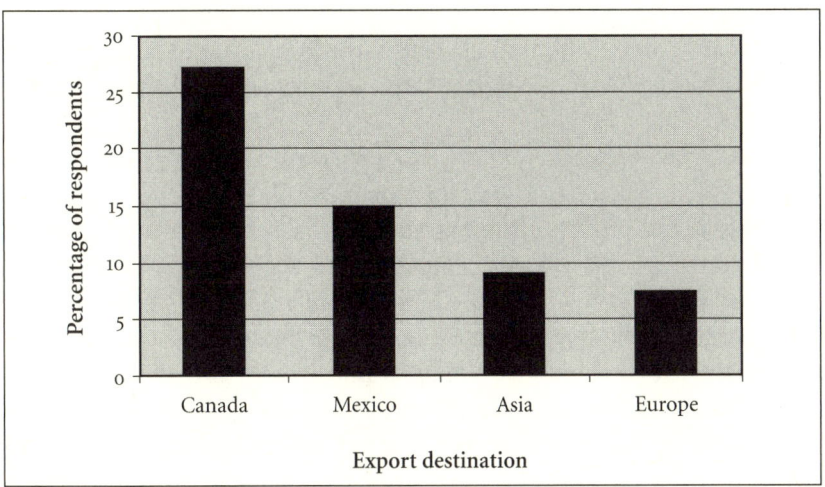

Figure 20. Top export destinations (percentage of respondents). (Source: Ronald Kalafsky.)

in terms of the surveyed firms, this finding does caution against linking R&D to firm-level growth.

Export intensity was also tested against company size, based on the number of employees. This metric was included given the long-standing body of research pertaining to firm size–export relationships, with equivocal findings by a number of researchers.[19] In the case of surveyed manufacturers, there was a significant correlation between firm size and export intensity. This relatively small sample suggests that in the case of Charlotte manufacturers, larger firms are more inclined toward increased international market activity. However, smaller firms can certainly also access export markets, as will be discussed below.

A final question pertains to the countries to which these manufactured exports were going. Figure 20 illustrates the top export destinations for the surveyed Charlotte manufacturers. Canada and Mexico are by far the top export destinations. Two main reasons play into this, as was explained in the open-ended survey responses and during the follow-up conversations. The first is obvious: these two countries are the closest large economies to Charlotte manufacturers. This finding confirms the work of Coughlin on the links between export activities and the countries to which companies ship their goods.[20] Most exporters will first ship to spatially proximate destinations because of familiarity with nearby markets. The second is the North American Free Trade Agreement. Given the relative ease of trade between these trading partners, shipping to Canada and Mexico is the path of least resistance with regard to regulations. The two other top destinations were "Asia" and "Europe." Admittedly, one of the limitations of an open-ended survey question is that respondents often listed regions rather than specific countries.

While the survey data indicate that a majority of the firms limit export sales to North America, it should be noted that the breadth of export destinations was surprising, including Australia, Saudi Arabia, and Singapore. Charlotte's exporters are not necessarily constrained spatially and some firms are successfully interacting with distant markets. Interestingly, the manufacturers who *did not* list either Canada or Mexico as their primary export destination reported an average export intensity of 17.7 percent, a figure well above the sample mean. Moreover, the distant export activities were not limited to larger manufacturers. Several producers shipping to some of the distant destinations such as Australia and Colombia employed fewer than twenty workers. One of the smaller firms involved in textile-related equipment mentioned that it was targeting Honduras and China for future growth. Incidentally, this firm is a smaller manufacturer (fewer than fifty employees). The consensus within this firm was that there is little domestic sales potential and that, at least in this industry, growth will be found abroad. This firm is following the geographical patterns of textile manufacturing. The non-Canada/Mexico exporter group averaged 58.3 employees, slightly smaller than the overall sample's mean firm size of 61.3 workers.

Discussion

The sample data reflect that, even now, Charlotte manufacturers derive a large percentage of sales from a relatively local customer base and that, on balance, the average company exports relatively little. Much of this stems from historical reasons, given that many textile firms produced for regional or domestic markets, but rarely for international customers. At the outset, then, there is a large group of firms that have not oriented their strategies toward a global buyer base. Firms are, without a doubt, facing difficult issues, much of it precipitated by international competition. Many Charlotte manufacturers have realized that regional (and even domestic) markets show few signs of potential growth.

To provide an example of the global changes affecting local firms, a machine shop from within Mecklenburg County asserted on the survey that offshore manufacturing and outsourcing by American companies is negatively impacting their establishment, taking away many of their prime customers. Firms need to look at export markets then as a potential answer to offset declining domestic sales, because many of the firms that they once supplied are no longer in business or have stopped buying locally. Another respondent (a machining company) alluded to this on the open-ended part of the survey, stating, "Now these customers are going offshore for their products. Trade issues have killed manufacturing." This same firm was attempting to move away from concentrating on the local textile industry and looking to export in order to save the firm. While these are just two cases from the survey participants, they are largely indicative of manufacturers who have relied heavily, if not entirely, on customers located locally or within the South. Given changes in the textile industry and in a number of other sectors such as metalworking, firms can no longer depend on these domestic buyers and are facing the global market. Are Charlotte-area manufacturers ready to take on the global market?

Given the promise of international markets and the decline of local manufacturers (many of which were longtime customers), exporting would appear to be a way to expand sales and remain commercially viable. Export activity is well within reach for manufacturers. According to recent data posted by the U.S. Department of Commerce's International Trade Administration, North Carolina's export of manufactured goods increased by $6 billion from 2002 to 2006. The survey data, moreover, indicated that export growth correlates significantly with other firm-level sales and market share growth metrics. The interviews also suggested that a number of firms are involved in exporting, if only to a small degree. The potential of exporting was epitomized by a survey respondent that produced industrial coatings. For this producer, interestingly, overall sales declined yet exports grew by over 15 percent. Export intensity was 75 percent and, as the respondent wrote next to the check-off boxes, "Growing rapidly!" For this manufacturer, at least, exporting was a means to address declining sales.

Where do Charlotte manufacturers fit in terms of the product life cycle? The products of many manufacturers appear to be decidedly toward the mature end of this cycle, which hinders entrance into dynamic, demanding international markets. Much of this stemmed from over-reliance on local customers in declining industries. Many firms need to export, but again, this requires a commitment to products that are competitive (i.e., innovative) for global buyers, rather than those for a select group of longtime customers. The response of the following respondent epitomizes the strategy to be taken by companies looking to export: "We have technically exciting products and markets that are very attractive to technically minded people."

Incidentally, this firm's export intensity was at 50 percent, having grown by 50 percent during the 2000 to 2005 period. Relatedly, the survey results showed a positive, significant relationship between research expenditures and exporting. This firm exemplifies the type of enterprise with potential to succeed in globally competitive markets.

Survey respondents preferred Canada and Mexico as export destinations due to proximity and ease of trade; these were the top two markets on the survey. New, non-NAFTA export markets are promising, if for no other reason than the potential expansion of sales. Indeed, many firms mentioned the pressing need to look to China and much of Asia as potential export markets. During discussions with several firms, many appeared to want to explore or initiate export activities, but were reluctant to do so due to a lack of market intelligence and potential language issues (especially the former). Regional or federal policy could provide for accessible market intelligence for small- to medium-sized firms. Additionally, firms themselves could explore risk-reducing options such as employing agents or distributors as local representatives in distant markets. One smaller manufacturer wrote, "You can not sell in Asia without a distributor or agent." For all survey respondents, the importance accorded to distributors and agents correlated positively with export intensity at a 95 percent level of confidence. As with general export market intelligence, finding reliable agents is also a task that is difficult for most firms, especially those with little or no export experience.

The export–firm size relationship is worth exploring in further studies. As mentioned constantly in the manufacturing community, smaller firms are particularly challenged in many facets of the manufacturing process. In their estimation, policymakers do not provide enough support for their plight. On the other hand, some of the higher-performing firms (and higher value-added producers as well) were some of the smaller firms in the sample. Further, U.S. Department of Commerce data show that smaller firms account for roughly 22 percent of all of North Carolina's exports of manufactured goods. These data demonstrate that export activities are not beyond the reach of the smaller firms. However, given some of the resource constraints mentioned above, these smaller producers may still need some form of export intelligence assistance. Interestingly, the survey data found no statistical relationship between export growth and employment growth. It could be that manufacturers are indeed becoming leaner in many ways.

Beyond market information, what other obstacles impede manufacturers looking to export? Export regulations, especially since the terrorist attacks on September 11, 2001, have harmed exporters. High-end equipment, such as machine tools, often receives higher customs scrutiny, particularly with regard to end use. As one high-end testing equipment firm mentioned on the survey, it's a "big headache — my European competitors are cleaning our clock with shipments." This respondent also added, "we are the good guys," so why is the government hindering U.S. exporters? This same firm is exploring relatively new emerging markets, such as Turkey and Indonesia, that often invite regulatory scrutiny. Many Charlotte firms want to export, but more could be done from a policy standpoint to provide export information about emerging markets and potential export license issues.

Although not discussed directly in this chapter, the workforce issue for manufacturers will need to be addressed. In order for firms to innovate and to expand their reach to global markets, a highly skilled workforce has become almost imperative. This stands to reason, as innovative firms must integrate new machinery and processes into their operations, which in turn drive the need for a higher-skilled workforce. The workforce was cited time and again as an obstacle to overall competitiveness, rather than other commonly held barriers to growth such as trade regulations or shortages of transportation linkages. That firms continue to cite this problem supports a point raised earlier by Glasmeier and Leichenko, who suggested that the southern industrial transition was hindered by development decisions that were "designed to invest in location rather than people."[21] Firms need skilled workers if they intend to remain at the preferred end of the product life cycle.

Where do the firms stand now? On the open-ended part of the survey and during the follow-up conversations, the criticality of human capital issues for manufacturers was indeed expressed numerous times. Rather than any infrastructure issues, the shortage of advanced manufacturing workers was named as a problem central to regional manufacturer competitiveness. The survey data also indicated a statistically significant correlation between the importance Charlotte firms place on skilled labor and their perception of a labor shortage. The labor shortage is part of a larger national concern regarding the long-term viability and global competitiveness of manufacturers.[22] However, given the current issues and needs facing Charlotte manufacturers and the funding challenges facing the educational system at numerous levels, this competitive concern could thwart attempts by manufacturers to succeed in international markets.

For the firms to create advanced products for international markets, a skilled workforce is necessary. The survey responses regarding the severity of the labor shortage suggest that the shortage is a serious challenge, affecting not only exports but overall competitiveness. It would stand to reason, then, that current and projected skilled labor shortages could harm firms' internationalization efforts more than many of the other perceived impediments.

Conclusion

Overall, it appears that exporting demonstrates great potential for Charlotte manufacturers. Most manufacturers realize that geographical sales expansion has become a near necessity to survive the changes occurring across the southern industrial landscape. Are firms ready to make the transition to exporting? One difficulty is that many firms have waited almost too long, relying instead on longtime, nearby buyers. Much of this is rooted in the nature of the once-dominant textile sector and its myriad supporting industries. Now that this industry has, in most cases, disappeared across the region, firms are compelled to look at wider markets for growth and long-term viability.

Another difficulty is the mature product lines of many manufacturers. Export-led, sustained growth will have to come from firms introducing more innovative products and having access to information about the potential (and limitations) of international markets. Beyond increased international competition and other possible impediments, human capital issues, in the opinions of the respondents, are a significant obstacle to the innovation process and could be the greatest "infrastructure" barrier to firms making the transition toward new/improved products and serving geographically wider markets. From a policy perspective, addressing this issue would appear to be one of the best ways to help firms. Taking a long-term perspective toward improving the human capital base of the region may be one of the best ways to help not only manufacturers but also other sectors to remain internationally competitive.

It should be emphasized that a number of the surveyed manufacturers indicated export success across a number of product lines and international markets. For a majority of the firms, however, developing new product lines and skilled labor shortages provide some of the greatest barriers to internationalization.

Notes

1. J. C. Cobb, The Selling of the South: The Southern Crusade for Industrial Development, 1936–1990 (Urbana: University of Illinois Press, 1993).

2. A. K. Glasmeier and R. M. Leichenko, "From Free Market Rhetoric to Free Market Reality: The Future of the U.S. South in an Era of Globalization," Interna-

tional Journal of Urban and Regional Research 20, no. 4 (1996): 601–15; M. L. Johnson, "To Restructure or Not To Restructure: Contemplations on Postwar Industrial Geography in the U.S. South," Southeastern Geographer 37, no. 2 (1997): 162–92.

3. M. E. Porter, "The Economic Performance of Regions," Regional Studies 37, no. 6/7 (2003): 549–78.

4. G. Grabher, "The Weakness of Strong Ties: The Lock-in of Regional Development in the Ruhr Area," in The Embedded Firm: On the Socioeconomics of Industrial Networks, ed. G. Grabher, 255–77 (London: Routledge, 1993).

5. R. V. Kalafsky, "An Examination of the Challenges of Charlotte Manufacturers," Professional Geographer 59, no. 3 (2007): 334–43.

6. Cobb, The Selling of the South.

7. S. O. Park and J. O. Wheeler, "The Filtering Down Process in Georgia: The Third Stage in the Product Life Cycle," Professional Geographer 35, no. 1 (1983): 18–31; Johnson, "To Restructure or not to Restructure."

8. J. O. Wheeler, "Locational Factors in the New Textile Industry: Focus on the U.S. South," Journal of Geography 97, no. 4/5 (1998): 193–203; R. Kalafsky, "The Manufacturing Sector in the South: Status and Recent Trends," Southeastern Geographer 46, no. 2, (2006): 259–77.

9. Glasmeier and Leichenko, "From Free Market Rhetoric to Free Market Reality"; J. C. Cobb, "Beyond the 'Y'all Wall': The American South Goes Global," in Globalization and the American South, ed. J. C. Cobb and W. Stueck (Athens: University of Georgia Press, 2005), 1–18; S. Guthrie-Shimizu, "From Southeast Asia to the American Southeast: Japanese Business Meets the Sun Belt South," in Cobb and Stueck, Globalization and the American South, 164–84.

10. S. Hirsch, Location of Industry and International Competitiveness (London: Oxford University Press, 1967); R. Vernon, "The Product Cycle Hypothesis in a New International Environment," Oxford Bulletin of Economics and Statistics 41, no. 4 (1979): 255–68.

11. Vernon, "The Product Cycle Hypothesis."

12. I. MacLachlan, "Plant Closure and Market Dynamics: Competitive Strategy and Rationalization," Economic Geography 68, no. 2 (1992): 128–45.

13. Grabher, "The Weakness of Strong Ties."

14. Kalafsky, "An Examination of the Challenges of Charlotte Manufacturers."

15. R. Deitz and J. Orr, "A Leaner, More Skilled U.S. Manufacturing Workforce," Current Issues in Economics and Finance 12, no. 2 (2006): 1–7.

16. Kalafsky, "An Examination of the Challenges of Charlotte Manufacturers."

17. R. V. Kalafsky and A. D. MacPherson, "Input/Output Ranges and Performance: An Examination of U.S. Machine Tool Producers," Entrepreneurship and Regional Development 15, no. 1 (2003): 69–82; A. D. MacPherson, "The Role of International Design Orientation and Market Intelligence in the Export Performance of U.S. Machine Tool Companies," R&D Management 30, no. 2 (2000): 167–76.

18. Grabher, "The Weakness of Strong Ties."

19. E. Verwaal and B. Donkers, "Firm Size and Export Intensity: Solving an Empirical Puzzle," Journal of International Business Studies 33, no. 3 (2002): 603–13.

20. C. C. Coughlin, "The Increasing Importance of Proximity for Exports from U.S. States," (Federal Reserve Bank of St. Louis) Review 86, no. 6 (2004): 1–18.

21. Glasmeier and Leichenko, "From Free Market Rhetoric to Free Market Reality," 613.

22. National Association of Manufacturers, "2005 Skills Gap Report — A Survey of the American Manufacturing Workforce," http://www.nam.org/~/media/Files/s_nam/docs/235800/235731.pdf.ashx (accessed December 18, 2008).

Tyrel G. Moore and Gerald L. Ingalls

A Place for Old Mills in a New Economy
Textile Mill Reuse in Charlotte

Textile mill reuse builds tangible bridges between Charlotte's old nineteenth- and twentieth-century and new twenty-first-century economies. The place-defining continuity inherent in renewed functions for old mills wraps a sense of heritage, place, and community into new economic and social environments. Furthermore, mill reuse creates a mutually supportive intersection for diverse interests including developers, preservationists, and municipal and regional governments whose initiatives focus on economic revitalization to restore sagging tax bases and revitalize blighted industrial landscapes and neighborhoods. More recently, "smart growth" advocates who promote "green" planning processes that yield sustainable, vibrant communities have been added to the list. From their multiple motivations for preservation and for successful business ventures, these groups realize that old buildings' sense of place and architectural character provide amenities that draw people back to once-blighted, empty urban spaces.[1]

The places that Charlotte's old mills find in a new economy represent more than innovative business ventures and public sector initiatives. They evocatively reveal the layers of past geographies and economies that have shaped the city's transition toward becoming a global city. In their initial development and in their reuse, Charlotte's textile mills are emblematic of stages that first defined the city as a center in the industrial transformation of a rural agrarian South and, in their recent reuse, redefined the city's textile heritage in a maturing postindustrial urban landscape. This chapter provides a spatial perspective on that process of change. Key elements of Charlotte's path in the process involve the ways the city first adopted a textile economy and later made adjustments in embracing the heritage of its early economic landscape. Data for that analysis are derived from histories of the southern textile industry; the Charlotte-Mecklenburg Historic Landmarks Commission and the City of Charlotte Planning Commission; historic maps of Charlotte; fieldwork and interviews related to our previous research on the topic; and a content analysis of local news articles on the textile industry and the reuse of mills. We begin this chapter with details of the southern textile mill expansion and the ways that it was significant to Charlotte's emergence as an urban place within an economy in transition. That nineteenth-century coverage is followed by a discussion of Charlotte's contemporary potentials and challenges for mill reuse in its varied forms. Finally, we discuss the city's individual postindustrial reuse projects with an emphasis on place-specific attributes of mills that made some of them catalysts for nearby redevelopment and made others candidates for reuse by virtue of redevelopment initiatives already taking place around their sites. Charlotte's mill reuse is significant: it offers a case study of how solutions can be created as old city-forming industrial corridors become dormant, neglected landscapes in the wake of a postindustrial hollowing out of central cities that take jobs and people into the suburbs.

Charlotte's Transition in an Industrial South

Charlotte, and the more rural region around it, was a concentration of cotton textile mill activity during a formative period in the southern expansion of the industry that occurred at an accelerated pace from the early 1880s to the 1930s. Southern-born textile industrialist and engineer D. A. Tompkins, who designed or built many of the Charlotte region's mills during its industrial transition, was an early voice for economic change. As a newspaper publisher, he was a strident supporter of the industrial shift, vigorously promoting southern industrialization on the pages of his *Charlotte Daily Observer*.[2] Historian C. Vann Woodward summed the gravity of the late nineteenth-century rise of the southern textile industry in this way:

> The dramatic elements in the rise of the Southern cotton mill gave the movement something of the character of a "crusade." The successful competition with New England, the South's old political rival, the popular slogan "bring the factories to the fields," and the publicity that attended every advance, have combined to enshrine the cotton mill in a somewhat exalted place in Southern history. Burdened with emotional significance, the mill has been made a symbol of the New South, its origins, and its promise of salvation.[3]

Woodward also recognized the entrepreneurial skills of a group of southern businessmen who led the shift away from the long-standing southern colonial and antebellum planter economy. That group of southerners represented something of a rough-cut nineteenth-century Creative Class.[4] They clearly had the talent of vision needed to venture into the industrialization of an agrarian South. One of them boldly asserted their sense of territorial promotion and regionalism when he expressed that a New South ambition aimed "to out-Yankee the Yankees."[5]

In documenting that industrial transformation and its vast spatial extent (see figure 21), Lemert noted that between 1913 and 1931, the number of mills rose from 415 to 634 in North Carolina and from 103 to 226 in South Carolina.[6] Charlotte's centrality in the spatial pattern of this expansion created multiple advantages that launched an urban trajectory for the emerging city. By the early 1900s approximately three hundred mills had been built within one hundred miles of Charlotte; eighteen of those mills were in Mecklenburg County.[7] Charlotte's significance was enhanced by early rail connections that made the city a major transportation center in the emerging industrial region. As Hanchett pointed out, those advantages appeared as early as 1850 and solidified with time as J. P. Morgan's Southern Railway acquired the early trunk lines and ran its main line through Charlotte.[8] By 1913, the intersection of these routes focused on Charlotte and formed a distribution network that linked the southern Piedmont mills and Charlotte to the coast and to the northeast. That connectivity and the concentration of mills vastly extended the reach and magnitude of Charlotte's business connections. The impacts of these New South economic developments on Charlotte's growth were substantial: between 1870 and 1900, the city's population rose from 4,400 to over 18,000 and gained increasing momentum as its mills came on line. The 1910 population reached 34,000, grew to 46,000 in 1920, and continued to rise to 82,000 by 1930, when it became the largest city in the Carolinas.[9] Charlotte's urban primacy, its urban-industrial status, and the mill villages of a new industrial middle class that changed Charlotte's internal spatial structure clearly were established on the broad shoulders of its textile heritage. One of the wider legacies of this economic change was the emergence of ancillary enterprises, such as banking, that would later drive the transition to a postindustrial economy. The city's textile heritage remains as old mills find prominent places in the late twentieth- and early twenty-first-century postindustrial landscapes. Indeed, we suggest that Charlotte's textile mill reuse projects are emblematic of Charlotte's current transition toward a "newer," more global, New South.

Potentials and Challenges for Textile Mill Reuse

Our previous research, conducted in Mecklenburg County and the seven counties surrounding it, identified differing reuse potentials by answering two overarching questions: What impact does the population size of towns and cities have on reuse opportunities? What locational characteristics influence types of new uses and opportunities for reuse? The answers to those questions are embedded in geographic differences. When mill reuse occurs, place matters and it matters a lot. We found that textile manufacturing continued in just under half of the mills in smaller communities compared to larger ones, where fewer than one-third still held those functions (see table 4). Vacant mills were also twice as likely to occur in smaller communities. By contrast, nonmanufacturing reuses were three times more likely to occur in larger locales. Those differences were attributed in part to the inertia exerted by mills that continued to operate in single-industry towns in the

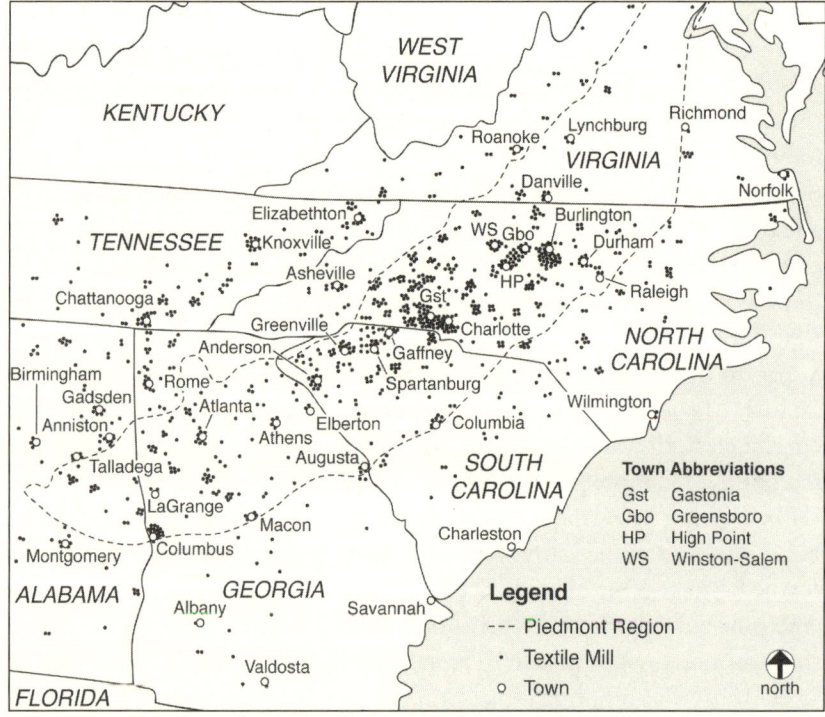

Figure 21. Adapted from Lemert (1933), this map shows the historic spatial extent of the Southern Piedmont cotton textile industry and Charlotte's central location in the region. (Source: UNC Charlotte Cartography Lab.)

Table 4. Disposition of mills by population size of places.

	Population less than 45,000		Population 45,000 or more	
Status of mill/type of use	Number	Percent	Number	Percent
Vacant, no proposed reuse	8	15	5	8
Vacant, some limited use	2	4	0	0
Demolished	7	13	9	14
Textile manufacturing	24	46	20	30
Other manufacturing	5	10	8	12
Adapted, nonmanufacturing	5	10	21	32
Adaptation/reuse proposed	1	2	3	5
Total	52		66	

Source: Gerald Ingalls and Tyrel Moore, "Old But New: An Inventory of Textile Mill Reuse in the Charlotte Urban Region," *Southeastern Geographer* 41, no. 1 (2001): 83.

larger region. The different potential for nonmanufacturing reuses related to population sizes of places seemed largely to be a function of the softer real estate markets that prevailed in smaller places. Those realities were evident in types of reuse that often involved commercial or mixed uses.[10] Some combination of office uses or warehouses accounted for almost one-fourth of reuse types (see table 5). These somewhat transient uses were most typical along railroads or industrial corridors that comprised the blighted, rough edges of urban spaces that discouraged long-term real estate investment. Furthermore, these rough edges defined perceived boundaries that created lingering risks for redevelopment and longer odds against reuse. That said, old industrial corridors were the sites of Charlotte's most visible nonmanufacturing reuse projects: the Atherton Mill complex on South Boulevard and the proposed reuse of Highland Park No. 3 Mill, in North Davidson Street's gentrifying NoDa Arts District.

Reuses along the city's old industrial corridors would have been even more unlikely without developers' access to federal and state preservation tax credits earmarked to stimulate the redevelopment of historically designated properties. When combined, the credits provided a tax incentive of 40 percent.[11] That fiscal support facilitated additional promising venture capital efforts and solidified public–private sector reuse partnerships. With crucial foresight, between 1985 and 1998 the Charlotte-Mecklenburg

Table 5. Types of adaptive reuse by land use.

Type of land use	Percent of sample
Commercial	27
Mixed use	33
Office	3
Office/warehouse	17
Warehouse	7
Residential	13

Source: Gerald Ingalls and Tyrel Moore, "Old But New: An Inventory of Textile Mill Reuse in the Charlotte Urban Region," *Southeastern Geographer* 41, no. 1 (2001): 86.

Historic Landmarks Commission had listed almost all of Charlotte's mills among the city's designated properties. The City of Charlotte supported the historic status, enacting a 50 percent reduction of the ad valorem tax rate on historically designated properties. Because of the tax burden related to their large size, this was especially critical to old textile mills.[12] Federally mandated brownfield tax incentives also buttressed reuse opportunities where sites were contaminated by previous industrial activities. These measures opened a door that otherwise might have remained closed, absent preservation incentives encouraging reuse. Accordingly, conclusions of our 2001 study recognized the importance of mills' historic status. We also expected that the city's "smart growth" policies would buttress the role of public–private sector partnerships in future reuse patterns. It also was obvious that, in the face of increasing offshore competition and a financially troubled domestic textile industry, the pool of vacant mills would increase. In comparison with other places in the region, Charlotte held promise in fiscal and municipal structures for finding new uses for old mills.

What we could not predict was that textile mill reuse would become so newsworthy in the immediate future. In researching the status and influence of reuse projects in the region in 2001, we uncovered just two recent newspaper articles on the topic. Since then, the region's leading newspaper, the *Charlotte Observer*, has carried upwards of seventy articles on the textile industry. Fallout from the post–September 11, 2001, economy and the regionally devastating impacts of globalization within the textile industry appropriately captured headlines. For example, Lunan reported that 62 mills closed in North and South Carolina in 2001, leaving 23,000 jobless. He added that from 1997 to mid-2002, 75,000 mill workers lost jobs as 236 of the area's mills were shuttered.[13] This post–September 11 freefall underscored the southern apparel and textile industries' vulnerability to import penetration, a threat that had been on the horizon since the mid- to late 1980s.[14] The majority of the closings occurred in small towns. Impacts were vividly captured in *Charlotte Observer* headlines: "Once Vital Textile Mills . . . Dying a Slow Death as Slumping Economy, Layoffs Fuel . . . Decline"; "Tiny Town Frets over Loss of Textile Mill"; "Despair in Mill Town"; "Future Is Uncertain for Vacant Factories"; "Empty Mills Burden Carolinas"; "Kannapolis Image as 'Dying Mill Town' Hurts"; and "Pillowtex Folds; 7,650 Go Jobless."[15] Collectively, these empty mills were remindful of what Jakle and Wilson identified as "derelict landscapes" within a place, such as New England's old textile centers.[16] The content analysis we employed revealed a timely and accurate lens for understanding the region's economic restructuring and also illuminated just how fragile the opportunities for mill reuse can be. The stark reality was that, in the wake of dramatic economic change, there were few opportunities for reusing old mills in many of the small towns.[17] These places had neither the money nor the population base to realize reuse options that depended on renters for apartments and offices. Mill conversions to condominiums represented truly bold ventures in rural markets.[18] A number of mills were lost to salvage in an environment where the value of their brick, pine heart beams, and pine, maple, or walnut flooring commanded top dollar as specialty upgrades for housing construction and renovation in urban markets.[19] The community heritage and sense of place of towns built and supported by a century-long textile mill economy were trucked away brick by brick and beam by beam, lost from the former mill town landscapes.

Even though textile plant closings and job losses were writing a tragic chapter in the region's economic and social history, half (thirty-five) of the textile industry–related news articles published in the *Charlotte Observer* between September 2001 and November 2007 highlighted ongoing or proposed textile mill reuse projects. Most of these appeared in the paper's business section. While reflecting hopeful outcomes for proposed developments, they also documented individual projects and their progress. Their focus on Charlotte's inner-city redevelopment also spotlighted a new development landscape instead of the typical suburban business and residential venues. In an environment where front-page columns were chronicling the demise of a regionally significant industry, almost as much print space was being devoted to mill reuse and to its tempo of development. The newsworthiness of the reuse of old mills makes equally significant statements about the role

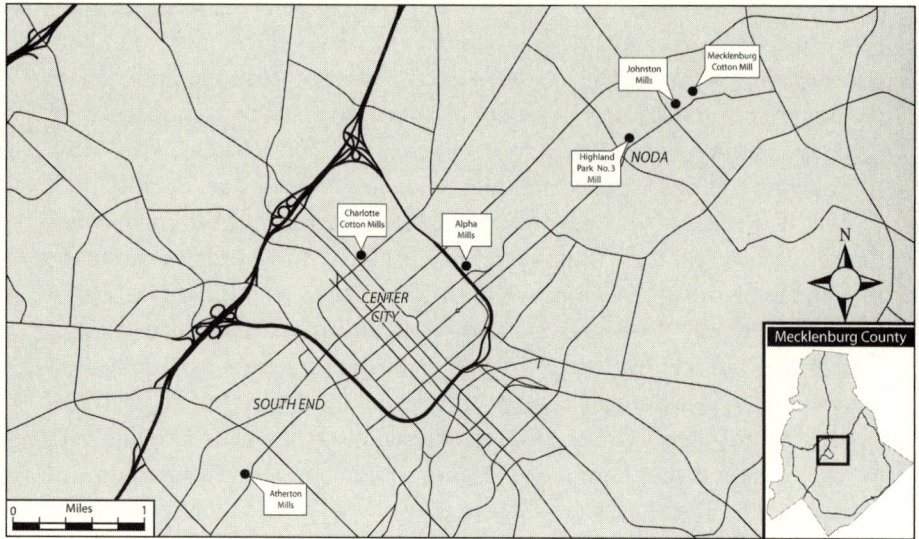

Figure 22. The map identifies the locations of Charlotte's Historic Mill Reuse projects. Each mill was designated a historic property by the Charlotte Mecklenburg Landmarks Commission. (Source: Martin Bunn, UNC Charlotte Department of Geography and Earth Sciences.)

their redevelopment was assuming in the new economy. In that transition, the nineteenth-century, industrial-economy mills were beginning to find their place in Charlotte's twenty-first-century, postindustrial economy.

A Place for Old Mills in Postindustrial Charlotte

The reuse of six of Charlotte's historic mills built between 1881 and 1904 are the focus of discussion here (see figure 22). The content of newspaper articles form data drawn from a geographic scale not comparable with our 2001 survey, but provide data permitting analysis of successful reuse efforts. The place-specific attributes of each mill reuse project illustrate the environments that promoted reuse. In some places, successful projects capitalize on corporate-community partnerships, which provide capitalization for investment and work with local governments and historic landmark commissions, and the attractions that come with heritage. In other cases old mills are catalysts for the redevelopment of industrial corridors beyond their own site.

It is important to note that Charlotte transitioned in two very important and nationally broad central city revitalization processes that could not be captured in the field surveys that generated our 2000 inventory of mill reuse: gentrification of central city neighborhoods and increased professional employment in the postindustrial economy. These trends generated significant demographic and economic changes that contributed to residential and commercial mixed land use changes on old mill sites and nearby land parcels.

Gentrification profoundly changed central Charlotte. Smith and Graves reveal that gentrification in Charlotte's Fourth Ward during the 1970s took on its own nuances, specifically beginning with third-wave gentrifiers — comprising working professionals with families — who departed from the longer, sequential process more typically begun by marginal or first-wave gentrifiers usually recognized in the literature on gentrification theory.[20] That aspect of the Charlotte gentrification process accelerated the production of what Ley identified as a new central city middle class reshaping central cities.[21] The North Carolina National Bank (NCNB), today's Bank of America, initiated the revitalization of the ward's mostly underdeveloped, vacant, previously industrial parcels. While the corporate leadership of Charlotte's Fourth Ward renewal was not unusual,[22] the local process was unique because it did not result in a rent-gap displacement of previous residents, which often occurs with gentrification. NCNB realized that civic investment paid dividends in a vital Center City that was a significant business amenity, especially in recruiting professionals with skills to grow the company's expertise and corporate standing.[23]

The Fourth Ward gentrification improved the climate for future mill reuse in two important ways. First, NCNB's corporate–public sector partnership served as a model and shaped public policy tools that facilitated revitalization initiatives across the city. In many ways, the forging of common corporate and municipal goals institutionalized the city's planning for redevelopment of inner-city and corridor industrial areas and adjacent neighborhoods, such as those around the Center City and in the historic South End.[24] Secondly, gentrification produced residual assets in these neighborhoods by attracting residents who created thresholds for the market entry of new businesses and services. In the process, old vacant mill sites created new urban spaces. Charlotte's central city redevelopment displaced no existing population, thereby avoiding a common criticism of gentrification processes.

Charlotte's success as a financial center also was a huge agent of change in attracting an increasing pool of younger, well-educated, and relatively affluent professionals. Richard Florida[25] identifies the presence of that college-educated, higher per capita income group as essential for regional competitiveness in economic and income growth. The growing numbers of these professionals in Charlotte enhanced not only its ascendancy as a global urban center but also produced a robust market for loft apartments and condominiums offered in the former textile mills. That connection was frequently conveyed in newspaper coverage of reuse projects: working professionals were often cited as a tenant pool for old mills' conversion to residential and professional office spaces and as a customer base for entertainment land uses. Collectively, these supportive environments also were integral elements in future textile mill reuse.

Charlotte Mills Then and Now

Located at 5th and Graham streets, Charlotte Cotton Mills, the city's oldest mill, was built in 1881 and enjoyed unique locational advantages. It was the only mill to be erected inside the city at what was then the edge of Charlotte's corporate limits in Fourth Ward, a location that permitted municipal property tax incentives to be granted for its first decade of operation. The location also was near existing residential areas of the city that housed the bulk of its labor force, which limited the investment of resources and time in providing employee housing. The company built only ten houses for mill workers.[26] Sanborn Insurance Company maps of Charlotte in 1896 and 1929 depict the mill's significance to spreading industrialization. Cottonseed oil plants, gingham mills, denim pants factories, textile machinery factories, and engineering businesses agglomerated within blocks of the Charlotte Cotton Mills complex.[27] The mill's operation ended with the Great Depression, but its buildings, by virtue of their attractive location, were occupied from 1936 to 1998.[28]

Charlotte Cotton Mills retained its nineteenth-century locational advantages in the postindustrial era. Its proximity to an emerging financial skyline amid twentieth-century economic restructuring and what would become Charlotte's Center City in the twenty-first century directly influenced its subsequent reuse. Corporate capital and strong community partnerships revitalized Fourth Ward. Just a few blocks from job-providing financial centers, it is now a vibrant neighborhood after being part of a Charlotte uptown vastly underutilized after the 1950s. The area underwent its own style of gentrification that, early on, brought people back to the central city and filled pockets of vacant industrial parcels.[29] In 2004, the mill was chosen for new offices by an architectural firm that paid $2.3 million for 12,700 square feet of space. They were attracted to the building's heritage and architecture. Its most recently developed space, CANS Bar, which has locations in Chicago and Milwaukee, occupies 13,300 square feet purchased for $2.3 million (see figure 23). The bar's owners were drawn to the building's architectural features, in-

Figure 23. CANS Bar is the entertainment center of the Charlotte Cotton Mills' adapted office, residential, and entertainment space. (Source: Tyrel Moore.)

cluding exposed brick walls, massive pine beams, and large windows.[30] The repurposed Charlotte Cotton Mills' marketability was supported by a large number of young professionals who work or live in the area. Renovation plans for 120 loft apartments, 20 of which rented at $1,500 per month, realized occupancy rates that were two times greater than those of recent new developments in Charlotte. Those successes offered proof of the reuse dividends accrued from the intersection of location and the public–private sector partnership of Duke Energy's real estate arm, Crescent Resources, Pappas Properties, and the Charlotte-Mecklenburg Historic Landmarks Commission.[31] Today the old mill contains 183 residential units[32] and blends seamlessly into the contemporary urban spaces and land uses around it.

Salvesen noted that mill reuse sometimes acts as a catalyst for urban redevelopment.[33] South Boulevard's historic South End, anchored by the reuse of the Atherton Mills, is a case in point. The 200,000-square-foot mill complex was built by D. A. Tompkins in 1892 and became Charlotte's sixth cotton mill. Like the Charlotte Cotton Mills, the Atherton Mill complex quickly became an industrial hub that comprised both related and diverse manufacturing sites. Unlike the Charlotte Cotton Mills, the mill's development included company-owned housing and city-forming elements created by adjacent mill communities in the Wilmore and Dilworth neighborhoods. Those residential areas remained after the mill ceased textile manufacturing in 1933.[34] By the mid 1970s, the old South Boulevard industrial corridor carried many of the negatives associated with blighted landscapes. Industrial and retail decline created pockets of vacant buildings, crime, and undesirable land uses such as X-rated video stores, all of which discouraged redevelopment and threatened the quality of life in the old mill neighborhoods. Two public initiatives, the 1976 formation of the Dilworth Community Development Association and Charlotte voters' 1987 approval of a $1.5 million bond referendum to fund infrastructure improvements along five urban corridors, including one in present-day South End, were vital to the area's redevelopment. From the private sector, local commercial real estate developer Tony Pressley of MECA Properties was at the vanguard of mill reuse as he reworked the Atherton Mill for a Spaghetti Warehouse restaurant in 1991.[35] The site now houses thirty-six loft apartments plus another eighty-five at Factory South and a restaurant supply and catering business.[36] In the interim, the South End Brewery opened and specialty shops were added within the same complex. Each of these drew upon a clientele attracted to the historic cachet of the old mill. The success of these projects showed not only the potentials that Charlotte's historic mills held in commercial real estate ventures, but also the effect they could have as redevelopment tools. The mill and its smokestack became the centerpiece of the South End Development Corporation logo, and were later used in the city's signage for the area.[37] This part of the old industrial corridor had become one of the city's most popular destinations.

Business uses around the complex emerged early; retail based on home furnishing and restoration specialties filled a market niche created by the established and gentrifying nearby historic neighborhoods such as Myers Park and Dilworth. These businesses specialized in supplying interior treatments and fixtures sought for architecturally and historically faithful renovation (see figure 24). This market was so robust that business spread effects extended beyond the mill site to encompass a one-and-one-half-mile-long, three- to five-block-wide stretch of the corridor. By 2000, thirty architectural and design firms established office space, showrooms, and studios that built on the momentum and vitality of the area and on the significance of its historic architecture. Their proximity within a relatively pedestrian-friendly setting was seen as an asset; the number of design-related firms mushroomed

Old Mills in a New Economy   131

Figure 24. Specialty retail shops focused on historic interiors and décor are key tenants in the Atherton Mill complex. (Source: Tyrel Moore.)

over the next five years to a total of 257.[38] Meanwhile, infill residential uses on the east side of the corridor added to the existing market.

The November 2007 opening of Charlotte's light rail system included an Atherton Mill transit station and a nearby New Bern stop as well as Charlotte Trolley stops. Despite its critics, the light rail has proven highly successful and is already running well ahead of projected ridership. The enhanced public access is another plus for the popular destination. Also new is the proposed five-story Chelsea at South End residential development. The $20 million project builds on South End's success and its modern design emulates the industrial architecture of the nearby Atherton Mill and that of warehouses in New York City's Chelsea neighborhood. Seventy-five residential units are planned to sit atop 8,000 square feet of retail and office space. Price points for the studio units are to range from the mid-$100,000s to the upper $300,000s. Pedestrian access to art galleries, restaurants, and nearby light rail transit stops influenced the developers' site selection.[39] The South End corridor's industrial heritage and its nineteenth-century sense of place have assumed a successful place in the city's twenty-first-century, postindus-

Figure 25. Highland Park No. 3 Mill's architecturally classic turret forms the centerpiece of the mill's new residential uses. (Source: Tyrel Moore.)

trial environment. In its transition, the emergence of the South End broke perceived barriers to redevelopment in ways that encouraged future projects elsewhere in Charlotte.

In North Charlotte, mill reuse also occurs along the gentrifying NoDa (North Davidson Street) corridor.[40] The earlier establishment of the NoDa Arts District and the gentrification of adjacent residential properties provided the impetus for redevelopment of the Highland Park No. 3 Mill. The mill fronted the Southern Railway and opened in 1903 as the predecessor of Charlotte's largest grouping of mills. Designed by Charlotte textile mill architect Stuart Cramer, its prominent multistory turret makes it Charlotte's most architecturally significant mill. It is on the National Register of Historic Places (see figure 25). When it closed in 1975 it was the city's last fully functioning textile mill. Two other mills just blocks away, the Johnston Mill and the Mecklenburg Cotton Mill, were added to the industrial complex in 1913. Over two hundred houses, the city's largest concentration of mill housing, were built in support of the three mills. The mill communities and their commercial focus at Thirty-sixth and Davidson streets defined North Charlotte.[41]

The decline of North Charlotte's industrial prominence was well underway in the 1970s and by the 1980s it stood as one of the city's blighted corridors. The mills' architectural assets were intact but their redevelopment potential was essentially relegated to warehouse space along the railroad tracks. More pressing concerns lay in the corridor's old mill communities. Belmont, Optimist Park, and Villa Heights all were identified as problem neighborhoods that the city attempted to address in a series of small area plans in the 1980s. Issues such as land use, housing, and quality of life subsequently were treated more comprehensively in the City Within a City Plans adopted by the city in 1993 and 1997. These plans recognized several barriers to redevelopment: underutilized parcels and retail that underserved the neighborhoods and attracted criminal activities, low rates of home ownership, and blight in century-old neighborhoods.[42]

Adaptive reuse of the Highland Park No. 3 Mill began in 2001 and proceeded deliberately, slowed at first by the collapse of the dot-com and e-commerce economy shortly after Atlanta-based Winter Properties launched the $25 million renovation for a proposed phase-one development of ninety loft apartments[43] and later by an unsuccessful attempt at mixed-income pricing. In a spatial sense, the site had little of the centrality that made the Atherton Mill a hub in the revitalization of a comparatively compact South End, nor the centrality enjoyed by Charlotte Cotton Mills, which stood in the shadows of the city's banking centers. The Highland Park project, marketed as NoDa Mills, has gained momentum with the sustained interest in the NoDa Arts District and the new $10 million phase two, which focused on preservation and reuse of the mill's tower. Striking views of the Charlotte skyline appear as major phase-two selling points on the project's website. The related retail conversion of the mill's 11,000-square-foot dye house also has attracted new retail tenants. Local firm Tuscan Development is converting the old bleachery to space for restaurants and entertainment.[44]

The Highland Park No. 3 Mill's redevelopment, and especially the growth of the NoDa Arts District, has renewed interest in nearby Johnston Mills at Davidson and 36th streets. Previous reuse attempts were truncated by management issues that later ended in bankruptcy for the Johnston Mill. That outcome left the City of Charlotte with nothing to show for a $6 million investment. The future of the mill seemed bleak when structurally damaging termite infestation closed the apartment complex housed in the old mill. Sadly, what began as a public sector effort to provide affordable housing ended in failure. The popularity of the NoDa area now affords a second chance for the Johnston and Mecklenburg mills' redevelopment, led this time by private sector initiatives from Tuscan Development.[45]

Figure 26. The Alpha Mill's award-winning turret restoration is a landmark of mill reuse that broke perceived redevelopment barriers beyond the I-277 Loop. The fence, which extends to a gated entry, addresses security concerns and is emblematic of gentrification on the old brownfield site. (Source: Tyrel Moore.)

The Alpha Mill represents the most recent example of spread effects that the renewal of the Center City has had on mill sites and their attractiveness as loft residences and condominiums (see figure 26).[46] The site had few, if any, advantages that favored redevelopment and accordingly faced the greatest barriers of any of Charlotte's historic mills. It was separated from the Center City by the I-277 Loop, which defined a hard boundary of the city's rough, blighted edges. Second, the I-277 Loop also formed a perceptual boundary that only discouraged redevelopment possibilities. Finally, the site was classified as a brownfield contaminated by industrial pollution from a textile engraving operation that operated from 1955, when textile production ceased, until 2001.[47]

Construction of the mill began at Brevard and 12th streets in 1888 by D. A. Tompkins and, with investments by other Charlotte businessmen, opened in 1889 to become Charlotte's second textile mill. It is registered on the National Register of Historic Places and is the only surviving mill among three that were built in the immediate area. Located at the northern edge of the city, each mill featured a related village.[48]

The initial interest in renovation of the Alpha Mill began in 2002 and increased with news of the proposed trolley line that would connect its loft apartments with uptown offices.[49] Although delayed by remediation of environmental problems, solutions to those issues made the site attractive for development. Successful remediation carries benefits including liability protection that passes to subsequent owners and a brownfields property tax incentive that greatly reduces property tax obligations for five years after completion of needed improvements to the property.[50] The local historic properties designation provided further preservation tax incentives that made the Alpha Mill Charlotte's only reuse project to bundle both pools of incentives for its redevelopment.[51]

The 127,000-square-foot facility went on the market for $2.3 million after the textile engraving business shut down in 2002. MECA Properties found a buyer in another local firm, commercial and residential developer John Crosland Company. Crosland restored the mill as part of a 167-unit apartment community with monthly rentals from $600 to $1,800. The $23 million project was almost immediately successful, boasting an occupancy rate of nearly 100 percent. Its proximity to Charlotte's Center City and striking views of the uptown skyline were major selling points. Seventy-three of the apartments are in the renovated mill and others are in new buildings in the gated complex. For Crosland, which formally opened the mill on the seventieth anniversary of their business, the project won the Real Estate Industry's 2007 Historic Restoration Award.[52]

Charlotte Observer associate editor Mary Newsome saw different reasons to celebrate Crosland's restoration of the mill. First, she called attention to the city's placing greater value on the preservation of its past. Second, she noted that Crosland's new urban ventures represented a transition from their long history of suburban commercial and residential subdivision development. And, she applauded Charlotte's willingness to save a piece of the past, a place where Charlotte seems never to have wanted to linger. In its quest for newness, Charlotte had successively erased the city's previous status as a gold-mining and coin-minting center, and later, a railroad hub and textile center. Finally, Newsome saw a broader meaning in the reuse of old mills: they remind us of past and present landscapes that still shape the city.[53]

The city, and especially its Center City, had been reshaped dramatically in its postindustrial transition to a new economy. Once largely vacant after business hours, by 2008 Charlotte's Center City population was estimated at 8,400 in Fourth Ward and historic South End areas alone. Although the vast majority of these residents lived in the roughly fifty condominium and apartment complexes built in these areas over the past decade and a half,[54] Charlotte Cotton Mills and Atherton Mill played significant roles in making their respective areas attractive for revitalization. As heritage landmarks, the old mills assumed emblematic places in Charlotte's transition toward becoming a global city.

Conclusions

The new places these old mills have found in a new economy bring several benefits: they have brought people back into landscapes previously neglected and bypassed for suburban residential development; they have removed blight by filling dormant or underutilized urban spaces along old industrial corridors; and they have promoted a sense of heritage drawn from a longer process of urbanization. Those benefits stem from the intersection of a number of steps taken by strong public–private sector partnerships. The city's role in assigning historic status to the old mills paid off doubly. First, the reduced property tax liability that came with historic landmark status improved mills' survival rates as they stood silent or as they endured transient uses after the decline of the city's textile era. Second, the federal and local tax incentives for adaptive reuse and restoration reduced risk and improved investment support of developers' initiatives. Armed with those advantages, mill reuse permitted the revitalization of historic corridors and neighborhoods well beyond the footprint of their sites.

The final piece in the reuse process was the presence of a market. In that crucial area, Charlotte's ascendancy as a global financial center played a prominent role in the city's growth — especially growth that attracted working professionals who saw the unique possibilities of working and living in places with century-old exposed brick walls, pine heart beams, and pine, maple, and walnut flooring. A new central city middle class of professionals and gentrifiers, not unlike the nineteenth-century mill workers, formed the population of Charlotte's new neighborhoods built around the once and present cotton mills.

Woodward saw textile mills as symbols of an industrial New South; the reuse of some of those same mills is emblematic of Charlotte's global evolution as a New South city. The mills and their later reuse built tangible bridges from Charlotte's industrial past to its emergence in a global postindustrial economy. Perhaps one hallmark of truly global cities is their ability to embrace vestiges of past geographies and knit them into the cityscapes of their new and future geographies. Charlotte's old mills, vibrant once again, nicely illustrate the city's global coming of age.

Notes

1. William Hudnut III, "Promoting Reuse," *Urban Land* 58 no. 11/12 (1999): 69–75; Richard Moe and Carter Wilkie, *Changing Places: Rebuilding Community in the Age of Sprawl* (Boston: Henry Holt, 1997); David Salvesen, "A Catalyst for Development," *Urban Land* 58, no. 11/12 (1999): 77–81; John Vallani, "Saving the Past," *Urban Land* 58, no. 11/12 (1999): 111–15.

2. Thomas Hanchett, *Sorting Out the New South City: Race, Class, and Urban Development in Charlotte, 1875–1975* (Chapel Hill: University of North Carolina Press, 1998).

3. C. Vann Woodward, *Origins of the New South, 1877–1913* (Baton Rouge: Louisiana State University Press, 1951), 151.

4. Richard Florida, *The Rise of the Creative Class: And How It's Transforming Work, Leisure, and Everyday Life* (New York: Basic Books, 2002).

5. Woodward, *Origins of the New South*, 151.

6. Ben Lemert, *The Cotton Textile Industry of the Southern Appalachian Piedmont* (Chapel Hill: The University of North Carolina Press, 1933), 138, table 63.

7. Wade Harris, *Sketches of Charlotte: North Carolina's Finest city and the Recognized Cotton Milling Centre of the Southern States* (Charlotte: W. H. Harris, 1904), 22.

8. Hanchett, *Sorting Out the New South City*.

9. Woodward, *Origins of the New South*, 137; Hanchett, *Sorting Out the New South City*, 2, table 1.

10. Gerald Ingalls and Tyrel Moore, "Old But New: An Inventory of Textile Mill Reuse in the Charlotte Urban Region," *Southeastern Geographer* 41, no. 1 (2001): 74–88.

11. Tony Pressley, personal communication with Gerald Ingalls, May 2000.

12. Dan Morrill, Charlotte Mecklenburg Historic Properties, 1997. Available at (www.cmhpf.org/surveydesignationlist.htm).

13. Charles Lunan et al., "Despair in Mill Town: 1st in a Year-long Series," *Charlotte Observer*, February 24, 2002, 1A.

14. Norman Glickman and Amy Glasmeier, "The International Economy and the American South," in *Deindustrialization and Regional Economic Transformation: The Experience of the United States*, ed. Lloyd Rodwin and Hidehiko Sazanami (Boston: Unwin Hyman, 1989), 60–80.

15. Ken Morstisgugu, "Where Looms Have Ceased: Once Vital Textile Mills

in Carolinas Are Dying a Slow Death as Slumping Economy, Layoffs Fuel Their Decline," *Charlotte Observer*, September 17, 2001, 1D; John Poretto, "Tiny Town Frets over Loss of Textile Mill," *Charlotte Observer*, February 3, 2002, 1E; Lunan et al., "Despair in Mill Town"; Sharon White, "Future Is Uncertain for Vacant Factories," *Charlotte Observer*, March 31, 2002, 4B; >; Charles Lunan, "Empty Mills Burden Carolinas," *Charlotte Observer*, July 22, 2002, 1A; Ronnie Glassberg, "Kannapolis Image as 'Dying Mill Town' Hurts," *Charlotte Observer*, September 11, 2003, 1K; and Adam Bell, "Pillowtex Folds; 7,650 Go Jobless," *Charlotte Observer*, July 31, 2003, 1A.

16. John Jakle and David Wilson, *Derelict Landscapes: The Wasting of America's Built Environment*, (Savage, Md.: Rowman and Littlefield, 1992).

17. Charles Lunan, "Empty Mills Burden Carolinas," *Charlotte Observer*, July 22, 2002, 1A.

18. Doug Smith, "Will Old Mill's Condos Sell in Rural Area?" *Charlotte Observer*, October 1, 2002, 1D.

19. Charles Lunan, "Textile Heritage Stripped Away: Signature Buildings Being Harvested for Coveted Heart Pine, "*Charlotte Observer*, July 21, 2002, 1A.

20. Heather Smith and William Graves, "The Corporate (Re)construction of a New South City: Great Banks Need Great Cities," *Southeastern Geographer* 43, no. 2 (2003): 213–34.

21. David Ley, *The New Middle Class and the Remaking of the Central City* (Oxford: Oxford University Press), 1996.

22. Jason Hackworth, "Post Recession Gentrification in New York City," *Urban Affairs Review*, 2002, 815–43; Paul Knox and Linda McCarthy, *Urbanization: An Introduction to Urban Geography*, 2nd ed. (Upper Saddle River, N.J.: Pearson Prentice Hall), 2005.

23. Smith and Graves, "The Corporate (Re)construction of a New South City."

24. City of Charlotte, Mecklenburg County, and Charlotte Center City Partners, *Center City 2010 Vision Plan*, 2000.

25. Richard Florida, "The Economic Geography of Talent," *Annals of the Association of American Geographers* 92 (2002): 743.

26. Hanchett, *Sorting Out the New South City*.

27. Sanborn Fire Insurance Company, *Insurance Maps of Charlotte, North Carolina* (New York: Sanborn Perris Company, 1896); Sanborn Fire Insurance Company, *Insurance Maps of Charlotte, North Carolina* (New York: Sanborn Perris, 1929).

28. Doug Smith, "Architecture Firm Moving to Atypical Office Space Uptown: Historical Significance, Dramatic Features Make Cotton Mills Appealing," *Charlotte Observer*, June 2, 2004, 1E.

29. Smith and Graves, "The Corporate (Re)construction of a New South City."

30. Smith, "Architecture Firm Moving."

31. Doug Smith, "Beer-Can Bar to Pop Tops Uptown," *Charlotte Observer*, September 29, 2005, 1D.

32. City of Charlotte, Center City Partners, "Uptown Housing Summary," 2007.

33. David Salvesen, "A Catalyst for Development," *Urban Land* 58, no. 11/12 (1999): 77–81.

34. Hanchett, *Sorting Out the New South City*; Dan Morrill, Charlotte Mecklenburg Historic Properties, 1997 Available at (www.cmhpf.org/surveydesignationlist.htm).

35. Dorothy Waterfill and Karen Doyle, *Historic South End: Charlotte's South End; The Early Years* (Charlotte: South End Development Corporation, 1999).

36. City of Charlotte, Center City Partners, "Uptown Housing Summary," 2007.

37. Waterfill and Doyle, *Historic South End*.

38. Doug Smith, "Design District Thrives in South End: Convenient Location, Historic Architecture Have Helped Bring Businesses to Charlotte," *Charlotte Observer*, September 15, 2005, 8D.

39. Doug Smith, "Light Rail, Uptown Skyline Attract 2 New Projects," *Charlotte Observer*, November 7, 2007, 4D.

40. Doug Smith, "Big Redevelopment Project on North Davidson Has its 1st 30 Renters," *Charlotte Observer*, November 28, 2004, 1D; Doug Smith, "Phase 2 of Urban Village Nearly Aloft," *Charlotte Observer*, March 31, 2005, 1D.

41. Hanchett, *Sorting Out the New South City*.

42. The City of Charlotte's Charlotte-Mecklenburg Planning Commission developed five neighborhood plans in the 1980s and 1990s: *Optimist Park Special Project Plan* (1983), *Belmont Special Project Plan* (1987), *Villa Heights Special Project Plan* (1991), *Central District Plan* (1993), and *City Within a City Neighborhood Assessment* (1997).

43. Doug Smith, "Big Redevelopment Project on North Davidson."

44. Doug Smith, "Keeping Arts, Music in NoDa," *Charlotte Observer*, October 10, 2007, D4.

45. Karen Cimino, "New Life for NoDa Hulks: Timely Move Forward on Mecklenburg/Johnston Mills," *Charlotte Observer*, November 19, 2007, 14A.

46. Mary Newsome, "Past and Future: 21st Century May Bring New Life to 19th Century Mill," *Charlotte Observer*, February 16, 2002, 18A; Doug Smith, "Historic Mill Becomes Restoration Prospect: Building Near End of Proposed Trolley Line Goes on the Market," *Charlotte Observer*, October 29, 2002, 1D; and Doug Smith, "Restored Mill's Opening Marks Crosland 70th," *Charlotte Observer*, June 14, 2007, 1D.

47. Doug Smith, "Phase 2 of Urban Village Nearly Aloft," *Charlotte Observer*, March 31, 2005, 1D; and Hart and Hickman, "Brownfield Projects," 2008, www.harthickman.com/brownfieldprojects.html.

48. Hanchett, *Sorting Out the New South City*.

49. Newsome, "Past and Future"; Smith, "Historic Mill Becomes Restoration Prospect".

50. North Carolina Department of Environmental and Natural Resources, Division of Waste Management, Brownfields Program 2008, www.ncbrownfields.org/program_faq.asp#6.

51. Smith, "Restored Mill's Opening Marks Crosland 70th."

52. Smith, "Restored Mill's Opening Marks Crosland 70th."

53. Mary Newsome, "Wannabe City Celebrates its Authentic Self; Once Hidden Creek is Uncovered, and Old Mill is Reborn, Not Destroyed," *Charlotte Observer*, June 16, 2007, 17A.

54. City of Charlotte, Center City Partners, "2008 Population Estimates."

Heather A. Smith and
Emily Thomas Livingstone

Banking on the Neighborhood
Corporate Citizenship and Revitalization
in Uptown Charlotte

The good private or corporate citizen is imbued with [a] sense of charity—[a] sense of improving life for others while at the same time improving life for oneself."[1] Corporate citizenship comes in many forms. Frequently it offers a way in which businesses and their leadership can "give back" to the community "in which they reside or maintain offices" and do so in a manner that enhances their own interests and image.[2] In the context of contemporary globalization, the scope and breadth of corporate citizenship reflects the multinational scale at which many corporations now work. Corporate citizenship may also influence the character and fortune of the cities in which businesses are headquartered. A symbiotic relationship can exist between a corporation and its hometown or headquarters community, particularly if a company has been a constant and active presence for a significant number of years. A corporation's loyalty to its community and vice versa can create an entrenched dynamic that helps define the essence of a city and shape its built environment. Furthermore, such a dynamic can manifest itself in specific revitalization initiatives grounded in corporate commitment to local place but contextualized by global ambition.

This chapter explores the process of neighborhood revitalization through the lens of corporate citizenship and focuses on the experience of Charlotte's Fourth Ward as an illustration of how corporate-led, neighborhood-based revitalization successfully achieved the goals of "improving life for others while at the same time improving life for oneself." Drawing from a range of local and census-derived data, archival resources, and key informant interviews, we tell the story of how, beginning in the early 1970s, North Carolina National Bank (NCNB) provided conceptual and financial leadership to a process of gentrification in the blighted Fourth Ward. The transformation of the ward into a vibrant, center-city neighborhood provided an initiating mechanism through which the bank provided sustained leadership to a range of public-private partnerships that facilitated not only the ward's revitalization but eventually that of the entire Center City. Gentrification of the historic Fourth Ward ensured the existence of an upwardly mobile, pedestrian-scale neighborhood in close proximity to corporate headquarters. Such aesthetic, economic, and geographic characteristics were viewed as essential to attracting globally competitive financial service workers to the city and to the employment rolls of the ascendant corporations headquartered there.

We begin the chapter with a discussion of the evolution of corporate citizenship and public-private partnership in American cities, then document and assess the specific case of revitalization in Charlotte's Fourth Ward. Our discussion focuses on how the visionary leadership and corporate citizenship of NCNB (now Bank of America) initiated a process of neighborhood-based revitalization that became the first piece in the overall redefinition and restructuring of Charlotte's Center City. We also highlight the way in which Charlotte's case is perhaps unique, given the ambitions of the bank and their tangible expression in the process of revitalization.

The Evolution of Corporate Citizenship: From Check Writing to Direct Engagement

Corporate citizenship expressed as engagement with local communities has a long history and has undergone several shifts of focus and application. Up until the mid-1950s, corporate engagement with communities primarily took the form of "corporate giving [which] was legally limited to donations that could be justified as being closely related to stockholders' interests."[3] In 1954, however, a New Jersey State Supreme Court ruling allowed corporations "to make contributions to charitable recipients without regard to any strict relation to stockholders' interests."[4] As a consequence, corporations were freer to identify avenues of contribution that were purely philanthropic as well as those that would profitably serve the companies' interests. In the 1960s, "under pressure to demonstrate their social responsibility," many American companies established charitable foundations that operated somewhat independently from the company.[5] Frequently, a strategic distance existed between the corporation and the business' namesake foundation. Corporate engagement with the community through the foundation was tantamount to check writing for worthy and high-profile causes.

By the 1970s there was growing recognition that corporations could or should have a dual purpose — "to be economically successful and to be socially responsible."[6] Throughout the subsequent decades of economic and public sector restructuring, many firms continued to embrace this dual purpose. Such companies manifested corporate citizenship through philanthropic endeavors as well as through a broadening range of community partnerships. They also became more engaged in the financial and strategic leadership of initiatives addressing social problems and became more directly involved in supporting community development.[7] As Craig Smith explains in his article "The New Corporate Philanthropy,"

> In addition to cash, [corporations] are providing nonprofits with managerial advice, technological and communications support, and teams of employee volunteers. And they are funding those initiatives not only from philanthropy budgets but also from business units . . . In the process, companies are forming strategic alliances . . . [and becoming] corporate citizens . . . cultivat[ing] a broad view of their own self-interest while instinctively searching for ways to align self-interest with the larger good.[8]

One element of this alignment comes in the form of improving the community context in which a company is based or has a significant business presence. As Porter and Kramer explain,

> corporations can use their charitable efforts to improve their competitive context — the quality of the business environment in the location . . . where they operate. Using philanthropy to enhance context brings social and economic goals into alignment and improves a company's long-term business prospects.[9]

This community-focused, spatially based model of corporate citizenship has been utilized in different forms by several corporations and across many U.S. cities. The Atlanta Project (TAP), for example, was founded in October 1991 by former President Jimmy Carter. TAP was a "five-year effort to confront the issues of urban poverty" through the combination of community empowerment, volunteerism, and public, private, and nonprofit collaboration.[10] Fragile neighborhoods were partnered with major Atlanta-based corporations such as Delta Airlines, IBM, Equifax, Bell South, Coca-Cola, Atlanta GasLight, NationsBank, Arthur Andersen Consulting, and Turner

Broadcasting. These companies provided partnered communities with pro bono executive expertise, targeted program development (loans for minority-owned business development, personal finance seminars), and resource provision (technology centers in local classrooms).[11]

More recently (in 2000), FleetBoston Financial initiated its Community Renaissance Initiative (CRI). Through CRI, FleetBoston combined philanthropic monetary contributions with its industry expertise in venture capital, mortgages, and small business lending to stimulate economic development, home ownership, and job creation. CRI focused efforts in six cities representing core markets for the company. Across impoverished communities in Brooklyn and Buffalo, New York; New Haven, Connecticut; Lawrence, Massachusetts; and Camden and Jersey City, New Jersey, CRI successfully leveraged over $10 million in private, public, and in-kind resources that helped support neighborhood, government, and business partnerships that collaboratively developed community revitalization interventions and programs.[12]

In the case of Hallmark Cards in Kansas City, Missouri, we see an example of a single company drawn to involvement in downtown redevelopment as a means to "protect their headquarters location."[13] As described in the fact sheet for Crown Center, the catalyst development for Kansas City's center city revitalization,

> In the early 1960s, the Halls [Hallmark's founders] looked out over the area surrounding their company's Kansas City headquarters and did not like what they saw: rutted parking lots, abandoned warehouses, the sorry remains of failed or failing Kansas City's Crown Center — 2 businesses, and a limestone hill cluttered with signs and tarpaper shacks. They believed the industry leader in personal expression deserved a better setting for its home — and that the city which had given much to them deserved better than the blighted landscape stretched before them. They had two choices: follow the stream of businesses fleeing the city for the suburbs; or stay and make the city environment better. They chose to stay.[14]

The impetus for Hallmark's corporate leadership was a form of "enlightened self-interest"[15] that recognized

> a parallel interest between business and communities because they have the same goals — low crime, higher property values, educated population, improved physical conditions ... both benefit from reaching those goals ... what is good for the community is also good for business.[16]

This enlightened self-interest initially gave rise to the development of the Crown Center Redevelopment Corporation — a wholly owned Hallmark subsidiary whose raison d'être was to alleviate blight and oversee the development of a mixed-use complex with housing, retail shops, hotels, and cultural venues. The aim was to attract and retain a sufficient number of middle-class residents and consumers to ensure continued vitality and economic growth in downtown Kansas City. Crown Center has continued to act as a catalyst and anchor for further revitalization initiatives. Hallmark has also continued to exercise community-focused corporate citizenship through property acquisition, financial lending, and support of low- to moderate-income housing in the communities surrounding its headquarters.[17]

As critical as corporate leadership may be in selected processes of central city revitalization, private sector "citizens" rarely act alone. Indeed, partnership or collaboration between a corporation, the constituency being served, and local government agencies is often *the* mechanism through which tangible change in urban communities is implemented.

Corporate Citizenship and Public-Private Partnerships

The merging of different private and public sector groups to rally around urban revitalization or redevelopment is not a new phenomenon. As Davis points out in his work, the look and trajectory of economic and physical growth of early twentieth-century Chicago was a consequence of the collaboration between a group of the city's most prominent business leaders and the work of architect and planner Daniel Burnham.[18] Similarly, in Pittsburgh in 1943 one of the country's most successful and long-lasting public-private partnerships, the Allegheny Conference, was formed. This partnership addressed the city's needs ranging from urban blight to industrial air pollution and flooding, from postwar economic shifts to new road development.[19] The Allegheny Conference brought city government officials together with the heads of major local corporations, academic scholars, and community members to leverage resources, institutional expertise, and leadership. This approach was so successful it became embedded in the city's long-term "problem-solving framework" and "came to permeate the local civic culture."[20] Even today, the Allegheny Conference occupies "a position at the heart of Pittsburgh's civic activity. As initiator, broker, supporter, monitor or facilitator, it touches nearly every major civic or development undertaking in the city."[21]

By the late 1970s, public-private partnerships were being considered as an explicit federal-level policy tool to address urban challenges and "advance specific economic development and downtown redevelopment and revitalization projects in which business was perceived to have an essential interest."[22] In the context of severe economic crisis and urban decline, the federal government began to look at ways to tap into private resources and corporate leadership to help address some of America's most pressing urban problems. The partnerships formed in places like Pittsburgh, Kansas City, and, as we will see, Charlotte made it clear that "business [could] play other roles besides creating wealth. They [could] widen economic opportunity and participation, invest in human capital, promote environmental sustainability, and enhance social cohesion."[23] Additionally, the private sector could supply "entrepreneurial zeal and skill" as well as resources and organizational expertise to significantly advance the cause and clout of a partnership.[24] It was also recognized that corporate involvement in a public-private partnership tended to be particularly effective — and enduring — when the partnership was dedicated to urban revitalization in a corporation's hometown.

While many public-private partnerships form due to an inclination toward social responsibility, they do not necessarily arise out of the sheer altruism of their business partners. As noted earlier, even corporate philanthropy is viewed as a form of enlightened self-interest in which life is improved for others while at the same time also improved for oneself. This, of course, does not negate the tangible and intangible contributions that corporations make to private-public partnerships and the initiatives they undertake. It does, however, encourage scrutiny of the motivations that give rise to corporate citizenship and the development of public-private partnerships that have been at the core of many revitalized American downtowns.

Linking Corporate Prosperity to a Vibrant Urban Environment

The balance of this chapter explores the case of Charlotte and the corporate-led revitalization of a historic neighborhood adjacent to NCNB/Bank of America corporate headquarters. In many ways, the story of Fourth Ward and the bank's leadership in the neighborhood's renaissance parallels the story of Hallmark in Kansas City. In both cases, the businesses were aware that the "corporation's headquarters [could] be jeopardized by deteriorating surrounding neighborhoods."[25] Beyond this, both cases highlight the importance of public-private partnerships and corporate citizenship as manifested in "special ties between the compan[y] and communit[y]."[26] In Hallmark's case the company's founder stated that "the atmosphere of Kansas City was in part responsible for the company's success and that made giving something back to the city a personal and corporate mission."[27] Hugh McColl, former CEO of NCNB/Bank of America who led the corporate charge in revitalizing Charlotte's Center City, echoed this sentiment: "I'd like to see the city reinvent itself. [Bank of America] does have an interest in making this the most exciting inner city in the U.S. That is my personal goal. That is our corporation's goal."[28] There is, however, a key difference between the two cases. While Hallmark's commitment to urban revitalization in Kansas City appears to come from a place of reciprocity and social responsibility, in Charlotte, NCNB's initiation and leadership of revitalization flows more from corporate ambition and a recognition that the health and image of the headquarters community was (and remains) central to achieving its expansionary goals.

Banking on the Neighborhood: Citizenship, Partnership, and Revitalization

In telling the story of how NCNB banked on the revitalization of a single neighborhood to kick-start the broader redevelopment of Charlotte's Center City in a way that aligned with the company's corporate goals, we begin with the city's early political geography. In 1869, to ensure fair political representation among city residents, Charlotte's urban core was divided into four wards. Through to the first half of the twentieth century, these wards were characterized by both established residential neighborhoods and thriving commercial corridors that were increasingly populated by burgeoning local banking institutions. In the latter half of the twentieth century, however, Charlotte's urban landscape experienced significant reorganization due to the top-down, federally funded Urban Renewal plan and the city's full embrace of suburbanization.[29]

By the 1970s, both First Ward and Second Ward had been directly impacted by the policy and process of federally sanctioned Urban Renewal. In Second Ward starting in 1960, the independent and once prosperous African American neighborhood called Brooklyn was erased from existence in a multiphased razing, only to become the city's government district, as it remains today. Shortly thereafter, the prominent African American heart of First Ward was also razed and replaced in 1967 with the Earle Village public housing project. The project itself was eventually torn down in 1997 to make way for HOPE VI redevelopment. Third Ward, the Center City's more industrial area, was largely left alone by urban renewal efforts. So by the early 1970s, processes of urban transition and renewal had left the only true opportunity for urban revitalization in the northwestern quadrant of the urban core, in Fourth Ward.

From approximately the 1880s to the 1940s, Fourth Ward was Charlotte's premier residential address. It was a predominantly white neighborhood where many of the city's elite professionals and political leaders lived. Charlotte's society tastemakers set social standards on the porches of Fourth Ward's grand Victorian homes. By the 1950s and 1960s, the trends of automobile infatuation (and later, dependency) and suburbanization rolled across Charlotte. Fourth Ward slipped into dereliction. Many of the once stately, ornately adorned homes were either torn down, converted to commercial or institutional use, divided into multiunit rental apartments, or left to decay. In addition to the neglected built environment, Fourth Ward became widely considered as dangerous and known as a hotspot for drugs, prostitution, crime, and vagrancy. It was also the neighborhood most closely adjacent to NCNB headquarters.

Although NCNB was undoubtedly the key corporate citizen in Fourth Ward's revitalization, it is important to acknowledge that initial efforts to address dereliction of the neighborhood flowed from preservation-oriented citizen groups (Citizens for Preservation, Friends of Fourth Ward, and the Charlotte Junior League) and the Charlotte-Mecklenburg Planning Commission. Between about 1972 and early 1975, these groups focused on how best to save and restore the remaining Victorian-era housing stock. They advocated for the redevelopment of the neighborhood in a less destructive, more creative way than the urban renewal paradigm that had reshaped the character and fortunes of First and Second wards.

The scope and pace of revitalization in Fourth Ward expanded when key members of Charlotte's Center City business community — most notably members of the executive leadership of NCNB — realized that revitalizing this neighborhood was the "key to survival of the city's central business district"[30] (see figure 27). Initially the bank was tentative about declaring the extent of its involvement in and commitment to a preservation and revitalization plan. When asked by the media about NCNB's involvement in the initiative, Joe Martin, then director of public policy for NCNB, said, "we support it but we are not behind it . . . we've provided advice and handholding, but of course that's essentially the same service we would afford any customer or potential customer."[31] Later that same year, it was clear that

Figure 27. Uptown Charlotte in the mid-1970s. (Source: J. Dennis Rash.)

NCNB was not only supporting the initiative but stepping fully into a role of collaborative corporate leadership.

In the early to mid-1970s, NCNB was gaining momentum as a national banking leader and positioning itself for greater representation in selected global markets (before stepping into the role of CEO, Hugh McColl had led the bank's national and international lending division). This trajectory was impinged in part because of the bank's headquarters location in Charlotte, whose provincial, suburban, automobile-dependent image was a hindrance to the bank's hiring of professional talent from other, more cosmopolitan, amenity-rich cities such as New York, San Francisco, and London. Explained former NCNB executive J. Dennis Rash, "we were bringing people in from London who didn't know how to drive" and the fact that there were no suitable neighborhoods for relocated professionals within walking distance of the office was problematic. People hired from the money markets, he explained, "needed to feel like they were in a headquarter city."[32] In order to attract and retain the human capital necessary to achieve their corporate goals, NCNB executives realized that revitalizing both the reality and the image of Charlotte's Center City was imperative. They additionally realized that the historic preservation efforts already underway in Fourth Ward provided an ideal springboard from which to launch that revitalization. With proper oversight and support, Fourth Ward could become a vibrant, upwardly mobile, residential neighborhood. Such a community in walking distance to bank headquarters could offer the geographic, financial, and aesthetic characteristics viewed as necessary to attracting globally competitive financial service workers to the city and to the employment rolls of the ascendant corporation(s) headquartered there.

The public-private partnership that evolved to revitalize Fourth Ward was described as

> a curious mixture of the Junior League, people interested in living there, people who attend churches in the area, people in the human service and delivery components, city-county planning staffs, bankers ... People ... beginning to realize that urban renewal is just too damn complex for anyone to do by themselves.[33]

In early summer 1975, NCNB's leadership of the corporate elements of the partnership was highlighted in a *Charlotte Observer* editorial:

> NCNB is helping plan financing for the renovations; other banks are expecting to join in. Private developers and uptown businessmen, mindful of what 2,500 people in Fourth Ward would mean, are cooperating ... the progress of the project suggests that government, business leaders and ordinary citizens with a good idea may be able to work together to make the idea become reality.[34]

By early 1976, following NCNB's lead, six additional local banks — City National, First Citizens, First Union National, Northwestern, Southern National, and Wachovia — each loaned $100,000 to the city. The money was used "to make low-interest loans to people who want[ed] to buy and renovate old houses in Fourth Ward."[35] When this low-interest loan money — coordinated by NCNB — became available, dedicated Fourth Ward proponents and their families borrowed for mortgages and renovations and moved into the deteriorating neighborhood — either to an existing dilapidated Victorian or to one transplanted via flatbed truck from another part of Charlotte, the county, or region (see figure 28). In parallel, the city in conjunction with local utility companies such as Duke Power agreed to underwrite infrastructure improvements (brick sidewalks, granite curbs, decorative lighting, landscaping, and underground power cables); the Planning Commission developed a plan for urban residential living in Fourth Ward; and the neighborhood gained sanctioned Historic District status.

For the population that the bank and partnership sought to attract to

Figure 28. Moving Victorian-era housing stock into the Fourth Ward. (Source: J. Dennis Rash.)

Fourth Ward, this historic designation was significant. It further contributed to an image of distinction essential to making the ward desirable for upwardly mobile and status-conscious financial service workers coming from both within and beyond Charlotte. Additionally, it provided a mechanism through which the historic character of the community and personal revitalization efforts could be guided and neighborhood stability guaranteed. Individuals who agreed to live in Fourth Ward (not speculate or rent out) and work to renovate its historic housing stock and community character were given priority access to the below-market-rate mortgages and rehabilitation loans administered by NCNB.[36] The allure of Fourth Ward was clear. When the original $700,000 ran out in 1976, the partnering banks came up with an additional $800,000 to replenish the fund so that the neighborhood renaissance could continue.

It is important to recognize that although Fourth Ward may have been a largely derelict and crime-ridden community, it was a community nonetheless, even before revitalization efforts began. Newspaper coverage of the process as it began occasionally captured the realities of class- and race-based disparity and displacement that typically accompany neighborhood-based revitalization. In reference to the low-income loan program, one about-to-be-evicted Fourth Ward resident was quoted as saying "none of the renting residents has enough income to qualify for the loans." Another observed, "when the white people were here, they wanted to move to Myers Park. Now, they want to come back to Fourth Ward. This is our home. Why don't they fix it up for us? We're the ones that's been living here all the time."[37] And then there were stories of interactions between incoming and outgoing residents:

> When [the incoming home owners] found the sagging, rat-infested house early this year, more than 20 people called it home crowded into poorly furnished one-room efficiencies with haphazard heat and inadequate plumbing. The two made their commitment to restoration, then set about finding adequate housing for the occupants and sharing their moving problems. They paid the first month's rent for at least one.[38]

The kind of support these "revitalizers" offered to the previous residents of their property was not uncommon in Fourth Ward, leading some observers to comment that the process of revitalization here was "kinder," "more humanitarian" than experienced elsewhere.[39] In keeping with this sentiment, J. Dennis Rash, by now a Fourth Ward resident and Friends of Fourth member, emphasized, "From the outset ... the Friends of Fourth Ward worried about getting — or deserving — a reputation for displacing people ... our objective from day one was to build a multi-racial, multi-income level neighborhood base."[40]

In 1978, the scope of Fourth Ward's revitalization expanded markedly when NCNB, under the leadership of Hugh McColl, announced the creation of a nonprofit subsidiary called the Community Development Corporation — the first of its kind in the United States. The formation of the CDC was authorized through an interpretive ruling by U.S. Comptroller of the Currency John Heimann and was praised as an exemplary way to model President Carter's urban policy goal of forming public-private partnerships to help ameliorate inner-city blight. One objective of the NCNB CDC was "to assist in revitalizing inner-city residential neighborhoods."[41] Charlotte's Fourth Ward was the initial focus of efforts so that it could continue to thrive "as the anchor for growing [overall] prosperity downtown."[42] A second objective was "to demonstrate to other developers and lenders that investment in the district [Fourth Ward] could be profitable and that young, middle-income professionals and their families could be attracted to an inner-city neighborhood"[43] The intersection between this goal and the tenets of corporate citizenship are apparent in the words of Hugh McColl:

> We believe the Fourth Ward represents an unusual opportunity to restore a neighborhood that affects the quality of life for our whole community...

initial efforts will focus mainly on developing middle-income housing to generate money for future projects for low- and moderate-income families ... We believe that developing housing units for middle-income people ... will attract private investment in neighborhood shopping and amenities for central city residents of all income levels.[44]

Media coverage and marketing of the initiative was careful to point out that even though the NCNB CDC would "acquire, develop, and manage property in Fourth Ward and perhaps other inner city areas ... NCNB [wouldn't] profit directly from it. But the bank profits, as the city does, from promoting private investment in the center city."[45] This emphasis on the fact that the bank wouldn't profit in conventional terms from its leadership and administration of the CDC is significant. By statute, the CDC had to retain any profits within the subsidiary to be redirected back into other community revitalization initiatives. Knowing this requires us to look beyond capital profit to understand NCNB's interest and motivation in taking leadership of Fourth Ward's revitalization.[46]

From "Grits and Stock Cars" to "Wall Street of the South"

At first glance, there is the expected indirect "profit" that flowed from the "public perception of the [bank's] civic-mindedness." As NCNB's then director of public policy further explains, "if the cooperation [facilitated by the CDC] can strengthen the economy of the inner city, obviously that makes a better climate to do business in, so that's good for us."[47]

But there was also something more intangible — the value of shifting the city's character and identity. Charlotte, previously seen as a place of "grits and stock cars"[48] was now developing an image more in keeping with the bank's ambition to become "Wall Street of the South."[49] As Smith and Graves explain,

> The bank's motivation in the Charlotte case requires a rethinking about traditional definitions of profit. Here "profit" derives not from the monetary gains made through rent-gap facilitated local real estate investment, but rather from the less tangible benefits of the bank's enhanced ability to compete in the "global" marketplace for human capital. Profit derives from the competitive, but image based, advantages gained through central city revitalization. When asked to illustrate the bank's motivational prioritization of image over profit, a former bank executive cited the small size of capital profit derived from the entire central city's revitalization

relative to the bank's total annual revenue... The profit generated from investments in Fourth Ward were so small in fact that they could be considered "rounding errors."[50]

Charlotte then, illustrates an unusual case of corporate citizenship and urban revitalization. NCNB's leadership in the private-public partnership that facilitated Fourth Ward's transformation took on a complex, perhaps more "enlightened" and forward-thinking tone than other examples detailed in the literature. Through its direct involvement in the revitalization of a derelict and decaying center city neighborhood and in the creation of a model CDC that encouraged and facilitated upgrading in neighborhoods in other U.S. cities, NCNB was able to significantly enhance its position as a bank in ascendance. It was not simply a case of the bank revitalizing Fourth Ward because it was doing the right thing philanthropically, protecting headquarters, or demonstrating awareness that "the atmosphere of [the city] was in part responsible for the company's success."[51] It was also a case of the bank creating a particular type of urban space that could help reshape the city's overall image in a manner that aligned with corporate business goals. In the words of Hugh McColl, "You can't have a great bank without a great city."[52]

The creation of a vibrant historic neighborhood within walking distance of NCNB headquarters was one of the mechanisms through which the bank was able to attract and retain the human capital necessary to achieve its desired status in the financial services sector (see figure 29). It is not unimportant that the successful revitalization of Fourth Ward was also the catalyst for the eventual wholesale revitalization and redevelopment of all four of Charlotte's central city wards—an additional boon to the city's globalizing image.[53] The revitalization of Charlotte's Fourth Ward, then, is a clear case of corporate citizenship and enlightened self-interest in which NCNB achieved the goal of "improving life for others while at the same time improving life for oneself."

Conclusion

The "alchemy that generates public-private partnerships" and associated revitalization "works differently in every city," but the key to success is often visionary leadership—something "that does not appear to be readily manufacturable or transferable."[54] It is impossible to overstate the importance of NCNB and its executive leadership team in the transformation of Charlotte's Center City. As one commentator explains, "NCNB has been able to influ-

Figure 29. Revitalized houses and streetscape in Fourth Ward with Hearst Tower and Bank of America's headquarters tower in the background. (Source: William Graves.)

ence the direction and personality of [Charlotte's] growth, working steadily to make it more cosmopolitan, more like London and less like, well, Charlotte."[55] The extent to which this image of Charlotte as a globally ascendant city is permanent or fleeting remains to be seen. Continued economic restructuring and the transitioning of political and societal realities may well translate into a waning of corporate influence in the arena of urban revitalization and redevelopment:

> shifting economic forces have diminished the capacity of ... CEO-led organizations, potentially stripping cities of a significant advocate. Mergers and acquisitions have reduced the number of home-grown CEOs, with their personal commitment to their hometown. The loss of major banks following deregulation has affected both financial contributions to civic

causes and leadership in the corporate community. CEOs today also have less autonomy than in the past in their ability to commit resources ... [this corporate disengagement] comes at a time of growing reliance on the private sector to solve urban problems as federal aid to cities is curtailed, leaving many cities with limited means to undertake major initiatives.[56]

This is particularly salient in the case of Charlotte banks who in the context of the recent economic crisis have seen major changes in the ownership, leadership, and structure of their corporations. Charlotte is a city for which the presence and leadership of upwardly mobile banks and other key corporate entities remains a fundamental component of its identity and psyche. That Wachovia has been purchased by San Francisco–based Wells Fargo and that Bank of America's purchase of Merrill Lynch might destabilize its position as an industry leader is unsettling. Despite these and other changes, however, we can still discern the enduring legacy of NCNB's specific brand of urban-focused corporate citizenship. There continues in Charlotte an unwavering expectation that corporations headquartered or centrally located here *should* play a leading and highly visible role in city growth and development dynamics. This was most recently evidenced in the language used by Duke Power's CEO Jim Rogers in reference to his company's 2009 decision to relocate its corporate headquarters to the forty-eight-story Wachovia Tower still under construction, but now under the ownership of Wells Fargo. "We thought it was a good time to demonstrate our commitment to uptown ... this is an important time to demonstrate some positive achievements with respect to the future of the city."[57] The extent to which Charlotte will be able to retain its hard-won and carefully crafted image as the globally ascendant Wall Street of the South may well rest on the extent to which other locally based CEOs adhere to the unique brand of corporate citizenship modeled by NCNB and its visionary leadership team.

Notes

1. Archie Carroll, "The Four Faces of Corporate Citizenship," *Business and Society Review* 100/101 (1998): 5.
2. Ibid.
3. Louis W. Fry, Gerald D. Keim, and Roger E. Meiners, "Corporate Contributions: Altruistic or For-Profit?" *Academy of Management Journal* 25, no. 1 (1982): 95.
4. Ibid.
5. Craig Smith, "The New Corporate Philanthropy," *Harvard Business Review*, May 1994, 107.

6. Barbara W. Altman, "Transformed Corporate Community Relations: A Management Tool for Achieving Corporate Citizenship," *Business and Society Review* 102/103 (1998): 43.

7. Ibid., 46.

8. Craig Smith, "The New Corporate Philanthropy," 106–7.

9. Michael E. Porter and Mark R. Kramer, "The Competitive Advantage of Corporate Philanthropy," *Harvard Business Review*, December 2002, 58.

10. Michael W. Giles, "The Atlanta Project: A Community-Based Approach to Solving Urban Problems," *National Civic Review* 354 (Fall 1993): 355.

11. Ibid., 359.

12. Porter and Kramer, "The Competitive Advantage of Corporate Philanthropy," 66. See also *Transformational Philanthropy: Celebrating Fifteen Years with TPI* (Boston: The Philanthropic Initiative, 2004), 5.

13. George E. Peterson and Dana R. Sundblad, *Corporations as Partners in Strengthening Urban Communities: A research report*. Report Number 1079-94-RR (New York: The Conference Board, 1994): 9–10.

14. Crown Center, "Kansas City's Crown Center: A Model Mixed-Use Community," http://www.crowncenter.com (accessed February 24, 2009).

15. Gerald Keim, "Corporate Social Responsibility: An Assessment of the Enlightened Self-Interest Model," *Academy of Management Review* 3, no. 1 (1978): 32–39.

16. Peterson and Sundblad, *Corporations as Partners in Strengthening Urban Communities*, 9–10.

17. Ibid., 13.

18. Perry Davis, "Why Partnerships? Why Now?" *Proceedings of the Academy of Political Science* 36, no. 2 (1986): 1.

19. Roger S. Ahlbrandt, "Public-Private Partnerships for Neighborhood Renewal," *Annals of the American Academy of Political and Social Science* 448 (1986): 120–34.

20. Ibid., 125; John Portz, "Supporting Education Reform: Mayoral and Corporate Paths," *Urban Education* 35 (2000): 408.

21. Portz, "Supporting Education Reform," 407.

22. Katharine C. Lyall, "Public-Private Partnerships in the Carter Years," *Proceedings of the Academy of Political Science* 36, no. 2 (1986): 5.

23. Akhtar Badshah, "Building Corporate Sector Partnerships," *Public Management* 79, no. 1 (1997): 2.

24. James Austin and Arthur McCaffrey, "Business Leadership Coalitions and Public-Private Partnerships in American Cities," *Journal of Urban Affairs* 24, no. 1 (2002): 44.

25. Badshah, "Building Corporate Sector Partnerships," 1.

26. Peterson and Sundblad, *Corporations as Partners in Strengthening Urban Communities*, 12.

27. Ibid.

28. Heather Smith and William Graves. "Gentrification as Corporate Growth Strategy: The Strange Case of Charlotte, North Carolina and the Bank of America," *Journal of Urban Affairs* 27, no. 4 (2005): 407.

29. Thomas Hanchett, *Sorting Out the New South City: Race, Class and Urban Development in Charlotte, 1875–1975,* (Chapel Hill: University of North Carolina Press, 1998).

30. Mark Brock, "Fourth Ward Called Vital," *Charlotte News*, May 28, 1975.

31. "Local Real Estate Dealer Gets Options in 4th Ward," *Charlotte Observer*, May 3, 1975.

32. J. Dennis Rash, personal interview with author, February 2003.

33. Pat Borden, "A Case of Love at First Blight," *Charlotte Observer*, February 3, 1977.

34. Editorial, "Fourth Ward: A Choice Place to Live?" *Charlotte Observer*, June 2, 1975.

35. Jerry Shinn, "Banks to Loan City 4th Ward Money," *Charlotte Observer*, January 10, 1976.

36. City of Charlotte, Charlotte City Council, *Fourth Ward special project plan,* 1987; J. Dennis Rash, "*The Improbable Success: Redevelopment of Downtown Charlotte . . . with a Corporate Twist!"* (keynote speech, annual meeting of the Southeastern Division of the American Association of Geographers, Charlotte, N.C., November 23, 2003).

37. Vanessa Gallman, "4th Ward Houses Being Saved, but the Poor Feel Pushed Away," *Charlotte Observer*, August 9, 1976.

38. Ellen Scarborough, "Restoration Men," *Charlotte Observer*, December 25, 1976.

39. Pat Borden, "4th Ward Took a Kinder Approach," *Charlotte Observer*, January 29, 1978.

40. Ibid.

41. Nancy Brachey, "Bank's New Business Partner the Inner City: NCNB Subsidiary Is Unique in U.S.," *Charlotte Observer*, April 14, 1978.

42. Philip Hayward, "Turning the Tables on Charlotte's Blight," *Preservation News*, August 1978.

43. "Follow the Leader," *Apartment Life*, June 1980, 23.

44. Brachey, "Bank's New Business Partner the Inner City."

45. Editorial, *Charlotte Observer*, September 1, 1978.

46. Rash, interview.

47. George Stein, "Fourth Ward Cheers NCNB Land Plan," *Charlotte News*, April 14, 1978.

48. D. Vrana, "Charlotte: A New U.S. Behemoth of Banking," *Los Angeles Times*, May 28, 1998.

49. Jamie Coomarasamy, BBC World Service radio broadcast, February 10, 2009.

See also "Downturn Bites in U.S. Financial Hub," BBC, http://news.bbc.co.uk/1/hi/world/americas/7880283.stm (accessed February 28, 2009).

50. Heather Smith and William Graves, "The Corporate (Re)construction of a New South City: Great Banks Need Great Cities," *Southeastern Geographer* 43, no. 2 (2003): 191. Rash points out that in the mid 1970s, the bank's interest in "going global" was more focused on replicating the urban characteristics of global cities in Charlotte, than in expanding the bank's influence in the global economy. J. Dennis Rash, personal communication with author, June 2009.

51. Peterson and Sundblad, *Corporations as Partners in Strengthening Urban Communities*, 12.

52. Rash, *"The Improbable Success."*

53. Smith and Graves, "The Corporate (Re)construction of a New South City," 191. See also Heather Smith and William Graves, "Gentrification as Corporate Growth Strategy: The Strange Case of Charlotte, North Carolina and the Bank of America," *Journal of Urban Affairs* 27, no. 4 (2005): 403–18.

54. Donald Haider, "Partnerships Redefined: Chicago's New Opportunities," *Proceedings of the Academy of Political Science* 36, no. 2 (1986): 138.

55. R. Yockey, *McColl: The Man With America's Money.* (Atlanta, Ga.: Longstreet, 1999), 241.

56. Royce Hanson, Hal Wolman, David Connolly, and Katherine Pearson, "Corporate Citizenship and Urban Problem Solving: The Changing Role of Business Leaders in American Cities," (discussion paper prepared for the Brookings Institution Metropolitan Policy Program, Washington, D.C., September 2006), v, 1.

57. Adam Bell and Rick Rothacker, "Duke Taking More Space in Wells Building," *Charlotte Observer*, February 26, 2009.

Gerald L. Ingalls and Isaac Heard Jr.

Developing a Typology of African American Neighborhoods in the American South
The Case of Charlotte

African American neighborhoods of southern cities grew at a slower pace, from more varied spatial foundations, and under different social, economic, and historic conditions than did black neighborhoods in northern cities. While, at first glance, the present-day pattern of African American neighborhoods of southern cities such as Charlotte resembles that of their northern counterparts, beneath the surface lies a rich historical diversity. In this chapter we contend that the longer history of African American residential experience in southern cities offers a fertile research opportunity to understand how such communities are affected by the efforts of cities to position themselves within the developing global economy. Cities such as Charlotte provide a rich laboratory for exploring diversity in the residential experiences of African Americans in urban America. Our investigation in Charlotte suggests that the African American residential experience is not as one-dimensional as is often depicted in the literature. In fact, Charlotte offers a range of residential types, and we have developed a typology of African American residential areas based primarily on the timing of their initial development.

We propose a typology of five African American residential types: In-Town Residential Concentrations, Rural Villages and Concentrations, Separate Villages (Rim Villages and Streetcar Suburbs), and more recent, Auto-Oriented Suburbs. All of these types saw their genesis during the period from immediately after the end of the Civil War until about 1920. In Charlotte black suburbs did not emerge until the late 1890s and early 1900s. However, all five neighborhood types underwent significant changes in spatial form and character as Charlotte and most of North Carolina experienced its own brand of economic (industrial) development around the turn of the century. And in Charlotte's current explosive urban growth, generated in large measure by Charlotte's efforts to compete within a restructuring, internationalizing economy, these neighborhoods are seriously threatened. Beginning in the mid to late 1960s, most, but not all, of the African American neighborhoods in our typology witnessed significant changes induced by significant urban restructuring under way in Charlotte's urban core, some of its older suburbs, and its new suburbs exploding outward into surrounding rural areas. We describe each of these five types of pre-urban, pre-1965 African American neighborhoods, offer examples of each type taken from the present-day landscape of Charlotte, and describe the changes currently under way.

African American Residential Patterns in the Literature

The separation of African Americans into distinctive and segregated residential communities has long been a dominant theme in urban America. African American residential patterns, particularly the ghettoes that characterized the nation's largest metropolitan areas from the latter half of the nineteenth century until today, have attracted considerable attention from social scientists. The focus on the ghetto as the worst manifestation of black residential patterns, and on the northern cities that hosted them, was a natural consequence of both the "context and historical roots" and the quest for understanding on the road to potential amelioration strategies.[1] The issue of how to frame policy to address the problems of the ghetto has, of course, been the focus of considerable debate.

During the decades of the 1960s, 1970s, and 1980s, social scientists broadened the conceptual framework for the examination of the African American urban residential experience to include urban poverty, social isolation, concentration, and dislocation.[2] However, during this period much of the debate swirled around conservative or liberal views of the problem of the concentration of the urban poor. Conservatives tended to blame the growth of urban poor on "persistence of a culture of poverty and/or the liberal social policies inaugurated by the civil rights movement and the Great Society programs."[3] Scholars such as Wilson framed the worsening plight of the urban poor on the structural transformation of the national economy. Under his definition, ghettoes became places of concentrated poverty and joblessness. In *When Work Disappears*, Wilson framed his argument in terms of changing technologies and growing internationalization that induced a demand for a different kind of worker, one unlikely to be found in the low-skilled, under-schooled, high-poverty populations of the inner cities of metropolitan America.[4] Increasing levels of economic segregation produced ever-more-isolated minority populations, which were concentrated into high-poverty, largely Hispanic and African American inner-city residential areas.[5]

Throughout the debate, the literature on the African American urban residential mosaic has mainly focused on large concentrations of urban poor in the centers of North American cities, especially the biggest metropolitan areas of the northern and western United States. A less pronounced theme in the literature on black residential experiences in urban America has been the residential mosaic of African Americans in the American South, where the concept of ghetto is much less applicable. Silver and Moeser argued that the remarkable similarity in African American residential patterns that characterized the three southern cities they chronicled — Atlanta, Richmond, and Memphis — were distinctive of the urban South and that these developmental patterns formed in a manner unlike their counterparts in the urban North. They suggested that both patterns formed from segregation, but that the term *ghetto* was far less descriptive of the African American residential experience in the South.[6] The fact that most African Americans have resided in the South over a longer period would seem to offer a rich laboratory for exploring diversity in their residential experiences in urban America, particularly as many southern cities have experienced rapid population growth and structural expansion in an effort to respond to a restructuring, globalizing economy.

This paper addresses the residential patterns of African Americans in Charlotte, North Carolina, as a case study. We move the scale of our examination of the African American residential pattern from large ghetto concentrations to smaller, much more diverse, and less spatially concentrated neighborhoods. We develop a typology of five African American neighborhoods in Charlotte, North Carolina, based largely on the timing of their primary development, which occurred predominantly during the turn-of-the-century, Jim Crow, and pre-Depression eras when Charlotte was growing from a small southern town into a southern city. We describe these neighborhood types and offer evidence of their historic distinctiveness from one another and from the patterns of African American residential experiences described in much of the literature on urban America. We also suggest that vestiges of many of these historic African American neighborhoods remain, at least for now, visible on the landscape. Finally, we suggest that the manner of development in Charlotte, a post–World War II, classically automobile-dominated city characterized by high rates of population and spatial growth and with aspirations of connection to a globalizing economy, has threatened or overwhelmed some of these historic African American neighborhoods while protecting others. We suggest that while sprawl envelops and threatens what were once small, rural, African American communities on Charlotte's urban edge, in a delicious irony, inner-city decay from the 1960s through the 1980s actually wrapped a protective cocoon around some of the others. However, the prosperity of the 1990s and the early years of the twenty-first century ultimately imperiled them all, especially as *inner-city redevelopment* and *infill* became buzzwords in the drive to make Charlotte a "world class city."

Variation in African American Residential Patterns

Social scientists, and geographers in particular, have a long-standing interest in the variation in African American urban residential experiences. Geographers such as Harold Rose, Joe Darden, George Davis and Fred Donaldson, Larry Ford and E. Griffin, Paul Groves and Edward Muller, and David Ward contributed markedly to our understanding of the development, growth, and maintenance of African American ghettos in major metropolitan areas of the United States.[7]

In an early effort to describe patterns of African American residential settlement, Rose argued that African Americans were present in other places in the city than ghettos. He classified outlying racial concentrations of American cities into two distinct spatial forms:

The colonized black suburbs, which were small but stable residential pockets that originated as shack towns on the edge of the city.
The ghettoized black suburbs, which were advancing spillover communities that were a direct result of sectoral expansion of the central city ghetto.

Rose emphasized that black suburbanization was confined to fewer than a dozen Standard Metropolitan Statistical Areas (SMSAs) that contained central cities with large, growing, nonwhite populations.[8]

Both Rose and Muller suggested that the black suburbanization movements of the 1960s and early 1970s involved blacks moving into lower quality suburbs already abandoned to them by whites.[9] Muller argued that blacks had been largely denied access to the suburbs and that their numbers there were far less than might have been expected given unlimited access. He suggested that "a goodly proportion of suburban black population still inhabits tiny, widely dispersed, and highly segregated traditionally black areas with settlement histories of five decades or more."[10] He pointed to the satellite towns adjacent to large central cities such as Evanston, Illinois; Pasadena, California; and Mount Vernon, New York, and stressed that in the 1980s suburbia remained largely off-limits to nonwhites.

O'Hare and Frey offer images of slightly more complex patterns when they observed that "black Americans run the gamut from poor to wealthy, and so do their neighborhoods."[11] They pointed out that the pace of African American suburbanization had accelerated from the 1960s to the point where approximately three in ten African Americans were suburbanites by 1990.[12] Owens and Wright argued that majority-black neighborhoods, even within the inner cities of the nine largest Primary Metropolitan Statistical Areas (PMSAs) of the United States, were diverse and changing. They suggested that:

> The stereotype of majority-black neighborhoods as distressed, deviant and dangerous urban underclass communities is misleading . . . One would not know it from the academic literature or the popular media, but this nation's metropolitan areas host a complex array of majority-black neighborhoods . . . Many are fragile and threatened; others are vibrant and thriving.[13]

Sociologist Mary Pattillo reinforced the argument for a more diverse definition of the African American ghetto. Her definition broadened the picture of concentrated poverty to include working- and middle-class black neighborhoods. Pattillo's definition became: the entirety of the spatially segregated and contiguous black community.[14]

Hartshorn also described variation in African American residential experiences outside the ghetto. He suggested that black residential space in cities exhibited one of two characteristic patterns: dispersed residences located on grounds or alleys adjacent to employers or clusters of housing near rail or industrial zones or corridors.[15]

A good deal of the description and analysis offered by geographers of the residential experience of African Americans has been based on examples drawn from larger metropolitan places, particularly in northern or midwestern settings. However, there are several key efforts by geographers to observe the urban residential experiences of African Americans in the South. Charles Aiken identified a slightly different type of black ghetto, one that developed as the population of the Yazoo Delta in a nonmetropolitan region of Mississippi realigned, producing increasingly higher concentrations of black population within municipalities of the Delta.[16] The consequence was the same: high poverty concentrations and lack of employment and job opportunity. Kellog examined clusters of African Americans in the postbellum South before the advent of Jim Crow and Lee examined black communities in southern Florida at the turn of the century.[17] Kellog suggested that black settlement patterns and their relationship to those of whites should be traced historically. He went on to suggest that in the antebellum southern city, four patterns of black housing existed:

1. small black districts on out-of-the-way streets,
2. houses of free blacks who were homeowners;
3. shantytowns near a city edge where slaves not needed in agricultural or domestic activities were quartered; and,
4. back-alley sites.[18]

Both Kellog and Lee suggest that the black residential pattern is a function of history and we should expect to note significant differences in the residential experiences of African Americans in northern and southern cities since each evolved at very different times and under very different social and economic conditions.

Difference is a key theme in our analysis. In agreement with the developing literature on the African American urban residential experience, we argue that diversity and change are quite characteristic of that experience. Second, we suggest that the differences in northern and southern urban development and the disproportionate concentration of African American population in the American South dictated similarly marked variations in the development of African American urban residential experiences in both regions. Indeed, in southern cities such as Charlotte it is not uncommon to find historic and persistent poor and middle-income, working-class black neighborhoods adjacent to and surrounded by historic and persistent upper-income, silk-stocking, white communities. Such examples appear to defy conventional wisdom, and some classic economic and social theory, and do not fit well the long-standing models of urban structure that focus on the ghetto as the major African American residential experience and seldom recognize that poor black and rich white neighborhoods can share common boundaries in today's urban space. However, in cities such as Charlotte, these seeming anomalies are simply a reflection of historical differences between southern cities and the development of northern cities, on which most of the classic urban models were developed.

What Made Southern Cities Different from Northern Cities?

The roots of the differences in northern and southern cities can likely be traced to the antiurban bias of the colonial and antebellum South. As Goldfield has suggested, "the southern city is different because the South is different. In that region, the city is much closer to the plantation than it is to Chicago and New York."[19] At least initially, southern cities developed as market centers to service local hinterlands rather than as focal points for industry and international commerce as in northern cities. While the South had its advocates of urbanization, such as J. B. D. DeBow, who saw urban development as a means of countering the "threat" of northern domination, the dominant voices parroted that of Thomas Jefferson, who equated cities with "vice and wretchedness" and labeled them "sores on the national body."[20]

For the first century of U.S. history, most of the South was firmly grounded in a highly traditional culture dominated by a planter and merchant class resistant to change and to any threat to their dominance. The antiurban bias was as much a statement of fear of the change that urbanization would entail as it was a rejection of cities. Most southern cities remained small until the late nineteenth and early twentieth century when the attitude about economic development and even industrialization changed and cities such as Charlotte became the focus of intensive development. The growth of the textile industry during the latter part of the nineteenth century catalyzed significant rural-to-urban migration and the eventual development of Charlotte into North Carolina's largest city by the late twentieth century.

African American rural-to-urban migration took a different form in the North and Midwest versus the South. In northern and midwestern cities African Americans crowded into dense, spatially confined areas. Gotham's examination of Kansas City indicates that social and economic forces often combined to produce racially homogenous neighborhoods through the use of restrictive covenants.[21] Unlike ethnic communities, which served as refuges or villages in the city where immigrant groups could adapt to the customs of the larger society, black communities, which developed during the massive black migrations of the 1920s, did not later disappear.[22] The result was, more often than not, the growth of large, expansive ghettos.

However, not all African Americans moved to northern cities; with the conclusion of the Civil War, African Americans began a migration to southern cities as well. Granted, the migration of rural blacks to southern cities occurred on a much reduced scale and intensity than the massive movements creating the ghettoes of the North and Midwest during the early twentieth century. As Myrdal argued, "Negroes did go to Southern cities but not nearly to the same extent as did the whites."[23] He pointed out that the rate of growth of blacks moving to southern cities was just far slower than that of whites.

The process of black concentration and growth in the urban South was different from that of northern cities not only in overall volume, but also in two very important physical and spatial characteristics. In northern cities blacks crowded into dense central sections recently occupied by foreign-born immigrants. In southern cities, the black residential pattern was of lower density and occurred over a wider area with greater spatial dispersion of black neighborhoods within and around the city.[24] Brownell suggested black settlements in southern cities in 1900 were "scattered," and the increased in-migration of rural blacks over the next four decades conformed to this dispersed pattern.[25] At the same time, however, the pattern in all southern cities during the twentieth century was one of advancing racial segregation: increasing concentration of blacks in fewer, larger residential areas nearer the urban core. Racial segregation was the rule in both northern and southern cities. But as Silver and Moeser suggested, southern cities involved a "purer form of apartheid" that constituted nothing less than the formation of a "separate city" within the context of the rapidly expanding southern metropolis. This separate city reached its most mature manifestation in a rapidly urbanizing South after World War II.[26]

The range of and opportunity for variation in the residential experiences of African Americans seem more pronounced in southern cities. African American neighborhoods of southern cities grew at a slower pace, from more varied spatial foundations and under different social, economic, and historic conditions than did black neighborhoods in northern cities. While at first glance the current pattern of African American neighborhoods of southern cities such as Charlotte resembles its northern counterparts, beneath the surface lies a rich historical diversity reflecting different growth patterns during their initial development and a longer history of African American residential experience. In Charlotte, population growth and explosive spatial expansion was delayed until after the civil rights movement of the 1960s. As a consequence of this late development, many of these African American neighborhoods remain on the landscape and offer a rich laboratory for exploring diversity in the residential experiences of African Americans in urban America.

Charlotte and Mecklenburg County as a Study Area

According to the 2008 estimates of population, Charlotte' population was 683,541 and Mecklenburg County had a population of 877,007.[27] Together the city and the county are the center of a Metropolitan Statistical Area of nearly 1.7 million and have been the economic and demographic engines that have fueled a rapid regional population expansion. Most of the expansion has taken place since 1970 with the automobile as the catalyst for an aggressive spatial expansion from the urban center of Charlotte into the surrounding rural areas in Mecklenburg County and the eight contiguous counties. Based on the 2000 Census, the population of Mecklenburg County grew by 96 percent from 1970 to 2000; Charlotte's population grew by 124 percent. By 2008 North Carolina State Data Center estimates indicated that Charlotte had grown by 170 percent (see table 6). More recently the six other small towns in Mecklenburg County have absorbed a good deal (about a third) of the population growth in the county.

Since much of our discussion of African American neighborhoods will focus on the period in which they were created and reached their zenith, we offer a relative location of the limits of Charlotte during the growth of the textile industry from 1880 to 1930. Until the growth of streetcar suburbs in the second and third decades of the twentieth century, Charlotte's urban outline was largely confined to the original four wards of present-day downtown Charlotte (see the map of Charlotte's regional location at the front of this volume). Most of the neighborhoods we develop in our typology are either within or immediately adjacent to this area.

In this paper we offer Charlotte as an example of a rapidly growing south-

Table 6. Demographic profile of the study area, 1970-2008.

	Population			Population Change (%)
	1970	2000	2008*	1970-2000
Metropolitan Statistical Area	409,370	1,499,293	1,675,495	63.5
Mecklenburg County	354,656	695,454	877,077	96.1
Charlotte	241,178	540,828	683,541	124.2

*State Data Center Estimates.
Source: Authors, based on U.S. Census, North Carolina State Data Center, and Charlotte Chamber of Commerce data.

ern city. Its growth is typical of cities across the postbellum South that received a substantial influx of African American population. Finally, we suggest that Charlotte is typical of the auto-centered economic and population expansion that has characterized much of the urban South since 1960. Charlotte in particular, with its diverse economy focused on the role of banking, financial services, and other services characteristic of a globalizing economy, has seen major population, economic, and spatial expansion. It is the latter attribute, rapid spatial growth, that we suggest threatens the continued existence of all of the neighborhood types we discuss.

A Typology of African American Residential Experiences

We base our typology of African American residential areas primarily on the timing of the development of these black communities in relationship to the evolution and solidification of Jim Crow institutions from 1880 to 1960. While one of these, the In-Town Concentration, involves residential areas that developed within the city of Charlotte over a period of two hundred years, from the latter part of the eighteenth to the middle of the twentieth century, our focus is primarily on the changes that occurred during the onslaught of Jim Crow and the long-term consequences of total, macro-level segregation through the first half of the twentieth century. Thus, in developing our typology we focus mainly on the vestiges of residential patterns and types of neighborhoods that developed within and adjacent to Charlotte in the aftermath of Jim Crow. One of our neighborhood types — the Auto-Oriented Black Suburb — is more reflective of the decline of Jim Crow and the dawn of the civil rights era. What is truly critical, at least in our view, is that we can still see evidence of these neighborhoods in the current urban fabric.

Our five African American residential types are: 1) In-Town Residential Concentrations; 2) Rural Villages and Concentrations; 3) and 4) two types of Separate Villages usually springing up at the edge of the town limits; and finally, 5) the more recent development of the Automobile-Oriented Suburb. Elsewhere in the literature Separate Villages are referred to as Rim Villages.[28] In Charlotte we observed that the Rim Village had more than one form, hence we label the two types collectively as Separate Villages: one was the Black Streetcar Suburb; the other was more like the traditional Rim Village. Timing is important since the critical elements in the emergence of both Separate Villages and In-Town Concentrations were the emergence of the Jim Crow movements of the late 1890s and early 1900s. Again, our objectives are twofold. First, we wish to call attention to the rich diversity of African American neighborhoods and propose a typology to be tested elsewhere. Second, we wish to catalog the threats to their continued existence as a means of prompting the actions needed to preserve them.

The Typology: In-Town Residential Concentrations

In the antebellum South, African Americans lived within and near the edge of many southern cities both as slaves and as freedmen. Kellogg listed three types of in-town settlement: Negro enclaves in the back alley; servants living along out-of-the-way streets near the homes of their owners; and free Negroes with skills or trades and the financial independence to live in a cluster separate from the other two types. His in-town concentrations reflected the "old, classic," southern, pre–Civil War, urban pattern of houses for whites fronting on the major streets with residences for slaves and free servants clustered nearby and often fronting onto alleys and side streets.[29] As Lee describes it, this form of black residential settlement was "the most universal of the patterns, interspersed blacks in white residential districts. Those blacks were usually domestics who were housed near the residences of their masters."[30] In-town, black residential areas were probably better defined and more easily recognizable in places that were substantial cities before the Civil War, such as Charleston, Richmond, Atlanta, and New Orleans. In smaller places such as Charlotte the pattern was less obvious despite a substantial black population.

At the close of the Civil War as freed slaves migrated to southern cities, Charlotte, with a refugee center or Freedman's Bureau, saw considerable increases in black population.[31] As we shall see when we examine the other types of settlement, not all of these new African Americans settled inside the town limits. However, from 1865 until the beginning of the twentieth century Charlotte saw significant increases in the in-town African American population and, at least initially, it was fairly evenly distributed throughout each of the town's four wards following a long-established pattern of settlement of black and white residents that existed before the Civil War.[32] Hanchett notes that there was no distinct "color line between black and white residents . . . blacks and whites lived side by side, often on the same block." Where small clusters of African Americans did develop, they tended to be in the low-lying and thus less expensive parts of town. He further noted that, "While this constituted more segregation than in antebellum times, there remained a surprising amount of intermingling by today's standards."[33]

In the 1890s and early 1900s these patterns began to change and the color lines began to sharpen. Like most of their southern brethren, Charlotte's white community caught Jim Crow fever. In the center city black districts hardened into self-contained enclaves. By the end of the first decade of the new century, distinctive black neighborhoods developed into what we label as In-Town African American Residential Concentrations. Large residential areas of African Americans emerged in all but the Fourth Ward. And as whites increasingly limited black access to virtually every facet of town life, In-Town African American Concentrations slowly became more and more self-contained. As Clark notes, "in southern cities, where the pattern of segregation is so complete that the dark ghettos must be almost self-sufficient, there are a number of Negro-owned stores, restaurants, and banks."[34] Charlotte was no exception to this general pattern. In the period after 1890, Charlotte's Second Ward saw the concentration of an increasing number of black-owned business and social/political institutions such as meeting halls. By the turn of the century, a strong community consciousness had developed and the community took on the name of Brooklyn. A number of three- and four-story buildings rose in Brooklyn and black entrepreneurs formed black-owned businesses and developed black office, commercial, and meeting space to replace the spaces that were increasingly inaccessible in white-owned downtown centers.[35] The resulting pattern of segregation into large-scale black and white communities dominated Charlotte's inner city until the end of the twentieth century.

By the 1960s the inner city's four wards had undergone a spatial reordering into virtually totally segregated communities. First and Second Wards had seen substantial growth in black population. Second Ward had become overwhelmingly black and Brooklyn was its identifiable, all-black center (see figure 30). This is the pattern that confronted Charlotte's white business leaders as the city began its demographic and spatial explosion propelled by the automobile.

Facing substantial increases in black population near the Central Business District (CBD), witnessing the beginnings of a massive flight of business to the suburbs, and fearing further decline of the CBD, Charlotte's white business and political leadership saw Second Ward and Brooklyn as threats to the city's retail and commercial heart. Whites failed to see vibrant and viable communities; they saw what looked like urban blight. In a move du-

Figure 30. A view of homes along East Eighth Street in Brooklyn in the Second Ward. (Source: Robinson-Spangler Carolina Room at the Public Library of Charlotte and Mecklenburg County.)

plicated countless times in cities all across the United States, Second Ward was almost completely demolished using federal funding in the "bulldozer" renovation era of the 1960s. Many of its residents were offered housing in the newly built public housing complex of Earle Village in First Ward, which was built under the auspices of urban renewal federal programming. Second Ward was effectively depopulated, dropping from 3,569 residents in 1960 down to 1 person in 1970.[36]

It is possible to argue that this was the Charlotte business leadership's first effort toward restructuring the inner city to position it for future national and international competition. It was certainly not the last effort to seize upon federal programming to restructure the African American In-Town Concentrations.

The erosion of Charlotte's In-Town Concentrations of African Americans continued, using different renewal strategies, into the next century. Beginning in the 1970s a successful gentrification of Fourth Ward, underwritten at least initially by the two major banks, resulted in the economic exclusion of most of its poor black residents within a decade. A new stadium for a professional football franchise would anchor Third Ward in the 1990s, and the subsequent development of this ward would attract large numbers of white residents, thereby eroding the relative presence of African Americans in this ward as well.

The final threat to In-Town African American Concentrations, indeed to any substantive presence of blacks in the original four wards of the city, would come in the form of the Clinton Administration's HOPE VI Program. This renewal effort was used to eliminate First Ward's 409-unit public housing project, Earle Village, and replace it with First Ward Place, a mixed-income development. The project was largely high density and the plan for the 406 units included 255 that were public housing, 50 that were available for low-income housing tax credit, and 101 that were market rate. An additional 68 apartments for seniors and 55 units for sale as townhouses and single-family homes completed the First Ward Project.[37] NationsBank served as development consultant and partner and created a mixed-finance development under HOPE VI auspices. In 2001 First Ward Place's 283 rental units included 18 percent designated for residents earning less than 55 percent of median income, 35 percent for market rate, and the remaining units were leased to public-housing-eligible households through the Charlotte Housing Authority.[38]

In the four decades from 1960 to 2000, urban renewal and gentrification reduced the African American presence in the original four wards. Overall population in the four census tracts that approximate Charlotte's original four wards fell from 17,547 to 5,233, and African American population has fallen from 12,272 to 2,882.[39] The reconstituted First Ward moved from an area dominated almost exclusively by public housing units to one in which the average house value climbed to $266,264 in 2005.[40] In 2008, the project contained fifty units of affordable housing — far less than the original plan suggested.[41]

Charlotte's In-Town Concentrations have vanished from the landscape of the inner city. All that remains are "landmark" vestiges of the once thriving African American communities. Of the forty-three landmark properties within the original four wards of downtown Charlotte, four are remnants of its African American heritage. Two are churches and two are examples of shotgun houses that characterized communities such as Brooklyn. Of the expansive area of Brooklyn, only the Grace A.M.E. Zion Church (1902) remains. The two shotgun houses (1898) were moved to the site of the other remaining African American church downtown, the Little Rock A.M.E. Zion Church (1911).[42]

None of the other four African American residential types in Charlotte and Mecklenburg County experienced this degree of degradation. Charlotte's drive toward becoming a global city has worn most heavily on the In-Town Concentrations. Housing projects such as First Ward's Earle Village, which in 1996 was only 60 percent occupied, with relatively high crime and poverty rates and deteriorated landscape, did not complement the image of an emerging global city that central city business leaders wished to project. HOPE VI funding helped to burnish that image. With a major financial institution as its investment partner, Charlotte and central city business leaders have reached out beyond the CBD to restructure the landscape. It is a pattern of capital investment in the urban core and reinvestment pushing well beyond established enclaves recognized in numerous other metropolitan areas of the United States.[43] The result seems to be a much less economically and culturally diverse urban core. That is certainly the case in the four wards of downtown Charlotte.

The Typology: Rural Concentrations

Moving from the urban core to the other end of the urban-to-rural continuum, we find another form of African American settlement. The Rural Concentration has been quite pervasive since 1865 on the landscape surrounding Charlotte. These small rural communities began several miles from the city of Charlotte, and in the rapid suburbanization of the last three to four decades have become rural enclaves. In a number of instances, the formation of these enclaves involved grants of land to former slaves; in other cases these communities were formed by purchases of land by freed slaves who had either lived in the area before the Civil War or migrated from farther away. Either path to formation usually resulted in a small African American community, often no more than a cluster of families with at least a church, occasionally a school, and perhaps a general store. These were normally located at some distance from Charlotte's town limits and were often far removed from those areas where significant white settlement and development was taking place. Figure 31 shows the location of the African American Rural Concentrations in Mecklenburg County.

In their earliest form these were primarily agricultural settlements. It was not until a general decline in the agricultural economy and/or the loss of interest in farming by the children of the original inhabitants that these areas began to change in character. In many instances, they evolved into rural enclaves of residences for older persons (homesteads for the younger) that occasionally saw additional residential growth as children built their own homes on inherited portions of their parents' farms.[44] All of these communi-

African American Neighborhoods   175

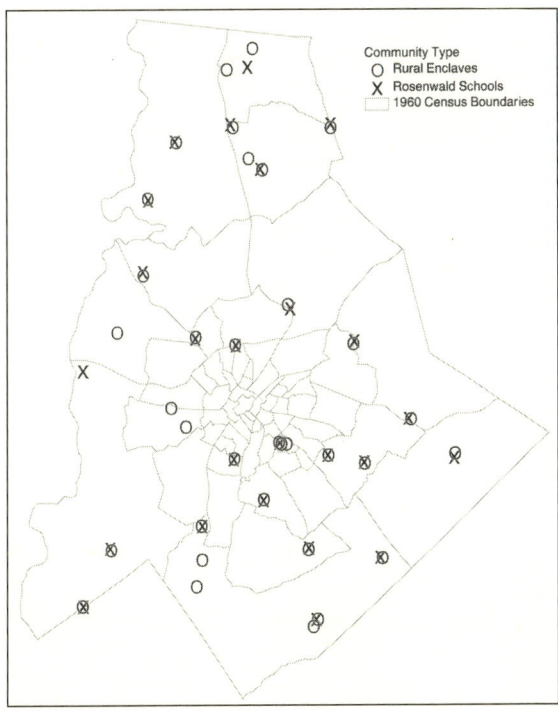

Figure 31. African American Rural Concentrations in Mecklenburg County. (Source: Gerald Ingalls.)

ties were far enough away from the old Charlotte limits that they were rural until relatively recently. In the last four or five decades they have become part of the urban fabric of Charlotte and Mecklenburg County.

As the economy and population of the county have exploded over the past four decades, the growth of Charlotte or one of the six suburban towns in Mecklenburg County has enveloped most of these Rural Concentrations. We can trace their envelopment by examining maps that depict the percentage of black population in the census tracts that made up Mecklenburg County in 1960 and 2000 (see figures 32 and 33). We can see that since 1960 these rural, black enclaves comprised less and less of the total population of the county's outlying census tracts. Eventually, the growth of new, suburban, and largely white tract developments or of the central city (Charlotte) overruns these Rural Black Concentrations and they either disappear or become tiny islands of African American settlement in a sea of white suburbs.

A surprising number of these Rural Concentrations have remained reasonably cohesive and identifiable on the urban landscape. Using the presence of a Rosenwald School as an indicator (see figure 34), we were able to identify

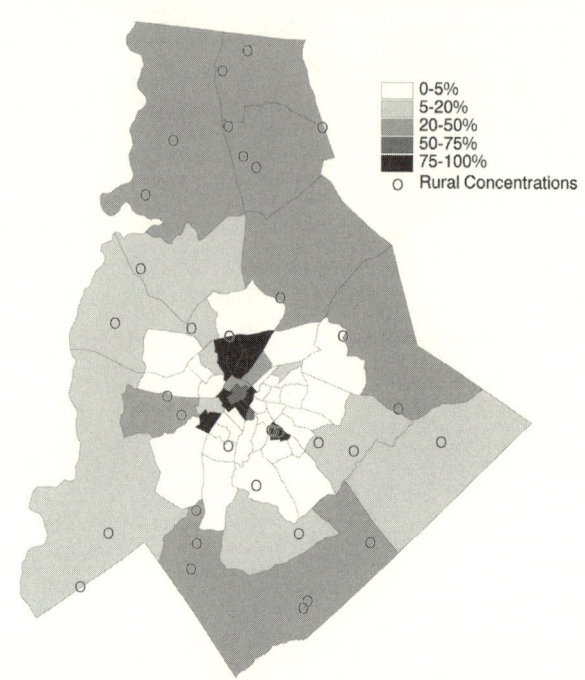

Figure 32. Percentage of black population by Mecklenburg County Census Tract, 1960. (Source: Gerald Ingalls.)

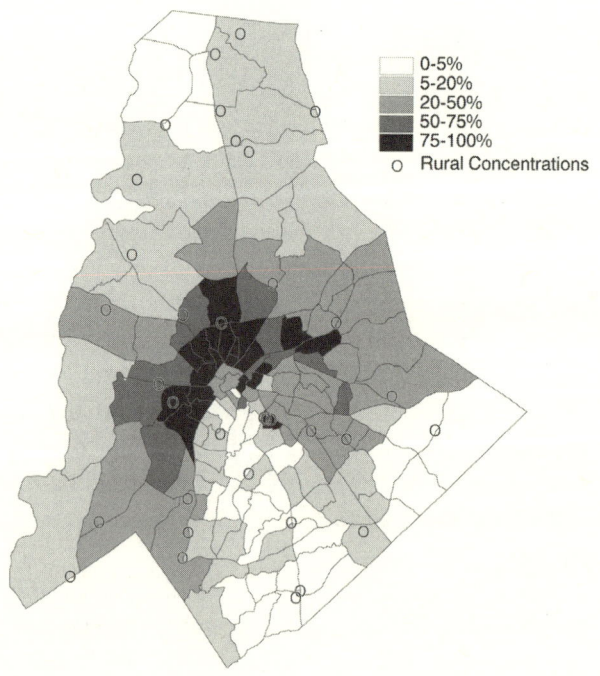

Figure 33. Percentage of black population by Mecklenburg County Census Tract, 2000. (Source: Gerald Ingalls.)

Figure 34. One of twenty-six Rosenwald schools built in Mecklenburg County, the Billingsville School opened in 1927 and is representative of the rural concentrations across the county. (Source: Robinson-Spangler Carolina Room at the Public Library of Charlotte and Mecklenburg County.)

more than two dozen remaining Rural Concentrations within Mecklenburg County.[45] One of these, Grier Heights, not only survived, but actually expanded. It is located well within the current inner city of Charlotte. It is a former farming community founded in the late 1870s about four miles south of (what was then) Charlotte, but squarely in the developmental path of what would eventually become Charlotte's premier high-income housing sector. By 2000 Grier Heights had evolved into a substantial, inner-city, African American urban concentration surrounded by much higher socioeconomic, primarily white neighborhoods that are themselves at the edges of the highest income sector of Charlotte (see figure 35). In today's urban fabric, Grier Heights appears an anomaly, at least until we appreciate the history of African American residential development.

Many of the remaining Rural Concentrations are located outside of the City of Charlotte in territory that was, as recently as 1990, part of rural Mecklenburg County. Abundant greenfield space has, at least as of this writing, insulated these communities from the pressure of development. However, within the last ten years, most of these Rural Concentrations have been annexed into one of the six small towns that are absorbing a sizable

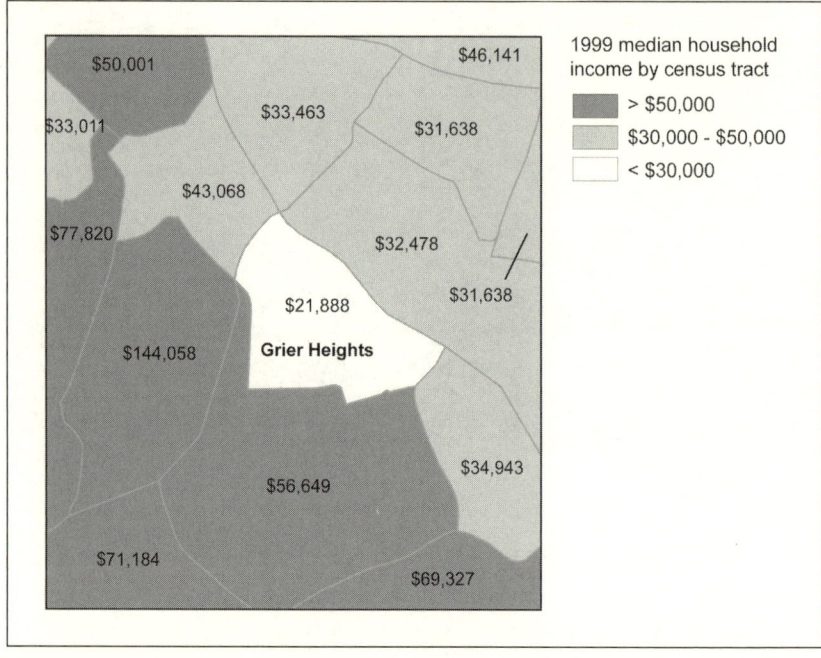

Figure 35. Grier Heights as an island of poverty. (Source: Gerald Ingalls.)

portion of population growth of the urban region. In an interesting irony, some of these Rural Concentrations are threatened by sprawl, while others, such as Grier Heights, are threatened by Charlotte's potential answer to sprawl — infill, redevelopment, and gentrification. The substantial profits to be had in building higher-density, expensive residential and/or commercial infill developments is as significant a threat to Grier Heights, now enveloped by Charlotte's high-income corridor, as the automobile-oriented, cul-de-sac development is to the Rural Concentrations located in suburbia.

The Typology: Separate Villages

In-Town Residential Concentrations and Rural Concentrations were created out of the demographic, social, and economic consequences of the collapse of the antebellum South. Jim Crow morphed the In-Town Concentrations of the antebellum era into all-black enclaves. Rural Concentrations took on a new dynamic by the sheer volume of migration of African Americans to the Charlotte region in the post–Civil War era. However, neither of these residential types could possibly have absorbed all of the demand for housing required by the thousands of new African American migrants coming to

Charlotte after the end of the Civil War. As a consequence, many migrants simply moved into the open land adjacent to what was then the town limits, creating small, separate, African American villages around the edges of the town. These were distinguished from Rural Concentrations by the livelihood of the residents. As with the In-Town Residential Area of Brooklyn, these separate villages were small, segregated, and occasionally self-supporting concentrations consisting of persons of different social classes. The genesis of these villages varies from land purchased by former slaves to land given by former slave masters. In Charlotte and Mecklenburg County there are sufficient differences in this type of settlement that we offer a distinction between what we label as Rim Villages and Black Suburbs.

Separate Villages — The Rim Village

The Rim Villages approximate what Lee referred to as "the classic southern pattern" of "black districts of substandard housing . . . located in marginal areas on the outskirts of town that were often poorly drained or otherwise unesteemed sites."[46] Wade suggested some Rim Villages were created before the Civil War by slaves "hired out" by planters to urban employers such as railroads needing labor for track work.[47] In Charlotte, a community known as Dulstown, located near the town's rail yards, and Greenville and Irwinville, located near the railroad line and its developing industrial and commercial corridor, seem to fit the pattern suggested by Wade.[48] Irwinville was part of a large farm dating from the antebellum era. Another of Charlotte's Rim Villages may have begun as a mining camp; Hanchett suggests that Blandville could have started as a labor camp for Rudisill and St. Catherine gold mines.[49] Blandville and Irwinville were lost in the continuing development of Charlotte's warehousing, light industrial, and commercial development. Greenville was razed to the ground in 1968, lost to urban redevelopment. In the last few years plans for Greenville have delivered on the promise for a rebirth: new housing is springing up on the site of the old village.

However, in Charlotte there were also Rim Villages located in more desirable locations with fewer of the negative locational and housing features suggested by Lee. One such village, Cherry, was located on relatively prime land, neither poorly drained nor undesirable. In fact, it is currently adjacent to Myers Park, a premier, silk-stocking, late streetcar–early automobile neighborhood of Charlotte. As Hanchett describes its evolution, Cherry was a village of relatively poorer blacks that probably began as a farming community. However, in the early 1890s, a wealthy white landowner living nearby (Colonel W. R. Myers) took an interest in the settlement and expanded it into a modern neighborhood. Eventually, because of its convenient location near a premier white neighborhood, its black residents served as servants of the wealthy whites of Myers Park. As with the In-Town Residential area of Brooklyn, Cherry developed a measure of self-sufficiency, including stores, schools, churches, boarding houses, and housing stock that ranged from substantial and sound to the shanty and shotgun shacks.[50] Cherry still exists today (see figure 36).

Separate Villages — The Streetcar Suburb

Our fourth type of black residential area is the Streetcar Suburb. Like the Rim Village, it was located at the edge of the Charlotte town limits around the beginning of the twentieth century. Unlike the Rim Village, this took the form of a purposeful suburban development with higher-quality housing and superior quality of life. Charlotte had at least two Black Streetcar Suburbs.

Charlotte's first Black Streetcar Suburb was Biddleville, named after Biddle Institute (now Johnson C. Smith University) founded in 1871 as a Presbyterian-supported, African American college for preachers and teachers (see figure 37). Colonel W. R. Myers, the aforementioned developer of a white streetcar suburb called Myers Park, donated land for Biddle Institute. The college is situated on high ground and offers one of the most stunning views of the

Figure 36. Present-day Cherry Village business corner at the intersection of Baxter Street and Baldwin Avenue. (Source: Gerald Ingalls.)

Figure 37. Johnson C. Smith University was the center of the first African American streetcar suburb. (Source: Isaac Heard Jr.)

current Charlotte CBD available. This is hardly the undesirable land most often occupied by Black Rim Villages. Quite the contrary, Biddleville, along with (In-Town) Brooklyn's Brevard Street, became one of the most desirable residential areas for the city's black elite around the turn of the twentieth century. Indeed, the area's intellectual atmosphere centered around the college, which with its cultural offerings made Biddleville one of the premier black communities in the Carolinas.[51] Eventually, the streetcar line from Charlotte was expanded up the hill to link this black suburb to the town.

Washington Heights, a black neighborhood constructed in 1913 by a white developer, was the second Black Streetcar Suburb. This development was built in response to the high demand for better-quality housing for African Americans demonstrated by the success of Biddleville.

By the time most of these Black Streetcar Suburbs were constructed, the primary growth patterns of Charlotte were well established. White streetcar suburbs were moving south; black streetcar suburbs were moving north. This pattern of segregation, institutionalized and codified in the aftermath of Jim Crow, would prevail through the end of the twentieth century and is evident in current residential patterns. As Charlotte grew, white neighborhoods developed in the south and east; black neighborhoods moved north and west. In today's urban landscape, the remnants of these African American suburbs are hard to distinguish in the midst of the decay that characterizes the current African American residential fabric in this part of the inner city. However, the relentless outward redevelopment of the CBD has pushed up against the last remaining barrier between the integrity of Biddleville and urban restructuring: the interstate.

The Typology: The Modern African American Suburb

At about the same time that the older Streetcar Suburbs and Rim Villages associated with Johnson C. Smith University were beginning to go into steep physical and economic decline, a number of new suburban-style subdivisions were developed in the vicinity. These new developments, built in the automobile era, were intended to satisfy the continuing demand for housing for Charlotte's professional and middle-class black households. Since these new developments came on line in the 1950s and 1960s, they emerged as black suburbs rolling outward to the north and west from the traditional African American core of Biddleville and Washington Heights in what was a totally segregated pre–civil rights, southern city.

McCrory Heights was developed in the mid to late 1950s to serve a black college that was having difficulty recruiting new faculty and staff when little suitable housing was available. McCrory Heights became the quintessential 1960s-style suburban subdivision with rolling lawns and carports. It was soon joined by a number of more modest developments. The process was completed during the late 1960s and early 1970s when the last of the exclusively black residential developments of University Park, Northwood Estates, and Hyde Park were developed.

These "modern" African American subdivisions are now in their fourth, fifth, and sixth decades. As a consequence, they are beginning to suffer from the same maladies of any housing development of that vintage. Developed to modest standards in a short time frame, they have become functionally obsolete and relatively undesirable in today's housing market. Their problems are compounded by the fact that with the demise of formalized economic segregation in Charlotte, the resale market for these homes has fallen considerably among the upwardly mobile, professional black households for whom they had been the only choice before the 1970s. As this housing aged, it created pressures on existing residents to reinvest in maintaining and upgrading their property. But as those residents aged and moved into their retirement years, the likelihood of this dwindled. All of these historic black suburbs have been subsumed into the highly segregated and spatially cohesive African American sector of Charlotte today.

These middle- and upper-income African American suburbs have often stagnated economically as their residents aged and retired. In a very few instances, Afrocentric community-minded activists have moved into housing in these neighborhoods as it has become available, almost as a way of conserving and showcasing the strength and stability that these suburbs represented from times of legal and sanctioned segregation. However, these newer residents often find themselves "strangers in a strange land" when they realize that many of their perspectives are viewed as extreme by the often surprisingly politically and socially conservative older residents. Where these neighborhoods are close enough to new growth centers of the community, they often become the targets of gentrification. Where these neighborhoods are far enough away from those new growth centers, and particularly if they suffer from extensive structural and functional obsolescence, they slowly slip from ownership into rental housing and begin the much-documented downward spiral into deterioration as they house increasingly poor, often single-parent households plagued by the physical and behavioral chronic nuisances that eventually destroy their desirability to any households with the freedom of choice.

Summary, Conclusions, and Implications

We have developed and presented a typology of five categories of black residential patterns using one case study of one southern American city—Charlotte, North Carolina. The African American communities there are products of the period from the end of the Civil War to the 1970s; however, most of them were well developed by the 1920s. What we find significant is that they are strong evidence of the diversity of the African American residential pattern and, even more to the point, that many remain on the landscape of Charlotte today.

These African American communities formed in response to white efforts to separate from their black neighbors. They were a direct result of the Jim Crow movement of the 1890s and 1900s and its consequences were felt well into the 1970s. While many of these neighborhoods were formed in adversity, they have endured as monuments to the resistance, resiliency, and creativeness of Charlotte's African American community. These communities are a major part of our southern heritage and our community identity. However, those that have not already disappeared are in considerable jeopardy.

Time has not been generous to Charlotte's historic black neighborhoods, but neither have they vanished from the landscape. The In-Town Concentrations are gone, victims of the bulldozer renovations of the 1960s and the spurt of economic growth during the 1980s and 1990s that saw considerable expansion of Charlotte's CBD and a strong market for downtown residential opportunities. All that remains of the In-Town Concentrations are a few scattered buildings fortunate enough to obtain historic landmark status.

However, a sizable segment of the historic African American residential communities remain on the landscape of Charlotte and Mecklenburg County. These include a number of Rural Concentrations and superb examples of Rim Villages and Streetcar Suburbs. While there is still time to preserve these segments of Charlotte's cultural history, the pressures of population growth, economic redevelopment of the inner core, and the economic pressures of Charlotte's drive to become a global city work steadily against all historic preservation — not just that of African American culture.

All too often urban communities fail to appreciate the rich heritage and diversity that lies directly before them. Unfortunately many communities are all too often blinded by the decay and depredation of what exists now. Since many of these neighborhoods are now in inner-city locales that have seen better days, most communities only see blight. Since many African American neighborhoods (Rim Villages, Rural Enclaves, and some In-Town Residential Areas) were built for poorer owners or renters, current residents often see little apparent architectural merit. Since many of the rural neighborhoods have been surrounded and subsumed by large-scale urban growth in primarily white suburbs, what remains of the rural American legacy does not seem to fit what the new community has become. New residents either fail to appreciate or choose to ignore the community history and conclude there is little worth saving. Despite these failures to see, understand, and protect, vestiges of these communities remain clearly visible on the landscape. Whether they will continue to remain is quite another issue.

Even in situations where there is little architectural or historic significance to the physical location of African American neighborhoods, as in the Sweet Auburn neighborhood of Atlanta where Dr. Martin Luther King Jr. was born and later preached in the Ebenezer Baptist Church, African American neighborhoods play an important role in the life of the community and are worth preserving. For those who have not been lifted into the middle- or upper-income groups by the progress of the last half century, these places serve the same purposes as the "old neighborhoods" of the European immigrants of earlier generations: common use of language, nearby kin, stores and services specially tailored to a certain group's tastes, and institutions important to the group — churches and lodges. Where the forces of globalization and general economic change work to restructure these neighborhoods, they undermine much of the infrastructure that supports the economically and socially unassimilated and unacculturated population of underemployed, impoverished, and struggling African Americans that still call these communities home.

Notes

1. Truman A. Hartshorn, *Interpreting the City: An Urban Geography*, 2nd ed. (New York: Wiley, 1992), 289.

2. Alford A. Young, "Social Isolation, and Concentration Effects: William Julius Wilson Revisited and Re-applied," *Ethnic and Racial Studies* 26, no. 6 (2003): 1073–87.

3. Harold M. Rose, "Are Non-race Specific Policies the Key to Resolving the Plight of the Inner-City Poor?" *Policy Studies Review* 7, no. 4 (1988): 859–64.

4. William Julius Wilson, *The Declining Significance of Race: Blacks and Changing American Institutions*, 2nd ed. (Chicago: University of Chicago Press, 1980); William Julius Wilson, *The Truly Disadvantaged: The Inner City, the Underclass and Public Policy* (Chicago: University of Chicago Press, 1987); William Julius Wilson, *When Work Disappears: The World of the New Urban Poor* (New York: Knopf, 1996).

5. Douglas S. Massey and Nancy A. Denton, "Suburbanization and Segregation in U.S. Metropolitan Areas," *American Journal of Sociology* 94, no. 3 (1988): 592–626; Paul A. Jargowsky, "Take the Money and Run: Economic Segregation in U.S. Metropolitan Areas," *American Sociological Review* 61, no. 5 (1996): 984–98; John B. Strait, "The Impact of Compositional and Redistributive Forces on Poverty Concentration: The Case of the Atlanta, Georgia, Metropolitan Region: 1980–1990," *Urban Affairs Review* 37, no. 1 (2001): 19–42.

6. Christopher Silver and John V. Moeser, *The Separate City: Black Communities in the Urban South, 1940–1968* (Lexington: University Press of Kentucky, 1995).

7. Harold M. Rose, *Social Processes in the City: Race and Urban Residential Choice*, Commission on College Geography, Resource Paper No. 61969; Harold M. Rose, *The Black Ghetto: A Spatial Behavioral Perspective* (New York: McGraw-Hill, 1971); Harold M. Rose, *Black Suburbanization: Access to Improved Quality of Life or Maintenance of the Status Quo?* (Cambridge, Mass.: Ballinger, 1976); Joe T. Darden, *Afro-American in Pittsburgh* (Lexington, Mass.: Lexington Boos/Heath, 1973); Joe T. Darden, "Blacks and Other Racial Minorities: The Significance of Color in Inequality," *Urban Geography* 10, no. 6 (1989): 562–77; George Davis and O. Fred Donaldson, *Blacks in the United States: A Geographic Perspective* (Boston: Houghton Mifflin, 1975); Larry Ford and E. Griffin, "Ghettoization of Paradise,"

Geographical Review 69, no. 2 (1979): 140–78; Paul Groves and Edward Muller, "The Evolution of Black Residential Areas in Late Nineteenth Century Cities," *Journal of Historical Geography* 1, no. 2 (1975), 169–91; David Ward, *Cities and Immigrants: A Geography of Change in Nineteenth Century America* (New York: Oxford University Press, 1971); David Ward, *Poverty, Ethnicity and the American City, 1840–1925: Changing Conceptions of the Slum and the Ghetto* (New York: Cambridge University Press, 1989).

8. Rose, *Black Suburbanization*, 14–15.

9. Rose, *Black Suburbanization*; Peter O. Muller, *Contemporary Suburban America* (New Jersey: Prentice-Hall, 1981).

10. Muller, *Contemporary Suburban America*, 82.

11. William O'Hare and William Frey, "Booming, Suburban, and Black," *American Demographics* 14, no. 9 (1992): 30.

12. Ibid.

13. Michael Leo Owens and David J. Wright, "The Diversity of Majority-Black Neighborhoods," *Rockefeller Institute Bulletin* (Albany, N.Y.: 1992), 1.

14. Mary Pattillo, "Extending the Boundaries and Definition of the Ghetto," *Ethnic and Racial Studies* 26, no. 6 (2003): 1046–57.

15. Hartshorn, *Interpreting the City*, 290.

16. Charles Aiken, "A New Type of Black Ghetto in the Plantation South," *Annals of the Association of American Geographers* 80, no. 2 (1990): 223–46.

17. John Kellogg, "Negro Urban Clusters in the Postbellum South," *Geographical Review* 67, no. 2 (1977): 310–21; David Lee, "Black Districts in Southeastern Florida," *Geographical Review* 82, no. 4 (1992): 375–87.

18. Kellogg, "Negro Urban Clusters in the Postbellum South," 311.

19. David Goldfield, *Cotton Fields and Skyscrapers: Southern City and Region, 1607–1980* (Baton Rouge: Louisiana University Press, 1982), 3.

20. Jefferson's opinion is summarized in L. H. Larsen, *The Rise of the Urban South* (Lexington: University Press of Kentucky, 1985), 2.

21. Kevin Fox Gotham, "Urban Space, Restrictive Covenants and the Origins of Racial Residential Segregation in a U.S. City, 1900–50," *International Journal of Urban and Regional Research* 24, no. 3 (2000): 616–33.

22. Harold M. Rose and Charles M. Christian, "Race and Ethnicity: A Competitive Force in the Evolution of American Urban Systems," in *Modern Metropolitan Systems*, ed. Charles M. Christian and Robert A. Harper (Columbus, Ohio: Merrill, 1982).

23. Gunnar Myrdal, *An American Dilemma: The Negro Problem and Modern Democracy* (New York: Harper, 1944), 88, quoted in Silver and Moeser, *The Separate City*, 188.

24. Silver and Moeser, *The Separate City*.

25. Blaine A. Brownell, "The Urban South Comes of Age, 1900–1940," in *The*

City in Southern History: The Growth of Urbanization in the South, ed. Blaine A. Brownell and David R. Goldfield (Port Washington, N.Y.: Kennikat, 1977).

26. Silver and Moeser, *The Separate City*, 6.

27. North Carolina State Data Center. Data Services Unit, Office of State Budget and Management. http://sdc.state.nc.us.

28. Kellogg, "Negro Urban Clusters in the Postbellum South"; John Kellogg, "The Formation of Black Residential Areas in Lexington, Kentucky, 1865–1887," *Journal of Southern History* 48, no. 1 (1982); Thomas W. Hanchett, "Sorting Out the New South City: Charlotte and Its Neighborhoods" (PhD diss., University of North Carolina-Chapel Hill, 1993); Richard C. Wade, *Slavery in the Cities: The South, 1820–1860* (New York: Oxford University Press, 1964), 275.

29. Kellogg, "Negro Urban Clusters in the Postbellum South," 311.

30. David Lee, "Black Districts in Southeastern Florida," *Geographical Review* 82, no. 4 (1992): 375.

31. In 1860, Charlotte had 2,265 people, of whom 40 percent were black. There were 825 slaves and 74 free blacks in the city. In 1880 Charlotte's black population reached 3,338 for an all-time high of 47 percent of the total population. Hanchett, "Sorting Out the New South City," 3.

32. Until the coming of the first streetcar suburb, Charlotte was basically a rectangular town divided into four wards simply numbered one to four (see figure 3). From 1865 to the early 1890s every one of the town's four wards had a significant percentage of black residents. Hanchett, "Sorting Out the New South City," 262.

33. Hanchett, "Sorting Out the New South City," 262.

34. Kenneth Clark, *Dark Ghetto: Dilemmas of Social Power* (New York: Harper and Row, 1965), 22.

35. Hanchett, "Sorting Out the New South City," 129–34.

36. U.S. Bureau of the Census, *Census of Population and Housing: 1970 Census Tracts*, Final Report PHC (1)-41, Charlotte, N.C. SMSA (Washington, D.C.: U.S. Government Printing Office, 1972), 1–64.

37. ULI-Urban Land Institute, *Engaging the Private Sector in HOPE VI* (Washington, D.C.: ULI-The Urban Land Institute, 2002), 35–41.

38. Ibid.

39. U.S. Bureau of the Census, *Census of Population and Housing: 1970 Census Tracts*, 1–64; U.S. Bureau of the Census, *Census of Population and Housing: 2000 Census Tracts*, Final Report PHC (1)-41, Charlotte, N.C. SMSA (Washington, D.C.: U.S. Government Printing Office, 2002), 1–45.

40. *Charlotte Neighborhood Quality of Life Study, 2006*, Metropolitan Studies Group, UNC Charlotte Urban Institute, http://www.ui.uncc.edu.

41. Charles Woodyard, written testimony submitted to the U.S. House of Representatives Committee on Financial Services, Subcommittee for Housing and Community Opportunity, 2007.

42. Charlotte-Mecklenburg Landmarks Commission, 2002, http://www.historiccharlotte.org/.

43. Elvin K. Wyly and Daniel J. Hammel, "Gentrification, Segregation, and Discrimination in the American Urban System," *Environment and Planning A* 36, no. 7 (2004): 1215–41.

44. Hanchett, "Sorting Out the New South City."

45. Rosenwald Schools are a great aid in locating these Rural Concentrations. From 1917 to 1938 the Julius Rosenwald Foundation financed 4,977 of these schools for African American schoolchildren, mostly across the South, and many of these distinctive buildings dot the landscape today. They can serve as a reasonable approximation of where African American communities once existed.

46. David Lee, "Black Districts in Southeastern Florida," *Geographical Review* 82, no. 4 (1992): 375–87.

47. Wade, *Slavery in the Cities*, 275.

48. Hanchett, "Sorting Out the New South City," 285.

49. Hanchett, "Sorting Out the New South City," 43–45.

50. Hanchett, "Sorting Out the New South City," 134–39.

51. Ibid.

Stephen Samuel Smith

Development and the Politics of School Desegregation and Resegregation

> The success of Charlotte, N.C. and Mecklenburg County, all this economic success... has been based on what I would call racial harmony... Had we taken a different course in 1972 (when schools were desegregated), then we would not be enjoying the prosperity that we now have.[1] — Statement prior to the 1999 reopening of the *Swann v. Charlotte-Mecklenburg School Board* litigation by C. D. Spangler Jr., business executive, member of Charlotte's school board in the 1970s, and subsequently one of North Carolina's wealthiest individuals, President of the University of North Carolina, and President of Harvard's Board of Overseers.

> Almost immediately after we integrated our schools, the southern economy took off like a wildfire in the wind. I believe integration made the difference. Integration and the diversity it began to nourish became a source of economic, cultural, and community strength.[2] — Statement a year later by Hugh L. McColl Jr., at the time CEO and chairman of Charlotte-based Bank of America and the person widely credited for spearheading the bank's emergence as global financial powerhouse.

These statements by two of Charlotte's most preeminent business executives have been widely echoed by numerous other civic leaders as well as by virtually every journalist and scholar (including me) who has written about the Charlotte-Mecklenburg Schools (CMS). CMS gave rise to the *Swann* litigation in which a 1971 Supreme Court decision upheld the constitutionality of mandatory busing for school desegregation. That landmark decision facilitated desegregation nationwide, and CMS developed one of the nation's most successful mandatory busing plans.

Given that contemporary Charlotte is much more of a global city than it was in the 1970s and 1980s — the heyday of the mandatory busing plan — and that desegregation is usually touted as preparing students to deal with the increasingly diverse workplaces and societies resulting from globalization, one might assume that school desegregation would be even more necessary for Charlotte's development at the start of the twenty-first century than it was a generation ago. But that assumption is contradicted by Charlotte's recent history, which has been characterized by ongoing economic growth but increasing school *re*segregation, not *de*segregation. Accompanying that resegregation has been concern that CMS schools are becoming increasingly differentiated in other ways as well. A 2004 report by CMS' equity committee said, "We fear the growing schism — and the proximity of a yawning chasm out of which we may never climb — between both 'have' and 'have not' segments of our population and the 'have' and 'have not' schools their children attend."[3]

The course of recent events suggests one of the main issues discussed in this chapter: given the important role that school desegregation played in facilitating Charlotte's development a generation ago, why has recent resegregation not adversely affected development and probably even helped it? The answer to this question largely exemplifies a slightly modified version of what Derrick Bell has called the "interest-convergence thesis," whose two rules he summarizes as:

> Rule 1: The interest of blacks in achieving racial equality will be accommodated only when that interest converges with the interests of whites in policy-making positions...
>
> Rule 2: Even when interest-convergence results in an effective racial remedy, that remedy will be abrogated at the point that policymakers fear the remedial policy is threatening the superior societal status of whites, particularly those in the middle and upper classes.[4]

I say *slightly modified* because rather than talk generally (and perhaps more ambiguously) about the societal status of middle- and upper-class whites, my discussion focuses on the economic interests of Charlotte's business elite, the politically and economically most influential social formation of whites in Charlotte.[5] In such a discussion, CMS' recent desegregation history provides considerable support for Bell's thesis.

The nature of this support can be sketched by putting Charlotte's experience in a broader perspective. In the post–World War II era, the South's economic development, the political stability of the region, and Cold War competition with the Soviet Union required transformation of many aspects of southern race relations, especially because of the determination with which African Americans were challenging these relations. This transformation's national aspects included landmark court decisions and legislation such as *Brown v. Board of Education* and the 1964 Civil Rights Act. But the particular route this transformation took in any given locality was heavily affected by the specifics of the local situation. In Charlotte, these specifics involved school desegregation. However, once the transformation of race relations together with Charlotte's political and economic development had crossed certain thresholds, the city's future development no longer hinged as heavily, if it hinged at all, on school desegregation. Thus, although CMS' desegregation accomplishments once facilitated development, education in Charlotte increasingly resembles that in the many other U.S. cities whose successful participation in the global economy is scarcely affected by their public school systems' heavy de facto segregation.

This chapter develops the argument sketched in the previous paragraph in five sections. The first provides some brief background material, and the second summarizes the *Swann* era, showing how mandatory busing initially benefited Charlotte's development and then summarizing developments that led to the reopening of the *Swann* litigation and a court order vacating the original *Swann* orders. The third section covers the early years of the post-*Swann* era, delineating a sharp jump in resegregation, changes in the way CMS envisions itself, and key political differences between the *Swann* era and the initial years of the post-*Swann* era. The fourth section discusses three themes that emerge from the earlier historical narrative: the new politics of school desegregation; development, resegregation, and the interest-convergence thesis; and the shadow cast by the era of white supremacy onto the era of globalization. The concluding section briefly considers two factors that might change CMS' current politics of education.

Two additional prefatory comments are appropriate: first, since my discussion focuses heavily on CMS' recent problems, it is important to emphasize that in these same years CMS could justifiably point to many noteworthy accomplishments.[6] Significant numbers of its schools received national and other kinds of recognition, as did significant numbers of students, teachers, and administrators. Moreover, the district's students benefited on a daily basis from the work of thousands of CMS employees who fulfilled their responsibilities with skill, care, and dedication despite the legal and political turmoil with which the district was dealing.

The second prefatory comment involves the chapter's characterization of schools as *inner-city* and *suburban*. That characterization follows the common practice of using *inner-city* as shorthand for schools relatively close to downtown whose enrollments consist of large percentages of students of color, many of them from poor families. By contrast, *suburban* is shorthand for schools in more outlying areas with higher percentages of non-Hispanic white students, most of whom are from middle-class or economically comfortable families. Such blanket shorthand has problems for several reasons including the dispersion of Charlotte's black population and the long-standing existence of some very affluent and overwhelmingly white neighborhoods close to downtown. Such problems notwithstanding, the shorthand is sufficiently accurate and stylistically convenient to justify its use. So, too, is the term *mid-ring* which is typically used in Charlotte to describe schools that lie, geographically and demographically, between suburban and inner-city schools and whose demographic composition has, in many cases, recently changed. Such changes arise from changes in the demographic composition of these schools' neighborhoods and/or the new student assignment plan that, as discussed below, relies much more heavily than the previous plan on assigning students to schools near their homes.

The Demographic and Electoral Context

As amply documented elsewhere in this volume, over the past generation, Charlotte has gone from a regional economic center to an increasingly important player on the national and international scene. Accompanying this economic transformation has been a growth in population that has seen public school enrollment increase significantly — from 76,000 K–12 students in 1991–92, to 106,000 in 2001–02, to 132,000 in 2007–08. In addition, CMS' demographic composition has also changed dramatically. In 1991–92, CMS' student population was 57 percent non-Hispanic white, 39 percent black, 3 percent Asian, and 1 percent Hispanic.[7] In 2007–08, it was 35 percent non-Hispanic white, 42 percent black, 4 percent Asian, 15 percent Hispanic, 1 percent Native American, and 3 percent multiracial/ethnic. The surge in Hispanic enrollment is the most obvious manifestation of how CMS has been affected by globalization.

Just as CMS' racial/ethnic composition has changed, so too has the rate of poverty. In 2007–08, 47 percent of CMS' students received free or reduced-price lunch (FRL), compared with 36 percent a decade earlier.

As its name suggests, CMS is a consolidated school system that covers all of Mecklenburg County, including Charlotte and the county's six towns.[8] CMS is led by a nine-person school board. Until 1995, all board members were elected at-large, but in that year CMS switched to a hybrid system, with three board members elected at large and one elected from each of the six districts into which the county is divided. Board members serve four-year terms, and elections are staggered so that the three at-large seats are on the ballot in one year, and the six district seats are on the ballot two years later. Although board members are elected independently of county commissioners, the latter influence CMS policy because the school district lacks taxing authority and must rely on the county commission to issue bonds and provide a significant portion of its operating revenue. CMS is not similarly financially dependent on the governments of the seven municipalities within Mecklenburg County, but education politics are frequently related to developments in municipal politics, especially those of Charlotte.

The *Swann* Era

In the legal and political struggles preceding the Supreme Court's 1971 ruling in *Swann*, most of the city's influential business elite stood on the sidelines and/or opposed any comprehensive desegregation efforts. But once the Supreme Court ruling settled the legal issues, the business elite threw its considerable political clout behind the implementation of desegregation and the election of school board members who would support desegregation. Despite hopping on the desegregation bandwagon relatively late in the game, the business elite soon found itself benefiting from it. With Charlotte's desegregation accomplishments receiving praise in national media, the business elite successfully drew on the city's reputation for progressive and tranquil race relations in the competition to attract mobile capital. Moreover, at least through 1985, test scores suggested that desegregation improved educational outcomes.

Business elite support for the busing plan was part of a broader political alliance between these executives and the political leadership of the black community. This alliance was a defining characteristic of Charlotte's urban regime through the 1970s and most of the 1980s and played a frequently decisive role in the election of pro-growth local officials and the successful passage of bond referenda for roads, sewers, and other infrastructure necessary for Charlotte's growth. The political clout of the alliance was exemplified by the mayoral elections of 1983 and 1985, in which Harvey Gantt became the first black to be elected mayor of a large, predominantly white southern city.

Undoubtedly moral and ideological considerations played a part in the business elite's support for the busing plan. But as the interest-convergence thesis would suggest, when desegregation conflicted with development, the latter typically won, as illustrated by the debate over the location of the outerbelt freeway in southern Mecklenburg.[9] Beginning in the mid-1970s and not fully resolved for a decade, the debate saw the Chamber of Commerce and most of Charlotte's major developers and builders push for the more southern of the two proposed routes despite the fact that this route would greatly lengthen the bus rides necessary for desegregation between outlying white neighborhoods and closer-in black neighborhoods. The deal over the outerbelt's location was finally resolved with the help of Johnny Harris, an influential developer who wanted to develop his vast landholdings in southern Mecklenburg into the two-thousand-acre residential, commercial, and recreational development called Ballantyne. Harris took advantage of his fund-raising activities in the 1984 gubernatorial campaign to secure appointment to the state Board of Transportation. Once on the board, the *Charlotte Observer* reported, Harris "pushed for completing the southern leg of the outerbelt ... It will border Ballantyne, increasing the land's value. Harris donated 110 acres in Ballantyne for the outerbelt, U.S. 521, and other roads. In return, the state will relocate and widen U.S. 521 through Ballantyne. That is how the system works ... Harris's advantage over most developers is the family land."[10] The eventual opening of the southern leg of the outerbelt in the 1990s helped suck development from mid-ring neighborhoods and contributed to widespread demographic changes in these neighborhoods' schools.[11]

The importance of the outerbelt's opening in the 1990s notwithstanding, both the busing plan and Charlotte's regime had begun unraveling in the 1980s. In the 1987 mayoral election, Gantt, a Democrat, was upset by Republican Sue Myrick. His defeat had many reasons, the most relevant here being the changes in Charlotte's electorate and political geography wrought by the development that attracted newcomers from the North and Midwest. The white Republicans among the newcomers were more likely than others to settle in outlying areas of the county, whose incorporation into the city of Charlotte was facilitated by North Carolina's liberal annexation laws. Myrick's victory signaled a sea change in local politics. In the twenty-five years prior to her victory 1987, the Democrats had won all but one mayoral election, but in that contest the Democratic Party was divided and the Republican benefited from significant Democratic support. However, in the twenty years after her 1987 victory, no Democrat was elected Charlotte's mayor. During this twenty-year period, Democrats frequently constituted a majority of other elected bodies such as the Mecklenburg County Commission, Charlotte City Council, and the (nominally) nonpartisan school board. But Republican dominance of Charlotte's mayoralty was a telling indicator of the post-1987 decline in the electoral clout of the coalition between black political leaders and the business elite. No coalition with comparable hegemony emerged to take its place.

Education politics were also significantly affected by the white newcomers. Moving to Charlotte from outside the South, many were accustomed to predominantly white, suburban school districts; and, not having lived through CMS' desegregation battles, newcomers lacked the pride of more-established Charlotteans in the busing plan. Local unhappiness with busing resonated with the national dissatisfaction with public education triggered by the 1983 publication of *A Nation at Risk*, and these two developments contributed to growing criticism of CMS and a large turnover in school board membership. In response to this criticism, and under the leadership of a revamped school board and new superintendent, in 1992 CMS scrapped much of the busing plan in favor of a system of magnet programs that were aimed at hitching CMS' wagon to the rising star of school choice and appeasing (primarily white) opposition to busing.[12] But in 1997, a white parent challenged the use of racial guidelines in the assignment of students to a magnet school. With six other white families subsequently joining the litigation, the case became one about the constitutionality of CMS' continuing to pursue desegregation more than a quarter century after the Supreme Court's ruling in *Swann*.

In the 1999 trial, CMS fought to preserve its desegregation efforts almost as vigorously as it had opposed such efforts a generation earlier. Indeed, few, if any, school boards have ever fought to remain under desegregation orders as vigorously as CMS did in that trial. The vigor of that effort notwithstanding, the school board was sharply divided, with three of the nine members generally opposing the effort. Hearing the case was Federal District Court Judge Robert Potter, a Reagan appointee who, while an attorney in private practice, had headed Reagan's local campaign efforts in the 1970s and been active in Charlotte's anti-busing movement in the 1960s. Given that background, it is hardly surprising that Potter's September 1999 ruling vacated the original *Swann* orders and ordered CMS to abandon its desegregation efforts.

The Adoption of a New Assignment Plan

Potter's ruling ushered in several years of turmoil as CMS struggled with the ruling's aftermath. Key aspects of this turmoil were prefigured by a rally in downtown Charlotte featuring many key political and business leaders that took place between the trial's conclusion and Potter's ruling. Resulting from fears that the trial had exacerbated doubts about the quality of education and the stability of pupil assignment, the Unity Rally was billed as an event that would unite Charlotteans whatever the outcome of the court case. "The business community is anxious to get on with this business of education," said Allen Tate, a leading local realtor, chair of the Charlotte Chamber, and one of the main organizers of the rally. "We know we've got to move on."[13]

However, efforts to "move on" were stymied by other dynamics, many of which were illustrated by another rally several months later that packed one of Charlotte's largest black churches. Called the Faith Community Rally on Public Education and initiated by black religious, civic, and political leaders, this rally reflected alarm at the widespread resegregation portended by Potter's ruling. With a spirit reminiscent of the civil rights era, the prevailing sentiment of the rally was exemplified by one of its organizers, Reverend Casey Kimbrough: "We will not go back to a segregated system. There is a storm in Charlotte, and there can be no peace without justice."[14]

All four black members of CMS' school board attended this rally, as did one of its white members. Constituting a (bare) majority of CMS' nine-member board, these five people fought — during the subsequent exhaustive courtroom appeals of Potter's ruling and intense local controversy about a new pupil assignment plan — to preserve as much of CMS' historic commitment to desegregation as the changed legal environment would allow. The board majority's ability to wage this fight, indeed the continued existence of the majority, was made possible by the November 1999 election. Occurring a month after the board's vote to appeal Potter's ruling, the election was one in which the three at-large seats were at stake. The board's two black at-large members, Arthur Griffin and Wilhelmenia Rembert, retained their seats despite their strong advocacy of this appeal and the high-profile campaigns of two challengers who opposed the appeal. One of these challengers was Larry Gauvreau, the most outspoken of the victorious white plaintiffs in the 1999 trial.

Initially, the board majority's efforts to preserve as much desegregation as was legally possible were accompanied by significant supportive grassroots mobilization, but this mobilization progressively diminished. With the legal appeals largely failing; CMS superintendent Eric Smith, the business elite, and most city and county elected officials pushing to "move on"; and increasing numbers of citizens dismayed by the ongoing uncertainty over pupil assignment; the school board adopted a new assignment plan in July 2001.

The Family Choice Plan can be summarized as a race-neutral choice plan that employed a complex system of magnet schools and geographically determined attendance areas. These areas gave every student a "home school," one near his or her residence, at which attendance was guaranteed. Students who did not wish to attend their home school could apply to other schools. But if a school lacked capacity to accommodate all applicants, preference went to those for whom it was the home school. Admittance to magnet schools was determined by a lottery, but in keeping with Potter's ruling, neither the lottery nor any other aspect of the pupil assignment plan took race into account.

The board's decision to adopt the plan lowered some of the stakes for the six district seats that were on the ballot in the November 2001 election. But important issues remained. The pivotal contest involved a challenge to Louise Woods, the white member of the five-person board majority that had sought to mitigate the district's pending resegregation. With considerable support from the business elite, Woods's challenger raised more than three times the campaign funds that she did. But strong neighborhood organization and the advantages of incumbency helped her stave off the challenge by a 58–42 percent margin. The board's five-person majority thus remained intact.

However, that same election saw Larry Gauvreau win a seat on the board from the district in northern Mecklenburg. Several past and present school board members shared Gauvreau's opposition to CMS' desegregation policies. But none did so with the combative scorn for what, in a pre-election statement in the *Observer*, he called the "diversity hucksters roaming the hallways of American education, business, and government."[15] His election augured the even greater political changes that would soon affect CMS.

The Early Years of the Post-*Swann* Era

From the perspective of late 2007, a discussion of the five-plus years of the new assignment plan can be grouped under three categories: resegregation, changes in CMS' understanding of itself and in its superintendent, and changes in the politics of education.

Resegregation
Racial
Although it is important to consider segregation from multiethnic/racial and socioeconomic perspectives, good reasons remain to begin the discussion with reference to blacks and non-Hispanic whites. The two groups are

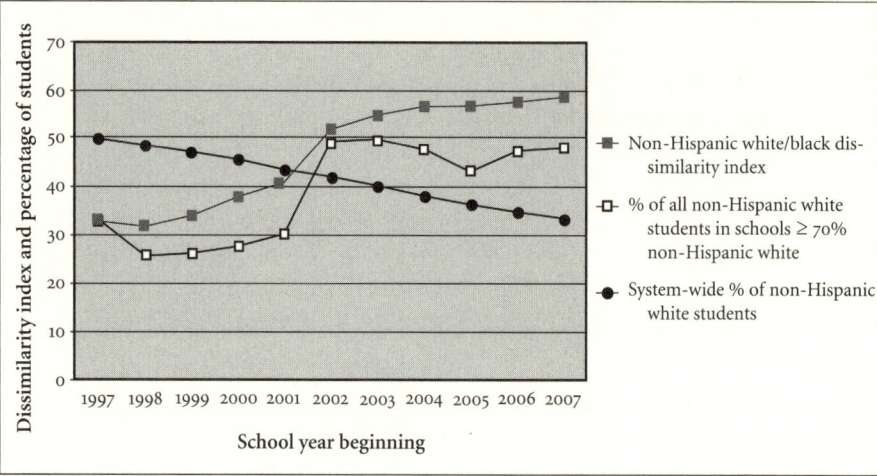

Figure 38. Racial resegregation, CMS elementary schools. Calculated from data obtained from North Carolina Department of Public Instruction and the National Center for Education Statistics. (Source: Stephen Samuel Smith.)

still the largest in CMS' increasingly diverse student population and much of the local politics of color continues to revolve around a black/non-Hispanic white axis. Using the index of racial imbalance or racial dissimilarity,[16] figure 38 charts black/non-Hispanic white segregation in CMS elementary schools, which because of their typically smaller enrollments and attendance zones are a more sensitive measure of segregation than middle or high schools. As the figure indicates, black/non-Hispanic white segregation drifted upward through the 1990s, jumped sharply in 2002–03 (the first year of the new pupil assignment plan), and has inched up since then. Figure 38 shows that the new plan increased black/non-Hispanic white segregation, which, of course, is the very kind of segregation that *Brown*, *Swann*, and a host of legal and policy initiatives were designed to decrease.

The dissimilarity index could be computed for any two groups of students, but it is initially more useful to look at racial/ethnic segregation from a perspective that takes account of the importance many non-Hispanic white families attach to keeping their children from attending schools with "too many" children of color.[17] Thus, figure 38 also presents data on the percentage of non-Hispanic white students who attend schools in which at least 70 percent of the students are non-Hispanic white. As can be seen, the figure presents a picture that is even starker than that presented by the dissimilarity index. There are relatively small fluctuations before and after 2002–03, but that year, the first of the new assignment plan, sees a very sharp change. In the five years prior to the implementation of the plan, 29 percent, on average, of non-Hispanic white students attended schools whose enrollment was at least 70 percent non-Hispanic white. In the years since the implementation of the plan, such schools have enrolled, on average, 48 percent of all the non-Hispanic white students who attend elementary school. The increase in the percentage of non-Hispanic white students in these heavily (≥ 70 percent) non-Hispanic white schools is especially significant because, as figure 38 also shows, the non-Hispanic white share of the district's total enrollment has dropped.[18] In other words, even though non-Hispanic whites now constitute a smaller percentage of CMS' total enrollment than in the *Swann* era, a much larger percentage of them are enrolled in elementary schools whose non-Hispanic white composition greatly exceeds the system-wide average.

As might be suspected from the high concentration of non-Hispanic whites in schools with very high percentages of non-Hispanic whites, there is considerable segregation between such students and all students of color, not just blacks. In 2007–08 the dissimilarity index between non-Hispanic whites and all students of color was 58 and that between non-Hispanic whites and Hispanics was 64 (which was higher than that for blacks/non-Hispanic whites of 59). By contrast, the dissimilarity index between blacks and Hispanics was 33, which indicates considerably less segregation between the two largest groups of students of color than between non-Hispanic whites and blacks, Hispanics, or all students of color.

The globalizing Charlotte of the post-*Swann* era is different in many ways from the more provincial Charlotte of the pre-*Swann* era. But when it comes to education and segregation, in many ways the more things change, the more they are in danger of becoming the same. The CMS of the pre-*Swann* era with its brutally sharp segregation between blacks and whites may be a thing of the past. But the CMS of the post-*Swann* era with its increasing segregation between non-Hispanic whites, on the one hand, and blacks and Hispanics, on the other, is very much a thing of the present.

Socioeconomic

In recent years CMS has increasingly viewed segregation in socioeconomic terms. The change is a result of the outcome of the 1999 trial, CMS's increasing ethnic/racial diversity, and the well-known fact that schools with high percentages of low-income children pose daunting educational challenges. Figure 39 displays trends in socioeconomic resegregation in CMS elementary schools by presenting data on the FRL/non-FRL dissimilarity index and the percentage of all elementary students in high poverty schools (FRL population ≥ 80 percent). The figure also presents data on the system-wide percentage of elementary school FRL students.

As figure 39 indicates, the single sharpest increase in the FRL/non-FRL dissimilarity index occurred upon the implementation of the new pupil assignment plan. The data on enrollment in high poverty schools presents the same picture, only more sharply. Prior to the implementation of the new plan, the percentage of students in high poverty schools was basically constant. It has also been largely constant in the years since the plan was implemented. However, between these two plateaus, the percentage of students in high poverty schools jumps approximately threefold. Moreover, the magnitude of this jump cannot be attributed to the system-wide increase in the percentage of FRL students, since that percentage increased only slightly between 2001–02 and 2002–03.

The data on racial and socioeconomic resegregation present very similar pictures. As measured by dissimilarity indices, both kinds of segregation have generally increased in recent years. However, the single sharpest increase in both indices occurred upon the implementation of the new assignment plan. As measured by the concentration of non-Hispanic white students in schools with high non-Hispanic white enrollments and by the concentration of FRL students in schools with high FRL enrollments, the picture is starker. The new assignment plan resulted in large jumps in both figures 38 and 39. Before and after those jumps, the data shows little change. Thus, on the basis of all four measures (two kinds of resegregation, two ways of measuring each kind), it is safe to conclude that independent of demographic trends and other changes, the implementation of the new assignment plan increased resegregation.

Changes in CMS' Understanding of Itself and in Its Superintendent

In 2006, CMS revised its vision statement in a way that codified and inscribed on the district's self-definition the changes in pupil assignment that were taking place. For at least fifteen years, the statement had included the lofty aspiration of being "the premier, urban integrated school system in the nation in which all students acquire the knowledge, skills, and values" necessary to live full, enlightened, and productive lives. But the revised statement made no reference to integration or even implied the commitment to diversity and racial justice that was inherent in *integrated*'s inclusion in the abandoned statement. Rather, the revised statement says the district "provides all students the best education available anywhere, preparing every child to lead a rich and productive life."[19]

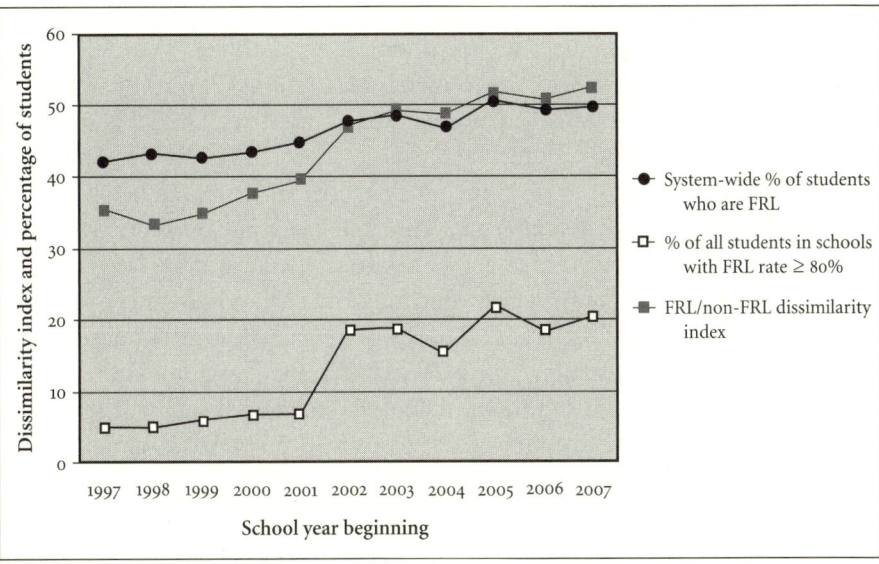

Figure 39. Socioeconomic resegregation, CMS elementary schools. Calculated from data obtained from Charlotte-Mecklenburg Schools. (Source: Stephen Samuel Smith.)

The abandonment of that lofty goal resembled another change that also recognized how CMS' reality now differed from its previously more grandiose aspirations. Whereas the post-*Swann* pupil assignment plan was initially called the Family Choice Plan, it is now simply the Student Assignment Plan. The change reflected the fact that, as an assistant superintendent commented in 2005, the plan's initial name erroneously conveyed that families had more choice than they actually had. That was because, with so many families choosing to exercise their guarantee of attendance at their home school, there were very few choices other than high poverty schools available to students who did not want to attend their home schools.[20]

The limited choice options were a salient issue for James Pughsley, CMS' superintendent. While urban superintendents typically face many challenges, those facing Pughsley were especially daunting. Previously CMS' deputy superintendent, he was appointed superintendent in May 2002 after Eric Smith announced that he was leaving CMS. Superintendent since 1997, Smith possessed formidable political skills, and successfully drew upon them in the battle to secure board support for the new pupil assignment plan. But with the plan not scheduled for implementation until the start of the 2002–03 school year, he left the district before it took effect and any of its consequences could be assessed.

Smith's political skills allowed him to flourish in the goldfish bowl that came with being CMS superintendent. Possessing a different kind of personality, Pughsley preferred, in his own words, "to fly below the radar."[21] That preference, critics charged, helped explain why CMS, under his leadership, was not adequately addressing the many challenges it faced. Several of these challenges stemmed from the political changes discussed below, and Pughsley did not like these changes. Although a year remained on his contract, he announced his retirement in April 2005, calling attention to how "'the climate has shifted' away from commitment to equal education for all children."[22] That shift, he explained, was illustrated by recent decisions of the school board to change the guidelines for pupil assignment in a way that further strengthened the home school guarantee and that made it more difficult to address the dilemma of severe overcrowding at some schools and the concentrated poverty at others.

Political Changes

There have also been landmark changes in the local politics of education. As noted earlier, the five-person board majority that had fought the resegregation portended by Potter's ruling remained intact in the 2001 election despite a well-financed attempt to unseat Louise Woods, the one white in the five-person board majority that had fought resegregation. But that year's election of Larry Gauvreau foreshadowed the changes that would sweep CMS in the 2003 elections. With two longtime incumbents, including Arthur Griffin, deciding not to seek reelection in 2003, that election would of necessity bring two new faces to the at-large seats. However, it brought three new faces because of the defeat of Wilhelmenia Rembert, who was then board chair. With Griffin not running, Rembert losing, and the other black candidates running far behind her, the 2003 election resulted in the number of black board members dropping from four to two. That was the lowest it had been since before the 1995 switch in school board electoral structure, even though in 2003 black students constituted a higher percentage of CMS' enrollment than ever before. More significant than the change in the board's racial composition was the obvious extent to which the election's outcome signaled how differently the political winds in CMS were now blowing.

Rembert's loss stemmed from a variety of factors, probably the most important of which were indicated by her postelection comment, "I believe there was a lot more anger in the suburbs and not the same sense of urgency in the African American community."[23] Indeed, black mobilization in support of her campaign — as was the case with many other aspects of education politics — was less in 2003 than it had been in 1999. Although her campaign was hurt by the fact that the overall turnout of black voters in 2003 was lower than in 1999, it also suffered from a more specific demobilization with regard to school board elections as measured by the fall-off between top-of-the-ballot offices (mayor and city council) and down-ballot offices (school board).[24]

Equally important as Rembert's defeat was the victory of Kaye McGarry, a first-time candidate and a white, who led the field with a stunning 18 percent more votes than the second-place finisher. She did especially well in Mecklenburg's outlying heavily white precincts, but in the heavily black precincts her vote total was less than 3 percent of Rembert's. Although voicing support for equity of resources in all schools, McGarry also claimed, "We do not have a funding problem, we have a spending problem. We do not need to be a transportation system; we need to be an education system."[25] Such claims, as well as her emphasis on preserving the home school guarantee, secured endorsements from prominent local conservatives, the Republican Party, and two recently formed parents' groups.[26] One of these groups was Parents for Education in Charlotte-Mecklenburg Schools, based in the south of the county; the other was Families United for North Mecklenburg Education (FUME), based in the north.

The acronym FUME accurately captured the feelings of a significant number of parents in northern regions of the county. Fueling those feelings — and similar sentiments in the south — was severe overcrowding in many of the two areas' schools. Contributing to anger about the overcrowding was the claim by Gauvreau and other conservative activists that this overcrowding arose largely because CMS was spending too much money on renovating and building schools in neighborhoods of color in order to pursue desegregation and/or to please these neighborhoods' representatives.[27]

Contentious and salient as overcrowding and other problems had become, FUME's approach to CMS was generally to try to fix it by campaigning for candidates like McGarry, serving on task forces, and mobilizing parents to attend board meetings. However, about fifteen months after the 2003 election, North Mecklenburg gave rise to another movement that was less concerned with fixing CMS than about dumping it — the group's website was titled dumpcms.com — by breaking it into smaller districts. Fueling the movement were the severe overcrowding as well as complaints about discipline, safety, and the district's large size, many of the latter coming from newcomers to Charlotte who were accustomed to the smaller districts in other parts of the country. The group's initial meeting drew more than four hundred people. Larry Gauvreau supported deconsolidation, as did other conservative political officials including the county commissioner who represented northern Mecklenburg and the mayor of Matthews.[28] However, deconsolidation required the approval of the state legislature, which has generally promoted consolidation between a county district and any city district(s) located within the county. Thus, the state House education committee killed the proposal with a near unanimous vote accompanied by statements from some members that deconsolidation would further segregate the district.

Despite the failure of deconsolidation in the state legislature, the secessionist movement provoked enough alarm among political and business leaders to trigger the formation in March 2005 of a high-profile task force. However, unlike similar groups in CMS history this one was neither publicly chosen nor publicly funded. Instead, local corporations contributed $500,000 to support the group's work. Cochaired by one of Charlotte's most prominent African Americans, former mayor Harvey Gantt, and Cathy Bessant, a white, high-ranking Bank of America executive, the leadership of the task force embodied the alliance between the business elite and Charlotte's black political leadership that had dominated local politics during the heyday of the busing plan and prior to Harvey Gantt's upset in the 1987 mayor's race. But the task force's main concerns only minimally reflected the concerns that had given rise to the busing plan. Rather its focus was on the governance issues that were especially dear to those seeking to dump CMS. While rejecting deconsolidation, the report's first four recommendations calling for the sweeping decentralization of CMS testified to the influence of the Dump CMS movement, as did the recommendation calling for CMS "to modify its K–8 student assignment plan toward a fixed assignment based on residence."[29]

Whatever hopes the task force and its sponsors may have had that the group's work would calm the political waters roiling CMS, its report was issued in December 2005, which was too late to affect the previous month's election. In that election a large CMS bond package was defeated, the first time a school bond package had failed since 1995. But in 1995, the margin was a close 51–49; in 2005, the margin was larger (57–43), with much of the opposition spearheaded by conservative elected officials. These efforts were exemplified in a letter published in the *Observer* that was signed by, among others, Gauvreau, McGarry, the county commissioner who represented northern Mecklenburg, and the county commissioner who represented southern Mecklenburg. Claiming that CMS had disastrously wasted its construction funds on inner-city facilities that now had many empty seats, the letter urged voters to reject the bond package and instead use alternatives to fund new school construction.[30] Such arguments along with concern about taxes necessary to pay for the bond package resonated with other complaints about CMS, especially in northern and southern regions of the county, where the margin of defeat exceeded the countywide margin even though more than 60 percent of the bond package would have been spent in those regions.

The ability of white opponents of the bonds such as Gauvreau and McGarry to mobilize their supporters contrasted sharply with that of black opponents. Although most black leaders and elected officials endorsed the bonds, they were opposed by the head of the education committee of the Black Political Caucus — one of Charlotte's most important black political organizations — on the grounds that they did not adequately anticipate growth in inner-city neighborhoods and that passage would facilitate even more resegregation.[31] But that opposition failed to sway most African Americans, and the bonds passed in the heavily (> 95.0 percent) black precincts with 57 percent of the vote.

Five months after the 1995 school bonds were defeated, a smaller package was put before the voters, and it passed easily. But CMS' political situation a decade later was much more perilous, and so it was not until two years after the 2005 defeat, in the November 2007 general election, that another school bond package appeared on the ballot. By this time, CMS had a new and politically astute superintendent. The size of the package as well as the location of the projects that it would fund resulted from lengthy negotiations within CMS and with the county commission (whose approval was necessary for the bonds to appear on the ballot). These negotiations secured the support of many people and groups that had opposed the 2005 package and blunted the opposition of others. The package passed easily with 68 percent of the vote.

The same election day that saw the bonds pass also saw the reelection of all three incumbent at-large board members. However, in this election, as in many other aspects of life, what did not happen is also of great interest: no people of color were on the ballot even though students of color comprised a higher percentage of CMS enrollment than ever before. Insofar as Hispanics, Asians, and Native Americans had rarely, if ever, sought election to the board, their absence on the 2007 ballot was perhaps not especially remarkable. But the 2007 school board election was the first board election since 1968 in which no African American appeared on the ballot, another indication of the black political demobilization over education issues.[32]

Discussion

A discussion of these recent events can be grouped under three headings: CMS and a new national politics of desegregation; resegregation, development, and the interest-convergence thesis; and the long shadow of the Jim Crow era.

CMS and the New National Politics of School Desegregation

Since CMS' mandatory busing plan was one of the nation's most successful, a discussion of the district's increased resegregation would do well to comment about resegregation nationally. While scholars disagree about how much resegregation has taken place nationally, even those who challenge claims of extensive resegregation acknowledge that progress toward desegregation "has faltered since the early 1990s."[33] The reasons for this faltering include court rulings by Potter and other conservative federal judges appointed by Republican presidents, the inability of even relatively successful experiences such as Charlotte's to fulfill more than a handful of desegregation's many promises, and increasing doubts among blacks and other peoples of color about the importance of (fighting for) desegregation as opposed to obtaining adequate resources for schools with large percentages of students of color. This faltering is unfortunate because of the growing scholarly evidence that desegregation improves educational outcomes both in Charlotte and nationally.[34]

But in Charlotte, there are additional reasons for viewing resegregation as unfortunate involving public opinion and electoral politics, especially in the years immediately before and after the 1999 trial. While many black Charlotteans had been disappointed by the shortcomings of desegregation, this disappointment was generally trumped by their opposition to Potter's ruling and the widespread resegregation that it portended. Not surprisingly, white Charlotteans viewed possible resegregation with greater equanimity, but public opinion surveys from 1995 to 2001 showed that between 15 and 20 percent of whites consistently supported busing to achieve racial balance and an additional 30 percent were ambivalent about neighborhood schools if this would result in considerable racial segregation.[35]

The reasons involving electoral politics are even more striking. At least ever since Richard Nixon first talked about how "the great silent majority of Americans" shouldn't feel guilty "about wanting your children in good schools close to home" and that it was not racist to object to having children "taken away from a neighborhood school and transported miles away,"[36] desegregation proponents worried that most communities, if left to themselves and not subject to the intervention of the federal courts, would abandon desegregation efforts. But CMS' experience provides support for the exact opposite view. The two school board elections (1995 and 1997) prior to the 1999 trial saw the formation of the school board majority that would fight Potter's ruling. More importantly, despite the political turbulence that resulted from his ruling, the two school board elections (1999 and 2001) immediately after his ruling saw that majority remain intact. Many factors were at work in these elections, and it would be wrong to interpret any of them as a referendum on desegregation. Moreover, there is no doubt that CMS' desegregation efforts faced increasing local opposition. But despite this opposition, it was not until the 2003 school board election — by which time the Supreme Court has issued its final ruling in the case and Charlotte's black community experienced considerable demobilization over educational issues — that the school board's majority was dismantled and that the board's political perspective and racial composition changed dramatically.

In other words, the situation in Charlotte in the years immediately preceding and following Potter's ruling was the very opposite of the desegregation politics characteristic of the civil rights era. In that era, desegregation proponents had to rely on the federal courts because local political arenas were so hostile. But in Charlotte in 1999 it was the ruling of a federal judge that limited, if not ended, CMS' desegregation efforts, and it was the workings of local politics that resulted in a democratically elected school board that fought to continue these efforts. Whereas in the 1960s there was generally a conflict between the pursuit of desegregation and the long-standing U.S. tradition of local control over education, in Charlotte in 1999, there was no such conflict. In this respect, just as original *Swann* litigation portended national changes in the school desegregation landscape, the court actions in the reopened *Swann* litigation were a portent of what would happen eight years later when, in high-profile cases arising in Seattle and Louisville, the Supreme Court struck blows against both desegregation and local control of education by ordering the two districts to abandon policies they had voluntarily adopted in order to increase racial/ethnic balance in the districts' schools.[37]

Resegregation, Development, and the Interest-Convergence Thesis

As indicated by the history of Charlotte's nationally touted busing plan, the link between it and Charlotte's economic growth was never primarily educational; the link was primarily political. To be sure, the best available evidence indicates that in Charlotte, as in many other instances, school desegregation improved educational outcomes. But to the extent that improved educational outcomes contributed to economic development, the length of time required for that improvement to measurably affect the actual skills of the local workforce was of necessity too long to explain the much quicker effect that school desegregation had on Charlotte's growth. School desegregation fueled Charlotte's reputation for having the kind of tranquil and progressive race relations that made the city a good place in which to live, raise a family, do business, and invest. Also consistent with the interest-convergence thesis was how the business elite's support for school desegregation contributed to the political alliance between it (the business elite) and black political leaders that was necessary for the election of pro-growth candidates and the passage of the bonds needed to pay for the infrastructure necessary to support economic growth.

Given that the primary link between Charlotte's economic development and the mandatory busing plan of the 1970s and 1980s was political, it becomes easier to understand why subsequent resegregation has not adversely affected local economic development. From a political perspective, the corporate, local, and national scene is now very different from what it was in the years of struggle that gave rise to Charlotte's busing plan. In the business world, Charlotte's major players are no longer regional upstarts trying to shed the image of southern backwardness. Rather, by the dawn of the twenty-first century, many of them — especially Charlotte's two preeminent businesses, Bank of America and First Union (subsequently Wachovia) — had become global powerhouses to whom workplace diversity was important and whose efforts to promote such diversity were widely hailed.[38] Moreover, these businesses' efforts to promote workplace diversity are as little affected by the resegregation of the public schools in Charlotte as they are by the even greater segregation of the public schools in many other cities where these businesses also have a major presence.

Moreover, the local political situation has changed. Whereas the events that led to the mandatory busing plan reflected the widespread and strong mobilization of black Charlotteans and their white political allies, these groups' recent political efforts have been dwarfed by those of whites —

especially in outlying areas of Mecklenburg — opposed to desegregation efforts. Potter's 1999 decision triggered, as noted earlier, an African American mobilization reminiscent of the civil rights era that was manifest in the Faith Community Rally on Public Education and the results of the 1999 at-large board elections. But that mobilization was short-lived, and much of it had disappeared by the time the board adopted the new pupil assignment plan in July 2001. That demobilization subsequently extended even into electoral politics, as indicated by the fall-off in votes for Rembert in black precincts in the 2003 election and the absence of any black candidates on the ballot in the 2007 election. To be sure, between 2003 and 2007 black and liberal white activists made periodic efforts to mobilize their presumed constituents for meetings, rallies, and attendance at school board meetings. Similarly, parent groups at several mid-ring schools mounted efforts to maintain diversity and obtain resources for these schools. But few, if any, of these efforts resulted in the impassioned mass participation that characterized the efforts to deconsolidate CMS, and to defeat the 2005 bond package.

Not surprisingly, the most immediate effect of this changed political climate has been on CMS itself. Thus, while Superintendent Pughsley expressed sympathy with the goals of desegregation proponents in private meetings with them, the paucity of political mobilization by these proponents' presumed constituency made it difficult for that sympathy to be translated into policy. Almost as importantly, the changed political situation affected the activity of Charlotte's business elite, whose support for any desegregation efforts was at least as necessary in the post-*Swann* era as it was thirty years earlier. Indeed, in the post-*Swann* era, Charlotte's business elite may have promoted workplace diversity, preached in many high-profile venues about diversity's importance to the community, and supported resource equity among the district's schools, but as the interest-convergence thesis leads one to expect, the changed local political situation provided considerable disincentive to challenge the resegregation of the schools. As opposed to the 1970s, which saw leading corporate executives push for desegregation, thirty years later the squeaking wheels most requiring the business elite's political grease were not those of Charlotte's black leadership and its white allies.

The business elite's approach to the politics of education is exemplified by the privately financed and chosen 2005 task force whose recommendations reflected its origins as a response to efforts led by whites in outlying areas to deconsolidate CMS. That generally collective approach is mirrored in the activities of many individual executives, including Hugh McColl, generally viewed as Charlotte's most influential business executive of the past twenty-five years. As noted by one of this chapter's epigraphs, the former Bank of America CEO and chairman touted the effects of the school desegregation of the 1970s and 1980s and its consequences for economic development. Moreover, absent a scheduling conflict, in the 1999 trial he would have testified, at CMS' request, about the importance of diversity.[39] But given the outcome of the trial, he was unwilling to lend any significant support to the effort to avoid the resegregation facing CMS, since there was scant political incentive to do so. Moreover, in the 2003 election he threw his considerable political weight behind Kaye McGarry, donating a thousand dollars to her campaign and lavishly praising her in a letter to the *Observer*.[40]

Moreover, even brief reflection about the national situation leads to the realization that Charlotte is hardly the only locality in which resegregation has not undermined local economic growth when the latter is measured by population and employment growth, corporate profits, or elite prosperity. According to these indicators, the United States did reasonably well from the early-1990s through 2007, even though these years saw little advance — if not considerable backsliding — in desegregation. Similarly, the nation's metropolitan areas are filled with localities in which development has surged and business elites have prospered despite the segregation of many of these areas' public school systems. Perhaps no locality better indicates how school segregation has been compatible with local economic growth than Atlanta, the paradigmatic New South city with which Charlotte, in the eyes of its civic boosters, has long been playing catch-up. At the same time that Charlotte was embarking on its busing plan, Atlanta was witnessing what has often been called the Atlanta Compromise, an arrangement in which blacks accepted segregation of the city of Atlanta's public school system in exchange for political and administrative control of the system. This arrangement had questionable if not disastrous educational consequences for the black children in Atlanta itself, but did not preclude extensive economic development in the Atlanta area.[41]

The Shadow of Jim Crow on Globalizing Charlotte

As the first decade of the twenty-first century draws to a close, it is clear that the past thirty years of development in Charlotte have increasingly eroded the conditions and support that facilitated adoption of the busing plan and its successes of the 1970s and 1980s. However, it is worth stressing that this development did not result primarily from impersonal demographic changes that, like the weather, occur largely independent of human activity. Rather Charlotte's development and the way in which it undermined school desegregation were affected by a long series of political and economic decisions made by human beings, including, as noted earlier, decisions involving the location of the southern route of the outerbelt.[42]

The construction of the southern leg of the outerbelt also indicates the persistent legacy of Jim Crow. As noted earlier, developer Johnny Harris's vast landholdings in southern Mecklenburg played an important role in his ability to influence the outerbelt's construction. Much of that land had been passed down through the family after its acquisition by Harris's grandfather, Cameron Morrison. An attorney of initially modest means, Morrison played a leading role in the disenfranchisement of blacks in North Carolina at the turn of the twentieth century, became one of the state's most prominent attorneys and influential politicians, and touted his advocacy of white supremacy in a successful campaign for governor in 1920.[43] Thus, the history and clout of the Morrison/Harris family illustrate how events rooted in the era of white supremacy can cast a long shadow over the course history subsequently takes, including Charlotte's desegregation efforts to redress some of the consequences of white supremacy.

Conclusion

In explaining the events that facilitated CMS' resegregation, this chapter has noted how the strong mobilization of African Americans and their white allies in the immediate aftermath of Potter's decision increasingly gave way to demobilization. It is thus appropriate to conclude by considering two factors that affect the possibilities of remobilization.[44] The first is greater clarity and unity by advocates for children of color about the extent to which equal educational opportunity requires desegregation. This issue antedates *Brown* by many years, but in the wake of *Brown* and *Swann*, the importance of desegregation to achieving educational equality became a fundamental tenet of education policy in Charlotte and remained so until the rulings of the federal judiciary in the reopened litigation. Not surprisingly, the changes in the legal situation and in CMS policy in the post-*Swann* era greatly exacerbated divisions among Charlotte's advocates for children of color about the importance and feasibility of desegregation. In particular, some previously strong advocates of desegregation argued that, with the exception of some mid-ring schools, the struggle for desegregation had been lost. Instead of fighting an already lost battle, they argued, it makes more political sense to focus on getting additional resources for segregated schools, especially since that goal is often supported — in principle at least — by whites hostile to desegregation and a business elite that currently has no political incentive to seek desegregation. And in contemporary Charlotte, as in many other places and at many other times, the counterclaim has been that attempts to make "separate" anywhere near "equal" are as doomed as efforts to pursue desegregation. Moreover, the counterclaim goes, there are few legal restrictions on pursuing desegregation using socioeconomic or academic criteria, or the judicious use of race-neutral attendance zones and magnet options.

A key aspect of evaluating these two sets of arguments is comparing the educational outcomes for students who attend segregated schools with the outcomes of other students, a task well beyond the scope of this chapter (even though, as noted above, there is increasing scholarly evidence for the educational benefits of desegregation). But it is not the educational benefits of desegregation that have recently divided local advocates for children of color. Rather it is sharp differences over the political feasibility of desegregation that have sometimes precluded more cohesive political action on important issues, such as the 2005 bond referendum. Politically speaking, that referendum turned out to be the worst of both worlds for such advocates. A majority of them supported the referendum, but it lost. A minority opposed it, but their opposition, as indicated by the vote in the heavily black precincts, had relatively little effect. It thus behooves advocates for children of color to try to gain greater clarity and unity about the extent to which it is worth fighting for desegregation and how to wage that fight.

Unlike the first factor, the second has only recently become important, and it has done so because of globalization's most marked effect on CMS: the surge in Hispanic enrollment. This surge raises the question of the extent to which mobilization for equality of educational opportunity might be fueled by increased cooperation between Hispanics and blacks. Although some efforts have been made to develop such cooperation in Charlotte, so far these efforts have been relatively few in number, tentative, and/or not especially successful. Research on other school districts suggests that such cooperation is difficult on issues involving scarcity, such as teaching and administrative jobs, because in these areas one group's gains frequently lead to the other's losses. But on issues where scarcity is not a factor, such as student achievement, both groups gain simultaneously.[45] Given that disproportionately large percentages of Hispanic and black students are often found in the same schools, there would seem to be a strong basis for increased cooperation between blacks and Hispanics around policies that would benefit students in these schools, such as increased resources and/or greater desegregation via, among other things, more choice and magnet options at non–high poverty schools than currently exist.

To the extent such cooperation manifested itself in the electoral arena, it might reverse the developments in at-large school board elections that began in 2003, when no African American was elected, and 2007, when no African American ran. The reason no African American sought election in 2007, according to some black political activists, was that Rembert's defeat in 2003, as well as that of two other African Americans in recent elections for at-large seats to the county commission, provided strong evidence of the difficulties facing blacks trying to win a countywide election. An electoral alliance over education between blacks and Hispanics might increase the electoral prospects of African American candidates and/or facilitate the election of the first Hispanic to the school board. However, given that Hispanics constitute less than 2 percent of Mecklenburg's electorate and many recent Hispanic arrivals cannot vote, such an alliance may be able to exercise more clout outside the electoral arena.

Of course, there is no guarantee that increased mobilization will significantly affect the course of education policy in Charlotte. The success of such efforts also depends on many other things including the acumen with which advocates for low-income children of color draw upon a panoply of approaches ranging from (the threat of) political disruption to normative appeals for individuals to look beyond their particular interests to the welfare of the whole. But while such remobilization is hardly sufficient, it is almost certainly necessary if Charlotte — once distinguished by its school desegregation successes — is to avoid becoming just another city whose pursuit of globalization's promises of increased prosperity and cultural diversity involves willful amnesia about *Brown v. Board of Education's* loftier promise of social and racial justice.

Notes

Earlier versions of this chapter were presented at the 2007 Annual Meeting of the American Political Science Association, Chicago, Illinois, and the 2008 Annual Meeting of the South Carolina Political Science Association, Orangeburg, South Carolina. In discussing events prior to 2002, I draw heavily on my *Boom for Whom? Education, Desegregation, and Development in Charlotte* (Albany: State University of New York Press, 2004). Because of space limitations, this chapter's summary of pre-2002 events generally omits citations to the relevant sources. The citations and a much fuller discussion of these events can be found in *Boom for Whom?* I am grateful to Jerome McKibben, Roslyn Mickelson, Carol Sawyer, and Stephanie Southworth for helpful comments. Any errors are solely my responsibility.

1. Debbie Cenziper and Celeste Smith, "School Plan Is Greeted Cautiously," *Charlotte Observer*, February 14, 1999.

2. Hugh L. McColl Jr., "What Is, and What We Hope For," (speech, Governor's Emerging Issues Forum, Raleigh, N.C., February 24, 2000).

3. *Second Annual Report of the CMS Equity Committee to the Charlotte-Mecklenburg Board of Education*, (Charlotte, N.C.: Charlotte-Mecklenburg Schools, February 2004), 4.

4. Derrick Bell, *Silent Covenants:* Brown v. Board of Education *and the Unfulfilled Hopes for Racial Reform* (New York: Oxford University Press), 69.

5. Even in 2007, Charlotte's business elite was overwhelmingly white. In the heyday of the busing plan, it was almost entirely, if not entirely, white. For a fuller definitional discussion of Charlotte's business elite, see Smith, *Boom for Whom?*, especially 259 n. 66.

6. Steve Lyttle, "130 CMS Teachers Earn Certification — Charlotte-Mecklenburg Now Has 516 Who Are Board Certified," *Charlotte Observer*, January 1, 2003; Betsy Schiffman, "The Best Education in the Biggest Cities," *Forbes*, February 13, 2004, http://www.forbes.com/2004/02/13/cx_bs_0213home.html (accessed June 29, 2007); "2003–04 Record: Highs and Lows," *Charlotte Observer*, August 1, 2004; Steve Lyttle, "Educators Honor CMS Middle Schools," *Charlotte Observer*, March 5, 2005; Editorial, "CMS Grads Rake in Awards," *Charlotte Observer*, July 14, 2007; "The Top of the Class: The Complete List of the 1,300 Top U.S. High Schools," *Newsweek* Web Exclusive, May 17, 2008, http://www.newsweek.com/id/39380 (accessed October 27, 2009).

7. In keeping with the way CMS and my other sources have reported data for many years, when discussing the demographic composition of schools, I will use the categories non-Hispanic white, black, Hispanic, Asian, and Native American. As is well known, these categories conflate race and ethnicity and, moreover, fail to distinguish among different Hispanic peoples and heritages. However, both the nature of the data and limitations of space preclude more precise categories. Data for the 2007–08 school year was obtained from CMS. Data for earlier years obtained from the National Center for Educational Statistics, Common Core of Data, available online at http://nces.ed.gov/ccd/bat (accessed October 27, 2009).

8. Despite these six towns and some remaining unincorporated areas, residents of Mecklenburg County are, in local discourse, often referred to as Charlotteans, and this chapter will follow that admittedly imprecise usage. For similar reasons, it will also use phrases such as "Charlotte's development" as shorthand for development that extends beyond the city of Charlotte to these six towns, unincorporated areas of Mecklenburg, and/or nearby parts of adjoining counties.

9. For a fuller discussion of the outerbelt and other examples of how develop-

ment trumped desegregation in conflicts between the two, see Smith, *Boom for Whom?*, especially 92–96, 221–230.

10. Ricki Morell, "Couple Symbolize City's Ambitions," *Charlotte Observer*, December 15, 1991.

11. Located six and one-half miles from downtown in the Independence Boulevard corridor, East Mecklenburg High School is about one quarter mile from three shopping centers on Independence. In the mid-1990s, those shopping centers included a Target, Circuit City, Office Depot, Toy-R-Us, Barnes and Noble, Harris-Teeter supermarket, and Eckerd drug store. As the opening of the outerbelt spurred growth on Mecklenburg's periphery, the first three of those stores closed their locations near East Mecklenburg High School in favor of ones further out Independence. The other four closed, replaced, if at all, by lower-end stores. Similarly, the demographic composition of East Mecklenburg High also changed: in 1994–95, enrollment was 65 percent white, 31 percent black, 1 percent Hispanic, 3 percent Asian; in 2004–05, the enrollment was 39 percent white, 46 percent black, 11 percent Hispanic, and 3 percent Asian.

12. Typically located in schools in predominantly African American neighborhoods, the magnet programs sought to increase white enrollment at such schools by providing a specialized and attractive curriculum (e.g., science and technology) that would motivate whites to apply for admission to these schools.

13. Jennifer Wing Rothacker and Celeste Smith, "Busing as We Know It Today Will End," *Charlotte Observer*, August 24, 1999.

14. Jen Pilla, "1,500 People Attend Rally for Schools," *Charlotte Observer*, October 4, 1999.

15. Larry Gauvreau, "Diversity: America's Irrational Rationale," *Charlotte Observer*, March 7, 2001.

16. The racial dissimilarity index is independent of the racial composition of a district and indicates the proportion of a district's students that would have to be moved to ensure that the racial composition of each school would be the same as the racial composition of the entire district. This index ranges from 0 (perfect racial balance) to 100 (complete segregation). There is a wide range of opinion about what constitutes "high" or "low" levels of racial balance, but a good working definition comes from the database on racial balance in districts nationwide maintained by Brown University's American Communities Project: "A value of 60 (or above) is considered very high ... [v]alues of 40 or 50 are usually considered a moderate level of segregation, and values of 30 or below are considered to be fairly low." (See http://www.s4.brown.edu/schoolsegregation/index.htm, accessed June 21, 2006).

17. The definition of "too many" hinges on numerous considerations, including where whites reside and their racial attitudes. My definition involving a threshold of 30 percent students of color accords with impressionistic and anecdotal evidence, including conversations with CMS personnel who deal with whites worried about how changes in attendance zones may affect a school's demographic composition.

Moreover, 70 percent non-Hispanic white provides an intuitively plausible threshold because it is currently double CMS' non-Hispanic white enrollment of 35 percent (2007–08 school year).

18. In some ways, the decrease in the percentage of non-Hispanic white CMS students is not surprising because the non-Hispanic white share of enrollment has also dropped nationally, primarily because of the surge in the nation's Hispanic population and differential birth rates. However, as I've shown elsewhere, the decrease in CMS' non-Hispanic white enrollment has been greater than it has been in most adjacent counties as well as in Wake County, which is home to Raleigh and vies with Mecklenburg for having the largest school system in the state, and in North Carolina generally (Stephen Samuel Smith, "Resegregation, Development, and Regime Politics in Charlotte, North Carolina," paper presented at the annual meeting of the American Political Science Association, Chicago, Ill., September 2, 2007). Possible explanations for these differences between CMS and the comparison school systems, including housing prices, tax rates, and perceptions about public education, require further evaluation.

19. *Strategic Plan 2010: Educating Students to Compete Locally, Nationally, and Internationally* (Charlotte, N.C.: Charlotte-Mecklenburg Schools, 2006), 7.

20. By 2006–07, students who wanted to attend a school other than their home school the following year faced the following situation: of the nine nonmagnet options, the school with the lowest poverty rate had a rate that was approximately 1.3 times the system-wide poverty rate, and the average of the poverty rates in these nine schools was approximately 1.8 times the system-wide rate. Of the twenty-nine schools with magnet options, only two had poverty rates below the system-wide rate. (Computations based on data from Charlotte-Mecklenburg Schools *Open Seat Option 2007–2008*, http://www.cms.k12.nc.us/studentassignment07–08/information/PDF/NewChoiceForm2007–08OpenSeat.pdf, accessed June 26, 2007.)

21. Ann Doss Helms, "Pughsley Points to Shifting 'Climate,' CMS Chief Says Those Who Remain Need to Will to Do the Right Thing," *Charlotte Observer*, April 22, 2005.

22. Helms, "Pughsley Points to Shifting 'Climate.'"

23. Celeste Smith and Ann Doss Helms, "With Rembert Loss, Chair Is Up for Grabs," *Charlotte Observer*, November 5, 2003.

24. In 2003, Patrick Cannon, a prominent African American, sought election to city council, and in 1999 another prominent African American, Ella Scarborough, ran for mayor. In two groups of precincts (turnout > 99 percent black, turnout > 95 percent black), the fall-off in 2003 between Cannon and Rembert was greater than between Scarborough and Rembert in 1999. Generalizing from these precincts to the entire county is difficult, but there are good reasons for thinking that had the fall-off been the same in 2003 as it was in 1999, Rembert would have been reelected (Stephen Samuel Smith, "Resegregation, Development, and Regime Poli-

tics in Charlotte, North Carolina," paper presented at the annual meeting of the American Political Science Association, Chicago, Ill., September 2, 2007).

25. "Charlotte-Mecklenburg Board of Education, Part II," *Charlotte Observer*, October 16, 2003.

26. "Conservative Crowd Endorses Madans," *Charlotte Observer*, October 31, 2003; campaign literature distributed by Republican Party, in author's possession; and "N. Mecklenburg Group Endorses 3," *Charlotte Observer*, October 18, 2003.

27. Tucker Mitchell, "Say a Prayer, Send More Mobiles," *Huntersville Herald*, August 12, 2004, http://www.huntersvilleherald.com/articles/2004/08/12/col umns/ mitchell_tucker/Mitchell_column01.txt (accessed March 16, 2008); Kaye McGarry et. al., "Bonds Not Best Way to Build Schools — Defeat the Bonds to Ensure Schools are Constructed Where Most Needed," *Charlotte Observer*, November 5, 2005.

28. Erica Beshears, "Talk Builds of School Split for N. Meck — 400 People Meet in Church and Are Asked to Sign Petition," *Charlotte Observer*, February 18, 2005.

29. American Institutes for Research/Cross & Joftus, *Findings and Recommendations of the Citizens' Task Force on Charlotte-Mecklenburg Schools* (Charlotte: Foundation for the Carolinas, 2005), i.

30. McGarry et al., "Bonds Not Best Way."

31. Carrie Levine, "Criticism of Bond Package Crosses Party, Racial Lines — For Different Reasons, Urban, Suburban Leaders Urge 'No' Vote," *Charlotte Observer*, November 5, 2005.

32. To be sure, the 2007 elections involved only the three at-large seats because the six district seats were not on the ballot. Two of these districts continued to be represented by African Americans, as they had since the hybrid system of representation was implemented in 1995. In accord with legal and political considerations, these two districts' boundaries had been drawn to facilitate the election of African Americans, and it is likely that blacks will continue to be elected from them. However, given the many political differences between running in these two districts and running at-large, the absence of blacks on the 2007 (at-large) ballot is significant because it represents a marked change from the political situation during the heyday and the waning of the mandatory busing plan. From 1970 until 1992, a period when all school board seats were at-large, at least one African American was on the ballot in every election, and an African American was elected in all but two of those elections (1970 and 1974). In the first three at-large elections (1995, 1999, and 2003) after the switch to the hybrid system, at least one African American was also on the ballot, and in two of these (1995 and 1999) at least one African American candidate was victorious.

33. John Logan, *Resegregation in American Public Schools? Not in the 1990s* (Albany, N.Y.: Lewis Mumford Center for Comparative Urban and Regional Research, 2004), 15.

34. For CMS, see R. Kenneth Godwin, Suzanne M. Leland, Andrew D. Baxter, and Stephanie Southworth, "Sinking *Swann*: Public School Choice and the Resegregation of Charlotte's Public Schools," *Review of Policy Research* 23 no. 5 (2006): 983–97; Roslyn Arlin Mickelson, "Subverting *Swann*: First- and Second-Generation Segregation in Charlotte, North Carolina," *American Educational Research Journal* 38, no. 2 (2001): 215–52; and Roslyn Arlin Mickelson, "The Academic Consequences of Desegregation and Segregation: Evidence from the Charlotte-Mecklenburg Schools," *North Carolina Law Review* 81, no. 4 (2003): 1512–63. In general, see Richard Alba et al., "Brief of 553 Social Scientists as *Amici Curiae* in Support of Respondents," in *Parents Involved in Community Schools v. Seattle School District No. 1*, 127 S. Ct. 2738 (2007), http://www.civilrightsproject.ucla.edu/research/deseg/amicus_parents_v_seatle.pdf (accessed July 27, 2007); and Robert L. Linn and Kevin G. Welner, *Race Conscious Policies for Assigning Students to Schools: Social Science Research and the Supreme Court Cases* (Washington, D.C.: National Academy of Education, 2007).

35. Smith, *Boom for Whom?*, 215.

36. As quoted in Matthew D. Lassiter, *The Silent Majority: Suburban Politics in the Sunbelt South* (Princeton, N.J.: Princeton University Press, 2006), 5.

37. *Parents Involved in Community Schools v. Seattle Sch. Dist*, 551 U.S. 701 (2007).

38. For example in 2007, as in previous years, *Black Enterprise* included both banks in its list of the forty best companies for diversity. Also included was TIAA-CREF, whose largest office is now in Charlotte and which plays an important role in the local political economy (Sonia Alleyne, "Best Companies for Diversity," *Black Enterprise*, July 2007, 106–34).

39. Jim Morrill, "Ruling May Keep McColl Off Stand," *Charlotte Observer*, May 1, 1999.

40. Richard Rubin and Ann Doss Helms, "Campaigns Have Raised 1.2 Million," *Charlotte Observer*, October 31, 2003; Hugh McColl Jr., "Charlotte Needs Schools, Schools Need McGarry," *Charlotte Observer*, October 31, 2003.

41. Gary Orfield and Carole Ashkinaze, *The Closing Door: Conservative Policy and Black Opportunity* (Chicago: University of Chicago Press, 1991).

42. See Smith, *Boom for Whom?* chapter 8 for a fuller version of the argument about the importance of human agency, rather than impersonal demographic forces, in explaining Charlotte's history.

43. *Does North Carolina Reward Her Servants? Cameron Morrison Fought A Glorious Fight For the Cause of White Supremacy in North Carolina in 1898–1900 in Company with a Number of the State's Greatest Leaders and Statesmen*, 1920 North Carolina gubernatorial campaign leaflet, Cameron Morrison file, Robinson-Spangler Carolina Room, Public Library of Charlotte and Mecklenburg County.

44. In discussing various political considerations, as this section does, I do not wish to deny the importance of legal and technical considerations, but politics is

this chapter's focus and the other considerations are not decisive. Although recent court decisions sharply limit the use of race in pupil assignment, these decisions do not preclude desegregation whose criteria involve the socioeconomic or academic characteristics of students. Nor do these decisions preclude the use of plans that avoid the explicit use of race, socioeconomic, and/or academic characteristics of students but seek to promote diversity through the use of magnets, the way in which attendance zones are drawn, and so forth. Similarly, while technical issues such as traffic congestion (which affects transportation times between home and school), are relevant, they can be addressed by the location of school construction, the drawing of attendance lines, and the acquisition of more buses. Moreover, while housing patterns undoubtedly affect school desegregation, it is worth remembering that Mecklenburg County is less residentially segregated now than it was during the heyday of the busing plan.

45. Kenneth J. Meier, Paula D. McClain, J. L. Polinard, and Robert D. Wrinkle, "Divided or Together: Conflict and Cooperation between African Americans and Latinos," *Political Research Quarterly* 57, no. 3 (September 2004): 399–409.

David Walters

Centers and Edges
The Confusion of Urban and Suburban Paradigms in Charlotte-Mecklenburg's Development Patterns

The discussions in this chapter focus on two dichotomous types of urbanism within Charlotte, North Carolina, and its hinterland, and on the forces that create these distinct urban environments. These conditions are characterized in Charlotte and several other American cities by: 1) reinvigorated central areas, comprising the downtown core and older, close-in urban neighborhoods, often with revived transit options; and 2) new, fast-growing and far-flung suburbs located and laid out in ways that require an automobile for all elements of daily life.

These two conditions are especially significant in a fast-growing metropolitan area such as Charlotte, which includes several towns in Mecklenburg County and surrounding counties. The focus on central areas at the same time as expanding the suburban periphery illustrates conflicting ways of building American cities, and as such, creates a potentially debilitating confusion of public policies. The quest for the kind of substantive and sustainable urbanity that can be provided by compact, walkable, mixed-use developments linked by transit (often referred to as "urban villages") is diametrically opposed to other consumer preferences for low-density living in car-dependent and single-use suburban developments that extend around the perimeter of the city into the wider metro area of surrounding counties. Accordingly, the chapter examines some of the originating concepts behind the urban village typology that fits well with Charlotte's transit-oriented development vision, and, secondly, puts the city's continued suburban expansion into a wider perspective of conflicting city policies and political preferences.

Center versus Edge

This chapter was written in a setting typical of the former condition, in a book-lined workspace in a suite of small but well-lit studios shared with the author's artist wife on the second floor of an old brick building that was once a local grocery store with apartments above. Below the studios at sidewalk level are a picture framing shop and a beauty salon. Next door are digital animation studios and some trendy clothing stores for the fashionable *flaneurs* who form an increasing presence on the block. Across the street is an artists' cooperative and a coffee shop heavily patronized by a squadron of kamikaze skateboarders who weave alarmingly between the traffic. On that same side of the street are the offices of Charlotte's weekly African American newspaper and a funky Tex-Mex restaurant, highly popular with the lunchtime downtown banking crowd.

The busy tracks of the city's first light rail line run fifty yards from the front door of the author's studio, with the neighborhood station less than one hundred yards away. Beyond the tracks stands a block of residential condominiums and small commercial spaces for architects, financial advisors, interior decorators, and an Italian restaurant, all opposite some older buildings containing a high-style modern furniture store (see figure 40).

More apartments have been built and others newly started on the next block, adjacent to the neighborhood fried chicken take-out restaurant (awarded in 2008 the honor of being the best such establishment in the whole nation!). At the south end of the street a cluster of converted textile mills and warehouses are home to a coterie of design firms with new live-work units infilling vacant spaces. Here also, new office condominiums have recently been completed and a group of twelve-story residential towers are under construction immediately adjacent to the train tracks.

One or two blocks north of the author's studio are more bars, art galleries, and offices, an alternative music venue, a Greek restaurant, two large apartment complexes, and some cleared sites along the rail line prepared for yet more residential and mixed-use development. A pharmacy, bank, office supply store, and several sandwich shops are also within a five-minute walk. In the seventeen years we've rented space in the building, we've seen the neighborhood gradually transform from a bleak and dangerous part of town, where we left our studio hurriedly before it got dark, into the "Main Street" of South End, Charlotte's best-known "urban village" with a diverse and fast-growing population.

The most dramatic catalyst for this urban redevelopment has been the

Figure 40. Camden Road, Charlotte. Stores and offices line the sidewalk while new condominiums face onto the light rail line running behind the single-story building. (Source: David Walters.)

new light rail line, the first of five proposed transportation corridors radiating from the center city. This transportation initiative followed hard on the heels of a historic trolley that ran between the South End neighborhood and the edge of downtown, just over half a mile to the north. This much-loved tourist attraction spurred some of the early rounds of development in the area; in a very effective manner it laid the groundwork for the city's major investment in the new, integrated system of light rail transit and appropriate land use planning.

However, at the very same time as the city, the state of North Carolina, and the federal transportation authorities were investing over $400 million in the South Corridor light rail line, nearly three times that amount was being spent on Charlotte's outerbelt freeway, I-485. This sixty-seven-mile ring highway, still many years from completion despite nearly two decades of construction, has opened up vast new areas for suburban development, almost always in conventional auto-dominated forms of separated uses — office parks, shopping centers, residential subdivisions, and apartment compounds. This growth is spreading into surrounding counties at a faster rate than either planning or local politics, with their very inefficient system of fractured and competitive municipal jurisdictions, can manage.[1] The Charlotte region has thus created a confusing situation for itself: at the same time that it's establishing a new *centripetal* pattern focusing on the thriving city center, it is hard at work building an opposing *centrifugal* suburban pattern of continual expansion at the periphery, thereby creating tensions and conflicts in development policies and politics.

One of the newest developments around the periphery is Ballantyne, in deepest south Charlotte, nearly at the South Carolina state line. This development would not exist without specific extra interchanges being constructed on the outerbelt with city approval. These extra interchanges slow the speed of through traffic and increase local congestion, thereby undercutting the original premise of the outerbelt as a high-speed traffic corridor avoiding the central city. The intensity of local trips and traffic movements along this stretch of the interstate have turned it instead into a clogged local access road for expanding suburban development.

The Ballantyne master plan, although it contains a variety of uses, arranges them in a spread-out and auto-dominated pattern; moreover, it was created by very influential private developers and approved by the city in full knowledge that it made very little sense in terms of connections to public transportation or the adopted transit and land use plan. Whereas from his studio the author can walk to several restaurants, sandwich shops, bars, a coffee shop, an office supply store, bank, and pharmacy, a worker or resident in Ballantyne must get behind the wheel of his or her car for almost every errand. A trip to lunch for most workers involves negotiating by vehicle a complex system of four-lane divided highways, perhaps with some illegal U-turns, even if the destination is visible and within easy walking distance.

Ironically, a later phase of Ballantyne has incorporated fragments of the urban village development type with some townhomes around a collection of restaurants, a few offices, and a cinema. However, this fragment of potential urbanity is just that, an urban stage set — high on image but short on substance in terms of the fabric of true community life.

The Importance of Place

While developments such as Ballantyne's "Village Center" fail the tests of authentic urbanity, they do enjoy considerable commercial success. Consumers are attracted to even the faintest semblance of an urban place, giving the lie to Melvin Webber's famous thesis of the 1960s that "place doesn't matter any more," and the predictions of techno-futurists that "geography is dead."[2] In fact, evidence from places such as Charlotte's South End increasingly demonstrate the opposite: place itself is fast becoming the main organizing feature of economic activity. Even while arguing that electronic space is more important than physical place, Kevin Kelly, a leading prophet of the "geography is dead" theme, qualifies this assertion by admitting that distinctive places retain their value, and that this value will increase despite the nonspatial dimension of information technology.[3]

Given their flexible and unpredictable work schedules, creative professionals in today's economy require access to recreational and entertainment opportunities at a moment's notice. They increasingly act "like tourists in their own city" and require amenities close at hand, within walking distance if possible.[4] Reinforcing this theme in 2001, author Joel Garreau, best known for his seminal book *Edge Cities*, noted that cities are changing faster today than at any time for 150 years, and that computers are reshaping our urban world to favor places that provide and nourish face-to-face contact. Garreau expressed his belief that the urban future could "look like the eighteenth century, only cooler." Edge cities and downtowns "that are sterile and charmless will die."[5]

The resilience of certain urban areas, and the related increased concentrations of economic power in places such as New York, London, Hong Kong, and Frankfurt have been extensively explored by Sassen and others.[6] This research explains why such urban concentrations, or "knowledge clusters,"[7] persist and succeed in the face of contrary pressures of decentralization derived from the spread of ubiquitous information technology. Such cities are the command and control centers for what Sassen identifies as the leading industries of our postindustrial period: finance and its related services. These cities are "national and transnational marketplaces where firms and governments can buy financial instruments and specialized services,"[8] and as the second largest banking center in the country, Charlotte is becoming a growing presence on this world stage, with Sassen's clustering of financial services and professional workforce evident in the center city.

Sassen goes on to argue that physical place, the kind of focused urban area that supports the active mingling and association of people, is central to this process, as it provides the physical locale through which pass the "multiple circuits" that comprise the fabric of economic globalization.[9] As noted by Storper and Venables, "employers gain access to a large pool of specialized labor," and "workers gain access to a greater number of potential employers, allowing them to minimize periods of unemployment, and make more rapid progression up a career ladder, with greater lifetime learning and wage growth. Underpinning these dynamics, however, are detailed processes of signaling and screening which occur largely through face-to-face contact," an ancient but still primary human need.[10]

Technological innovation is facilitated by the "spillover" effect that comes with regular face-to-face contact between professionals located in close geographical proximity, where "the circulation of knowledgeable workers between firms [enhances] the ability of these firms to recombine knowledge, imitate best practices, and otherwise improve their products."[11] Knowledge literally "rubs off" as workers absorb information from contact with skilled individuals, and denser city districts, fueled by clusters of specializations backed by the diversity of the mixture of uses needed to support daily life, provide excellent opportunities for both planned and serendipitous contact.

In this context of dense urban clusters of activity, Garreau believes the primary purpose of future cities will be to provide optimum conditions for this fruitful face-to-face contact. This contention is further amplified by Storper and Venables, who argue that "[f]ace-to-face contact remains central to the coordination of the economy, despite the ... variety of information ... which can be communicated near instantly." Moreover, because face-to-face contact is "the most fundamental aspect of proximity," these authors maintain that it's a basic reason for "the persistence of urbanization and localization,"[12] which in urban design terms are synonymous with key elements of spatial order and focused patterns of activity required for making places. In a similar vein, William Mitchell argues in his book, *E-topia: "Urban Life, Jim — but not as We Know It,"* that physical places and urban spaces will retain their relevance in the Internet society specifically because people still care about meeting face-to-face and gravitate to places that offer particular cultural, urban, scenic, or climatic attractions that can't be experienced at the end of a wire and a computer screen.[13]

In this context, good urban design and traditional public spaces are crucial in providing the appropriate environment for these human activities, and realistically, the best kind of urbanism to meet this need is the traditional mix of street and square, park and boulevard — all in the context of a walkable and transit-connected urban village or neighborhood.[14]

Beyond its value as a necessary component of place, the concept of higher density urban villages linked by transit is also critical to visions of urban sustainability, and was first revived from historical precedent by Douglas Kelbaugh and Peter Calthorpe as "Pedestrian Pockets" (later renamed Transit-Oriented Development or TOD) during the late 1980s.[15] Another key study in the quest for a usable definition of sustainable urban form came from Australia in 1989, where two planners, Peter Newman and Jeffrey Kenworthy, compared the use of energy by urban Australians, Americans, and Europeans.[16] Not surprisingly, Americans used most energy, Australians came in second, and Europeans were the most frugal of the three study groups. The researchers related this energy use to the spatial character of cities and the availability of public transport, and concluded that the compactness of European cities combined with the high standard of public transport largely accounted for the lower figures of energy consumption. From this conclusion came the oft-repeated wisdom that the most sustainable form of urban development was one that restricted the geographical spread to a defined area and then served this area with good public transportation.

This conclusion has not gone unchallenged,[17] but the generally accepted corollary to this research was that cities and neighborhoods should be denser and have a mixture of uses within walking distance. In combination with Calthorpe and Kelbaugh's Transit-Oriented Development, Dauny and Plater-Zyberk's contemporaneous Traditional Neighborhood Development in America and the work during the early 1990s of the Urban Villages Group (later The Urban Villages Forum) in the United Kingdom further validated the concept of the urban village.[18] More recent studies in America have shifted the debate into the arena of public health, calculating the considerable cost savings and health benefits to a variety of age groups that accrue from walkable, compact development.[19]

By the early years of the twenty-first century, many developers had become alert to the market opportunities provided by urban village development, and the Urban Land Institute published detailed guidance and case studies on the theory and practice of this type of development.[20] In other countries, this planning concept is even more advanced. In Great Britain, for example, the concept has become planning orthodoxy and is enshrined in government policy for "sustainable communities."[21]

Urban versus Suburban in Charlotte

The development of transit-linked urban villages has become one staple of Charlotte's long-range transportation and land use planning. However, the urban village, with its increased densities and mixture of uses, is not without its detractors in American public and political opinion. This opposition often comes from the conservative end of the political spectrum, but also from residents of existing neighborhoods, and this mix of resistance forces has been very active in Charlotte's recent development history. The varieties of American conservative opinion heard loudly in Charlotte decry the urban transit village as social engineering, by which opponents mean that "elitist" planners and architects are "dictating how Americans live."[22] The opposition from residents of existing neighborhoods is less ideological. It generally falls within the classic NIMBY variety, where increased density is erroneously equated with crime, traffic, and lower property values.

Despite this combined opposition, urban villages have one very powerful ally — national and regional demographics. As is now well known, the number of American households that conform to the conventional profile of a married couple with children, typical consumers of single-family housing in suburbia, fell to less than one quarter (24.3 percent) of the total number of households as recorded in the 2000 census, and is expected to keep falling for the next several decades. By contrast, the numbers of aging baby boomers who are downsizing to urban dwellings in more compact, walkable urban areas is increasing, as is the number of echo boomers, the generation that comprises the children of baby boomers. Both generations are seeking an urban setting that supports their changing lifestyle expectations as an alternative to conventional suburbia, and as a market indication of this trend, the price per square foot for condominiums and town houses in the United States in 2003 exceeded that of conventional detached dwellings for the first time in the nation's history.[23]

These trends are illustrated in Charlotte-Mecklenburg, where the average sales prices of smaller condos and town homes in the city center in March 2008 ($466,302) exceeded the average sales price of larger single-family homes everywhere in Mecklenburg County with the exception of only the two listing areas that included Charlotte's wealthiest suburbs (Eastover, Myers Park, and the SouthPark area) where the average single-family home sales prices were $482,737 and $697,359.[24]

The armature for all Charlotte's efforts at developing new typologies of urban growth and transportation options to suit these local demographic trends and create a more sustainable urban future is the *2030 Transit Corridor System Plan*, adopted by Charlotte-Mecklenburg in November 2006. This comprised a revision to the previous *2025 Transit Corridor System Plan*, itself adopted in 2002 and developed from studies in the 1990s led by consultant architect-planner Michael Gallis. These studies established the principle of five multimodal transportation corridors, each with associated and intensified land uses, radiating from the center of Charlotte and extending approximately twenty-five miles into neighboring counties as far as a ring of surrounding towns. These corridors neatly correlated new transit options for bus and/or rail with the area's major highways and some existing railroad rights-of-way, and this plan concept was adopted by the City of Charlotte and Mecklenburg County in 1994.

The encircling communities and the highways linking them to Charlotte comprise the following: Mooresville and I-77 to the north; the twin towns of Concord-Kannapolis and I-85 to the northeast; Monroe and Hwy 74 to the southeast; Rock Hill, South Carolina, and I-77 to the south; and Gastonia and I-85 to the west. Inside this fifty-mile-diameter ring, six smaller towns within Mecklenburg County lie along one or another of the corridors: Huntersville, Cornelius, and Davidson are situated along the northern corridor with its planned commuter rail line parallel to I-77; Matthews sits adjacent to Hwy 74 to the east at the end of either a rapid busway or light rail line; and Pineville lies close to I-77 to the south, just beyond the terminus of the first operational light rail line (see the map of metropolitan Charlotte at the front of this volume).

In support of this concept, the *2025 Integrated Transit/Land Use Plan for Charlotte/Mecklenburg* was completed in 1998. The key elements of this plan comprised "the development of a regional rapid transit system that would improve mobility, encourage more compact development and support the proposed land use initiatives in each of the ... growth corridors."[25] In 2002 this plan was updated as the *2025 Transit Corridor System Plan*, which identified five distinct corridors.

> *South Corridor*: This comprises light rail transit to I-485 (the Town of Pineville myopically rejected the extension of the tracks into their community in part due to a fear of increased crime). This light rail line utilizes an existing rail right-of-way adjacent to the heavily trafficked South Boulevard and paralleling I-77, one of the busiest stretches of interstate in North Carolina, and one that has limited capability for widening.

North Corridor: The plan here is for a commuter rail to Mooresville (Iredell County) with enhanced bus services on HOV (high occupancy vehicle) lanes along I-77. However, in 2006 the Iredell County Commissioners refused the requests of the Mooresville Town Council and the Metropolitan Transit Commission (the locally appointed body that oversees the transportation plan) to participate in funding the construction of this line. (These county commissioners are renowned for their conservativism and represent largely rural interests. Their hostility to any integrated urban land-use and transportation planning illustrates the profound difficulties that exist in American politics for any coherent form of regional planning). Accordingly, this commuter rail service will either be funded by tax increment financing arrangements relative to new private development along the line, or, lacking this funding source, the line will by necessity terminate awkwardly at the Town of Davidson on the Mecklenburg side of the county line.

Northeast Corridor: Light rail transit is planned to extend to the campus of University of North Carolina at Charlotte and terminate just within the I-485 beltway loop. This light rail line would be a direct extension of the South Corridor light rail. In addition to the light rail, enhanced bus services would connect with selected train stations and travel on I-85 to serve the nearby University Research Park and the thriving commercial areas around Concord Mills in Cabarrus County farther to the northeast.

Southeast Corridor: This corridor would be served by bus rapid transit along Independence Boulevard to the Town of Matthews and I-485. The bus rapid transit would operate in dedicated guideways with grade-separated infrastructure where necessary, much like a light rail line. (More recent political pressure from leaders on the east side of Charlotte has revived the possibility of light rail transit for this corridor, but the economics and ridership are not likely to support this option).

West Corridor: Originally this corridor was to be served by bus rapid transit to the Charlotte-Douglas International Airport with enhanced bus services on adjacent main streets in the area. This concept has since been upgraded to a streetcar serving the airport and Westside neighborhoods, but not until 2018. Until that time, enhanced bus services will improve the transit options on the west side of the city.

In addition to these five spokes radiating out from the Center City, the plan proposes a cross-town streetcar running from Beatties Ford Road at its intersection with I-85 on the west, through the center of downtown, linking the various rail and bus hubs and extending to the Eastland Mall area in the east.

The clear focus of this transportation and land use plan was Charlotte's Center City, conceived in the 1990s by planners and by corporate executives such as Bank of America former Chairman Hugh McColl as the burgeoning business, civic, and cultural hub of the region. If the Charlotte region was to thrive economically, so their logic went, then it must have a flourishing and prosperous center at its heart. Charlotte's city center must provide not only jobs in abundance, but also a civic and cultural quality of life that would attract the best and the brightest talent to live and work in the city. During the decade since its adoption in 1998, this central concept of the Transit Corridor Plan has been borne out by the tremendous pace of development in the center city and along the south corridor rail line. An article in the *Charlotte Observer* in January 2008 recorded with pride a record number of construction cranes, twenty-five in all, towering over development sites within and just outside the I-277 freeway loop around the city center.[26]

Downtown Charlotte and its in-town neighborhoods have experienced a prolonged period of intensive growth, with new high-density residential towers and mid-rise infill construction, new office buildings, hotels, major sports stadia, and several new museums either built or under construction. The downtown residential population of eleven thousand (in 2007) was expected to reach a critical mass of approximately twenty thousand people by 2012, when all the new high-density and high-rise projects currently under way would be finished.[27] However, at the time of writing, the incipient 2008 recession is slowing (but not stopping) this fast rate of growth.

New development is also proceeding apace along the transit corridor adjacent to the highly successful light rail line, where new high-density, low- and mid-rise housing has flourished to a degree that has confounded the skeptics. By 2007, the rail line had already attracted an estimated $257 million in new investment (built projects or projects under construction) with another $1.58 billion in other announced projects, not counting those in the Center City.[28] These new developments will add $24 million annually to city and county tax revenues and provide some valuable insulation against rises in property taxes (see figure 41).[29]

These developing successes of the original transit and land use plan concepts dovetailed with a series of Major Investment Studies for each corridor

Figure 41. Typical new transit-oriented development. Despite the 2008–09 recession, more than one thousand new apartments and condominiums are being built adjacent to the LYNX Blue Line in Charlotte's South End district. (Source: David Walters.)

as required by the Federal Transportation Authority for federal funding. These studies led to the consolidation and reinforcement of the plan by the 2006 adoption of what was then re-titled the *2030 Transit Corridor System Plan*. However, this plan proved increasingly controversial during construction of the South Corridor light rail line prior to its completion in November 2007. This opposition was due partly to:

1) the increasing expense of the light rail project, although these increased costs were due largely to inflation and the steeply rising costs of key building materials such as concrete and steel that affected all construction projects;
2) the disappointment and anger of communities and community leaders along the southeast and west corridors that they were not slated to receive light rail service (nearly universally perceived by citizens and politicians as superior to bus rapid transit); and
3) vociferous opposition to rail transit and its associated high-density urban village style development by energetic groups of far-right-wing Republicans and Libertarians.

This third element of the opposition crystallized into an organized political effort to undo the most important source of funding for Charlotte-

Mecklenburg's transportation plan, the half-cent sales tax passed by voters in 1998. In 2006 this tax raised approximately $68 million and its status as a secure revenue stream is a key component of approval for federal funding. The tax does not apply to food, gasoline, or prescription medicines, and as the tax is paid by all who shop in Mecklenburg, irrespective of where they live, revenue is raised without affecting property taxes paid by city and county residents. Ironically, roughly 65 percent of the tax goes toward the city's expanding bus system, the backbone of any successful urban transit system, with only a minority of the money funding the South Corridor light rail line.[30]

Despite the small percentage of tax money that goes directly to the light rail line, it was this tax, coupled with the trains themselves, that attracted the ire of right-wing activists. For these politically motivated groups, light rail represented everything that was perceived as wrong with "big government," and the South Corridor line became the whipping boy of some frenetic propaganda on Charlotte's AM talk radio and in the city's free weekly "newspapers."[31] By paying a subcontractor to collect sufficient petition signatures, these opposition groups succeeded in placing a referendum on the half-cent sales tax on the November 2007 local ballot in a concerted effort to derail the whole transit plan. One stated aim of the petition organizers and Libertarian supporters was to reduce public transit in Charlotte to a minimum, designed to serve only those poorest segments of the population without access to private cars.[32]

Despite very aggressive politicking by the coalition of local libertarian antitax campaigners with their state and national backers such as the John Locke Foundation in Raleigh, North Carolina, and other right-wing organizations such as the Reason Foundation, the anti-rail advocates were routed at the polls by a margin of 70 percent to 30 percent in favor of retaining the half-cent sales tax for the transportation plan. They were defeated by a more powerful alliance of pro-business Republicans, rallied by the Chamber of Commerce, local developers, and a broad base of Democratic support, including the crucial African American vote from communities where public transport provided a much-needed social and economic service.

Just a few days later, Ron Tober, the triumphant CEO of the Charlotte Area Transit System, who had been the target of much personal venom from anti-transit factions in the community during the campaign, drove the first train of scheduled service from Charlotte's main Center City station to the applause of hundreds of dignitaries and local supporters.

This symbolic act was a fitting acknowledgment of the efforts made by planners in Charlotte to introduce policies of integrated transportation and land use after decades in which these two facets of urban policy were distinctly compartmented in the minds of planners, politicians, and the public alike. The fact that these efforts have been only partially successful, and only in relation to the downtown, its adjacent in-town neighborhoods, and the South Corridor rail line, is mainly a testament to the lack of political will by elected officials to enact these policies over a wider area in the face of concerted opposition from the development lobby.

Outside the transit corridors, planning in Charlotte still remains the handmaiden of private development. A working planner in one of the small towns in the Charlotte region remarked: "All I do is make the developers' lives easier. It's what my elected officials want. They don't seem to care about the future."[33]

In cities like Charlotte, where private developers and other professional groups within the building and real estate industries have historically been able to influence elected officials to do their bidding — by financial contributions to their election campaigns, and by assiduously cultivating personal relationships to curry favors in return — more progressive ideas of development control have tended to get sidelined by elected officials.

This is a familiar story in towns and cities across America. In a lengthy editorial analysis in the *Charlotte Observer* about alternative sources of income to pay for growth-related needs in Mecklenburg County (such as impact fees, a land transfer tax, or an adequate public facilities ordinance), the newspaper editors simply state as a matter of basic political fact that local elected officials won't explore these options in any meaningful way as they "aren't willing to endure political pressure from developers — who contribute heavily to City Council, county commission and state legislative campaigns."[34]

The story is the same at the state level. According to an earlier report in the *Charlotte Observer* during the 2002 election cycle, political action committees representing real estate agents and homebuilders in North Carolina gave $255,450 and $223,159 respectively to legislative candidates, making these two organizations the largest sources of campaign funds in the state, ahead of lobbyists for health-care groups, bankers, and lawyers.[35]

In cities such as Charlotte, therefore, growth happens the way developers desire, rather than as directed by elected politicians or planning staff. Generic auto-dependent suburban expansion thus continues largely unchecked around the city's periphery, but ironically, the singular success of planners along the South Corridor rail line is due to this same developers' impetus for profits. The more compact and sustainable patterns of transit-oriented development flourish in Charlotte because enough developers have found they can make handsome profits from this type of development in the new market environment where consumers increasingly value qualities of placemaking and an urban lifestyle. In locations such as the South Corridor there has been a happy convergence of progressive public policy and business-driven economics. Public policy has been matched by the private sector's realization that there is a lot of money to be made following behind the public sector's investment in transit.

While this transit-oriented success offers hope for the future of Charlotte and similar cities in other parts of America, the scale of the problem of managing growth in a more comprehensive manner is daunting. New development at the urban edge of most American cities is still chiefly shaped by conventional use-based zoning ordinances, with very little in the way of progressive policies or Smart Growth ambitions.

A study of land use regulation in the State of Illinois, for example, verified the extent to which planning is a victim of its own devices.[36] An analysis of the regulations of 168 cities and counties found that Smart Growth tools were almost nonexistent, and the prescriptive requirements for lot sizes, setbacks, road widths, and parking decidedly favored low-density sprawl and urban fragmentation.[37]

Form-Based Planning at Charlotte's Suburban Fringe

But suburban expansion doesn't have to follow these outmoded and problematic patterns and regulations. The Charlotte region is fortunate in being able to provide a progressive counterpoint to these outdated policies and attitudes. Since the mid-1990s, the three adjacent and contiguous towns in north Mecklenburg, Davidson, Cornelius, and Huntersville, have managed their growth through compatible sets of form-based zoning ordinances that embody New Urbanist and Smart Growth principles of urban design and planning.

Form-based codes focus first on the physical form of development and secondarily on use, exactly the opposite emphasis of conventional zoning. The uses of buildings can change much faster than their physical form, and form-based codes place more emphasis on the long-lasting physical character of public spaces and buildings within which uses may change according to market conditions and community priorities.

The keys to the success of form-based planning in these three edge towns have been that they are relatively small communities, each less than thirty thousand population, and that they are self-governing, flexible municipalities able to control their own destiny to a large degree.

While the practice of zoning reform in larger cities such as Charlotte can be excruciatingly slow and frustrating, this author's experience of working with these and other small towns to reform and rewrite their zoning ordinances around form-based principles has indicated that smaller communities on the urban fringe are often more amenable to this difficult change of direction and concept. In these smaller communities, elected officials are known to a larger proportion of the population and are more directly accountable. Gathering public interest in matters of community governance and future planning is easier in smaller towns and participation is more effective.

The process of working with the three north Mecklenburg towns was exemplary in this regard. Faced with an oncoming tide of suburban expansion headed north toward them from Charlotte's outer boundaries, these towns made common purpose by completely rewriting their zoning ordinances around form-based New Urbanist and Smart Growth principles in the mid-1990s. In so doing, they took a clear regional lead in planning reform.

A brief review of this work in north Mecklenburg helps clarify the scope, content, and operation of form-based codes in America and provides a useful contrast with the market-driven approach adopted by default by elected officials elsewhere in the Charlotte region. The contiguous towns of Davidson, Cornelius, and Huntersville worked sequentially to craft new town master plans and new form-based zoning ordinances to replace existing conventional documents.[38] Unlike the famous New Urbanist "Seaside Code" that established the precedent for form-based zoning in 1982, and which operated initially as a controlling mechanism for eighty acres of private development, the new codes for the three north Mecklenburg towns comprehensively regulate all manner of private and municipal development in an area covering approximately eighty square miles. These codes specifically emphasize the preservation of rural areas wherever possible and promote transit-supportive development along the planned commuter rail line specified in Charlotte-Mecklenburg's *2030 Transit Corridor System Plan*.

Several key lessons were learned from this process of code creation, especially the relationship between urban morphology (the sense of overall grain and character of an area) and building typology (a lexicon of different types of buildings based on their formal characteristics). Drawing from European morphological urban analysis, and in particular the work of

M. R. G. Conzen on historical urban transect studies,[39] a way of coding based on hierarchical geographic zones of urban or rural character rather than separated uses was established. As such, "character zones" dictated the overall scale and arrangement of building types within their areas.[40] This same logic forms the basis of the more sophisticated "Transect" classification developed later and separately by Duany and Plater-Zyberk.[41] Within this morphological urban categorization, new development was regulated by building types (with flexible patterns of use); design standards for streets, parking areas, and public open spaces; and provisions covering landscape and signage.

A second and essential strategy was for the code to be developed around design concepts relevant for particular locations. In the mid-1990s there were few contemporary developments to use as precedents, so as part of this multiyear public process, alternative designs were developed for contentious tracts of land as a focus for discussion and public education[42] (see figure 42). Many of these designs were combined into a large map depicting a build-out scenario for the whole area covered by the contiguous jurisdictions of the three towns.

This map established a comprehensive vision of collaborative growth management and featured extensive interconnected street and open space networks along with transit village centers along the proposed North Corridor commuter rail line to and from Charlotte (now scheduled to start operation in 2012).[43] Most importantly, the vision embodied in the plan was backed by form-based zoning that was compatible across all three jurisdictions.

These principles of form-based coding are now enshrined in the increasingly familiar "Smart Code" developed by Duany and Plater-Zyberk with its Transect methodology. This code format is significant because instead of morphological study being used to analyze historical examples (as with Conzen and others), New Urbanists use the Transect to describe the way things *ought to be*.[44] This same predictive quality, and the use of urban design concepts and categories of urban or rural character to define and manage the future, is characteristic of most form-based zoning codes, and was at the heart of the north Mecklenburg codes from their inception.

However, even after more than a decade of operation, planners in the three towns still find that some elected officials and developers struggle to understand design ideas contained in the code. Having decent examples on the ground helps, but planners are required to engage in a constant process of educating developers, elected officials, and the general public about the concepts and requirements of the code. In Huntersville, for example, members

Figure 42. Urban design layout for land in Cornelius, North Carolina. This design plan was typical of many created by the author as part of the lengthy public participation process involved in writing and adopting new form-based codes in the three north Mecklenburg towns from 1994–97. (Source: David Walters.)

of the planning staff are developing a picture book of urban design concepts specifically for their elected officials and planning board members. This educational process will continue as new elected officials take office, planning staff come and go, and new residents enter the community. The author's experience in Huntersville has shown this continuing educational mission to be extremely important: without such a commitment, it's likely that the code would have been overturned by politically motivated opponents.

Modifications to the code should be expected over time, and these must also be explained to everybody involved. All municipalities operating a form-based code must have professional design expertise on staff in the person of an urban designer, architect, or landscape architect, or else a design consultant retained to work with elected officials, developers, and builders to help implement the code's objectives. This requirement was borne out in Huntersville when, about five years after the code was adopted, key members of the town staff who had been involved in writing the document left for other employment. Without this institutional memory, or a planner with design qualifications, there was a very steep learning curve for new staff. These difficulties were overcome, and the normative operation of the planning department in 2008 had evolved to the point where an interdisciplinary team of town employees, comprising generalist planners, an urban designer, a transportation planner, a traffic engineer, and a civil engineer, meet weekly for several hours to discuss the design ramifications of new projects submitted for approval.

Having a fully qualified urban designer on staff is considered by the Huntersville planning director to be essential. The Huntersville team keeps a definitive "interpretation file" from their weekly discussions, whereby any interpretations of the code by town staff concerning innovative design or previously unmet planning conditions are recorded and filed. This establishes precedents and a reference source for future discussions and seeks to avoid conflicting interpretations of similar matters. Even with a tightly drafted code such as the Huntersville example, there is always interpretation involved, and this takes time. Review of major schemes that seek a conditional rezoning approval is never as simple as staff "checking the box" and issuing a quick permit.

The experience of Huntersville staff and other planners in the Charlotte area working with form-based codes does not bear out the oft-quoted claim that form-based codes expedite permitting and provide incentives for developers with a quick and less expensive approval process. In theory, because the code establishes a clear physical vision and standards for new development, projects that meet those standards can be quickly approved. This may happen in some jurisdictions, but in Huntersville, a town well equipped to deal with these matters with an expert staff sympathetic to the principles of form-based coding, the design basis of the regulations injects a greater degree of subjectivity into the approval process. However carefully worded and illustrated the code might be, this subjectivity needs careful handling, politically and legally. The approval process is "streamlined" and effective, but not necessarily any faster than conventional zoning practices. However, the town staff was unanimous in stating that the design content of the code had brought about a big improvement in the quality of new development in the town since its inception in 1996.[45]

While quicker permitting may not be realistic, Huntersville has benefited unexpectedly from form-based coding. The town has developed a reputation as a national leader in progressive zoning reform, and this forward-thinking image has transcended the planning world into the realms of economic development. The town is now home to companies that would not normally consider a community of thirty thousand people for their corporate headquarters, and has been included in lists of the best places to live in America.[46]

Planning in a "Globalizing" City

The experience of these communities on the suburban fringe of a large metropolitan area demonstrates that smaller municipalities can be more flexible and change policies more quickly and completely than large cities. This is due in part to the more intimate scale of local politics, where the community as a whole can become involved in major decisions more easily, leading to a public process of consultation and involvement that is manageable within twelve to eighteen months overall. By contrast, Charlotte's development of form-based TOD regulations that initially involved only a small part of the city along the South Corridor light rail line was begun in 2001 and these regulations were still under active reconsideration in 2007 after much neighborhood opposition.

This lengthy, drawn-out adoption and revision process for these TOD codes is different in one important respect from Charlotte's normal process of trying to improve and update its zoning provisions to include better urban design principles. As noted earlier, any improved codes are normally opposed strongly by the development community, who reflexively see them as onerous requirements that increase their costs, and who have been generally unwilling to play their part in improving the standard of Charlotte's infrastructure and public spaces. In the case of the TOD codes however, opposition and consequent delay has come more from neighborhood groups who oppose additional density on land near them rather than from developers, who actively support the code changes, as they stand to gain from these same increased densities.

While the north Mecklenburg towns established the precedent of using form-based codes several years before Charlotte moved in that direction, the city's TOD codes have some immediate local precedent in the municipality's use of "Pedscape" plans as zoning overlays that put primary stress on the creation of an attractive and safe public and pedestrian realm along the streets within certain neighborhoods. The modest but sensible urban design principles within these Pedscape plans — including buildings fronting streets with smaller front yard setbacks, narrower streets and medians where appropriate,

Figure 43. Streetscape improvements on East Boulevard in Charlotte include bicycle lanes and planted medians with clearly marked pedestrian crosswalks and controlled vehicle turn lanes. (Source: David Walters.)

bike lanes, wider sidewalks, street trees in planting strips, on-street parking, and screened on-site parking behind buildings — were controversial at first, even in historic neighborhoods that would benefit from the higher quality streetscapes. However, the first such zoning overlay for Charlotte's historic Dilworth neighborhood was eventually adopted in 2002, with the first constructed street improvements carried out in 2006 (see figure 43).

These urban design principles have been extended into more detailed dimensions of building massing and density within the TOD overlay code provisions initiated by the city along the light rail line, and the proactive land assembly and progressive zoning actions taken by Charlotte planners and elected officials has provided an excellent example of design policies and standards that fit the New Urbanist model. Essential elements in the plans for this transit corridor are new urban villages clustered around the train stations along the line, but most of the land where these new communities will be constructed was previously zoned for industrial or commercial use. To assist developers to create more fitting new development on these sites, the city rezoned large tracts to allow the range of mixed urban uses required for an urban village of high-density housing, shops, and offices. The city investment was too large, and the plans too vital to the city's future, to leave this new urban development to chance, or to require developers to bear the economic cost and political burden of major rezonings, often in the face of local opposition. In certain strategic locations, the city purchased key parcels of land, rezoning them and then "flipping" them to developers in order to stimulate the desired development.

By standards elsewhere in the city, the City of Charlotte and its planners have been very proactive in the transit corridor with TOD zoning: the public sector has been leading development, identifying sites, preparing standards for density and urban design, and facilitating master plans for private developers to implement. It is a good and professionally well-managed process that reflects credit on the city, but it is not the norm in other suburban areas where the same planners' efforts at upgrading design principles have met with solid and consistent resistance from developers. Without the political will or courage from elected officials to face down the city's development lobby, the good work by planning staff often goes to waste.

"Failure" and Future of Planning in Charlotte

Planning in the Charlotte metropolitan area, including the former rural counties around Mecklenburg that are now being swamped by waves of suburban growth, is often described by the press and public at large as having "failed," implying that planners haven't being doing their job, or doing it badly. In Charlotte's case, and in many other American cities, this conclusion is unfair and simplistic. Charlotte area planners are quite smart enough to work out what is going on and what needs to happen to manage growth in a more orderly and sustainable manner. However, the actions and attitudes of elected officials often fail to reach the same standards, and their limited views of development are often warped by the "advice" of the development lobby.

In rare conjunctions where planners' objectives and developers' profit motives align, such as in the South Boulevard light rail corridor, experience has shown that elected officials will back the planning staff: they will take the necessary decisions on transportation, infrastructure, land use, and urban design they know will meet with the approval of the development industry that helps fund their election coffers. In suburban situations, however, and particularly around the I-485 outerbelt, these circumstances rarely pertain. Suggested improvements put forward by planning staff, be they changes to the city's General Development Principles that suggest more sustainable and integrated patterns of development, or upgraded street standards that would require higher design provisions for pedestrian safety and multimodal travel, were forcibly opposed by the real estate and development communities, who applied pressure to elected officials to turn down these recommendations. As a result, well-intentioned planning policies designed to improve the patterns of growth throughout the city can languish in bureaucratic limbo for months and years.

But there are some small signs that this situation is changing and that elected officials in Charlotte are becoming a little more independent of developers' wishes. On October 22, 2007, after many months of dedicated opposition by developers, home builders, and real estate agents, the city council eventually approved Charlotte's Urban Street Design Guidelines, which are intended to create "complete" streets — that is, "streets that provide capacity and mobility for motorists, while also being safer and more comfortable for pedestrians, cyclists, and neighborhood residents."[47] However, this approval is only the beginning of the process of better street design throughout the city: these guidelines are simply recommendations without the force of law. Now comes at least another year of haggling with developers about the zoning and subdivision code changes necessary to implement the guidelines, providing a whole new set of opportunities for the real estate and development interests to delay and obfuscate the process.

Clearly, despite their ambitions to be more proactive in shaping the city into more sustainable patterns, most planners in Charlotte (and in the nation) remain facilitators to the development industry and subservient to the political will of their local elected officials, who in turn largely remain committed to unrestrained growth and free market capitalism. The irony of this market-oriented, pro-growth strategy is that it results in an urban form considered by critics such as Sassen and Garreau as undesirable to the next generation of global city residents; indeed, Charlotte's unrestrained growth seems likely to mortgage the city's future to an unsustainable degree. However, experience in Charlotte's South End and in its northern suburban fringe shows that it *is* possible to overcome the politics of failed planning in the region, and these examples may present a more viable model for Charlotte as it enters its global era.

The compromised performance of planning in Charlotte is due to nothing less than the political structure and ideology that defines the American system of governance; within this system, good planning can only occur when it suits the bottom line of the marketplace, and many Americans would not have it any other way. The schizophrenic attitudes of Charlotte, actively funding environmentally sensible, high-density mixed-use transit corridors while at the same time spreading unsustainable, car-dependent, and low-density developments across the surrounding counties, look set to remain a conflicted mess of policies for the foreseeable future. It is unlikely to improve until such time as major cultural, technological, economic, or environmental changes force much-needed transformations in American political values and attitudes about development, growth, and the environment.

Above all, the ability of private capital interests to purchase the decisions they desire from elected officials in local government would need to be drastically abridged. Such practices have led foreign commentators to describe local government in the United States as a "balkanized" system "where corruption is regularly rewarded"; however, within the American political system spending money for political gain and influence is firmly and legally regarded as a form of "protected speech."[48] This paradox suggests that while many American planners and architects understand the changes that need to be implemented, any meaningful political reform along the lines of more ecological and sustainable development will be a long time coming.

Notes

Portions of this chapter have been adapted from two of the author's previous books, *Design First: Design-based Planning for Communities*, 2004 (with Linda Luise Brown), and *Designing Community: Charrettes, Master Planning and Form-based Codes*, 2007, both published by Architectural Press and used with permission.

1. R. Sulock, "Sewer Shortage Stunts Growth: Many Developers Put on Hold as Counties Scramble to Catch Up," *Charlotte Observer*, September 13, 2007, 1A.

2. See M. M. Webber, "The Urban Place and the Nonplace Urban Realm," in *Explorations into Urban Structure*, ed. M. M. Webber et al., 79–153 (Philadelphia: University of Pennsylvania Press, 1964); and M. M. Webber, "Order in Diversity: Community without Propinquity," in *Cities and Space: The Future Use of Urban Land*, ed. L. Wingo Jr., 23–153 (Philadelphia: University of Pennsylvania Press, 1964). See also M. Dear, "Prologomena to a Post Modern Urbanism," in *Managing Cities: The New Urban Context*, ed. P. Healey et al., 27–44 (London: Wiley, 1995); G. Gilder, *Telecosm: How Infinite Bandwidth Will Revolutionize Our World* (New York: Free Press, 2000); K. Kelly, *New Rules for the New Economy: 10 Radical Strategies for a Connected World* (New York: Viking, 1998); and W. J. Mitchell, *City of Bits: Space, Place, and the Infobahn* (Cambridge, Mass.: MIT Press, 1995).

3. Kelly, *New Rules for the New Economy*, 94–95. The theme of "place-led" urban redevelopment is examined more fully in David Walters and Linda Luise Brown,

Design First: Design-based Planning for Communities (Oxford: Architectural Press, 2004), 75–93.

4. R. Lloyd and T. N. Clark, "The City as Entertainment Machine," in *Critical Perspectives on Urban Redevelopment: Research in Urban Sociology*, vol. 6, ed. Kevin Fox Gotham, 375–78 (Oxford: JAI Press/Elsevier, 2001).

5. Joel Garreau, "Face to Face in the Information Age," paper presented at the conference "City Edge 2: Centre vs. Periphery," Melbourne, Australia, April 19–20, 2001.

6. S. Sassen, *The Global City: New York, London, Tokyo* (New York: Princeton University Press, 1991); S. Sassen, *Cities in a World Economy* (Thousand Oaks, Calif.: Pine Forge/Sage Press, 1994); S. Graham and S. Marvin, *Telecommunications and the City: Electronic Spaces, Urban Places* (London: Routledge, 1996).

7. Steven Pinch, Nick Henry, Mark Jenkins, and Stephen Tallman, "From 'Industrial Districts' to 'Knowledge Clusters': A Model of Knowledge Dissemination and Competitive Advantage in Industrial Agglomerations," *Journal of Economic Geography* 3 (2003), 373–88.

8. S. Sassen, "Urban Economy and Fading Distance," The Second Megacities Lecture, The Hague, Netherlands, November 1, 1998, http://www.megacities.nl/.

9. Sassen, "Urban Economy and Fading Distance."

10. Michael J. Storper and Anthony J. Venables, "Buzz: Face-to-Face Contact and the Urban Economy," in *Institutions, Incentives and Communication in Economic Geography*, ed. Michael Storper (Stuttgart: Franz Steiner Verlag, 2004), 48.

11. Ibid.

12. Ibid.

13. W. J. Mitchell, *E-topia: "Urban life, Jim — but not as we know it"* (Cambridge, Mass.: MIT Press, 1999), 141.

14. D. Walters, *Designing Community: Charrettes, Masterplans and Form-based Codes* (Oxford: Architectural Press, 2007), 135–59.

15. D. Kelbaugh, ed., *The Pedestrian Pocket Book* (New York: Princeton Architectural Press, 1989).

16. P. Newman and J. Kenworthy, "Gasoline Consumption and Cities: A Comparison of U.S. Cities with a Global Survey," *Journal of the American Planning Association* 55 (1989): 24–37.

17. J. Gómez-Ibáñez, "A Global View of Automobile Dependence — Cities and Automobile Dependence: A Source Book," *Journal of the American Planning Association* 57 (1991): 376–79.

18. A. Duany and E. Plater-Zyberk, *Towns and Town-Making Principles* (New York: Rizzoli, 1991); T. Aldous, *Urban Villages: A Concept for Creating Mixed-use Urban Developments on a Sustainable Scale* (London: Urban Villages Group, 1992); T. Aldous, ed., *Economics of Urban Villages: A Report by the Economics Working Party of the Urban Villages Forum* (London: Urban Villages Forum, 1995).

19. R. Ewing, K. Bartholomew, S. Winkleman, J. Walters, and D. Chen, *Grow-

ing Cooler: The Evidence on Urban Development and Climate Change (Washington, D.C.: Urban Land Institute, 2007).

20. Charles C. Bohl, *Place Making: Developing Town Centers, Main Streets, and Urban Villages* (Washington, D.C.: Urban Land Institute, 2002).

21. ODPM (Office of the Deputy Prime Minister), *Delivering Sustainable Development PPS1* (London: The Stationery Office, 2005); ODPM, *Sustainable Communities: People, Places, Prosperity* (London: The Stationery Office, 2005).

22. E. S. Achenbaum, "Hot Debate Erupts after CATS Report," *Charlotte Observer*, September 19, 2007, 1B.

23. Ewing et al., *Growing Cooler.*

24. http://www.carolinahome.com/statistics/stats_area.cfm?order_by=area%20DESC (accessed September 2007).

25. Charlotte Area Transit System (CATS), *Corridor System Plan: Staff Recommendations*, 2002, 1.

26. M. Price, "Building Boom Brings Bumper Crop of Cranes," *Charlotte Observer*, January 22, 2008, 1A.

27. http://www.charlottecentercity.org/nav.cfm?cat=21&subcat=115&subsub=79 (accessed September 2007).

28. R. Morgan, "Why Chamber Is Backing Transit Half-Cent Sales Tax," *Charlotte Business Journal*, August 24, 2007, 67.

29. Presentation by city staff to Charlotte City Council, August 27, 2007.

30. http://charlotte.about.com/od/governmentcityservices/a/transit_tax.htm (accessed October 21, 2009)

31. M. E. Pellin, "A Train Wreck Transit Study," *Rhinoceros Times*, August 2, 2007, 1; J. Capo, "CATS' Light Rail, Agenda 21, the U.N. & You," *Rhinoceros Times*, May 20, 2004; J. A. Taylor, "Tober Leaves Fiscal Train Wreck in Wake," *Rhinoceros Times*, August 16, 2007.

32. S. Harrison, "Answers to Those Taxing Questions," *Charlotte Observer*, August 12, 2007, 1A.

33. Interview with planner, October, 2007.

34. "Finding Money for Growth," *Charlotte Observer*, August 12, 2007, 20–21A.

35. R. Hall, "Why the Sprawl Lobby Has Clout," *Charlotte Observer*, May 19, 2003.

36. E. Talen and G. Knaap, "Legalizing Smart Growth: An Empirical Study of Land Use Regulation in Illinois," Annual Conference of the Association of Collegiate Schools of Planning, Atlanta, Ga., November 2, 2000; E. Talen and G. Knaap, "Legalizing Smart Growth: An Empirical Study of Land Use Regulation in Illinois," *Journal of Planning Education and Research* 22 (2003): 345–59.

37. E. Talen and A. Duany, "Transect Planning," *Journal of the American Planning Association* 68, no. 3 (2002): 245–66.

38. These form-based codes were developed under the guidance of the author,

an architect and urban designer. During the 1980s and 1990s, few planners had any training in or understanding of design, and the early form-based codes in America derived from the architectural and urban design expertise of their various authors.

39. M. R. G. Conzen, "The Use of Town Plans in the Study of Urban History," in *The Study of Urban History*, ed. H. Dyos, 113–30 (New York: St. Martin's, 1968).

40. *Davidson Land Plan: Part I, Policy Guide* (Davidson, N.C.: Town of Davidson, 1995).

41. Duany Plater-Zyberk & Company (DPZ), *The Lexicon of the New Urbanism, Version 3.2* (Miami, Fla.: DPZ & Co., 2002), A.4.1.

42. The importance of these designs cannot be overestimated. The depiction of new buildings, spaces, and street networks in clear pictorial graphics was a major factor in the public education process. These were *architectural* drawings by the author and not typical planners' abstract diagrams. This level of detail was a key factor in persuading the public to accept new planning concepts.

43. http://www.charlotte.com/local/story/510022.html (accessed September 2007).

44. S. Brower, "The Sectors of the Transect," *Journal of Urban Design* 7, no. 3 (2002): 313–20.

45. Interviews with Huntersville, N.C., planning staff, 2006–2007.

46. Ibid.

47. Charlotte, N.C., Department of Transportation, "What Are the Urban Street Design Guidelines?" http://www.charmeck.org/departments/transportation/urban+street+design+guidelines.htm.

48. R. Wakeford, *American Development Control: Parallels and Paradoxes from an English Perspective* (London: HMSO, 1990), 000; J. B. Cullingworth, *The Political Culture of Planning: American Land Use Planning in Comparative Perspective* (New York: Routledge, 1993), 18.

Tom Hanchett

Salad-bowl Suburbs
A History of Charlotte's East Side and South Boulevard Immigrant Corridors

Asurprising new residential pattern seems to be taking shape in American cities. Historically, dating back to the nineteenth century, newly arrived immigrants clustered in tight-packed inner-city neighborhoods, often denoted as Little Italy, Chinatown, or the like. Today, in contrast, foreign arrivals are heading outward, scattering into post–World War II suburbs. Settlement geography seems to be dispersed and multiethnic, usually mingling the fresh arrivals among longtime residents.

These "salad-bowl suburbs" have been most remarked upon in Chicago, New York, Los Angeles, and Atlanta. The *Chicago Tribune*, for instance, reported in 2005:

> For the first time, more Latinos live in Chicago's suburbs than in the city ... Latinos now make up a fifth of the six-county region ... Latino-owned businesses have helped revitalize broken business strips in towns such as Waukegan, Cicero and Melrose Park. And Latino homeowners account for nearly half of a recent surge of 89,000 suburban houses sales since 2000.[1]

The trend also appears in smaller metropolitan areas, even in Pennsylvania's depressed Allentown where Latino suburbanites quadrupled between 1980 and 2000.[2] All ethnic groups seem to be taking part, as demographer William Frey noted in his pioneering essay, "Asians in the Suburbs."[3] Intermingling of groups is evident in the suburbs of New York and Los Angeles, according to a 2000 study led by David Halle.[4] Likewise in Dallas, writes reporter Pala Lavigne, old parts of the city have identifiable Latino "barrios," but in the suburbs "roots are spread more evenly among Mexico, India, China and other places abroad."[5] Evidence of this polyglot pattern is coming from census data and also from observers on the ground.[6] It is especially visible in business areas where roadside signs shout in a multitude of languages, such as in suburban Phoenix as observed by Alex Oberle, or along Atlanta's busy Buford Highway, as chronicled by Susan Walcott.[7]

Salad-bowl suburbs is a good name for this new phenomenon. A handful of specialists in geography and demography have proposed other labels for these places and the processes that unfold there — ethnoburbia, melting pot suburbs, heterolocalism — but no name has yet stuck, perhaps because none captures the multiplicity of old and new cultures coexisting side by side.[8] The metaphor of the salad bowl was coined in 1959 by historian Carl Degler, who sought a better image of cultural change than the older *melting pot*.[9] Most scholars now agree with Degler that immigrants' cultural distinctiveness seldom melted completely away, but rather contributed flavorful fresh components to American society. The residential intermingling now happening in suburbia takes the salad bowl metaphor to a new level.

Salad-bowl suburbs are very evident in Charlotte. Two immigrant areas in Charlotte developed rapidly after 1990 — the East Side (along Central Avenue, North Tryon Street, and adjacent streets) and South Boulevard. Both are very suburban in aspect, characterized by ranch houses, garden apartment complexes, and small strip shopping centers built mostly during the 1950s to 1970s. Newcomers of every background live and shop here, including Latinos, Asians, Middle Easterners, Africans, and eastern Europeans. Although immigrants are highly visible, native-born whites and blacks still remain the majority of the population.

This chapter traces the history that produced Charlotte's East Side and South Boulevard corridors. Both areas got started in the mid-twentieth century as workers who had gained a little prosperity in the city's textile mills and other factories moved outward into modest new suburban housing. These white families were joined by African Americans as civil rights movement victories took hold in the 1970s, a process that resulted in some all-black areas, but more mixed-race neighborhoods. History produced an array of affordable housing opportunities by the 1990s. And that was precisely what immigrants needed when they began arriving in that decade.

A Family Story, to Begin

Roy and Polly Grant are the sweetest couple, old fashioned salt-of-the-earth white southerners who will not let a stranger visit without taking away a jar of homemade peach preserves. I first sat with them in the 1980s in the parlor of their modest two-bedroom brick home on The Plaza in Charlotte's Eastside, gathering tales about Roy's life working in Carolina cotton mills and playing stringband music. Recently I asked them to recall the places they've lived over the years, and their story offers a useful starting point for understanding the evolution of the Eastside and also South Boulevard.

Born on a Carolina farm in 1916, Roy Grant took part in the farm-to-factory migration that redefined the South in the early twentieth century. He moved to the mill town of Gastonia in 1935 to find a job in the massive Firestone textile mill. There he lived "on the mill hill," in the company housing that most southern mills provided for their workers.

When Grant's musical career, playing on the radio for millhand audiences, brought him to Charlotte, he and Polly again chose a factory neighborhood. Settling near friends, they lived in humble housing just outside the Highland Park No. 3 Mill village. This working-class district known as North Charlotte (now called NoDa) huddled off North Tryon Street immediately northeast of downtown.

In the 1950s Roy took a job with the post office. The steady income allowed the family to qualify for a mortgage and buy their own home. Roy and Polly purchased a small, new, two-bedroom brick ranch house on The Plaza. It was part of a just-created suburban area between Central Avenue and North Tryon Street, now the Eastside.

The couple raised three children and grew old together happily in their piece of the American Dream. Then in the late 1990s they made another move, to the Wilora Lake retirement facility a couple of miles away. Dealing with the vicissitudes of age was the main reason for the move.

But the fact that the community was changing also played a role. No longer was the neighborhood a place of familiar, old-fashioned southerners. Today a Spanish speaking family lives in Roy and Polly's old home. Cambodian and Mexican stores fill the small shopping center nearby.

"Zone of Emergence": Millhands as Immigrants

Roy Grant's move as a young man from Carolina farm to cotton mill was very typical of the southern labor force in general. Foreign immigrants were a rarity here, a marked contrast to the urban north. In big northern cities, huge steel mills, stockyards, and massive factories drew families off farms as far away as Italy, Hungary, and Russia. The smaller cotton mills of the Carolinas, however, were able to fill jobs with people from the farms of the American South. Charlotte, like most New South cities, attracted virtually no immigrants in the early twentieth century. The low-wage workers who left the farms to labor in the region's textile mills came from the hills and hollers of the American South itself.

It is interesting to explore parallels between millhands in the South and immigrants in the North in terms of housing patterns. When poor white southern farm folk arrived in the city, they were as segregated as any ethnic group in the metropolitan North. A downtown Charlotte minister wrote in 1903:

> Just at this period in the development of mill people it seems to be better to allow them to ... form a class to themselves ... If this tendency to become a separate class is not resisted, and churches and schools are provided to these people, all to themselves, they ... do better than where mill people and others are mixed promiscuously.[10]

Mill families were housed in carefully delimited company-owned villages set apart from the middle-class city — and also set apart from the city's African American neighborhoods. The North Charlotte industrial area, planned in 1903 around the Highland Park No. 3 cotton mill, was the largest of these blue-collar neighborhoods-of-arrival.

In northern cities, immigrant families who prospered and began to move up in the world often physically moved outward to a "Zone of Emergence."[11] First described by Robert Woods and Albert Kennedy in Boston in 1914, such a place included modest new suburban single-family cottages intermingled with small rental apartment dwellings (triple-deckers in the Boston example). Such areas offered less crowding, more green space, and better prospects for homeownership than the initial tenement districts. But they were decidedly less grand than the fine suburbs of the wealthy business-owning classes.

Geographers have offered various models of where the Zones of Emergence tend to locate in the city.[12] In the 1920s, Chicago scholars Robert Park and Ernest Burgess sketched a now-classic diagram showing a ring of "workingmen's" neighborhoods just outside the center city. In 1939, sociologist Homer Hoyt observed that residential zones often took the forms of wedge-shaped sectors, dividing the city like slices of a pie.

In Charlotte, the two pie-shaped wedges of neighborhoods on the East Side and along South Boulevard functioned as the city's Zones of Emergence. Former millhands and others on the cusp between blue-collar and white-collar economic levels moved outward into freshly constructed suburbs after World War II. Like in immigrant Boston, these areas mingled modest single-family dwellings with rental apartments — a budget version of the grander suburbs on Charlotte's southeast side.

Creating the East Side and South Boulevard Corridors

Suburbia has a somewhat different meaning in Charlotte than it does in most nonsouthern cities. State laws throughout much of the South make it easy for cities to annex outlying territory. In places such as Chicago and New York, suburbs became separate incorporated municipalities. Here, however, they were brought into the city soon after they were built. In governmental terms, this means that much of the urban-suburban battling that hurt metropolitan unity in the North was not evident here. But in terms of the built environment, Charlotte's suburbs look pretty much like those elsewhere in the United States. The car is king, sidewalks are rare, and strip shopping plazas line the main streets.

Charlotte grew rapidly in the years after World War II. As late as the mid-1940s, the city boundary ran barely two miles from downtown. It crossed Central Avenue a few blocks past The Plaza, bisected North Tryon Street at 36th Street, and hit South Boulevard at Remount Road. That compact city mushroomed over the next twenty-five years. By 1970 the boundary rested some four miles from downtown. Charlotte's land area tripled in these decades from barely twenty square miles to over sixty-five square miles.[13]

As in many U.S. cities, that growth was sectoral in character, resulting in a city of pie-shaped wedges closely identified by income and race. African Americans initially suburbanized to Charlotte's northwest, a pattern triggered partly by the nineteenth-century campus of Johnson C. Smith University (then known as the Biddle Institute), a historically black college. By the mid-twentieth century, if you drove out Beatties Ford Road, the major radial street running northward from the center city, you would see mostly black faces. Well-to-do whites settled southeast, drawn to new suburbs beyond the posh 1910s and 1920s garden suburbs of Myers Park and Eastover. If you traveled out Providence Road, the main southeast radial, upper-income white suburbia was what you would see.

For less elite whites, the east and the south became the favored sectors. On Charlotte's east side, Central Avenue, The Plaza, and North Tryon Street extended northeastward from the vicinity of the mills that clustered at North Charlotte. Similarly on the south side, South Boulevard ran southward from the mills at Dilworth, paralleling the industrial zone along the Southern Railroad. Suburban Charlotte looked like a pie with wealthy whites living

Figure 44. Eastside split-level homes built in the 1960s. (Source: Tom Hanchett.)

in the southeast slice, blacks residing in the north and west, and these less-well-to-do whites with working-class backgrounds located in two slices that extended south and east-northeast.

The sectors of lower-end white neighborhoods were nice places. Small one-story ranch houses appeared first, most around one thousand square feet. Rental units were also commonplace, including duplexes that looked like slightly larger ranch houses, and the occasional project that might contain half a dozen apartments. Over time, bigger and bigger dwellings appeared. The upward economic progress of the initial families, plus Charlotte's general growth, which attracted middle-income arrivals from all over the country, pushed newly constructed Eastside and South Boulevard houses into the two-thousand-square-foot range by the 1970s. Charlotte's truly wealthy still gravitated southeast, but for all other economic levels, the Eastside and suburban streets off South Boulevard were highly desirable places (see figure 44).

Businesses followed the general suburban trend of the 1950s to 1970s. Small-scale strip shopping popped up along the transportation arteries, usually as groups of two or three stores facing a parking lot. In 1968 an enclosed shopping mall anchored by a Woolco discount store went up on North Tryon, but soon foundered. In the mid 1970s the Eastside unexpectedly gained a grand regional mall. Eastland Mall boasted three major department store anchors, two levels of specialty stores, plus an ice skating rink and Charlotte's first multirestaurant "food court." Some observers wonder how it could compete with just-opened Southpark Mall in Charlotte's rich southeast sector. But to most people, Eastland Mall seemed a solid signal that this once humble side of town had really arrived.

And the Eastside and South Boulevard areas were also attracting major multifamily housing investment. During the 1970s and early 1980s, a nationwide trend in construction of "apartment communities" played itself out along arteries in these areas. Clusters of two- and three-story buildings set in attractive landscaping, often with swimming pools, fountains, and clubhouses, were marketed to young professionals. Developers of both the strip shopping and apartment complexes found it relatively easy to build on the Eastside and in the vicinity of South Boulevard. Posh southeast Charlotte had less such construction, because politically well-connected citizens could block development, and the majority-black west and northwest had even less than the southeast, owing to investor perceptions of marketability.

As the 1990s dawned, the Eastside and South Boulevard sectors possessed some of Charlotte's highest suburban residential densities and plenty of small retail space close to housing. Storefronts sometimes went vacant, losing out to big-box competition, and the smaller houses and 1950s duplexes sometimes struggled to find tenants, reflecting the rising aspirations of Charlotte residents. Yet even with the arrival of upwardly mobile African Americans since the 1970s, the Eastside and South Boulevard sectors of Charlotte remained solidly middle-class and desirable, exactly the sort of *Leave It to Beaver/Brady Bunch* suburbia celebrated on TV sitcoms.

From All-White to Racially Mixed

The racial integration of Charlotte's suburbs is worth examining in some detail. The American South is, of course, known for sharp racial separation in the early twentieth century and for staunch defense of segregation during the civil rights era of the 1950s and 1960s. But scholars have begun to note an impressive turnabout in racial patterns since the 1970s.

Beginning with the Fair Housing Act of 1968, "equal housing opportunity" became a watchword of lenders and real estate sellers nationwide. "Data from Census 2000 show that black-white segregation declined modestly at the national level after 1980," concludes an article in the journal *Demography*. And for reasons not fully understood, "declines were centered in the South and West."[14]

In Charlotte, civic leaders made a point of welcoming integration, especially after the local schools became the national test case for court-ordered busing: *Swann v Charlotte-Mecklenburg*, 1971. In 1970 Charlotte ranked as the United States' fifth most segregated city.[15] By 2000 the city had become the nation's second *least* segregated urban place.[16]

The Eastside and South Boulevard corridors, comfortably middle-class but not overly expensive, became desirable places for suburbanizing African Americans. This brought some tensions. Hidden Valley, a middle-income subdivision off North Tryon Street, tried to hold on to white residents but became all black, as did several other pockets on the Eastside. But more often, whites and blacks found ways to coexist.

A look at U.S. Census data for the six census tracts along the Central Avenue corridor, for instance, shows this transition. In 1960 the entire area was overwhelmingly segregated, every tract nearly 100 percent white. In the mid-1960s, the Belmont–Villa Heights neighborhood switched abruptly from all-white to all-black, apparently due to landlords who funneled in African Americans displaced by Urban Renewal projects elsewhere. After 1968, that kind of racial steering would no longer be legal. The Plaza-Midwood neighborhood, adjacent to Belmont–Villa Heights, became 77 percent white, 21 percent black by 1980. That was very close to the city-wide ratio of 79 percent white, 20 percent black.[17] It has held that mixture through 2000. Other tracts showed a similar pattern. Except for Belmont–Villa Heights, all neighborhoods along Central Avenue were between 71 percent and 86 percent white by 1990.[18]

So it seems that Fair Housing regulations worked — not perfectly, to be sure, but well enough to bring substantial racial integration. Racially mixed neighborhoods came into existence, with a fair amount of stability over time, rather than abrupt white flight.

Foreign Immigrants Arrive

Jose Hernandez-Paris still vividly remembers seeing the first Mexican restaurant actually run by Mexicans in Charlotte. Jose's parents had emigrated in the 1970s from Colombia, South America, rare foreigners in this overwhelmingly native-born town. Driving down South Boulevard one day in the 1980s, the family saw a sign for a restaurant called El Cancun about to open in a disused fast-food franchise building. Mexicans were at work renovating the interior. The Hernandez-Paris family were so excited they stopped the car and pitched in.

A few years later, Latino construction crews arrived to set the steel for the towering NationsBank (now Bank of America) skyscraper, completed in 1992, that still defines the uptown skyline. Bilingual English-Spanish speakers were still hard to find, and Hernadez-Paris was called upon to help translate construction documents. But things were about to change. Geographer Owen Furuseth suggests that the skyscraper crews returned to their homelands with news of a clean, economically thriving southern city where jobs seemed plentiful.[19] Whatever the exact mechanism, Latino movement to Charlotte quickly swung into high gear.

During the 1990s, this city that had experienced virtually no foreign immigration during the nineteenth and twentieth centuries suddenly emerged as a magnet for newcomers from around the globe. A hot economy led by banking — Charlotte became the nation's second-largest banking center circa 2000, second only to New York City — meant that there were plenty of jobs, including entry-level service positions. A Brookings Institution survey marked Charlotte as the fourth-fastest growing Latino city in the United States during the 1990s, and a subsequent Brookings study named it the nation's second-fastest during 2000–2005.[20] Mexicans were the largest single immigrant group, but Hispanic arrivals came from every Central American and South American nation. Charlotte's second-largest immigrant group was the Vietnamese, seeded in part by resettlement of Vietnam War refugees in the city by Catholic Social Services during the 1970s. Appreciable numbers of Asians also immigrated from Laos, Cambodia, Korea, and India. And still others newcomers arrived from eastern Europe, Africa, the Middle East, and elsewhere.

Suburbia, Not Inner-City Tenements

During America's massive immigrant influx of the late nineteenth and early twentieth centuries, new arrivals had flocked to tenement districts near the downtowns of America's biggest cities. Classic examples included South Philadelphia or New York City's Lower East Side. Old, high-density multi-story buildings, largely abandoned by the suburbanizing middle class, offered few amenities — tight living quarters, rudimentary plumbing, steep stairs to climb, no green space. But rent was cheap, and the very closeness of everything made it easy to walk to many different jobs, or to find customers or laborers when starting a business. Here immigrants could begin to forge a new life in America. In city after city, people began to speak of Little Italy or Chinatown or dozens of other ethnically identified low-income districts. Once these immigrants got their feet under themselves, they would move out to the suburbs, often leaving the inner city to be occupied by the next immigrant wave.

Charlotte, in contrast, had no tenements. In the nineteenth century, when tenement neighborhoods were created in big urban centers of the northern United States, Charlotte had been little more than a village, a place of fewer than twenty thousand people in 1900. What few old center-city buildings it did possess were largely demolished during the rapid growth of the late twentieth century. So when immigrants began arriving in Charlotte in the 1990s, instead of heading to the inner city, they found inexpensive housing in the older post–World War II suburbs. Sometimes the arrivals moved into black working-class districts located on the north and northwest or in pockets elsewhere in the city such as Grier Heights (an African American suburb where a number of Latinos settled), or Belmont–Villa Heights (where the city's Cambodians initially found rental quarters). A small number of foreigners who arrived with money scattered into middle- and upper-income areas throughout the city. But most of Charlotte's immigrants gravitated to the Eastside and South Boulevard.[21]

Today banners in Spanish advertise vacancies in the apartment communities. A look at people relaxing on the porches on a warm Sunday evening shows Africans, Arabs, and Southeast Asians as well. Because of the density of apartments and small houses, public transportation functions well here; on Central Avenue, the city's busiest mass transit route, buses run every ten minutes, an important amenity that attracts even more immigrants.

The once bedraggled small strip shopping centers, easily walkable from the apartment complexes, have flowered into vibrant miniature "downtowns." Most cater to not one but several ethnic groups (see figure 45). Latino *tiendas* (grocery stores) and Asian markets offer a mix of basic American and imported goods. As populations grow, restaurants and specialty stores pop up. On one corner on Central Avenue, a Bosnian grocery shares a parking lot with a Vietnamese pool hall within sight of an African coffee shop and a Mexican *taqueria*. Three stoplights further on, another cluster contains a Latino store specializing in Christian books and gifts, the Carneceria Mexicana butcher shop and grocery, a Vietnamese wholesaler servicing the city's nail-care salons, and the Jerusalem Barber Shop, whose customers are mostly

Figure 45. Ethnic entrepreneurs. Entrepreneurs from India, Vietnam, Mexico, and Greece share one Central Avenue plaza. (Source: Nancy Pierce.)

Middle Easterners visiting the nearby mosque. Even "American" businesses have an international flavor: Wal-Mart customers speak a dozen languages and Somali cab drivers sit in a circle under a tree outside Starbucks continuing an old African custom of coffee conversation.

The bustling entrepreneurial scene is beginning to stimulate new construction. In the 1990s, a Vietnamese family ambitiously converted the abandoned Woolco shopping center on North Tryon Street into Asian Corner Mall with new red-roofed "pagoda" towers (see figure 46). Today the mall is still struggling for solvency, but smaller projects are finding success. In half a dozen spots, developers have demolished older buildings and put up compact groups of stores intended to attract immigrant businesses. Go into those stores, and near the cash register you'll find business cards for other start-up entrepreneurs — painters, contractors, auto mechanics, and many real estate brokers.

Indeed, outsiders can get the erroneous impression that the Eastside and South Boulevard are all-immigrant. Remember the six census tracts adjoining Central Avenue noted earlier for their 1990 racial integration? In 2000, native-born whites remained the largest group in all those areas, followed by native-born blacks. Looking at the city as a whole, geographers Owen Furuseth and Heather Smith found only a single census tract in 2000 had a Latino majority.[22]

Will Charlotte's salad-bowl suburbs persist? Or is this just a temporary illusion of integration? It is possible that native-born residents will depart over time. Both the Eastside and South Boulevard are currently struggling to get adequate school resources, to deal with perceptions of crime, and with other challenges. Patterns will be clearer once counts are in for the 2010 census and those beyond.

A New South

Charlotte's new urban geography marks the years around 2000 as the emergence of yet another "New South." The term dates to the post–Civil War period when southern leaders sought to rebuild this formerly agricultural region as a place of cities and factories. Reinvention has continued apace over the years, and scholars now point to several successive New Souths.[23] The current era of change may be the most remarkable. Just a generation ago the South was known for segregation, blacks and whites kept separate both by deep-seated cultural attitudes and by law. That racial landscape has changed dramatically, but painfully and haltingly — as the current trend toward resegregation in the schools of Charlotte demonstrates.

If you had predicted a generation ago that the South would become a magnet for immigrants, most southerners would have expressed disbelief. That those ethnic groups would not be segregated, but rather intermingled into all areas where affordable housing exists, would have engendered even stronger skepticism. Yet that is precisely what has happened in the South Boulevard corridor and on the East Side of Charlotte. The post–World War II suburban neighborhoods that were once Zones of Emergence for blue-collar white southerners are now salad-bowl suburbs, places of both arrival and upward mobility for newcomers and longtime residents of the New South.

Figure 46. Ethnic entrepreneurs. Sisters Megan, Ivy, and Mimi (not pictured) Nguyen created Asian Corner Mall. (Source: Nancy Pierce.)

Notes

1. Antonio Olivo and Oscar Avila, "Latinos Choosing Suburbs Over City," *Chicago Tribune*, November 1, 2005. On Chicago, see also: Louis DeSipio, *Counting on the Latino Vote: Latinos as a New Electorate* (Charlottesville: University of Virginia Press, 1996); Sapna Gupta, "Immigrants in the Chicago Suburbs," (policy paper prepared for Chicago Metropolis 2020, February 2004); David A. Badillo, "Mexicans and Suburban Parish Communities: Religion, Space and Identity in Contemporary Chicago," *Journal of Urban History* 31, no. 1 (November 2004): 23–46; Richard P. Greene, "Chicago's New Immigrants, Indigenous Poor, and Edge Cities," *Annals of the American Academy of Political and Social Science* 551, no. 1 (1997): 178–90.

2. Lillian Escobar-Haskins and George F. Haskins, "Latinos in the Lehigh Valley: The Dynamics and Impact of This Growing and Changing Population," (Lehigh Valley, Pa.: Lehigh Valley Economic Development Corporation, 2005).

3. William P. O'Hare, William H. Frey, Dan Frost, "Asians in the Suburbs," *American Demographics* 16, no. 5 (1994): 32–38. See also Richard D. Alba, John R. Logan, and Shu-yin Leung, "Asian Immigrants in American Suburbs: An Analysis of the Greater New York Metropolitan Area" in *Suburban Communities: Change and Policy Responses*, ed. Mark Baldassare, 43–70, Research in Community Sociology 4 (Greenwich, Conn.: JAI Press, 1994).

4. David Halle, Robert Gedeon, and Andrew A. Beveridge, "Residential Separation and Segregation, Racial and Latino Identity, and the Racial Composition of Each City," in *New York and Los Angeles: Politics, Society and Culture: A Comparative View*, ed. David Halle, 150–93 (Chicago: University of Chicago Press, 2003). On Los Angeles, see also James P. Allen and Eugene Turner, "Spatial Pattern of Immigrant Assimilation," *Professional Geographer* 48 (2): 140–55; William V. Clark and Shila Patel, "Residential Choices of the Newly Arrived Foreign Born: Spatial Patterns and the Implications for Assimilation," (University of California—Los Angeles: California Center for Population Research, On-Line Working Paper Series, February 2004). On New York, see also Richard Alba, Nancy Denton, Shu-Yin Leung, and John R. Logan, "Neighborhood Change under Conditions of Mass Immigration: The New York City Region, 1970–1990," *International Migration Review* 29: 625–56; Richard Alba, John R. Logan, and Brian Stults, "The Changing Neighborhood Contexts of the Immigrant Metropolis," *Social Forces* 29, no. 2 (2000): 587–621.

Scholars agree there is ethnic intermingling in suburbia but debate its extent. Allen and Turner, for instance, assert that recent immigrants still cluster somewhat more than native-born residents. See also David Fasenfest, Jason Booza, and Kurt Metzger, "Living Together: A New Look at Racial and Ethnic Integration in Metropolitan Neighborhoods, 1990–2000," in *Redefining Urban and Suburban America, Evidence from Census 2000*, ed. Alan Berube, Bruce Katz, and Robert

Lang, vol. 3, 93–118 (Washington: Brookings Institution, 2005). For an overview of the debate, see Clark and Patel.

5. Pala Lavigne, "Opportunity Knocks In 'El Norte': Region Attracts Immigrants from All Over, and Their Ways of Life Are as Diverse as They Are," *Dallas Morning News*, October 25, 2005.

6. Perhaps the first writer to note the trend was reporter Alex Marshall, who observed intermingling of white, black, and Filipino families in post-1970s suburban areas of Virginia Beach, Virginia: "The Quiet Integration of Suburbia," *Virginian-Pilot*, July 25, 1993. More recently, see April Austin, "New School, New Town, New County — Immigrant Parents and Suburban Schools: Not Always an Easy Fit," *Christian Science Monitor*, January 13, 2004. An early scholarly analysis came from sociologists Richard D. Alba, John R. Logan, Brian J. Stultz, Gilbert Marzan, and Wenquan Zhang, "Immigrant Groups in the Suburbs: A Reexamination of Suburbanization and Spatial Assimilation," *American Sociological Review* 64 (1999): 446–60. Other scholarly works include William H. Frey, "Melting Pot Suburbs: A Study of Suburban Diversity," in *Redefining Urban and Suburban America*, 155–179; Roberto Suro and A. Singer, *Latino Growth in Metropolitan America: Changing Patterns, New Locations* (Washington, D.C.: The Brookings Institution, Center on Urban and Metropolitan Policy, 2002); Janet Rothenberg Pack, ed., *Sunbelt/Frostbelt: Public Policies and Market Forces in Suburban Development* (Washington, D.C.: Brookings Institution Press, 2005); Jon Teaford, *The Metropolitan Revolution; The Rise of Post-Urban America* (New York: Columbia University Press, 2006).

7. Alex Oberle, "Latino Business Landscapes and the Hispanic Ethnic Community," in *Landscapes of the Ethnic Economy* ed. David H. Kaplan and Wei Li, 149–63 (Lanham, Md.: Rowman & Littlefield, 2006); Alex Oberle, "Se Venden Aqui: Latino Commercial Landscapes in Phoenix, Arizona," in *Hispanic Spaces, Latino Places: Community and Cultural Diversity in Contemporary America*, ed. Daniel D. Arreola, 239–54 (Austin: University of Texas Press, 2004); Susan M. Walcott, "Overlapping Ethnicities and Negotiated Space: Atlanta's Buford Highway," *Journal of Cultural Geography* 20, no. 1 (2002): 51–75. See also Kirk Kicklighter, "Rainbow Atlanta: Census Shows Racial Barriers Disappearing in City, Suburbs," *Atlanta Journal and Constitution*, May 6, 2001.

8. Li Wei, "Ethnoburb Versus Chinatown: Two Types of Urban Ethnic Communities in Los Angeles," *Cybergeo* 10 (1998): 1–12; Wilbur Zelinsky, *The Enigma of Ethnicity: Another American Dilemma* (Iowa City: University of Iowa Press, 2001), 124–54; Frey, "Melting Pot Suburbs."

9. Carl N. Degler, *Out of Our Past: The Forces that Shaped Modern America* 3rd ed. (New York: Harper Perennial, 1984), 332. First edition published in 1959.

10. *Charlotte Observer*, August 2, 1903.

11. Robert Woods and Albert Kennedy, *The Zone of Emergence*, 2nd ed. (Boston: MIT Press, 1969). More recently, see Herbert Gans, *The Urban Villagers:*

Group and Class in the Life of Italian-Americans, 2nd ed. (New York: The Free Press, 1982); Douglas S. Massey, "Ethnic Segregation: A Theoretical Synthesis and Empirical Review," *Sociology and Social Research* 69, no. 3 (1985): 315–30; Robert Zecker, "'Where Everyone Goes to Meet Everyone Else': The Translocal Creation of a Slovak Immigrant Community," *Journal of Social History* 38 (Winter 2004): 423–53.

12. Robert E. Park, Ernest W. Burgess, and Roderick D. McKenzie, eds., *The City* (Chicago: University of Chicago Press, 1925); Homer Hoyt, *The Structure and Growth of Residential Neighborhoods in American Cities* (Washington, D.C.: Federal Housing Administration, 1939); Homer Hoyt, *Where the Rich People and the Poor People Live: The Location of Residential Areas Occupied by the Lowest and Highest Income Families in American Cities* (Washington, D.C.: Urban Land Institute, 1966). Scholars now caution that these models—reasonable approximations of urban form in the early and mid-twentieth century, respectively—have very limited viability beyond that period. Thomas W. Hanchett, *Sorting Out the New South City: Race, Class and Urban Development in Charlotte, 1875–1975* (Chapel Hill: University of North Carolina Press, 1998), 6–10; Zelinsky, *Enigma of Ethnicity*; Michael P. Conzen, "Morphology of Nineteenth Century Cities," in *Urbanization of the Americas: The Background in Historical Perspective*, ed. W. Borah, J. Hardoy and Gilbert Stetler, 119–42 (Ottawa: National Museum of Man, 1980); and Michael P. Conzen, "Historical Geography: Changing Spatial Structure and Social Patterns of Western Cities," *Progress in Human Geography* 7, vol. 1 (March 1983): 88–107.

13. James W. Clay and Alfred W. Stuart, eds., *Charlotte: Patterns and Trends of a Dynamic City* (Charlotte: University of North Carolina at Charlotte Urban Institute, 1987), 31. Hanchett, *Sorting Out the New South City*, 214, 234.

14. John Logan, B. J. Stults, and Reynolds Farley, "Segregation of Minorities in the Metropolis: Two Decades of Change," *Demography* 41, vol. 1 (2004): 1–22.

15. Annemette Soresen, Karl E. Taeuber, and Leslie J. Hollingsworth, *Indexes of Racial Segregation for 109 Cities in the United States, 1940 to 1970, with Methodological Appendix* (Madison: University of Wisconsin Institute for Research on Poverty, 1974), table 1.

16. Lois M. Quinn and John Pawasarat, "Racial Integration in Urban America: A Block Level Analysis of African American and White Housing Patterns," www.uwm.edu/Dept/ETI/integration/integration.htm. See also John Woestendeik and Ted Mellnik, "Fewer People Living in Racial Isolation, Mecklenburg More Diverse, More Integrated," *Charlotte Observer*, April 5, 2001.

17. Elise C. Richards, "Residential Segregation in Charlotte, N.C.: Federal Policies, Urban Renewal and the Role of the North Carolina Fund" (Terry Sanford Institute of Public Policy, Duke University, 2002), 29.

18. U.S. Bureau of the Census, Census of Population and Housing: 1960 Census Tracts PHC (1)-24, Charlotte, N.C. SMSA (Washington, D.C.: U.S. Government

Printing Office, 1961), 13–46; U.S. Bureau of the Census, Census of Housing: 1960 City Blocks HC (3)-293, Charlotte, N.C. SMSA (Washington, D.C.: U.S. Government Printing Office, 1961), 1-28; U.S. Bureau of the Census, Census of Population and Housing: 1970 Block Statistics HC (3)-165, Charlotte, N.C. Urbanized Area SMSA (Washington, D.C.: U.S. Government Printing Office, 1971), 2-42; U.S. Bureau of the Census, Census of Population and Housing: 1980 Block Statistics PHC80 1-116, Charlotte-Gastonia, N.C. SMSA (Washington, D.C.: U.S. Government Printing Office, 1981), 30–76; U.S. Bureau of the Census, Census of Population and Housing: 1990 Block Group Statistics, Charlotte-Gastonia, N.C.; and U.S. Bureau of the Census, Census of Population and Housing: 2000 Block Group Statistics, Charlotte-Gastonia, N.C.

19. Owen Furuseth, personal communication with the author, August 26, 2008.

20. Bruce Katz and Robert Lang, eds., *Redefining Urban and Suburban America: Evidence from Census 2000*, vol. 1 (Washington, D.C.: Brookings Institution Press, 2003), 191; and Audrey Singer, "Twenty-First-Century Gateways: An Introduction," in *Twenty-First-Century Gateways*, ed. Audrey Singer, Susan W. Hartwick, and Caroline Brettell, (Washington, D.C.: Brookings Institution Press, 2008), 26.

21. In addition to the following essay in the present volume, see Heather Smith and Owen Furuseth, "Making Real the Mythical Latino Community in Charlotte, North Carolina," in *Latinos in the New South: Transformations of Place*, ed. Heather Smith and Owen Furuseth, 191–216 (Burlington, Vt.: Ashgate, 2006); and David Goldfield, "Unmelting the Ethnic South: Changing Boundaries of Race and Ethnicity in the Modern South," in *The American South in the Twentieth Century*, ed. Craig Pascoe, Karen Leathem, and Andy Ambrose, 19–38 (Athens: University of Georgia Press, 2005).

22. Smith and Furuseth, "Making Real the Mythical Latino Community in Charlotte," 203.

23. James C. Cobb, "From the First New South to the Second, the Southern Odyssey through the Twentieth Century," in *The American South in the Twentieth Century*, ed. Craig Pascoe, Karen Leathem, and Andy Ambrose, 1–18 (Athens: University of Georgia Press, 2005); and Howard N. Rabinowitz, *The First New South: 1865-1920* (Arlington Heights, Ill.: Harlan Davidson, 1992), 1. Rabinowitz identifies four New Souths up through the 1970s.

José L. S. Gámez

Mi Reina
Latino Landscapes in the Queen City (Charlotte, N.C.)

It is late morning on a Thursday and I stop into a small convenience store to purchase an *agua fresca* (fruit-juice drink); I walk out with my drink in hand and a Club de Fútbol América cap. I was interested in the cap because of the logo that it carried — one that depicted a soccer ball as the globe with the North and South American continents located between the letters C and A. In my naïveté, I thought it might have been a cap for a new North American soccer team; what sold me on the item was the enthusiasm of the clerk behind the counter. As it turns out, Club América is one of Mexico's most successful teams, having won ten professional championships. The country's other success story, Chivas has eleven titles to its credit. "*No me digas,*" I say (You don't say). "*De veras,*" she tells me (It's true). So, I buy the cap. It is a hot, bright August day; I put my new cap on to shade my eyes and walk over to the *lonchera* (taco truck) to get a plate of *carnitas tacos* (fried pork tacos). I chat with the cooks (*"hace un calor hoy día . . . the heat today"*), I eat, and I get on with my day fully satisfied — hunger satiated, outfit complete.

I spent this late weekday morning conversing in Spanish, tooling around a commercial landscape in which Spanish-language signage appears on every available surface, and listening to Spanish-language radio. I am in Charlotte — Charlotte, North Carolina.

My morning in Spanish may not seem particularly interesting to people who live in major North American urban centers like Los Angeles, New York, or even Atlanta, but for many North Carolinians, this represents a significant and unfamiliar trend. The landscape through which I traveled is essentially invisible to most Charlotteans; this is an area often overlooked and forgotten by many within greater Charlotte due to the area's aging auto-oriented infrastructure. As such, it does not exist within the mental maps of many of the city's middle- and upper-class residents whose lives are oriented around often newer suburban landscapes. This is now the terrain of immigrants, many of whom are Latino, and their permanent settlement has begun to reshape this and several other areas of Charlotte — a city better known for its namesake, Queen Charlotte of Mecklenburg-Strelitz, than for its thriving ethnic communities.[1]

In fact, the growing number of Latinos within the Queen City (as Charlotte is often called) and its surrounding areas has given rise to some very visible forms of resistance. For example, the *Charlotte Observer* reported the appearance of an A-frame commercial roadside placard that encouraged drivers to "Honk if you hate Spanish."[2] The article ran at a time when increasing numbers of hate e-mails arrived at social service organizations catering to Latinos and English-only initiatives became fodder for city council debates. In Charlotte and many of its neighboring towns, the presence of a growing number of Latinos has given rise to a great deal of tension.

This tension stems in part from the fact that immigration is a relatively new phenomenon in this city and region. The southeastern United States has not been a significant part of global migration patterns historically, but this has changed since 1990.[3] In fact, southern states have experienced the country's most explosive Latino booms in the years between 1990 and 2005, during which Latino demographics experienced triple digit growth: 394 percent in North Carolina alone, while many neighboring states saw growth rates of over 100 percent.[4] One result of this new immigration trend is that the largest percent increases occurred in what Roberto Suro and Audrey Singer have called "new Latino destinations" — cities such as Atlanta, Orlando, and Charlotte.[5] In this sense, the Solid South is melting into the air of multicultural modernity in ways that challenge the region's long-standing black/white cultural binary.[6] States such as North Carolina, therefore, must confront the "complex nature of race relations in a post–civil rights era" in which biracial frameworks are "unable to grasp the patterns of conflict and accommodation among several increasingly large racial/ethnic groups."[7]

Despite resistance from some sectors of the local metropolitan population, Charlotte's Latino communities continue to grow. According to 2005 census studies, Latinos now make up approximately 10 percent of both Charlotte's and Mecklenburg County's total populations. Other estimates hold that the Latino populace is at least double what the official record claims, given the endemic under-counting in census reporting. This recent growth, which has helped push the total Latino population to over 4 percent statewide, has also contributed to emerging Latino cultural landscapes in several parts of the city.[8] "*Mi reina* (my queen)," it seems, is becoming as common a phrase in some areas of town as "Queen City" is in others.

Immigrant settlement (both permanent and temporary) has an impact on the social and physical landscapes of urban and suburban areas. Such impacts have been seen in places ranging from U.S. cities such as Los Angeles to European centers such as Duisburg-Marlox, Germany.[9] One result of these impacts has been the transformation of existing urban landscapes in ways that meet the cultural needs of immigrants and that produce new urban borderland conditions. And, it is in these areas that one is able to observe how identity construction can inform spatial reconstruction as immigrants inhabit and engage in the production of place in specific areas.

This chapter examines how the border is now inhabited in places far from geopolitical demarcations. Charlotte's relatively recent experience with Latino immigration puts in stark relief the emergence of a new set of border conditions that illustrate how space, place, and identity intersect within the contemporary transnational landscape. What one finds is a set of urban conditions previously unfamiliar to most southern cities—conditions of invisibility, of exile, of heterotopic spatiality, and of emergent or prototopic urbanism.

Sites of invisibility often occur in existing but overlooked parts of the city such as the one described in the opening vignette of this essay; such spaces are often characterized as former centers of economic and social activity that have been surpassed by newer urban or suburban developments elsewhere. These sites become invisible to many simply because they fail to attract the attention of middle- and upper-income groups. Sites of exile may overlap with invisible spaces or exist in more publicly visible locations; these locations, such as a storefront church or a city park, emerge as socially symbolic sites for specific transnational communities. These spaces become hybrid landscapes in which immigrant sociospatial patterns mix with existing conditions to create a new cultural borderland. Heterotopic spatiality refers to the heterogeneous sociospatial life (represented by a mix of uses and activities much more complex than allowed by conventional mixed-use zoning) exhibited in many Latino immigrant landscapes in which a vibrant public culture thrives despite the fact that many of the activities found there would be defined as "nonconforming" by local planning codes. Prototopic urbanism refers to the theoretical premise that the spatial characteristics found in immigrant landscapes represent a potential model for the reintroduction of fundamental aspects of urban life into aging auto-oriented areas.

Each of these conditions will be explored further as interrelated parts of Charlotte's changing metropolitan landscape in order to identify urban characteristics that hold promise for the design of civic, public, and urban spaces. It is my contention that the sociospatial dynamics of Charlotte's Latino landscapes do not represent areas in decline, but, rather, the emergence of a vibrant model of economic regeneration that may hold lessons for the redevelopment of other aging urban spaces. These landscapes illustrate a form of grassroots or organic urbanity that cannot be captured by conventional planning, design, or development patterns. Of particular importance, and a significant characteristic that differentiates the landscapes explored in this chapter from mainstream planning norms, is rooted in the transnational and hybrid nature of such sites. Such landscapes illustrate how North American midcentury urban fabric becomes infused with Latin American cultural attributes, thereby resulting in a sociospatial condition that is both border town and Main Street USA simultaneously.

(In)visible Cultures

Although Charlotte now plays host to a significant Latino population, the presence of that population has yet to physically transform the city in ways similar to those found in Los Angeles, East Los Angeles, or other cities of the American Southwest. In the QC (local slang for the Queen City), one has to seek out the spatial practices of the Latino community in order to understand how changing migration patterns have begun to transform new Latino destinations. In fact, it is in the invisible geographies, the in-between, overlooked, and often leftover spaces of the city, that one often finds the Latino metropolis as well as potential ties to cities like Los Angeles.

Such ties are, admittedly, difficult to identify upon first glance. Charlotte's Latino population is in its emergent stages while East Los Angeles, for example, is home to over a million of the five million–plus Latinos in the greater Los Angeles area.[10] The presence of successive generations of Latinos and the influence of continued migration flows have contributed to the development of a unique urban cultural landscape. The cultural vibrancy found in Latino Los Angeles has been well documented and the residential fabric of East Los Angeles has provided the clearest evidence of an urban Latino landscape. As the urban theorist Margaret Crawford has pointed out,

> These lived spaces, exuberant but overlooked, pose an alternative to the middle-class American house, actual or imagined. Taking control of

ordinary personal and social spaces, residents have transformed a stock of modest single-family houses into a distinctive domestic landscape. Extending their presence beyond the property lines to the sidewalk and street, they construct community solidarity from the inside-out, house by house, street by street.[11]

By contrast, Charlotte has not developed a residential landscape that one can easily identify with Latino immigrant communities. This is due in part to the relatively low percentage of Latinos within the city as a whole and in part to the patterns that immigration has taken in the context of cities such as Charlotte — cities whose morphology reflect the post–World War II urbanization of the Sun Belt. Here the conventional patterns of migration, in which central cities serve as initial homes to ethnic enclaves, no longer hold true; instead, Charlotte's recent migrants have helped bring new life to aging suburban landscapes (dating from the late 1940s to the 1970s) now landlocked within successive rings of urban growth.

Several factors have contributed to this change in settlement pattern. As with many urban cores that underwent significant reinvestment during the urban renaissance of the 1990s, Uptown Charlotte (as the central business district is known) has become a *landscape of power* not unlike that described by the urban theorist Sharon Zukin — a landscape in which downtown has become "synonymous with the city itself" primarily through the assertion of mainstream cultural and economic values.[12] The central city, in this paradigm, is often reinvented as the seat of not only economic capital but also regional cultural capital; Charlotte has followed this pattern by becoming the second-largest financial center outside of New York City and by developing a strong regional cultural infrastructure that includes various galleries and museums, performance spaces, and professional sports arenas. As one might expect, real estate values in Uptown Charlotte have skyrocketed and this has left only a limited range of affordable housing options.

In Charlotte's case, then, the central city lacks a residential fabric into which migrants might weave. This is coupled with the fact that much of the new suburban hinterland is often far removed from places of employment (with the notable exceptions of construction and landscape services), often organized around lifestyle neighborhoods (golf-community development, for example), and often out of the reach of most migrant pocketbooks. Thus, the middle-belt of urban development — the former suburban fringes from the late 1940s through the 1970s — have become the primary port of entry for local migrants. It is here that one finds several emerging "enacted environments" that mirror some patterns of spatial expression found in places like East Los Angeles but that also differ in other ways.[13]

These midcity, or middle-belt, urban areas have become accessible for several additional reasons: midcentury residential developments are now facing a stage of succession as elderly residents, the first wave of suburban home owners, slowly transition out; much of the housing facing commercial arterials in these areas comes in the form of multifamily apartment complexes that have begun to show their age, thereby providing a pool of rental units as middle-income renters seek newer housing stock; these areas have a low percentage of family growth relative to other parts of the city and, therefore, there is less competition for residential structures; and the commercial components of these areas are also aging, thereby providing affordable spaces for migrant entrepreneurs.

In one such area within Charlotte, that of the Central Avenue commercial corridor, Latinos are rapidly approaching a significant overall threshold of 13 percent of the residential population, which is considered a tipping point that will lead to an increasingly concentrated Latino landscape.[14] Here, one finds that an aging auto-oriented landscape no longer attractive to middle-class communities has become the landscape of opportunity for many migrant communities. While the Latino population count in the area may seem low, it represents the city's third-largest concentration. And, Central Avenue itself has areas in which Latino cultural life has taken root with greater vibrancy than other areas in the city with higher Latino population counts.

However, this vibrancy remains isolated within certain commercial areas of Central Avenue. Within the residential areas, a Latino presence remains largely invisible; the only tangible expressions of their presence seem bound to technology: technologies of communication, as represented by the omnipresent satellite antennae that adorn both apartment complexes and single family homes, and technologies of movement, as represented by the multiple passenger vans (an informal commuter network) parked in front of residential units. Therefore, the "housescapes" described by Daniel D. Arreola or the "East Los Angeles vernacular" found in the work of James T. Rojas have yet to develop in Charlotte, and it is unclear that they will.[15]

This is, in part, a consequence of Charlotte's relatively new experiences with Latino migration and Latino lifestyles and, in part, a consequence of the nature of Latino migration itself. Many of the Queen City's newest Latino residents represent a traditional model of first-wave immigrants that is predominantly made up of men establishing a foothold in the region. This group has yet to articulate a residential landscape reflective of their presence because they have not had the time or the resources to do so.

The lack of a tangible Latino residential landscape may also be a consequence of the material landscape itself or of the housing stock that has become available within this middle-belt of development rings. Specifically, the material fabric of these neighborhoods differs from those in places like California and the southwestern United States, making the adaptation of typical housing stock much more difficult. The predominant housing type along Central Avenue is the large apartment block. These multifamily apartment units deny inhabitants the ability to modify or transform spaces according to cultural preferences, since ownership of the unit is typically in the hands of an outside agent.

The single-family homes found in the middle-belt areas of Charlotte are also not easily transformed, due to their physical construction. Brick, which was a material of choice for developers in this region during the mid-twentieth century, is not easily painted; this makes the addition of color (a vehicle of personal and cultural expression) difficult. Additionally, much of the housing stock from this era represents a spatial typology that proves difficult to physically transform without significant financial investment. The typical suburban models of this era were often small split-level homes averaging fifteen hundred square feet; the split-level home, or a home with three levels separated by a combination of half and full flights of stairs, limits incremental home-owner-built additions because level changes within the house often restrict the expansion of any one level to a only a few options.[16] These factors, coupled with sloping terrain (these house types are often on sites with significant elevation changes), create a fairly rigid house type. Thus, within the residential landscape, Latinos in Charlotte remain largely out of sight.

In Exile on Main Street

As pointed out earlier, several areas along Central Avenue have begun to coalesce as Latino landscapes. Yet despite the growing presence of a Latino community, Charlotte does not have a specific "Latin Main Street" that one could compare with cities such as New York or East Los Angeles. In each of those contexts, a principal neighborhood commercial street takes on characteristics tied to the area's dominant cultural and ethnic group. According to the geographer Inés M. Miyares, such principal streets typically fall into one of three categories: "enclave streetscape," "multiethnic adaptive streetscape," or a "landscape of invasion."[17] It is through the introduction of signage and business names (and their accompanying businesses) alluding to countries of origin, color, national or ethnic flags and iconography, and religious symbolism that these areas are transformed into ethnic main streets or enclave streetscapes in which a single group seems to dominate.

Rather than enclave streetscapes, Charlotte, by contrast, has several commercial corridors that share attributes of the multiethnic streetscape and the landscape of invasion. As Miyares defines them, landscapes of invasion reflect urban succession patterns in which new groups begin to articulate urban areas as they occupy spaces left behind as a previous group moves on; multiethnic adaptive streetscapes emerge "on a commercial street where multiple groups take advantage of site and situation, particularly access to transportation. No single group dominates. Instead, the retail landscape is fashioned to reflect the ethnic dynamic of the city."[18]

Central Avenue appears to represent multiethnic adaptive streetscapes or streetscapes showing signs of ethnic invasion. There are several commercial nodes along Central's four-mile stretch from Uptown to its termination as it merges with Albemarle Road in eastern Charlotte. Geography, demographics, land use patterns, and building typology all serve to inform the specific shape of each node along the way. The Plaza-Midwood area serves a diverse middle-class and increasingly gentrified area; further east, various Asian commercial centers have emerged, often marked by recent construction or renovation; yet further east one finds several nodes in which Latino marketplaces seem to dominate. And, interspersed throughout, one finds vestiges of an African American commercial landscape. Similar patterns of occupation can be seen along two other major arterials in Charlotte: South Boulevard, which runs from Uptown to the southern suburban community of Pineville; and North Tryon Street, which runs from Uptown to the northern university area.

Within this context, several clearly defined Latino commercial nodes have developed that operate as public squares for the local community. For example, the intersection of Central Avenue and Rosehaven has developed into a *zocalo (town plaza)* — into a central public zone for a diverse Latino community from both the local neighborhoods and from across the city. The physical form of the intersection itself is nothing special; it exhibits the loosely knit urban fabric of a typical suburban intersection with gasoline stations, convenience stores, and strip commercial centers providing only a hint of spatial form. And, yet, each of these commercial entities plays an important role in the social shape of this Latin landscape.

It is in areas such as this that a parallel to Los Angeles and East Los Angeles may be drawn. The physical fabric of the area is not unlike much of that found in greater Los Angeles. This suburban, low-density fabric is common to many post–World War II urban landscapes and to many Sun Belt cities. However, the lack of density in places like East Los Angeles has given rise to the opportunistic occupation of urban space through the insertion of an *urban prop*, or of an urban element that both adds to the physical fabric of the place while (more importantly) contributing a social catalyst.[19]

A case in point: the Mexico-USA Xpress Mart, a convenience store serving the Latino community near this intersection, is a central component of a new borderland *zocalo* (see figure 47). The site of this store (its physical location) and its constituent parts work in concert to form an emergent public realm in a space previously designed for cars. Within the building, one finds the Mexico-USA Xpress Mart adjacent to Romero's Mexican bakery. Both shops offer staple items and a range of services. The Mexico-USA Xpress Mart serves (as the signage suggests) as a point of contact between the United States and Mexico by providing access to Western Union wiring services to not only Mexico but also Guatemala, El Salvador, Nicaragua, Honduras, and beyond; a convenient neighborhood location at which to purchase cellular telephone service; and sports-related paraphernalia from a variety of Latin American countries. The façade of the building and its ice vending machine double as billboards for touring Spanish language musical acts, as community notice boards, and as informal job banks (see figure 48).

Figure 47. The intersection of Central Avenue and Rosehaven Drive with a taco truck anchoring a new immigrant social space. Such low-density urban spaces are characteristic of post–World War II urban development. (Source: José Gámez.)

Figure 48. Mexico-USA Xpress Mart façade and detail of job announcement. The ice vending machine serves a secondary function as a notice board within an immigrant landscape. (Source: José Gámez.)

In its capacity as a job bank and bulletin board, the building and its associated elements concretize an invisible network that contains both the Mexico-USA Xpress Mart and Romero's Bakery. Each circulates information about social events, available apartments, and job openings in ways that respond to the fluid landscape occupied by many immigrants. It is in this fluid landscape that a variety of cultural inventions occur: commercial elements serve secondary functions as notice boards; community announcements catalyze social and economic networks; and mobile vendors and taco trucks formalize both social and physical spaces.

For example, in an effort to locate qualified help for local construction activity, "Everardo" placed a notice seeking carpenters for local apartment construction. In his search, Everardo has deployed a local slang term — "freimiar," an invented term that conflates the English construction activity "to frame" with Spanish verb conjugation (see figure 48). In this word, a form of *Spanglish* (a combination of Spanish and English) has emerged to fit the unique construction environment found within Charlotte and the Carolinas. This is a sector of the economy in which Latino labor dominates — over 90 percent of the construction labor pool in both the Charlotte and Triad areas is made up of Spanish speakers.[20] It is interesting to note the inter-state network that this job announcement represents; the area codes of the contact telephone numbers listed on the announcement (240 and 540) are not local to Charlotte or North Carolina. They are, in fact, both area codes from other eastern seaboard states. The 240 area code covers parts of western Maryland while the 540 area code covers southwestern Virginia, the Roanoke Valley and the upper Shenandoah Valley. The notice illustrates the role that Charlotte now plays both internationally and regionally within a network of migratory labor.

The Mexico-USA Xpress Mart is not an isolated instance; similar cases exist in various locations in and around the city. What is important to examine is the role of each element within such locations. The presence of the taco truck — a mobile commercial kitchen — is central to both the physical and social form of the space. In figure 49, the taco truck occupies an edge of a typical suburban shopping strip, thereby creating an active boundary to a formerly ill-defined space. In this sense, the taco truck not only creates a new edge condition, which helps to formalize and support a social space, but it also activates that edge through the introduction of culturally focused commerce that attracts both pedestrians and motorists alike.

The initial spatial form of the site (the preexisting commercial buildings

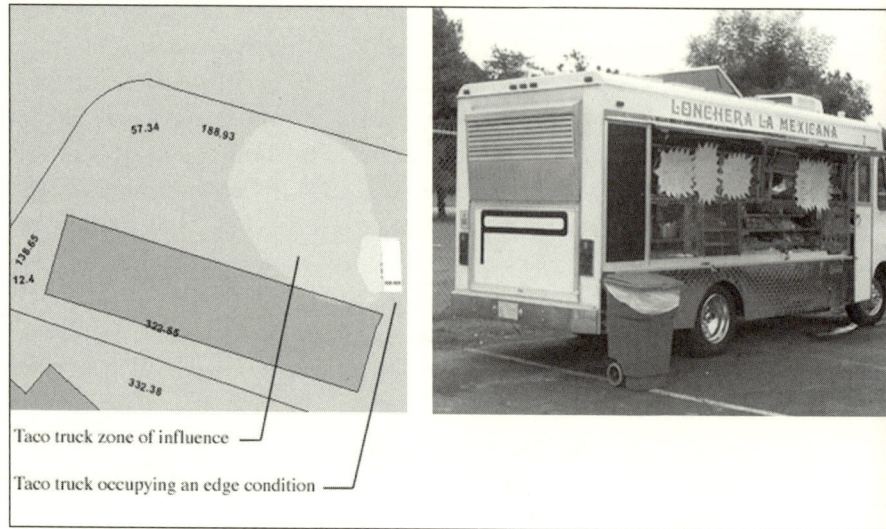

Taco truck zone of influence

Taco truck occupying an edge condition

and parking lots) couples with mobile commercial and social amenities to consolidate an emergent Latin urbanity. The site also benefits from a nearby bus stop, which is a source of constant foot traffic. At times, as many as four differently owned taco trucks arrive at this intersection (in addition to the one that typically occupies an edge of this building's parking lot), which contributes to a concentration of social activity that resembles a small marketplace or bazaar. This intersection, which is typical of many suburban landscapes, has become particularized through the introduction of a transnational community in much the same way that many similar sites have in East Los Angeles. This site has become a Pan-Latin plaza in which expatriates from various Spanish-speaking countries congregate.

Urban props play central roles in animating space and contributing to the emergent public life of this commercial strip. Ice machines serve as community bulletin boards while mobile structures add economic, social, and physical density to an urban landscape that remains largely invisible to many Charlotteans. It is invisible, in part, because commercial areas such as the one represented by this sector of Central Avenue do not overlap with the cognitive or social maps of most members of Charlotte's majority and/or middle classes. Nonetheless, intersections like the one at Central and Rosehaven represent an emergent Main Street condition within a community that finds itself in a state of exile — a community that has inhabited a new

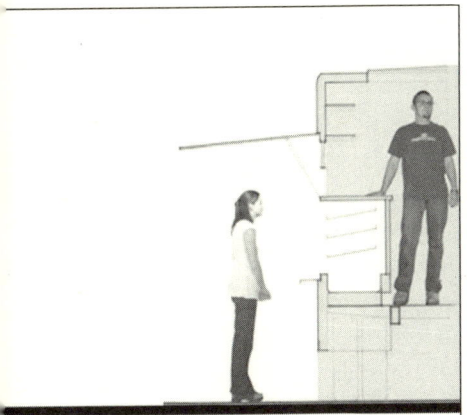

Figure 49. The taco truck as spatial activator on a typical strip center site. (Source: Kevin Williams, Charlotte Community Design Studio, UNC Charlotte School of Architecture.)

landscape far from home, often in an effort to rebuild and strengthen the home from which it came.

Consequent to the development of these ethnic streetscapes, an emergent borderland urbanity has developed and flourished precisely because it occupies a landscape largely overlooked by mainstream planning or urban design theories and by middle-class Charlotteans. The presence of these activities signals an insurgent urbanity not unlike that described by anthropologist James Holston — an urbanity that establishes place via occupation rather than through top-down planning or urban design initiatives.[21]

Hybridity and the Rise of a Pan-American South

Latino migration into southern states such as North Carolina presents a challenge to the structure of regional cultural politics, which is tied to the historically rooted black/white binary that has long characterized the southeastern United States. Such a challenge will put Charlotte into play with other cosmopolitan centers by reshaping this traditionally insular city into a more globally integrated and more culturally pluralistic urban node. In this sense, Charlotte is not just the Gateway to the New South (a title often cited in local civic booster and travel literature) — it is rapidly becoming a gateway into the new Pan-American South that will represent a hybrid of regional cultures. By contrast, Los Angeles has now become a post-minority city, a city in which no single demographic/racial/ethnic group represents a clear majority population. When Latinos became Los Angeles's largest minority group during the 1990s, the city crossed a threshold into a landscape of cultural pluralism that foreshadowed trends soon to emerge in many U.S. urban centers.

While on the surface Charlotte and Los Angeles may not appear to have much in common, views from their respective streets provide different perspectives. Latino Los Angeles has established itself culturally and spatially and a similar presence is now emerging in Charlotte. However, migrants in both contexts more often than not occupy invisible terrains that seemingly belong to both sides of the U.S.-Mexico border and neither simultaneously. Migrants often poach urban remnants left behind as majority and middle-class populations move on in search of greener pastures and newer suburban amenities. Despite the vibrancy exhibited by these landscapes, the spatial transformations that migrant communities initiate are often overlooked, or, in the worst cases, resisted; civic officials and local professionals (architects, planners, urban designers), for example, often view the emergence of ethnic landscapes as evidence of urban decline or nonconforming urban practices.[22] For these standard-bearers of middle-class values, Latino cultural landscapes are all too easily characterized as spaces that meet only a narrow interpretation of what Michel Foucault called heterotopias.

For Foucault, heterotopias were "something like counter-sites, a kind of effectively enacted utopia in which . . . all the other real sites that can be found within the culture, are simultaneously represented, contested, and inverted."[23] Historically, those in the seat of power often marked these sites of contestation as places of social deviance or crisis. The cultural landscapes of Latino communities (both established and migrant) are often categorized in much the same way.

Despite the fact that Foucault's terminology remains under-theorized, the promise of the counter-site described by Foucault provides a way to read the emergent sites of Latino urbanity in Charlotte. Rather than viewing the transformations occurring within aging commercial arterials such as Central Avenue as evidence of physical and social decline, it is possible to see within them the promise of an authentic form of urbanity that does not rely on conventional ideas of urban form for its potential. The promise of such a view has been articulated in the work of the cultural theorist Homi Bhabha. Bhabha's search for the *location of culture* is a search that, in many ways, begins in the heterotopic realms of which Foucault wrote. For Bhabha, such spaces provide moments (both spatial and temporal) in which the grid of dominant norms is disordered and a new spatiality comes into being; these new spaces offer a view into an *other* space:

> all forms of culture are continually in a process of hybridity. But for me the importance of hybridity is not to be able to trace two original moments from which the third emerges, rather hybridity to me is the "third space" which enables other positions to emerge... The process of cultural hybridity gives rise to something different, something new and unrecognizable, a new area of negotiation of meaning and representation.[24]

The in-between spaces and urban zones often defined as marginal by many professional standards are in fact quite the opposite; such places provide openings in the urban fabric for new social realms to be enacted and for new hybridized forms of American urbanism to take shape in precise places at specific moments in time. As such, they become nodes in an emergent urban landscape of contestation, resistance, and dialog that extend the spaces from which migrants travel into new settings.

Proto-Urbanity in the QC/LA

Spatial extension forms not only a transnational network but also a hybrid urbanity rooted in the performance of a traveling, translated, and transformed set of cultural expressions. Such places might be better seen as *proto-topias*, or as embryonic sociospatial zones, that point to ways by which the aging auto-oriented landscape might be made more vibrant.

These spaces also point to ways by which a civic dimension might be reintroduced within landscapes that often were built without this crucial component of public infrastructure. The migrant landscapes of places like Central Avenue in Charlotte point to the ability of social action to both occupy and transform physical space. These landscapes illustrate this process not through examples of material construction but, rather, through spatial practices that fill in the urban landscape with props, activities, and cultural meaning. These activities and interventions occur within urban landscapes that were minimally equipped to handle public social life at the time of their development. This, again, points to a process by which urban and suburban spaces may be transformed with little to no infrastructure; however, this process relies on an acceptance of differing spatial habits and what are often considered nonconforming uses.

However, these proto-topias also challenge conventional notions of a public realm. As emergent and hybrid spatial entities, proto-topias are "built" both of the local condition and of a global circuit while simultaneously remaining apart from each; they are deeply ingrained within a border culture that is both of the north and the south and neither at the same time. In part, this has to do with micro-scale economies rooted in migrant entrepreneurship and the micro/macro-communities that they serve. However, this dimension of commerce also has roots in the traditional urban and social fabric of many Latin American cities and towns in which culture is implicitly a part of public life. Despite the lack of physical fabric in the U.S. suburban condition, this thread of *Latinidad*, or emergent Latin identity, persists and begins to transform local space based on global cultural interests.[25] In this sense, the cultural location of public life is hybridized through the transformation and performance of public culture.

This chapter does not aim to romanticize the plight of many migrants or to minimize the degree to which mainstream societies limit accessibility of the city in general. However, migrant social life has begun to rearticulate the meaning of the urban landscape in Charlotte through spatial occupation, which can determine the value of places for specific groups of people. By extension, social occupation can and does *take place* through the performance of culture and through the enactment of daily social rituals. Culture takes place in two ways: first, culture, as an expression of social life, occurs in time and space (it *takes* place, it happens); secondly, culture, as a dimension of social occupation, articulates, appropriates, and activates space (it *takes* a part of the urban realm and redefines it as a specific site within a network of social relations and within an often invisible and imagined cultural geography).

This has been the case in East Los Angeles. As mentioned earlier, the cultural and physical landscapes of Los Angeles and East Los Angeles have been well documented; here, the typical Southern Californian suburban landscape has been transformed to reflect the cultural needs of folks from south of the border. Similar transformations can now be found in places like Charlotte. One result of this is that Charlotte must recognize that it is now home to a global mix of cultures, peoples, and spatial practices.

In this sense, the cultural location of many migrant landscapes lies somewhere between a local and a global condition and this illustrates a need for an expanded notion of the public realm — one that does not center around the values of a dominant or mainstream culture but rather supports a plurality of cultures equally situated within a public grid. Singular notions of the public and of the public realm no longer suffice; migrant landscapes demonstrate that urban space is made up of multiple publics who often occupy competing public realms. However, mainstream urban design and planning practices often fail to confront the complexities of an era marked by multiple publics, instead favoring a singular definition of the public and the public realm and advocating the spatial narratives that promote urban structures rooted in North American and Northern European village traditions.

As a result, the contemporary era is now dominated by model of urbanity in which public culture is envisioned as "an elaboration of a distinctive culture of civil society and of an associated public sphere" not unlike that which "was implicated in the process of bourgeois class formation."[26] Under this framework, culture itself is involved in the formation of social realms, often through practices that lie outside the realm of the rule of law but that nonetheless shape public actions, beliefs, and images. The implied model of the public is one that eliminates difference by discounting views that conflict with those of the mainstream; this model of the public seeks "zero-degree" cultural zones that veil social and material inequalities behind screens of shared values.[27] This model overlooks structural inequalities that maintain migrant landscapes (among others) as invisible at best or that label them as deviant in the worst cases. Under these circumstances, the public realm is not neutral, as the legal scholar Nancy Frazer has illustrated:

> public spheres themselves are not spaces of zero-degree culture, equally hospitable to any possible form of cultural expression. Rather, they consist in culturally specific institutions — including, for example, various journals and various social geographies of urban space. These institutions may be understood as culturally specific theoretical lenses that filter and alter the utterances they frame.[28]

The migrant landscapes explored in this chapter represent the possibility of a hybrid public realm that may mitigate the pressures of many recent trends in planning and urban design and that may point to a location of culture that lies outside conventional frames. In Charlotte, many new urban developments adhere to the frameworks of form-based planning and design. These guidelines promote mixed-use development and urban/architectural patterns that directly shape the space of the street, the aesthetics of the city, and the social norms expected of the occupants of both. As such, these guidelines promote conformity and homogeneity — two characteristics that effectively exclude cultural difference and, by extension, contribute to the invisibility of various sectors of the city's overall demographic.

While invisibility may be a particular consequence of often indeterminate legal, economic, and social status, such an invisibility can be both beneficial and tactical: tactical in the sense that invisibility allows for a form of spatial occupation that is fluid and dynamic, and beneficial in the sense that invisibility provides a space of exile and refuge, or a homeplace, that affords a measure of safety, of resistance, and of invention.[29] From this perspective, one of the most promising attributes of the emergent Latino spatial practices often found in Charlotte's migrant landscapes is that they manifest a counter-urbanity that is not contingent on physical representation in an aesthetic sense; rather, this emergent Latino urbanity is tied to spatial expression as a dimension of a critical imagination.[30]

The articulation of a proto-topia is, therefore, difficult to manifest under the auspices of conventional urban design or planning practices that privilege specific urban forms rooted in premodern townscapes over the spatiality of the present. Migrant landscapes reclaim existing space by imbuing them with new transnational and transcultural spatial expressions. In this sense, such spaces are characterized by a both/and condition in which cultural dimensions of a homeland are redeployed in a borderland and this redeployment results in a hybridization of cultural attributes that draw from the past and present. However, this is not a spatial practice rooted in the nostalgia of some lost condition; rather, this is a spatiality that fundamentally engages the present.

The tactical and strategic reuses of space found in both East Los Angeles's established and Charlotte's emerging Latino landscapes provide models for the rebuilding of our urban and suburban landscapes generally. By looking at the ways by which culture is spatialized, at the ways by which past and present are recombined, and by identifying the emergent qualities of a new form of public realm, one can begin to learn from the locations of cultures now present in our cities. The Latino landscapes examined in this chapter provide evidence that places can be taken over, reconfigured, rewritten, and revitalized through cultural expression. However, in order to capitalize on the opportunities that grassroots urbanity holds for the city, the public realm itself must be reclaimed as a multifaceted forum. This would require us to remember that "public life has always combined three characteristics: a common-wealth for the common good or benefit, open to general observations by strangers, and involving a diversity of people and thus engendering a tolerance of diverse interests and behaviors."[31]

Urban spaces can and should encompass a diverse set of publics that, when taken comprehensively, build toward a multifaceted public realm. Many Latino landscapes in Charlotte offer examples that such diversity can actually prosper in spaces otherwise thought inadequate by mainstream or middle-class standards. As such, a Latino urbanity should be nurtured and allowed to generate a form of the public realm that reflects the lived realities of a contemporary transnational condition. The uses of the pubic domain that both emergent and established Latino landscapes represent help illustrate how the city itself can be revived as a space of public engagement. They do so through the debates that they spawn, through the cultural values that they promote, and through the mental maps that they help establish. In this sense, the space of the city is enacted as the open geography of a border culture that is now a fundamental part of Charlotte as well as many other North American cities.

Notes

1. This ethnographically based research was funded in part by a Faculty Fellowship from the University of North Carolina at Charlotte's Urban Institute.
    Queen Charlotte was the wife of King George III of the United Kingdom and a distant relation of the current Queen of England, Elizabeth II.
2. Julia Oliver, "Store Owner Uses Sign to Criticize Latino Influx," *Charlotte Observer*, May 22, 2007, 1A.
3. Kavita Pandit, "The Southern Migration Turn-around and Current Patterns," *Southeastern Geographer* 37 (November 1997): 238–50.
4. Karen Martin, "A City Transformed," *Planning*, July 2002, 14–19.
5. Roberto Suro and Audrey Singer, "Latino Growth in Metropolitan America: Changing Patterns, New Locations," Brookings Institution Survey Series Census 2000, July 2002. See also Betsy Guzmám, *The Hispanic Population: Census 2000 Brief*, U.S. Department of Commerce, Economics and Statistics Administration, Census Bureau, May 2001.
6. *Solid South* refers to electoral history of U.S. southern states from the end of Reconstruction to the emergence of the civil rights movement. During this period the Democratic Party experienced large electoral wins in the southern states, giving rise to the notion that the South was a solid voting block upon which Democrats could depend.
7. Michael Omi, "Out of the Melting Pot and into the Fire: Race Relations Policy," *Policy Issues to the Year 2020: The State of Asian Pacific America — A Public Policy Report* (Los Angeles: LEAP Asian Pacific American Public Policy Institute/University of California, Los Angeles, Asian American Studies Center, 1993), 9.
8. *United States Census Bureau Report: 2005 American Community Survey Data Products for Mecklenburg County, North Carolina (15 August 2006)*; *United States Census Bureau Report: 2005 American Community Survey Data Products for Charlotte, North Carolina (15 August 2006)*. Latino community leaders base their popu-

lation estimates on the first-hand experience of local social service organizations, which often cite working with immigrants who did not participate in the census.

9. For the impacts of Mexican communities upon East Los Angeles, see the work of James Rojas, Margaret Crawford, and Mike Davis, among others; for an account of Turkish immigration in Duisburg-Marlox, see Patricia Ehrkamp, "Placing Identities: Transnational Practices and Local Attachments of Turkish Immigrants in Germany," *Journal of Ethnic and Migration Studies* 31, no. 2 (March 2005): 345–64.

10. Lawrence A. Herzog, *From Aztec to High Tech: Architecture and Landscape across the Mexico–United States Border* (Baltimore: Johns Hopkins University Press, 1999).

11. Margaret Crawford, "Mi casa es su casa," in *Urban Latino Cultures: La Vida Latina en L.A.*, ed. Gustavo Leclerc, Raul Villa, and Michael J. Dear, 117–24 (Thousand Oaks, Calif.: Sage Publications, 1999), 117.

12. Sharon Zukin, *Landscapes of Power: From Detroit to Disney World* (Berkeley: University of California Press, 1991), 180.

13. James T. Rojas, "The Enacted Environment: The Creation of Place by Mexicans and Mexican-Americans in East Los Angeles," (master's thesis, Massachusetts Institute of Technology, 1991).

14. Heather A. Smith and Owen J. Furuseth, "The 'Nuevo South': Latino Place Making and Community Building in the Middle-Ring Suburbs of Charlotte," in *Twenty-First-Century Gateways: Immigration and Incorporation in Suburban America*, ed. Audrey Singer, Susan W. Hardwick, and Caroline B. Brettell, 281–307 (Washington, D.C.: Brookings Institution Press, 2008).

15. Daniel D. Arreola, "Mexican-American Housescapes," *Geographical Review* 78, no. 3 (1988): 299–315; Rojas, "The Enacted Environment."

16. Although this type of residential unit is difficult to transform or adapt physically, it does easily subdivide to provide multiple semiprivate and autonomous spaces within the shell of a single home: a lower level that is set apart spatially by a full flight of stairs can easily be closed off from the upper areas, which, in effect, creates a second home within the larger structure. In this sense, split-level homes fit the needs of an immigrant landscape well by allowing a single home to encompass several residences within.

17. Inés M. Miyares, "Changing Latinization of New York City," in *Hispanic Spaces, Latino Places: Community and Cultural Diversity in Contemporary America*, ed. Daniel A. Arreola, 145–66 (Austin: University of Texas Press, 2004), 157–58.

18. Ibid., 157.

19. Rojas has used *urban prop* primarily in relation to the residential landscape of East Los Angeles, but it has implications for urban areas in general. As in the theater, the prop becomes a device to propel the action of the narrative and, in the case of East Los Angeles, the prop helps condition space to meet the social needs of the

community. See Rojas, "The Enacted Environment," 000; James T. Rojas, "The Enacted Environment of East Los Angeles," *Places* 8, no. 3 (Spring 1993): 42–53.

20. El Pueblo, Inc., "2002 Latino Legislative Agenda," www.elpueblo.org.

21. James Holston, "Spaces of Insurgent Citizenship," *Architectural Design* 66, no. 11/12 (November/December 1996): 54–59.

22. Several California municipalities have attempted to enact legislation aimed at suppressing the spatial expression of Latino cultural interests. This has led some state policy makers to consider the relationship between Latino cultural landscapes and urban policy. See Michael Mendez, "Latino New Urbanism: Building on Cultural Preferences," *Opolis: An International Journal of Suburban and Metropolitan Studies* 1, no. 1, (2005): article 5, http://repositories.cdlib.org/cssd/opolis/vol1/iss1/art5.

23. Michel Foucault, "Of Other Spaces," *Diacritics* 16, no. 1 (Spring 1986): 24.

24. Homi Bhabha, *The Location of Culture* (New York: Routledge, 1994), 211.

25. See Herzog, *From Aztec to High Tech,* especially 177–201.

26. Nancy Frazer, "Rethinking the Public Sphere: A Contribution to the Critique of Actually Existing Democracy," in *Between Borders: Pedagogy and the Politics of Cultural Studies*, ed. Henry A. Giroux and Peter McLaren (New York: Routledge, 1994), 78.

27. Ibid., 82.

28. Ibid., 86.

29. See bell hooks, *Yearning: Race, Gender, and Cultural Politics* (Boston: South End Press, 1990), especially 41–49.

30. Arjun Appadurai, "Disjuncture and Difference in the Global Cultural Economy," in *Colonial Discourse and Post-Colonial Theories: A Reader,* ed. Patrick Williams and Laura Chrisman, 324–39 (New York: Columbia University Press, 1994).

31. Michael Brill, "Transformation, Nostalgia, and Illusion in Public Life and Public Place," in *Public Places and Spaces,* Human Behavior and Environment: Advances in Theory and Research 10 (New York: Plenum Press, 1989), 20.

Owen J. Furuseth

Epilogue
Charlotte at the Globalizing Crossroads

In his 1941 landmark book, *The Mind of the South*, W. J. Cash probed the intellectual and sociological roots of the New South.[1] Over the course of his analysis, Cash dismissed the importance and place of urbanization and urbanism in the region's development and its future. Cash's perspective on contemporary city life was dark, shaped by images of crime, crowding, disease, and presided over by a self-serving economic and political leadership.[2] Although Cash had strong family connections to the Charlotte region and spent a portion of his newspaper career as a writer and associate editor with the *Charlotte News*, the city earned scant mention — aside from the dubious honor of having one of the two highest murder rates in the South, a title ironically shared with Atlanta, our longtime rival.[3] For Cash, Charlotte was but another middling southern town. Not very important, not very promising.

Fast forward almost seventy years and behold the transformation. As the authors in *Charlotte, NC* have documented, the city has become both important and promising. On a descriptive level, Charlotte has grown to be the largest urban center in the Carolinas and one of the most dynamic metropolitan centers in the South. More importantly, it is a city that has intentionally reinvented its image and its functions to take advantage of societal and economic trends while grasping for the cachet and superlatives applied to older and larger urban centers. Bodaciously, Charlotte represents itself as competing with America's largest metros as well as with international cities.

The malaise and plutocratic structures that surrounded urbanism in Cash's South have given way to a culture of growth, change, and progress. These qualities are easily measured and embraced by the Charlotte community, from the elites who have driven the growth machine apparatus to working-class whites and African Americans whose jobs and worldview equate growth and change with opportunity. Native Charlotteans may grouse about crowded highways and overbearing Yankee newcomers, but nativism and antigrowth politics have never taken hold.

Less precisely defined, however, is a community-wide vision of progress. If framed in economic terms, progress equates to new jobs, wealth creation, and enhanced recognition in the world of economic developers and their ranking schemes. But describing progress in social and ideological terms exposes the traditional fissures of class and race. For a globalizing Charlotte, where diversity and openness to a wide range of immigrants are fundamental, tensions play out in public discourse and political contests, ranging from episodic skirmishes to protracted painful epochs. Indeed, the short-lived rescue of Charlotte from the homosexual agenda by county leaders cutting off public monies to *Angels in America*, recounted by Goldfield, represents the former. The bulldozing of the Brooklyn neighborhood under the rubric of urban revitalization, discussed by Ingalls and Heard, and the long-running struggle for equality in public education, chronicled by Smith, illustrate the latter.

Beyond the steadfast bond between government and the corporate interests that undergirds all facets of public policy in Charlotte, religion is also a pervasive force that shapes the life of Charlotte. Until the recent globalizing period, religiosity in Charlotte was rooted in southern-flavored Protestantism. Although Southern Baptists are the largest single denomination in the city, mainstream Presbyterians and Methodists, combined, outnumbered their more evangelical brethren. In the most recent survey (in 2000) of religious congregations and adherents, Southern Baptists in Mecklenburg County numbered 75,026; United Methodists, 46,604; and Presbyterian Church (USA) members, 41,868.[4] Taken together, the three largest Protestant groups made up nearly one-half (49 percent) of all congregational adherents in the county.[5]

Among the Protestant denominations, the Presbyterian Church (USA) holds particular significance. With seventy-five active congregations in the county, the Presbytery of Charlotte centered in Mecklenburg County is reputed to be home to the second highest concentration of Presbyterians in the United States. Only Pittsburgh, Pennsylvania, has a higher concentration. But more important than numbers is the status of the laity. Starting with the early Scotch-Irish settlers and the subsequent influx of rural capitalists and mill owners, Charlotte's business and political elite have deep Presbyterian roots. A roster of Charlotte's elected officials, merchants, and financial leaders closely matches the membership rolls of Charlotte's oldest and most prominent Presbyterian churches: Covenant, First, and Myers Park.

One notable impact of globalization has been transition in the city's religious traditions. First, the overall level of religiosity, as measured by the number of adherents compared to the total population, has declined. The 1980 Churches and Church Membership survey reported Mecklenburg County's adherence rate was 60.1 percent, meaning six out of every ten Mecklenburg County residents were congregants of a church or temple.[6] By 2000, the adherence rate had declined to 48.0 percent.[7]

A second shift has been the decline in Protestant domination of the religious scene. One important impact of immigration from both international and domestic sources is the planting of new faith communities and religious traditions, including those previously not represented or underrepresented here. In the 2000 survey, for example, nine Buddhist, three Hindu, and five Muslim congregations were counted.[8] In 1990, none of these groups were reported. Jews have a long history in Charlotte, but over the last two decades, temple membership has increased nearly ten-fold, from 897 to 8,500 between 1980 and 2000.[9]

The most fundamental realignment in Charlotte's religious scene is Roman Catholicism. The influx of Latino and Southeast Asian immigrants has resulted in explosive growth in the Diocese of Charlotte. Consider that between 1980 and 2000, the number of Catholic adherents grew from 14,891 to 59,292, or nearly 300 percent.[10] During the same period, the proportion of overall religious adherents in Mecklenburg County increased a more modest 37.3 percent. Data developed by the diocese estimate that in 2000, Hispanic Catholics were 40.9 percent of all parishioners in Mecklenburg County.[11]

These shifts in religious practices and affiliations are certainly likely to affect civic leadership. This transition will likely be paralleled by the reality that religiosity will remain a part of the cultural core of Charlotte. After all, Charlotte is a part of the American South. Billy Graham Parkway, named in 1981 for the conservative evangelist and hometown boy, is a prominent piece of the city's roadway system. However, more recent namings (the Levine Museum of the New South in 1990, the Blumenthal Performing Arts Center in 1992, and the Levine Children's Hospital at Carolinas Medical Center in 2007) have elevated leaders with different roots and spiritual traditions.

As a leading destination for twenty-first-century international immigration and classified as a pre-emerging metro gateway, Charlotte is the site of intense debate over undocumented immigration and immigration reform. While anti-immigrant policies have been actively pursued by state legislators in North Carolina and local governments in the counties surrounding

Charlotte, efforts to target and turn away Latino immigrants to Charlotte have been largely unsuccessful.

In general, Republican leaders in Charlotte have shown little interest in joining with conservatives in the North Carolina and National GOP to make anti-immigrant policies a theme in the local party platform. The two exceptions to this pattern are U.S. Representative Sue Myrick and Charlotte Mayor Pat McCrory. Their efforts, however, have failed to rally broader Republican support. Representative Myrick, a former mayor of Charlotte, began her congressional career as a moderate Republican by North Carolina standards. As the national political debate over immigration heated up, she has emerged as a congressional leader against immigration reform. Myrick has authored a series of anti-immigrant bills and actively promoted ICE 287(g) partnerships across the region as a way to identify and remove "illegals" from her 9th Congressional District. The 287(g) program authorizes police and sheriff agencies to perform federal immigration law enforcement functions. Two of the three county sheriff departments in Myrick's district are 287(g) participants.[12]

Representative Myrick's highly visible campaign against undocumented immigrants has been complemented by Charlotte Mayor Pat McCrory. The mayor is progressive on land use planning and transit issues. And, early on, he supported immigrant settlement in Charlotte. By 2005, McCrory had reversed his support and authored legislation to sanction local action on Representative Myrick's anti-immigrant proposals. The legislation lacked support in city council however, and McCrory moved on to appoint the Mayor's Immigration Study Commission. The rationale for establishing the commission arose from McCrory's service on President Bush's Homeland Security Advisory Council and his exposure to the flow of "illegal" immigrants into San Diego.[13]

The commission was made up of community leaders, service providers, business interests, and Department of Homeland Security staff. Conservative activists on the commission sought support for a local anti-immigrant agenda. Pro-immigrant members argued for local and state immigration reform measures. The final report endorsed neither perspective. Early in 2007, the findings and recommendations were publicly presented. There was no implementation strategy. Lacking support on city council, the commission report produced no public action.[14]

Why has the anti-immigration agenda been a failure in Charlotte? I believe an explanation is found in the traditional alliance between the city's business interests, especially the dominating financial services sector, and local government leadership. On one level, immigrant rights have emerged as a twenty-first-century civil rights issue. International immigrants are the contemporary brethren of African Americans in the 1960s. The words and images used by immigrant opponents and their lineage have not changed from the earlier civil rights movement. So, just as Charlotte's civic leaders in the 1960s sought to resolve racial tensions, current city leaders have no interest in demonizing the new Latino immigrants, legal or undocumented. In fact, there is widespread recognition within the business community that an army of Latino laborers was a necessary component of the physical construction of the new Center City and expansive suburbs.

But there is another layer to the explanation. In globalizing Charlotte, business practices and images are transparent and scrutinized by customers and investors 24/7. Charlotte's corporate and business recruiters work in global markets. Business decisions surrounding compensation plans (gay employee benefits), investment areas (child labor practices, green energy), or client services (loans to low-wealth communities, bank services to undocumented populations) are made for national and international markets, not the headquarters city. Local policies that disadvantage immigrants in Charlotte would expose the city's corporate leaders to criticism and potentially damage business opportunities in markets beyond North Carolina.

Has Charlotte transformed itself again, moving in a socially and politically progressive direction? One datum point is the 2008 presidential election results. Although President Obama eked out a 14,000-vote North Carolina victory, his smallest margin in any state, Obama won Mecklenburg County in a landslide. His 100,000-vote margin was the largest in the state.[15]

The electoral popularity of a young, African American nonsoutherner was unprecedented in Mecklenburg County's election history. The deep extenuating circumstances of the 2008 election cycle may render the election an anomaly. Nonetheless, it does hint at a next step in the globalizing process seen in other maturing cities. Physical and economic shifts are often matched by political and social progress. The blurring between Charlotte's twentieth- and twenty-first-century culture and patterns is already well under way. What lies ahead is not certain. But whatever path Charlotte takes, it would surely perplex and challenge Mr. Cash's vision.

Notes

1. W. J. Cash, *The Mind Of The South* (1941; repr. New York: Vintage Books, 1991).
2. Cash, 413–17.
3. Cash, 414.
4. Dale E. Jones et al., *Religious Congregations and Membership in the United States: 2000* (Nashville: Glenmary Research Center, 2002).
5. The Association of Religion Data Archives, "2000 County Membership Report, Mecklenburg County, North Carolina," http://www.thearda.com/mapsReports/reports/counties/37119_2000.asp (accessed June 15, 2009).
6. The Association of Religion Data Archives, "1980 County Membership Report Mecklenburg County, North Carolina," http://www.thearda.com/mapsReports/reports/counties/37119_1980.asp (accessed June 15, 2009).
7. The Association of Religion Data Archives, "2000 County Membership Report Mecklenburg County, North Carolina."
8. Ibid.
9. The Association of Religion Data Archives, "1980 County Membership Report Mecklenburg County, North Carolina," and "2000 County Membership Report Mecklenburg County, North Carolina."
10. The Association of Religion Data Archives, "1980 County Membership Report Mecklenburg County, North Carolina."
11. Roman Catholic Diocese of Charlotte, "Catholics by County, 2000," http://www.charlottediocese.org/atlasofthediocese.html (accessed June 15, 2009).
12. Program critics note that 287(g) is not effective in removing dangerous and violent undocumented criminals from the United States — although that is a central intent of the program. Rather, most immigrants are picked up for minor crimes. The risk of racial profiling is also high. Indeed, the most recent data show that more than half of the aliens arrested and deported in Mecklenburg County since 2002 were originally charged with traffic or DWI offenses. See the *Charlotte Observer*, March 5, 2009.
13. The Mayor's Immigration Study Commission, *Immigration: Legal and Illegal Local Perspective — Charlotte, North Carolina* (Charlotte: City of Charlotte, 2007).
14. During the 2008 election cycle, Mayor McCrory was the Republican candidate for governor. McCrory was defeated in the Obama-led Democratic near sweep of statewide races.
15. North Carolina Board of Elections, Mecklenburg 2008 Election Results, http://results.enr.clarityelections.com/NC/7937/14537/en/summary.html, http://results.enr.clarityelections.com/NC/Mecklenburg/7997/14386/en/summary.html (accessed June 12, 2009).

Contributors

DEREK H. ALDERMAN is a professor of cultural and historical geography at East Carolina University and a former editor of the peer-reviewed journal *Southeastern Geographer*. He has written widely on the role of change, continuity, and contest in shaping the landscape of the American South, focusing particular attention on race relations, tourism, and public commemoration in the region. He is the coauthor, with Owen Dwyer, of *Civil Rights Memorials and the Geography of Memory* (2008).

OWEN J. FURUSETH is the associate provost for metropolitan studies and extended academic programs, and a professor of geography at the University of North Carolina at Charlotte. He received his Ph.D. in geography and resource planning from Oregon State University. His research interests are centered around community planning, especially social and community change associated with population growth. Over the past several years, his research has focused on examining Latino immigrant experiences in the state of North Carolina, and, more specifically, the Charlotte metropolitan region. This work has included research and community engagement activities addressing the receptivity of community groups and service providers to new immigrants, the spatial mismatch surrounding health care provision, and the impact of new immigrants as agents for economic development and community redevelopment. Dr. Furuseth is on the board of directors of the Latin American Coalition, Charlotte's largest Hispanic service organization. He also serves as UNC Charlotte's liaison to the Fundacion Comunitaria del Bajio (Bajio Community Foundation), an organization working in Guanajuato state, Mexico, to strengthen rural communities experiencing high rates of immigration to the United States, especially North Carolina.

JOSÉ L. S. GÁMEZ is an associate professor of architecture, a member of the Latin American studies faculty, and a Research Fellow with the Institute for Social Capital (2008–09) at the University of North Carolina at Charlotte. He also serves as the coordinator of the Design+Society Research Center for the School of Architecture and the College of Arts+Architecture. His research and design practices explore questions of cultural identity in architecture and urban design, the impacts of Latino immigration upon urban space, and critical practices in Chicano art. His research is published in *Aztlán: A Journal of Chicano Studies* and *Places: A Forum of Environmental Design*. He has also authored essays that appear in the edited books

Writing Urbanism: A Design Reader (2008) and *Expanding Architecture: Design As Activism* (2008). He has taught at Portland State University and the University of Nevada at Las Vegas prior to joining the faculty at UNC Charlotte. He received his Bachelor of Environmental Design from Texas A&M, his Master of Architecture from UC Berkeley, and his Ph.D. in architecture from the University of California at Los Angeles.

DAVID GOLDFIELD is the Robert Lee Bailey Professor of History at the University of North Carolina at Charlotte. A native of Memphis, he grew up in Brooklyn, New York, and attended the University of Maryland. He is the author or editor of fourteen books dealing with the history of the American South, including two works, *Cotton Fields and Skyscrapers: Southern City and Region* (1982) and *Black, White, and Southern: Race Relations and Southern Culture* (1991), nominated for the Pulitzer Prize in history, and both received the Mayflower Award for nonfiction. *Still Fighting the Civil War: The American South and Southern History* appeared in 2002 and received the Jules and Frances Landry Award and was named by *Choice* as an Outstanding Academic Title. His most recent book is *Southern Histories: Public, Personal, and Sacred*, published by the University of Georgia Press in 2003.

Goldfield is the editor of the *Encyclopedia of American Urban History*, published by Sage Publications in 2007. He is currently working on a reinterpretation of the Civil War, "Rebirth of a Nation: America during the Civil War Era," for Bloomsbury Publishing Co. The Organization of American Historians named him Distinguished Lecturer in 2001. Goldfield is the editor of the *Journal of Urban History* and a coauthor of *The American Journey: A History of the United States* (2009). He also serves as an expert witness in voting rights and death penalty cases, as a consultant on the urban South to museums and public television and radio, and works with the U.S. State Department as an academic specialist, leading workshops on American history and culture in foreign countries.

WILLIAM GRAVES is an associate professor and John H. Biggs Faculty Fellow in the Department of Geography and Earth Sciences at the University of North Carolina at Charlotte. During 2005–06 Dr. Graves was a GlaxoSmithKline Faculty Fellow in the Economic Development of North Carolina at the Institute for Emerging Issues at North Carolina State University. His research involves exploring the impacts of economic change in the southeastern United States, particularly the development of advanced services within the urban South. This work has been published in the *Professional Geographer, Urban Geography*, and *Southeastern Geographer*. A central theme of this research has been the role of financial systems in southern industrial transformation. Dr. Graves has a secondary line of research into Charlotte's urban transformation. This work has been published in the *Journal of Urban Affairs* and *Southeastern Geographer*. Dr. Graves has served as coeditor of the *Industrial Geographer* and on the editorial boards of *Southeastern Geographer* and the *Journal of Applied Geospatial Research.*

TOM HANCHETT earned his Ph.D. in U.S. history from University of North Carolina at Chapel Hill following degrees from Cornell University and the University of Chicago. His research interests range widely in urban history and southern history since the Civil War. He is author of *Sorting Out the New South City* (1998), an exploration of segregation in Charlotte, now in its second printing by UNC Press. Other writings have appeared in the *American Historical Review*, *Cornbread Nation: Best of Southern Food Writing*, and the *New Encyclopedia of Southern Culture*. Dr. Hanchett taught historic preservation and urban history at Youngstown State and Cornell before joining Charlotte's Levine Museum of the New South as staff historian in 1999. He has curated the museum's award-winning major exhibitions, including a permanent installation offering an overview of the region since 1865, an exploration of 1970s women's history, and a study of the Carolina roots of *Brown v. Board of Education,* which won the American Association of Museums' top national prize. The Levine Museum mission is to "use history to build community"; in 2005 Dr. Hanchett and others from the museum received the U.S. government's annual award for museum community service, presented at a White House ceremony by the First Lady.

ISAAC HEARD JR. is an adjunct lecturer in the Department of Geography and Earth Sciences at the University of North Carolina at Charlotte. As a practicing urban planner and member of the American Institute of Certified Planners, Mr. Heard has more than thirty years of experience in a variety of aspects of planning, with a particular emphasis on community economic development and neighborhood revitalization. He served as the executive director of the Northwest Corridor Community Development Corporation, a coalition of twelve inner-city neighborhoods in Charlotte, North Carolina, for nine years and as the Charlotte office director for the Enterprise Foundation for four years. In addition, Mr. Heard has provided training in strategic planning, economic development, and project development for community-based organizations on behalf of the U.S. Department of Housing and Urban Development, the Federal Home Loan Bank of Atlanta, and Branch Banking and Trust.

GERALD L. INGALLS is a professor of geography in the Department of Geography and Earth Sciences at the University of North Carolina at Charlotte. His research has focused on urban and political geography. Major themes of his research in urban geography include urban regional governance, the patterns of residential change, and adaptive reuse. His research in electoral geography has focused on themes such as election behavior patterns (particularly in the American South), the geography of campaigning, women in politics, and campaign financing. His work has appeared in *Southeastern Geographer, Political Geography, Women in Politics, Comparative State Politics, American Politics*, as well as in a number of books.

RONALD V. KALAFSKY is an associate professor in the Department of Geography at the University of Tennessee. His research interests include the geographies of manufacturing, human capital and industrial innovation, and export strategies of manufacturers. Of particular interest are the challenges and performance of manufacturers located in mature industrial regions, including Canada, Japan, and the southern United States. Research on these topics has appeared in journals such as the *Professional Geographer, Tijdschrift voor Economische en Sociale Geografie*, and *Southeastern Geographer*. Dr. Kalafsky is the coeditor of the *Industrial Geographer* and also serves on the editorial board of the *American Review of Canadian Studies*.

JONATHAN KOZAR is a Ph.D. candidate in geography and urban regional analysis at the University of North Carolina at Charlotte. He is a research specialist at the UNC Charlotte Urban Institute, an applied public policy research and community outreach institute of the university. His research interests include the many facets surrounding the economic transition from a manufacturing to a knowledge and service economy in the United States. With particular interests in the increase of business and producer services, his research examines emergent industries within business-to-business markets and the associated economic impact at geographic scales spanning the urban hierarchy from urban to rural.

MATTHEW D. LASSITER is associate professor of history at the University of Michigan, where he teaches courses on urban/suburban history, social and political history, and public policy. Dr. Lassiter is the author of *The Silent Majority: Suburban Politics in the Sunbelt South* (2006), winner of the 2007 Lillian Smith Award presented by the Southern Regional Council. His article for the *Journal of Urban History*, "The Suburban Origins of 'Color-Blind' Conservatism: Middle-Class Consciousness in the Charlotte Busing Crisis," was republished in *The Best American History Essays 2006*. Dr. Lassiter is also coeditor of *The Myth of Southern Exceptionalism* (2009) and *The Moderates' Dilemma: Massive Resistance to School Desegregation in Virginia* (1998). He is currently working on a book project titled "The Suburban Crisis: The Pursuit and Defense of the American Dream."

EMILY THOMAS LIVINGSTONE earned her master's degree in geography with concentration in urban regional analysis from the University of North Carolina at Charlotte in December 2008. Her thesis, "Contemporary Gentrification Processes in a Globalizing City: Super-gentrification, New-build Gentrification and Charlotte, North Carolina," focuses on traditional and contemporary gentrification, globalization, economic restructuring, perception, distinction and image — within the changing context of center city Charlotte. Her professional and academic areas of interest include urban restructuring trends, downtown (re)development strategies, issues of social equity, and contemporary gentrification. A native Charlottean, Ms. Livingstone is employed with Centralina Council of Governments.

RONALD L. MITCHELSON is a professor of economic geography at East Carolina University and chair of the Department of Geography. His primary research focus is transportation and economic development. He has written frequently about the structure of transportation and communications flows and their unique ability to reveal important insights concerning the transformation of landscapes and regions.

TYREL G. MOORE is professor of geography at the University of North Carolina at Charlotte. Dr. Moore's recent research interests focus on the impacts of economic restructuring on rural areas and small towns in the U.S. South. In particular, that research explores the issues faced by mining communities in Appalachia and textile mill towns in the Piedmont of North and South Carolina as those places struggle to reinvent their economies and to preserve elements of their place-defining heritage. The local transformation and survival of these communities are regionally significant public policy issues. Dr. Moore has published articles on regional development and planning in the *Journal of Geography*, the *Professional Geographer*, *Southeastern Geographer*, and *Progress in Rural Planning and Policy*. Dr. Moore serves on the editorial boards of *Southeastern Geographer* and the *Journal of Geography*.

HEATHER A. SMITH is associate professor of geography and director of the urban studies minor at the University of North Carolina at Charlotte. Dr. Smith also holds appointments as faculty research associate with the UNC Charlotte Urban Institute and senior researcher with the Canadian Metropolis Project, an international forum for research and policy on migration, diversity, and changing cities. As an urban social geographer her research interests revolve around issues of contemporary urban restructuring. Her work on revitalization and gentrification has been published in *Tijdschrift voor Economische en Sociale Geografie*, *Southeastern Geographer*, and *Journal of Urban Affairs*. Research on immigrant settlement and neighborhood poverty can be found in *Urban Studies* and the *Annals of the Association of American Geographers*. Dr. Smith's most recent writing on Latino migration into Charlotte and the broader U.S. South can be found in the edited volumes *Immigrants Outside the Megalopolis: Ethnic Transformation in the Heartland* (2008) and the Brookings Institution's *Twenty-First Century Gateways: Immigrant Incorporation in Suburban America* (2008). With Owen J. Furuseth, Dr. Smith is also the coeditor of *Latinos in the New South: Transformations of Place* (2006).

STEPHEN SAMUEL SMITH is a professor of political science at Winthrop University. He served as an expert witness for the NAACP's Legal Defense and Educational Fund in the reopened *Swann* litigation and is the author of *Boom for Whom? Education, Desegregation, and Development in Charlotte* (2004). His work on urban politics and education policy has appeared in the *Journal of Urban Affairs, Educational Evaluation and Policy Analysis, Perspectives on Politics, Teachers College Record*, and in many edited volumes. He also writes about problems in the social capital literature, including, with Jessica Kulynych, "It May be Social, but Why is it Capital? The Social Construction of Social Capital and the Politics of Language" (*Politics & Society*, 2002).

DAVID WALTERS is a British architect who has practiced and taught in the United States since 1981. He is a professor of architecture and urban design at the College of Arts and Architecture at the University of North Carolina at Charlotte and the program director of the Master of Urban Design program. Since the mid-1990s, Walters has worked extensively with small towns in the Carolinas helping them to craft master plans and zoning ordinances that balance property rights with managed and environmentally responsible growth. He is also senior urban designer with the Lawrence Group, a firm of architects and town planners with offices in St. Louis; Beijing; New York; Denver, Colorado; Austin, Texas; and Davidson, North Carolina. His practice experience over many years has provided material for two books on urban design and planning, *Design First: Design-based Planning for Communities* (2004), cowritten with his wife, Linda Luise Brown, and *Designing Community: Charrettes, Masterplans and Form-based Codes* (2007). Walters is also the coeditor, with Christopher Grech, of *The Future Office* (2008), an extensive review of trends in workplace design from neighborhood planning to information technologies.

Index

Adams Mark Hotel, 10
adaptability, 4, 5
AeroDyn Wind Tunnel, 68–69
African American communities, 6, 8, 184; aging of, 182–83; agricultural settlements, 174–75, 177; diversity, historical, 160, 183; globalization and, 185; Kansas City, 166; post–World War II, 13; redevelopment (inner city) as threat to, 163; residential types (*see* residential types, African American); "segregation nostalgia," 16; small size of, 174; southern cities, 167; stereotype of, 164; suburban, 251; textile industry and, 168; typology of, 160–85; urban renewal, 147–48
African Americans, 11, 173; as "involuntary immigrants," 22; migration, rural-to-urban, 166; race relations, transformation of, 190; slavery era, 11–12. *See also main entries, e.g., African American communities; Jim Crow era*
Aiken, Charles, 164–65
airline hub, 13; international flights, 36, 41; jets, 29–30. *See also main entries, e.g., Douglas Airport*
alcohol, 19. *See also* moonshine, NASCAR and
Allegheny Conference, 145
Alpha Mill, 134–35
Amick, Marvin, 61
Andretti, Mario, 61
Angels in America (Kushner), 19–20, 38, 285

architecture: building typology, urban, 235–36; firms, 130–31
arts and entertainment, 36, 39; civic fundraising campaign, 43. *See also* Highland Park No. 3 Mill; NoDa Arts District
Asian Corner Mall, 257
Asian immigration, 255
Atherton Mills, 123, 129, 130; transit station, 131
Atlanta, Georgia, 284; Atlanta Compromise, 210; bootleggers and, 55, 82nn17–19, 82n21; rivalry with, 34, 37, 39, 40, 55–57
Atlanta Project (TAP), 143–44
automobile manufacturing, 102; migrant communities near, 268
automobiles, as catalyst for urban expansion, 168

Bahre, Bob, 76
Baker, Buck, 54, 57; crew, 61
Bakker, Jim and Tammy Faye, 19, 38, 42
Ballantyne, 194, 223
BankAmerica, 90
Bank of America, 42; acquisitions, 91–92, 96–98; expansion, 90–95; Federal Reserve and, 97; nationalization, potential, 98; new markets, need to adapt to, 93–94
banks and banking, 1, 4–5, 11, 28, 121; acquisitions, 90–91; assets, 87, 91; attitude, oppositional, 91; autonomy, reduction of, 155–56; branching, intrastate, 88–89; consolidation, 20;

banks and banking (continued) corporate citizenship, 141–56; economy and, 87; employees, 127–28, 136, 255; financial crisis of 2008, 95–98; global economy, connection to, 87–99; growth of city, role in, 136; neighborhood revitalization, role in, 150; in the nineteenth century, 88; origins, 13; regulatory environment, 88; retail vs. investment, 94–95; social responsibility, 143; Sun Belt Banking Center, 34–40; Uptown area, support for, 42–43. See also Federal Reserve Bank; Southeastern Banking Compact; and specific banks
Barringer, Osmond, 58
Bell, Derrick, 190
Belmont-Villa Heights, 254, 256
Bessant, Cathy, 204
Bhabha, Homi, 276–77
Biddle Institute, 180–81, 251
Biddleville, 180–81
Black Political Caucus, 205
Blandville, 179
Blumenthal Center for the Performing Arts, 17–18, 286
Bristol, Chris, 77
Brookings Institution survey, 255
Brooklyn, 171
Brookshire, Stanford, 29
Brown v. Board of Education of Topeka, 15–16, 29, 191
Bryant, Don, 33–34
building typology, urban, 235–36
Burgess, Ernest, 250
Burnham, Daniel, 145
bus rapid transit, 229, 256, 274
business establishment, 29–30; black political leaders, alliance with, 208; diversity in the work-place, efforts to promote, 208; economic interests, 190; education task force, 209–10; school busing, support for, 193; Swann era, 193
Business Week profiles, 28
busing, school, 33, 189; business elite's support of, 193; economic development and, 208; rejection of, 6, 16. See also Swann v. Charlotte-Mecklenburg School Board
Byron, Red, 54

CANS Bar, 128–29
Carolina Panthers, 37–38
Carolinas Medical Center, Children's Hospital, 286
Carolinas Partnership, 40–41
Carter, Jimmy, 143
Carver College, 14
Cash, W. J., The Mind of the South, 284
Center City, 135–36, 230; NCNB's impact on, 154–55; preservation efforts, 149
Central Avenue corridor, 254, 256, 270, 277; Latino population, 268, 269–75
Central Business District (CBD), 171–72
Chamber of Commerce: Cold War, during, 26, 27; Community Relations Committee, 29; Foreign Trade Commission, 32; goal of selective growth, 33–34; international trade center, 36; promotional statements, 44; publications, 26. See also public relations campaigns
character zones, 236
charitable foundations, corporate, 142–43
Charles, Pat and Harvey, 56
Charlotte Coliseum, 37

Charlotte College, 14
Charlotte Cotton Mills, 128–29
Charlotte Douglas International Airport, 36, 229
Charlotte Junior League, 148, 150
Charlotte-Mecklenburg Historic Landmarks Commission, 120, 123–24, 129
Charlotte-Mecklenburg School Board, 6, 192–93; elections, 205–6, 207; post-*Swann* ruling reversal, 196. *See also Swann v. Charlotte-Mecklenburg School Board*
Charlotte-Mecklenburg Schools (CMS), 8, 189; accomplishments, 191; complaints about, 203–4; deconsolidation movement, 204, 209–10; demographic composition, 192; desegregation, 191, 195, 206–7; Family Choice Plan, 196–97; "home schools," 197; magnet programs, 195, 197; new assignment plan, 195–97, 199; overcrowding, 203; parent groups, 203; political changes, 202–6; post-*Swann*, 197–206; poverty enrollment, 200; resegregation, 197–200; self-definition, 200–2; Student Assignment Plan, 201; task force, 204–5, 209–10. *See also* Charlotte-Mecklenburg School Board; school system; *Swann v. Charlotte-Mecklenburg School Board*
Charlotte Motor Speedway. *See* Lowe's Motor Speedway
Charlotte Observer articles: Ballantyne recreational development, 194; Center City development, 230; growth-related needs, income sources for, 233; Latino population, increase of, 264; NCNB's role, revitalization of Fourth Ward, 150, 151; political action committees, 233; preservation, historical, 135; textile industry, 124–25; textile mill reuse, 125–26
Charlotte Repertory Theater, 20, 38
Charlotte Speedway, 56, 58, 59; stock car race, June 1949, 50
Chelsea at South End, 131–32
Cherry, 179–80
Chicago Tribune article, salad-bowl suburbs, 247
Children's Hospital at Carolinas Medical Center, 286
China Construction Bank, 94
Chip Ganassi Racing team, 79
churches, landmark, 173
Citizens for Preservation, 148
city planning, 6, 127; bond referendum to fund infrastructure improvements, 130; Center City, role of, 230; development, role of private, 232–34; form-based planning, 234–39; future of, 241–43; globalization process, during, 239–41; growth management, collaborative, 236; for multiethnic population, 279; opposition to, 227; redevelopment of blighted areas, 133, 145–46; "smart growth," 119, 124; transportation and land use, attempt to integrate, 232–33; urban design concepts picture book, 237. *See also* Planning Commission, City of Charlotte; Transit Corridor System Plans
civil rights, immigrant, 288
Civil Rights Act of 1964, 29, 191
Civil War: economic stagnation following, 21; "New South" defined, 258
climate, 26, 27
Club America, 263
Cobb, James, 52
Cohen, Sacha Baron, 79

Cole, Grady, 57
community: corporate citizenship and, 141–56; corporations, reciprocity with, 146–47; gentrification of neighborhoods, 126–27; heritage, loss of, 125; knowledge, 62–69; quality of life, 75; size of, and textile mill use, 122–23. *See also main entries, e.g., Latino community*
Community Development Corporation, 152, 153
computers, as influence on urban environment, 224
Concord Speedway, 59
Cone, Bonnie, 14
Confederate flag, 77, 78
construction crews, 255
Conzen, M. R. G., 235–36
Cornelius, 234–35
corporate citizenship and Uptown revitalization, 141–56; community reciprocity, 146–47; evolution of, 142–45; NCNB's legacy, 156; public-private partnerships and, 145–46; relationship, 141
"cotton mill" campaign, 12
cotton mills. *See* textile mills
Coulter, David, 91
Countrywide Financial, 96–97
Cramer, Stuart, 132
Crawford, Margaret, 266–67
Crescent Resources, 129
Crisler, Al, 57
Crown Center Redevelopment Corporation, 145, 146
Crutchfield, Edward, 39, 90
cultural change, 2, 4, 6; assimilation, 15; deficiencies, 28; growth and progress, 284; Latino, 276, 278; location of culture, 276–77

Darlington Raceway (South Carolina), 60

Daugherty, Brad, 77
Davidson, 234–35
Davis, Marc, 77
Daytona 500, 66
Degler, Carl, 248
demographics, 1, 6; late twentieth century, 14–15; Latino, 264; public school enrollment and, 192; urban villages, 227
desegregation, 15, 16; business elite's involvement in, 193; the "Charlotte Way," 29; educational equality and, 211; national, 210; politics, school-related, 191, 195; post-*Swann*, 196; school, 33, 189–214, 206–7
design firms, 130–31
developers, private, 232–34
Dilworth, 240. *See also* Dilworth Community Development Association
Dilworth Community Development Association, 130
disadvantages, regional, 1–2
distribution center, 25, 26; for eastern half of U.S., 28, 121; jet airplanes, role of, 29–30
Douglas Airport: imported products, port of entry for, 32; jet airplanes at, 29–30. *See also* Charlotte Douglas International Airport
Douglas, Ben, 13
Downtown Merchants Association, 47n26
Duke Power, 150
dumpcms.com, 203–4
Duncan, Michael Clarke, 79
Dunnaway, Glenn, 50, 57

Earle Village, 174
Earnhardt, Dale, 59; Dale Trail, 71
Earnhardt, Dale, Jr., 71, 79
Earnhardt, Ralph, 58, 61, 71
Eastland Mall, 253

East Los Angeles, California, 7, 266–67, 271, 276–78
East Side, 7, 248–49, 251–53, 256
economy, 1; banking's effect on, 87; financial crisis of 2008, 5, 95–98; Latino community, regeneration, 266; manufacturing's role, 103; mortgage defaults, 95; motorsports and, 62; place, importance of, 224–26; school desegregation and, 189, 208; school resegregation and, 190; stagnation, post-Civil War, 21
Eddleman's Garage, 71
Edge Cities (Garreau), 224
education, higher, 13–14, 16, 63. *See also specific schools*
education, public. *See* Charlotte-Mecklenburg Schools; school system
Elmwood Cemetery, 78
employment, professional, 1, 126–27; gentrification and, 149–51, 154
energy use, 226
entertainment. *See* arts and entertainment
environmental concerns, 76; pollution, 133, 135; "smart growth" advocates, 119, 124
ESPN, 66
E-topia: "Urban Life, Jim — but not as We Know It" (Mitchell), 225
exports from southern U.S., 102–16; company size and level of, 111, 114; destinations, 111, 114; regulatory restrictions, 114–15; sales growth, potential, 107–8, 114, 116

Fair Housing Act of 1968, 253–54
Faith Community Rally on Public Education, 196, 209
Families United for North Mecklenburg Education (FUME), 203
Family Choice Plan, 196–97
Federal Reserve Bank, 13
Ferrell, Will, 79
First National Bank (Lake City, Florida), 89
First Union, 35, 42, 90
First Ward, 174
FleetBoston Financial, Community Renaissance Initiative (CRI), 144
Flock, Bob, 55
food, 15
football, 18, 19, 37
Ford cars, 57, 61
Foreign Trade Zone, 36
Fortune 500 firms, 25
Fourth Ward, 8, 128, 171; gentrification, 5, 127, 142, 172; Historic District status, 150; history, 148; loan program, low-income, 151–52; preservation, 149; public-private partnership, 150; residents, incoming versus outgoing, 152; revitalization, 141–42, 146–48. *See also* Friends of Fourth Ward
France, Bill, 50, 55–57
France, Brian, 77
Franchitti, Dario, 79
freeway. *See* outerbelt freeway
Friends of Fourth Ward, 148, 152
fundraising campaign, civic, 43
Furuseth, Owen, 255

Gallis, Michael, 227
Ganassi, Chip. *See* Chip Ganassi Racing team
Gantt, Harvey, 25, 35, 36, 37, 193; election upset, 194; task force, 204
Garreau, Joel, *Edge Cities*, 224
Garrison, Wilton, 55
Gauvreau, Larry, 196, 197, 202, 204
gentrification, 5, 126–27, 149–51; advantages, 153–54
GI Bill, 14

Gibbs, Joe. *See* Joe Gibbs Racing (JGR)
globalization, effects of, 2, 3–4, 136; African American communities, 185; business practices and images, 288; post-*Swann*, 199; process, emphasis on, 3, 119–20; urban areas, 225; white supremacy and, 191
globalization, local effect on, 3, 4, 210–11; Latino communities, growth of, 275–76
global status, emerging, 1, 7, 8, 285; city planning, 239–41; Jim Crow era, 210–11
Golden West Financial (Oakland, California), 95
Grace A.M.E. Zion Church, 173
Graham, Billy, 19, 286
Grant, Roy and Polly, 248–49
Great Britain, sustainable communities, 226
Greenville, 179
Grier Heights, 177–78, 256
Griffin, Arthur, 196, 202

Hall, Randal, 80
Hall, Roy, 54, 55
Hallmark Cards (Kansas City, Missouri), 144–45, 146
Hall of Fame. *See* NASCAR, Hall of Fame
Harris, Johnny, 194, 211
Hartsfield, William B., 13, 55
Hendrick Motorsports, 63, 65
Heritage USA theme park, 38
Hernandez-Paris, Jose, 254, 255
Hidden Valley, 254
Highland Park No. 3 Mill, 123, 132, 133, 250
Historic District status, 150
history: cotton mill as symbol, 120–21, 136; Fourth Ward, 148; manufacturing industry, 103–6; preservation of, 135, 149; recent, 190; white supremacy's lingering effect, 211. *See also* Charlotte-Mecklenburg Historic Landmarks Commission; memory community, Charlotte as; Museum of the New South; National Register of Historic Places
Holman, John, 61
Holman-Moody shop, 61–62
Holston, James, 275
Homeland Security, 287
homosexuality, 19–20, 38, 285
HOPE VI redevelopment, 147, 173, 174
Hornets, 37, 43
housing, 128, 148, 250. *See also main entries, e.g., residential patterns*
Howell, Mark, 70
Hoyt, Homer, 250
Huntersville, 234–35, 236–37; urban designer, need for, 238–39

identity, southern, 52, 78
Illinois land use regulation, 234
image of city: banking industry and, 88, 89, 153–54, 156; mercurial nature of, 25–26, 39–40, 44; need to improve, 24–25, 121; in the press, 37–38; presumptions, national, 37–38; school desegregation's contribution to, 193, 208–10
immigrants and immigration, 2, 6, 20–21, 258; Americanization of, 21–22; anti-immigration campaigns, 286–88; Asian, 255; civil rights, 288; experience, local, 78; international migrants, 25; laborers, 249–51; Latino (*see* Latino community; Latino population); northern cities, 250, 255; religion, 286; residential pattern (*see* suburbs, salad-bowl); resistance to, 264; undocumented, 286–87. *See also* Zone of Emergence

import penetration, 32, 125
industrial transition of southern U.S., 104, 120–21
industry, local. *See* banking; knowledge, industry; manufacturing; NASCAR; textile manufacturing
Indymac Bank, 96
integration: NASCAR efforts toward, 76–77; suburban, 253–54
interest-convergence thesis, 190, 208–10
international marketplace, 103
international standing, quest for, 40–44; Mayor's International Cabinet, 41
International Trade Administration (U.S. Department of Commerce), 113
Irwinville, 179

James Madison University Center for Sports Sponsorship, 63
Jarrett, Ned, 58
Jefferson, Thomas, 166
Jim Crow era, 26, 169, 183; globalization and, 210–11; residential types, African American, 169–70, 183
job postings, 273
Joe Gibbs Racing (JGR), 77
John Crosland Company, 135
Johnson, Junior, 54, 58
Johnson C. Smith University, 180–81, 251
Johnston Mills, 132, 133
Judd, Ashley, 79

Kelly, Kevin, 224
Kennedy, Albert, 250
King, Martin Luther, Jr., 78, 184
knowledge: clusters, 224; communities, 62–69; industry, 5, 6
Kushner, Tony, 19–20, 38

labor supply, 2, 5, 21, 27; Latino, 255, 288; mechanics, 61; residential areas, 128, 250; from rural areas, 249–50; skilled, 105–6, 115; survey of manufacturers, 2005 (*see* manufacturing survey, 2005); textile industry and, 124–25. *See also* employment, professional
Lake Norman, 78
Lakewood Speedway (Atlanta, Georgia), 54–55
Latino community, 1; commercial nodes, 270; cultural landscapes, 276, 278; distinct landscape for, lack of, 268–70; economic regeneration, sites of, 266, 267; enclave streetscape, 269, 270; exile, sites of, 265; heterotopic spatiality, 265, 276; hybridity of, 277, 281; invisibility, sites of, 265, 266, 278, 279–80; job postings, 273; networking, 273, 274; prototopic urbanism, 265, 277–78, 280; shopping, 271–74; suburban residential areas, 7, 267–68; technology and, 268. *See also* Latino population; suburbs, salad-bowl
Latino population, 7, 21, 192, 263–81; Allentown, Pennsylvania, suburbs, 247; Chicago, Illinois, suburbs, 251; demographics, 264; East Los Angeles, California, 266–67, 271, 276, 278; growth of, 264–65; identity, emergent, 278; immigration of, 254–55, 275; resistance to, 264; school enrollment, 212
Levine, Leon and Sandra, 19, 286
Lewis, Ken, 93–94, 95
Little Rock A.M.E. Zion Church, 173
loan program, low-income, 151–52
Lorenzen, Fred, 61

304 Index

Los Angeles, California. *See* East Los Angeles, California
Lowe's Motor Speedway, 51, 60, 66; community, tensions with, 75–76

manufacturing industry, 5, 26; competitive issues, 105; crisis, ongoing, 102; economy and, 103; employment, 105–6, 115; export performance (*see* exports from southern U.S.); higher value-added manufacturing, transition to, 102–3, 105–6; history of, 103–6; international marketplace, 103; product life cycle, 104–5, 113, 115; sales, local, 112; survey, 2005 (*see* manufacturing survey, 2005). *See also* main entries, e.g., textile manufacturing
manufacturing survey, 2005, 106–12; employment and sales, 108–9; exports, 108, 110, 111, 114; innovation level of Charlotte firms, 110–11; research and development, effect of, 110; sales, 107, 108–9, 112; sales growth potential, 107, 114, 116; workers, skilled, 115
marketing firms, 74–75
Martin, Hoyle, 20
McColl, Hugh, 14, 16, 34–35, 37, 149; ambition, 90; arts initiative, 39, 43; BankAmerica, comments on, 90; Center City revitalization, 147; education task force, 209–10; Fourth Ward revitalization, 152–53, 154; merger talks, 42; resentment as fuel for ambition, 38, 88; school desegregation and the economy, 189; on Southeastern Regional Banking Compact, 89
McCrory, Pat, 287
McCrory Heights, 182

McFadden Act of 1927, 88–89
McGarry, Kaye, 203, 210
MECA Properties, 130, 135
mechanics, 61
Mecklenburg Cotton Mill, 132
media coverage, 74: Fourth Ward revitalization, 153; NASCAR, 66, 79; national, 39; school desegregation, 193; textile industry, globalization, 124–25
memory community, Charlotte as, 70–75
Merrill Lynch, acquisition of, 97
Metrolina and Metrolina Fairgrounds, 32–33, 59
Metropolitan Transit Commission, 229
Mexico-USA Xpress Mart, 271–73
The Mind of the South (Cash), 284
Mitchell, William, *E-topia: "Urban Life, Jim — but not as We Know It,"* 225
Miyares, Inés M., 269–70
Montoya, Juan Pablo, 51, 79
Moody, Ralph, 61
moonshine, NASCAR and, 53–54, 55, 57, 82nn17–19, 82n21
Morrison, Cameron, 211
mortgage defaults, 95
motorsports, economic impact, 62. *See also* NASCAR
Museum of the New South, 18–19, 286
museums, 18–19, 74, 286
Myers, W. R., 179, 180
Myrick, Sue, 194, 287

NASCAR, 2, 4, 5; Car of Tomorrow (COT), 69; Charlotte's emergence, 57–62; Confederacy and, 77; Drive for Diversity Combine, 76–77; economic impact, 52, 62;

environmental concerns, 76; events, national, 66; facilities (team), 63, 65; fan base, 66; financing plan (Charlotte's), 73; future of, 80; globalization of, 79; Grand National Division, 57, 61; Hall of Fame, 52, 73–74, 75; history, 53–57, 71; image modification, 78; integration efforts, 76–77; international expansion, 51, 78–79; litigation, 66; location of, reasons for, 53–57; market expansion strategies, 76; mechanics, 61; movie (spoof), 79; practice time, 65; purses, 56, 60; Research and Development Center, 69; revenue, 66; rivalries, 56; shop development, 62; sponsorship, corporate, 57, 63; Sprint Cup teams, 62–63, 69; television coverage, 66; tensions, local, 75–79; transcultural nature, 52. *See also* Charlotte Speedway; Daytona 500

NASCAR Images, 74
NASCAR Technical Institute (NTI), 67–68
National Basketball Association (NBA), 37–38
National Football League (NFL), 18, 37
National Register of Historic Places, 132, 134
NationsBank, 35, 38, 42, 90; construction of, 255; development consultant, 173; merger, 42
NCAA Final Four, 10–11
New Urbanist, 240; "Seaside Code," 235; "Smart Code," 236; Transect methodology, 236
New York Times travel section feature, 39
nightlife, 39
Nixon, Richard, 207
NoDa, 249
NoDa Arts District, 123, 132

NoDa Mills, 133
North American Free Trade Agreement, 111–12
North Carolina Motorsports Association (NCMA), 62
North Carolina National Bank (NCNB), 34–35, 96; acquisition of First National Bank, 88, 89; Center City restructuring, role in, 142, 148, 150–51, 153–54; corporate citizenship, 141–42, 156; corporate-public sector partnership, 127; employees, attracting, 154. *See also* Bank of America; Community Development Corporation
North Corridor commuter rail line, 236
Northeast Corridor, 229
Northerners, assimilation of, 16

O'Connor, Flannery, 22
outerbelt freeway, 193–94, 211; suburban development and, 223

Pappas Properties, 129
Parents for Education in Charlotte-Mecklenburg Schools, 203
Park, Robert, 250
Parks, Raymond, 54, 56
Pattillo, Mary, 164
Pearson, David, 61
Pedestrian Pockets, 226
Pedscape plans, 239–40
Penske Racing South, 76
Performance Instruction and Training (PIT), 67–68
Performance Racing Network, 74
Petty Enterprises, 65
Petty, Kyle, 79
Petty, Lee, 50, 56–57, 60–61
Petty, Richard, 58
place, importance of, 224–26, 265, 275

planning. *See* city planning; Planning Commission, City of Charlotte
Planning Commission, City of Charlotte, 120, 150
Plaza-Midwood, 254
politics: alliances with black political leaders, 208, 213; busing, rejection of, 6; Latino migration, effect of, 275–76; presidential election of 2008, 288; school board, 6, 205–6, 207; of school desegregation, and development, 189–214; white newcomers, effect on desegregation, 195, 208–9; zoning, 147
Polking, Paul, 89
pollution, 134, 135
population, 121, 136, 168; downtown residents, 230; public school enrollment and, 192–93; religious affiliation, 285
Potter, Robert, 195, 209
poverty, regional history of, 4
preservation: citizen groups, 148, 149; tax credits, 123–24, 135
presidential election of 2008, 288
Pressley, Tony, 130
product life cycle, 104–5
Protestant denominations, 285
public-private partnership for neighborhood revitalization, 5, 127, 129, 136, 142; Fourth Ward, 150
public relations campaigns, 2, 4, 24–44; "Action City," 30–31; "America's New Business Horizon," 40; "Charlotte: A City on the Move," 36; civil rights issues, 29; "A Good Place to Make Money," 24; "Industrial Center of the Carolinas," 27; international targets, 41; "Open Gateway to the New South," 27; "Queen City of the South," 27; "The Sky's the Limit," 35; "Spearhead of the New South," 28–29; "Visions for a Greater Charlotte," 35–36; "Watch Charlotte Grow," 24, 27; world-class city, 35. *See also* Carolinas Partnership
public relations firms, 74–75
Pughsley, James, 201–2, 209

Queen City, 27, 264, 265, 266
Queen City Speedway, 59

racing, stock-car, 4; Atlanta, Georgia region, 55, 56; bootleggers and, 82n16, 82n17, 82n19; corporate structure, 69; dirt track, 59; fairground tracks, 58–59; June 1949 race, 50; local influence, 75; media coverage, 74; organization, importance of, 55–56; pre-NASCAR, 54–55; technological advancement, 60. *See also* NASCAR; *and specific locations*
rail system, light *See* transit system, light
railroads, 11–12, 121; textile mills alongside, 123, 133. *See also* transit system, light
Raleigh, North Carolina, rivalry, 40, 43
Rash, J. Dennis, 149, 152
redevelopment process: African American communities threatened by, 163; corporate citizenship and, 141–56; corporate-led revitalization of Fourth Ward, 146–47; HOPE VI, 147; inner city, 125–26, 133; Kansas City, Missouri, 144–45, 146; mill use as catalyst for, 129–31; public-private partnership, 5, 127, 129, 136, 142
Reed, John Shelton, 22
religious belief, 7, 8, 19, 285–86; artistic expression and, 20

Rembert, Wilhelmenia, 196, 202–3, 209
resegregation, school: development and politics, 189–214; economy and, 190; interest-convergence thesis, 208–10; post-*Swann*, 191, 197–200; protests, 196; racial, 197–99; socioeconomic, 199–200
residential patterns, 251–52; sales, 227, 267. *See also* Fair Housing Act of 1968
residential types, African American: in the American South, 162; antebellum, 165, 166–67; case study (Charlotte, North Carolina), 160–67; changes in spatial form and character, 160–61; colonial, 166; development, primary, 160–61; diversity of residential patterns, Pughsley 183; ghetto, 161, 162, 164, 165, 166; Grier Heights, 177–78; In-Town Concentration, 169, 170–74, 184; Jim Crow era, 169–70, 183; Modern African American Suburb, 182–83; northern cities, 161, 162, 165; patterns, 161–63, 166; Rim Village, 179–80, 184; Rural Concentration, 174–78, 184; Separate Villages, 178–82; sprawl, 163; Streetcar Suburb, 180–82, 184; suburbs, 160, 163–64, 180, 182–83, 254; typology, 169–83; urban poor, unskilled, 161–62
residents: aging, 227, 268; immigrant, 227. *See also* suburbs, salad-bowl
retail industry, 130, 271–73. *See also* shopping malls
Roberts, Glenn "Fireball," 54, 61
Roediger, David, 21–22
Roman Catholicism, 286
Rosenwald School, 175, 177
Ross, Jimmy, 61
Rumph, Joe, 61

rural areas, preservation attempts, 235

school system, 6, 8; bond package, 205, 208, 212; construction, 205; desegregation, 15–17, 33, 189–214; economy after desegregation, 189; inner-city, 191–92; mid-ring, 192; resegregation, 189–214; suburban, 191–92. *See also* Charlotte-Mecklenburg Schools; *and main entries, e.g.,* busing, school
Sears, Roebuck, 27–28
Seay, Robert and Ray, 54
Second Ward, 171–72
segregation, 15; residential, 37, 171, 181, 254; "segregation nostalgia," 16
service center, 3
shopping malls, 253; international flavor of, 256–57; strip, 252–53, 256, 273–74
Shuman, Buddy, 54, 56, 58
slaves and slavery, 11–12; land grants to former slaves, 174
Smart Code, 236
Smart Growth, 35
Smith, Eric, 196, 202
Smith, Johnson C. *See* Johnson C. Smith University
Smith, O. Bruton, 56, 60, 66–67, 75–76
South Boulevard, 248, 251–53, 256, 270
South Business profile of Charlotte, 34
South Corridor, 7, 234, 239
Southeast Corridor, 229
Southeastern Banking Compact, 11
Southeastern Regional Banking Compact, 89–90, 91
South End Brewery, 130
South End corridor, 131–32, 221, 224
South End Development Corporation logo, 130

Southern Historical Association (SHA), 10, 23
Southern Railway, 121, 251
Southern States Fair Ground, 58–59
Southland Speedway, 60
Southpark Mall, 253
Spaghetti Warehouse, 130
Spangler, C. D., Jr., 189
Spanglish, 273
Speed Channel, 74
Speedway Motorsports, Inc. (SMI), 66
sports, professional, 36–37, 43; corporate sponsorship, 57. *See also main entries, e.g., NASCAR*
streetcar line, 181, 230
subdivisions, 17
suburban development patterns, 220–43; Allentown, Pennsylvania, 247; alternative to, search for, 227; centrifugal pattern, 223; Chicago, Illinois, 247; expansion, 220, 234–39; Latino, 267–68; northern versus southern, 251; outerbelt freeway and, 223; planning staff, resistance to, 241–42; polyglot, 247–48, 255–58; racial integration, 253; urban versus, 227–34. *See also* suburbs, salad-bowl
suburbs, salad-bowl, 7, 247–58; defined, 248; East Side, 248–49; regeneration of aging landscapes, 267, 280; South Boulevard, 248
Swann v. Charlotte-Mecklenburg School Board, 16, 189, 191, 195, 196, 207

Talladega Nights: The Ballad of Ricky Bobby, 79
Tate, Allen, 196
tax incentives: historically designated property redevelopment, 123–24, 136; municipal property, 128; preservation tax credits, 123–24, 135; property tax liability, reduced, 136
technology, 225, 268; "knowledge community," 62–69
televangelists, 38
television coverage, NASCAR events, 66
textile manufacturing, 12, 28, 128–36; globalization of, 124–25; history, 104, 120–21; import penetration, vulnerability to, 125; migration (rural-to-urban) and, 166, 250; newspaper articles, 124–25; pollution, 134, 135; residential villages, company-owned, 250; unemployment, 124–25
textile mills, reuse of, 5, 119–37, 221; advantages, 119; case study, 120; community heritage, loss of, 125; historic status, 123–24, 135, 136; newspaper articles, 125–26; nonmanufacturing potential, 123; postindustrial Charlotte, 126–28; potentials and challenges, 122–26; redevelopment, as catalyst for, 129–31; residential conversions, 125, 127–28, 130, 131–33, 135; restoration, award-winning, 135; salvage, 125; tax incentives, 123–24. *See also specific sites and renovations*
Third Ward, 172–73
Thomas, Herb, 57
Tober, Ron, 232
Tompkins, Daniel A., 12, 120, 129, 134
tourism, 74
trade center, international, 36
Transit Corridor System Plans, 227–28, 243; funding, federal, 231; Major Investment Studies, 230–31; Northeast Corridor, 229; Southeast Corridor, 229; West Corridor, 229
Transit-Oriented Development (TOD),

226; regulations process, 239–40
transit system, light, 13, 221, 222, 229, 230; development alongside, 235, 240; North Corridor, proposed, 236; South Corridor line, 231–32, 239–40
transportation hub, 222; development of, 25, 121, 234, 256; shopping areas, 252–53. *See also* Transit Corridor System Plans; Transit-Oriented Development
trolley line, 135, 222
Turner, Curtis, 54, 56, 60, 61
Tuscan Development, 133

UNC-Charlotte. *See* University of North Carolina
unionization, 69
Unity Rally, 196
University of North Carolina, 14, 229
Uptown, 10, 11, 22, 34; bank investments, 42–43; landscape of power, 267; transformation, 36
Uptown Merchants Association, 47n26
urban design: concepts picture book, 237; form-based code and, 237–38; Urban Street Design Guidelines, 242
urban environments: computer influence, 224; defined, 220; diversity, advantages of, 280–81; transit link, 226, 227
urban growth, 175; catalyst for, 221–22; development patterns, 220–43; landscapes of invasion, 270; morphology, 235–36; sustainability, 226
Urban Land Institute, 226
Urban Renewal plan, federally funded, 147, 172
Urban Street Design Guidelines, 242

urban villages, 220, 226; building typology, 235–36; suburbia versus, 227–34; transit-linked, 226, 227, 240

Victorian-era housing, 148
Villeneuve, Jacques, 79
Vinroot, Richard, 37, 41
visitors, 10–23
Vogt, Red, 54, 56
voters, nonsouthern, 6

Wachovia, 42, 88, 93, 95, 96
Wall Street Journal, on bank merger, 42
wards, downtown, 168, 170; churches, landmark, 173. *See also specific wards*
Washington, George, 26
Washington Heights, 181
Washington Mutual Savings, 96
Weatherly, Joe, 61
Webber, Melvin, 224
Wells Fargo, 96
West Corridor, 229
Westmoreland, Hubert, 57
Wheeler, Humpy, 79
When Work Disappears (Wilson), 161–62
White, Rex, 57–58
white supremacy and globalization, 191, 211
Wilson, William Julius, *When Work Disappears*, 161–62
Winter Properties, 133
Woods, Louise, 197, 202
Woods, Robert, 250
Woodward, C. Vann, 88, 98, 120
World Affairs Council of Charlotte, 36
world-class city, transition to, 24–44
World War II, changes following, 13, 251, 256, 271

Yazoo Delta (Mississippi), 164–65

Zone of Emergence, 250
zones and zoning: changes, resistance to, 239, 241; character zones, 236; Foreign Trade Zone, 36; form-based codes, 234–39; interpretation file, 238; ordinances, 234–35; Pedscape plans, 239–40; reform, progressive, 238–39, 240; Zone of Emergence, 250

Zukin, Sharon, 267